# JONATHAN EDWARDS

# Jonathan Edwards

## A PROFILE

EDITED BY

DAVID LEVIN

*AMERICAN PROFILES*

*General Editor: Aïda DiPace Donald*

 HILL AND WANG : NEW YORK

# Contents

# *Introduction*

Despite his vigorous leadership in one of the most powerful mass movements of the eighteenth century, biographers have consistently argued that "the real story of the life of Jonathan Edwards is to be found in the life of the mind." Edwards holds the attention of admirers and critics with the strength of his intellect and the intensity of his piety. Freethinking critics from Vernon L. Parrington to Peter Gay lament that this mind, which might have liberated men, worked instead to revive a cramping Calvinism. Perry Miller declares that Edwards surpassed Isaac Newton in divining the philosophical significance of atomic physics. Alan Heimert places Edwards' ideas among the chief influences on the American Revolution.

Scholar and poet, moreover, choose the same phenomena to suggest the intellectual and pious force of the man. Before he was twelve, they remind us, Edwards wrote a remarkable essay on the spiders he had observed about his father's Connecticut farm; and at Yale, in his early teens, he wrote his brilliant "Notes on the Mind," which reveal a profound comprehension of Locke's *Essay concerning Human Understanding*. To represent his piety scholars invariably cite one of the religious experiences of his youth that are recounted in his own "Personal Narrative":

The first instance that I remember of that sort of inward, sweet delight in God and divine things that I have lived much in since, was on reading those words, I Tim. 1. 17. *Now unto the King eternal, immortal, invisible, the only wise God, be honor and glory for ever and ever, Amen.* As I read the words, there came into my soul, and was as it were diffused through it, a sense of the glory of the Divine Being; a new sense, quite different from any thing I ever experienced before.

Jonathan Edwards would be a memorable historical figure if only because his religious experience typified the piety of revivalism, or if only because he achieved some of the best theological and philosophical exposition of his century. What makes him especially valuable is his consistent devotion to both rigorous thought and uncompromising piety. He stands before us as the exemplary Puritan, striving to think clearly in the world for the glory of God.

We must therefore recognize in Edwards not only the lad who, while reading Timothy and again later while walking in his father's pasture, was suddenly illuminated with "a divine and supernatural light" that gave him a new apprehension of all the things he perceived. We must also study the meticulous psychologist of religion who in his late thirties reconstructed these experiences in his "Personal Narrative." It is only through the narrative that we know Edwards' experiences of rapture, and in that context the boy's experiences are no more important than the man's precise observation and narrative. By lifting the boy's rapture out of the man's analytical narrative, we risk overlooking Edwards' conscientious effort to trace the distinguishing marks of a work of the Spirit of God.

For these reasons a modern biographical Profile will avoid the excesses of caricature if it takes some of its outlines from pious writers of the eighteenth century. The best descriptive commentary on Jonathan Edwards' religious experience is his own "Personal Narrative," and the best biographical account of his entire religious activity is the book by his disciple Samuel Hopkins, in which the "Personal Narrative" was first published a few years after Edwards' death. Hopkins takes care to distinguish the boy's experience from the man's narrative.

Hopkins' little biography has not been reprinted for more than a century, and it has never been reprinted without editorial improprieties that made substantive changes in both Edwards' and Hopkins' texts.[1] By presenting it to modern readers in a version that makes no changes except for normalizing spelling and capitalization, I hope to re-establish the best text of Edwards' famous narrative and also to suggest the value of considering piety in its own terms. Hopkins takes seriously Edwards' entire set of beliefs. He therefore gives us a chance to form a conception of the pious life without the mediation of a modern skeptic's explanatory comment, and according to the custom of early biographers he relies heavily on Edwards' own words. Readers should notice that the large space I have allotted to Hopkins in this Profile belongs almost equally to Edwards himself, for Hopkins gives Edwards' Resolutions, diary, and letters as much space as the "Personal Narrative."

In this representation we see Edwards' whole life under the rule of faith. From the time he wrote a solemn covenant a few months after his nineteenth birthday, he strove to dedicate all his effort to the service of God. His account of this action implies a control, a disciplined capacity to will, that seems to us far from the rapturous desire he has experienced at other times, far from the desire to be annihilated and swallowed up in Christ:

Saturday, Jan. 12 [1723]. in the morning. I have this day solemnly renewed my baptismal covenant and self-dedication, which I renewed when I was received into the covenant of the church. I have been before God; and have given myself, and all that I am and have to God, so that I am not in any respect my own: I can challenge no right in myself, I can challenge no right in this understanding, this will, these affections that are in me; neither have I any right to this body, or any of its members: no right to this tongue, these hands, nor feet: no right to these senses, these eyes, these ears, this smell or taste. I have given myself clear away, and have not retained any thing as my own. I have been to God this morning, and told Him that I gave myself *wholly* to Him. I have given every power to Him; so that for the future I will challenge

---

[1] I am indebted to Daniel B. Shea for pointing out the superiority of Hopkins' text of the "Personal Narrative"; so far as we know, all modern reprints of Edwards' narrative follow an incorrect nineteenth-century version. The chief differences are discussed briefly in Mr. Shea's excellent book *Spiritual Autobiography in Early America* (Princeton, 1968).

no right in myself, in any respect. I have expressly promised him, and do now promise almighty God, that by His grace I will not. I have this morning told Him, that I did take Him for my whole portion and felicity, looking on nothing else as any part of my happiness, nor acting as if it were; and His law for the constant rule of my obedience: and would fight with all my might against the world, the flesh, and the devil, to the end of my life. And did believe in Jesus Christ, and receive Him as a Prince and a Saviour; and would adhere to the faith and obedience of the gospel, how hazardous forever the profession and practice of it may be. That I did receive the blessed Spirit as my teacher, sanctifier, and only comforter; and cherish all His motions to enlighten, purify, confirm, comfort and assist me. This I have done. And I pray God, for the sake of Christ, to look upon it as a self-dedication; and to receive me now as entirely His own, and deal with me in all respects as such; whether He afflicts me or prospers me, or whatever He pleases to do with me, who am His. Now, henceforth I am not to act in any respect as my own.—I shall act as my own, if I ever make use of any of my powers to any thing that is not to the glory of God, and don't make the glorifying Him my whole and entire business; if I murmur in the least at affliction; if I grieve at the prosperity of others; if I am any way uncharitable; if I am angry because of injuries; if I revenge: if I do any thing, purely to please myself, or if I avoid any thing for the sake of my ease: if I omit any thing because it is great self-denial: if I trust to myself: if I take any of the praise of any of the good that I do, or rather God does by me; or if I am any way proud.

The written covenant had been a customary private act among Puritans for more than a century, and Edwards' mixture here of meditation with affirmation is also perfectly conventional. What seems remarkable in this document written by a young man soon after his nineteenth birthday is the degree of explanation, the insistence on enumerating the senses given over to divine command and on defining the many tempting ways of acting "as my own." Here Edwards follows both the advice and the practice of Cotton Mather, and with an intensity equaled by few eighteenth-century diarists besides Mather himself. Like Mather, moreover (though in a different tone), Edwards expresses two strongly paradoxical qualities. He casts his resolution of self-surrender in a language that asserts not only self-control but a very strong personality. The might of the character that will fight the world, the flesh, and the devil will also lead it sometimes to be proud.

By printing this critical passage from Edwards' diary, Hopkins thus gives us one of the best views we have of the Puritan mind. Here the Puritan mind achieves discipline, declares an exalted willingness to surrender the self to God, resolves to strive for His purposes, then begs that its devotion be certified as genuine, and at last warns itself of the kinds of action that will mark its devotion as counterfeit.

In Edwards' day as in Cotton Mather's, the Puritan could never be absolutely sure of his election. When Edwards looked back on these early days more than fifteen years later, he noted that his own experience had taught him a major lesson: that the more his sense of God's excellency increased, the more sensibly convinced he was of his own wickedness. Permanent self-doubt was built into the system. Just as selfish action made one question whether one had really submitted one's will to God's service, so a convicting awareness of one's selfishness was a sign justifying hope. And although strenuous action in the Lord's cause could not give anyone perfect assurance of his own salvation, it was a better sign than the selfish acts against which Edwards warned himself, and it left little time for them. Hopkins lets his biographical narrative and the less important quotations from Edwards show how Edwards' subsequent life was ruled by the early covenant I have quoted. Some of the Resolutions that Hopkins reprints have properly been compared to similar resolutions by Benjamin Franklin and Cotton Mather, whose *Bonifacius* (or *Essays to Do Good*) was surely one of young Edwards' models. What those Resolutions demand is a life saturated with pious effort, both in public and private action: study, worship, thoughts of parents and neighbors, family government, preaching, theological and philosophical dispute, pastoral duty in Northampton, leadership of the revival, writing on the psychology of conversion and the nature of true virtue.

Hopkins helps us to see, then, that the intellectual achievement for which we honor Edwards was an expression of his piety. He also helps us to see that the tragedy of Edwards' dismissal by the Northampton congregation after twenty-five years of service issues

from the same resolve foreshadowed in the renewal of the covenant that I have quoted. Serving the Lord, Edwards encourages the
religious revival of the 1730's and 1740's even though he is
troubled by its excesses, including the suicide of his despairing
uncle. Then, as the revival subsides, Edwards stands firm in his
role as teaching elder during a controversy over "lascivious and
obscene" reading among young boys in the congregation; by his
standards compromise on such matters is unthinkable, and he
provokes the resentment of many parishioners. When he tries a
few years later to re-establish serious tests of conversion as a
prerequisite to church membership, the congregation not only
votes for his dismissal, but also refuses to let him preach a group
of sermons explaining his theological reasons for insisting on the
tests! The greatest religious thinker of his day is silenced by
people who fear he might convince them. He teaches them any-
way, if only in his farewell sermon, and he warns them there that
their conduct and his own will be considered at the Judgment.

In all this activity the hellfire preacher who terrified the Enfield
community with the sermon that became known as *Sinners in the
Hands of an Angry God* seems not to be present. I have not meant
to hide him, but it is necessary to see him, as most scholars of the
last thirty years have come to see him, in the context that Samuel
Hopkins and Perry Miller have established. This Jonathan Edwards
is the man who had resolved in his youth "to endeavor to my
utmost to act as I can think I should do, if I had already seen the
happiness of heaven, and hell torments." Hellfire is not his characteristic mode of preaching, but to bring sinners to a sense of their
true danger he is willing to preach a sermon on the text "Their foot
shall slide in due time" and to fill every auditor with a sense of
heavy weight, pressing downward toward hell. You stand on a
rotten covering over hell, you tend downward with a great weight,
heavy as lead, he tells them in 1741, and the only thing that keeps
you from dropping into hell at this very moment is the merciful
hand of an angry God, who holds you up. Edwards hopes they
will act just as he had long ago hoped that he would act "if I had
already seen the happiness of heaven, and hell torments."

The strength of Edwards' intellect, and its significance in American history, have been more effectively studied in modern scholarship than in the writings of a Hopkins. Williston Walker, a liberal church historian of the early twentieth century, tries to set Edwards' thought in the history of Congregationalism; sympathetic but prevented by his liberal Christianity from sharing Hopkins' evaluation of Edwards' piety, Walker nonetheless presents a clear, brief exposition of Edwards' critique of free will and of Edwards' definition of virtue.

Walker also reminds us briefly that we must consider the tiny scale of Edwards' Northampton, with its population of only two hundred families, but I have relied on chapters from Henry Bamford Parkes and Ola Elizabeth Winslow to supplement Hopkins' biography with more modern accounts of Edwards' early life in Connecticut and Northampton. It is the nature of Edwards' religious experience, Parkes argues, that kept him from being tempted by deism and other freethinking. Ola Elizabeth Winslow deepens our sense of that experience by providing a clear description of the Edwards family—the father, the mother, and the sisters—in the years before Jonathan's conversion.

Perry Miller, John E. Smith, and James Carse represent here the intensive study that has been accorded Edwards' philosophical and religious ideas during the last thirty years. In different ways all three of these scholars treat Edwards as a historical figure whose ideas not only foreshadow modern attitudes but also speak intelligently about modern issues. In his chapter on "The Objective Good," Miller portrays the youth whose reflections on Newton and Locke propelled him into a new atomic world. There the very definition of the atom implies a power constantly exercised rather than a substance visually apprehended. Smith's exposition of Edwards' great *Religious Affections* commends us to a mind that refuses to oversimplify its hard-won observations of psychological reality. Carse, like Miller, insists on a modern portrait, but in the chapter reprinted here he gives generous space to the most terrifying "maledictions" in Edwards' sermons. He reads these as social criticism and as tributes to the crucial importance of the human will, and he places them beside Edwards' memoir of the saintly model, David Brainerd.

Peter Gay, though admiring and sympathetic, regards Edwards as a tragic figure not because he was the first modern American but largely because he was "the last medieval American—at least among the intellectuals." Concentrating on Edwards' projected history of the work of redemption, Gay has written one of the best briefs for the dissent in the argument over Edwards' modernity. His lucid essay stands here as representative of that dissent, other spokesmen for which are cited both in the Selected Bibliography below and in Gay's notes.

Perhaps the Edwards characterized in this Profile is too sweet to serve as a just representation of the historical actuality. Although his battle with his congregation expresses the political cost of the uncompromising toughness that Miller and Smith celebrate, to finish the portrait we ought to have some glimpse of the Edwards who rode joyfully into a polemical paragraph to demolish the enemies of truth:

So that, according to their [Arminian] notion of an act, considered with regard to its consequences, these following things are all essential to it, viz., that it should be necessary, and not necessary; that it should be from a cause, and no cause; that it should be the fruit of choice and design, and not the fruit of choice and design; that it should be the beginning of motion or exertion, and yet consequent on previous exertion; that it should be before it is; that it should spring immediately out of indifference and equilibrium, and yet be the effect of preponderation; that it should be self-originated, and also have its original from something else; that it is what the mind causes itself, of its own Will, and can produce or prevent, according to its choice or pleasure, and yet what the mind has no power to prevent, it precluding all previous choice in the affair.

So that an act, according to their metaphysical notion of it, is something of which there is no idea; it is nothing but a confusion of the mind, excited by words without any distinct meaning, and is an absolute nonentity, and that in two respects: (1), there is nothing in the world that ever was, is, or can be, to answer the things which must belong to its description, according to what they suppose to be essential to it; and (2) there neither is, nor ever was, nor can be, any notion or idea to answer the word, as they use and explain it. For if we should suppose any such notion, it would many ways destroy itself. . . .

The passion that could lead this mind to open new views of God's excellency and a new definition of true virtue could also exult in deadly combat. And in the power of such paragraphs one can see perhaps the best explanation of Edwards' strength in the revival pulpit. It is the sheer force of his cumulative argument, as much as the heat from incendiary images, that communicates emotion to auditor and reader. We feel the passionate strength of a pious mind, driving the intellect forward to the Lord's work. Some sense of a modern response to that strength is expressed through many of Edwards' own words in the poems by Robert Lowell that complete the Profile.

DAVID LEVIN

*Stanford, California*
*May 1, 1968*

# Jonathan Edwards, 1703–1758

Jonathan Edwards was born on October 5, 1703, in East Windsor, Connecticut, the son, grandson, and great-grandson of Protestant ministers. Educated under his father's care, he entered Yale College in his early teens and was graduated in 1720. It was during these undergraduate years that he read John Locke's *Essay concerning Human Understanding* and wrote his own "Notes on the Mind," in which he stated principles that affected the rest of his intellectual and religious life. "That which truly is the substance of all bodies," he declared, *"is the infinitely exact, and precise, and perfectly stable idea, in God's mind, together with His stable will, that the same shall gradually be communicated to us, and to other minds, according to certain fixed and exact established methods and laws."*

Edwards continued to study at Yale, spent one winter as a minister in New York, returned to Yale as a tutor, and was called in 1726 to join his grandfather, Solomon Stoddard, as pastor of the congregation at Northampton, Massachusetts. Edwards married Sarah Pierpont in 1727. For the next twenty-five years he served this congregation in "the most enthusiastical town in New England." Even before the religious revivals that made him famous, he made some stir in Boston with a lecture published under the title *God Glorified in the Work of Redemption by the Greatness of Man's Dependence upon Him in the Whole of It*

(1731). But the chief pastoral work for which he is known came in two swelling revivals, the first in 1734 and the second—part of the Great Awakening—in 1740–1742. He not only preached and counseled in these religious upheavals but also wrote major works in defense of the revival. Aware of the excesses that accompanied these remarkable works of redemption, he was nonetheless determined to find ways of distinguishing false from true conversions, and these experiences led him to write some of his most important tracts and books: *A Faithful Narrative of the Surprising Work of God* (1737), *The Distinguishing Marks of a Work of the Spirit of God* (1741), "Personal Narrative" (published only after his death), *Some Thoughts concerning the Present Revival in New England,* and *A Treatise concerning Religious Affections* (1746).

In 1744 Edwards made a number of enemies in his own congregation by refusing to compromise his belief in church discipline when a group of young people were discovered reading and exchanging "lascivious and obscene" books. The bad feelings continued to develop over more complex issues in the next few years, and in 1750 he was dismissed by the congregation because he insisted on maintaining a new set of requirements for church membership. He had become convinced that his grandfather Stoddard had erred in admitting every professing Christian whose behavior was not openly scandalous; after years of following Stoddard's practice, Edwards now contended that a new rigor had to be exercised by the elders in evaluating professed conversions. The struggle was protracted and devious, but in the end a special committee of ministers from the area ruled against Edwards, and although one of these men later published a posthumous apology to Edwards (confessing animosity as a leading motive for his negative vote), the forty-eight-year-old minister was forced to leave Northampton.

In 1751 Edwards accepted a position at Stockbridge, Massachusetts, as missionary to the Housatonic Indians and as pastor for the local congregation. This isolated assignment freed him to write several of the major works of his life: *A Careful and Strict Enquiry into the Modern Prevailing Notions of that Freedom of the Will which is supposed to be Essential to Moral Agency,*

*Vertue and Vice, Reward and Punishment, Praise and Blame* (1754); "The Nature of True Virtue" and "Concerning the End for Which God Created the World" (written 1755; published in 1765 as *Two Dissertations*); and *The Great Christian Doctrine of Original Sin Defended* (1758).

In 1758, Edwards reluctantly agreed to accept the presidency of the new college at Princeton, New Jersey, but soon after his arrival there he died after being inoculated for smallpox.

D.L.

# JONATHAN EDWARDS

✪

# The Life and Character of the Late
# Reverend Mr. Jonathan Edwards

## THE PREFACE

President Edwards, in the esteem of all the judicious, who were well acquainted with him, either personally, or by his writings, was one of the *greatest—best*—and *most useful* of men, that have lived in this age.

He discovered himself to be one of the *greatest of divines,* by his conversation, preaching and writings: One of remarkable strength of mind, clearness of thought, and depth of penetration, who well understood, and was able, above most others, to vindicate the great doctrines of Christianity.

And no one perhaps has been in our day, more universally esteemed and acknowledged to be a *bright Christian,* an eminently *good man.* His love to God and man; his zeal for God and his cause; his uprightness, humility, self-denial, and weanedness from the world; his close walk with God; his conscientious, constant and universal obedience, in all exact and holy ways of living: In one word, the goodness, the holiness of his heart, has been as evident and conspicuous, as the uncommon greatness and strength of his understanding.

And that this distinguished light has not shone in vain, there are a cloud of witnesses. God, who gave him his great talents, led him into a way of improving them, both by preaching and writing,

*The Life and Character of the Late Reverend Mr. Jonathan Edwards* was originally published in Boston in 1765.

which has doubtless proved the means of converting many from the error of their ways; and of greatly promoting the interest of Christ's church, both in *America* and *Europe*. And there is reason to hope, that though he is now dead, he will yet speak for a great while yet to come, to the great comfort and advantage of the church of Christ; that his publications will produce a yet greater harvest, as an addition to his joy and crown of rejoicing in the day of the Lord.

But the design of the following memoirs, is not merely to publish these things, and tell the world how eminently great, wise, holy and useful President *Edwards* was; but rather to inform in what way, and by what means he attained to such an uncommon stock of knowledge and holiness; and how, in the improvement of this, he did so much good to mankind; that others may hereby be directed and excited to go and do likewise.

The reader is therefore not to expect a mere encomium on the *dead,* but a faithful and plain narration of matters of fact, together with his own internal exercises, expressed in his own words; and is desired not to look on the following composure so much an act of friendship to the *dead,* as of kindness to the *living;* it being only an attempt to render a life that has been greatly useful, yet more so. And as this is designed for the reader's good, he is desired to remember, that if he gets no benefit hereby; is not made wiser nor better, gains no skill or disposition to live a holy and useful life, all is in vain as to him.

In this world, so full of darkness and delusion, it is of great importance that all should be able to distinguish between true religion and that which is false. In this, perhaps none has taken more pains, or labored more successfully, than he whose life is set before the reader. And it is presumed that his religious resolutions, exercises and conduct here exhibited, will serve well to exemplify and illustrate all that he has wrote on this subject. Here pure and undefiled religion, in distinction from all counterfeits, appears in life and practice, exhibiting a picture which will tend to instruct, strengthen and comfort all those, who in their religious sentiments and exercises, are built on the foundation of the apostles and prophets, of which Jesus Christ is the chief cornerstone; while their hearts and practice in some measure answer to it, as in water, face answereth to face. And here, they who have hitherto unhappily been in darkness and delusion, in this infinitely important affair, may have matter of instruction and conviction.

This is a point about which, above many other, the Protestant world is in the dark, and needs instruction, as Mr. *Edwards* was more and more convinced, the longer he lived; and which he was wont frequently to observe in conversation. If therefore these his remains are adapted to answer this end, and may be considered as a word behind all to whom they shall come, "saying, THIS IS THE WAY, walk ye in it," and shall in this view, be blessed to many, it will be a relief under one of the greatest calamities that attend the Christian world, and promote that important end, so worthy the attention and pursuit of all; and in which he from whom this mantle falls, was zealously engaged, and which he pursued to the end of his life.

In this view especially, is the following life offered to the public, with an earnest desire that every reader may faithfully improve it to this purpose; while he candidly overlooks any improprieties and defects which he may observe to be chargeable on the compiler; who is he knows, in a great degree unequal to what is here attempted.

*August 20, 1764*

**PART I** *Containing the* HISTORY *of his* LIFE, *from his* BIRTH, *to his* SETTLEMENT *in the Work of the* MINISTRY

Mr. Jonathan Edwards was born October 5, 1703, at Windsor, a town in Connecticut. His father was the Reverend Mr. Timothy Edwards, minister of the gospel on the east side of Connecticut River in Windsor. He began to reside and preach at Windsor in November, 1694, but was not ordained till July, 1698. He died January 27, 1758, in the eighty-ninth year of his age, not two months before this his son. He was in the work of the ministry above fifty-nine years: and from his first beginning to reside and preach there, to his death, are above sixty-three years; and was able to attend on the work of the ministry and preach constantly till within a few years before his death. He was very universally esteemed and beloved as an upright, pious, exemplary man, and faithful minister of the gospel; and was greatly useful. He was born at Hartford in Connecticut, May 14, 1669, received the honors of the college at Cambridge in New England, by having the degrees of Bachelor and Master of Arts given him the same day, July 4, 1694, one in the forenoon, and the other in the afternoon.

On the sixth day of November, 1694, he was married to Mrs. Esther Stoddard, in the twenty-third year of her age, the daughter of the late famous Mr. Solomon Stoddard of Northampton; whose great parts and zeal for experimental religion are well known in all the churches in America; and will probably be transmitted to posterity yet unborn, by his valuable writings. They lived together in the married state above sixty-three years. Mrs. Edwards was born June 2, 1672, and is now living in her eighty-ninth year, remarkable for the little decay of her mental powers at so great an age.

They had eleven children: all which lived to adult years, viz. ten daughters, seven of whom are now living, and this their only son and fifth child.[1]

[1] *As the following more large and particular account, of Mr.* Edwards's *ancestors may gratify some readers, 'tis inserted here in the margin.*

Mr. Edwards's grandfather was Mr. Richard Edwards. His first wife was Mrs. Elisabeth Tuttle, daughter of Mr. William Tuttle of New Haven in Connecticut, and Mrs. Elisabeth Tuttle his wife, who came out of Northamptonshire in England. His second wife was Mrs. Talcot, sister to Governor Talcot: by his first wife he had seven children, the oldest of which was the Reverend Mr. Timothy Edwards of Windsor, his father, before mentioned. By his second wife, Mrs. Talcot, he had six children.

The father of Mr. Richard Edwards was Mr. William Edwards, who came from England young and unmarried. His wife, Mrs. Agnes Edwards, who also came out of England, had two brothers in England, one of them Mayor of Exeter, and the other of Barnstable. Mr. William Edwards's father was the Reverend Mr. Richard Edwards, minister of the gospel in London. He lived in Queen Elisabeth's day, and his wife, Mrs. Anne Edwards, assisted in making a ruff for the Queen. After the death of Mr. Edwards she married to one Mr. James Cole. She, with her second husband and her son William Edwards, came into America, and all died at Hartford in Connecticut.

Mr. Edwards's grandfather (Mr. Solomon Stoddard, and his predecessor at Northampton) married Mrs. Mather, the relict of the Reverend Mr.

Mr. Edwards entered Yale College in the year 1716, and received the degree of Bachelor of Arts in September, 1720, a little before he was seventeen years old. He had the character of a sober youth, and a good scholar while he was a member of the college. In his second year at college, and thirteenth of his age, he read Locke on the human understanding, with great delight and profit. His uncommon genius, by which he was, as it were by nature, formed for closeness of thought and deep penetration, now began to exercise and discover itself. Taking that book into his hand, upon some occasion, not long before his death, he said to some of his select friends, who were then with him, that he was beyond expression entertained and pleased with it, when he read it in his youth at college; that he was as much engaged, and had more

Mather his predecessor, and the first minister at Northampton. Her maiden name was Esther Warham, daughter and youngest child of the Reverend Mr. John Warham, minister at Windsor in Connecticut, who came out of England, before which he was minister in Exeter in England: he had four children, all daughters; and Mrs. Warham survived him, and had two daughters by Mr. Newbury, her second husband.

Mrs. Esther Warham had three children by Mr. Mather, viz. Eunice, Warham, and Eliakim. And she had twelve children by Mr. Stoddard, six sons and six daughters: three of the sons died in infancy. The three that lived to adult years were Anthony, John, and Israel. Israel died in prison in France. Anthony was the Reverend Mr. Anthony Stoddard, late minister of the gospel at Woodbury in Connecticut, who lived to a great age, and was in the work of the ministry sixty years: he died September 6, 1760, in the eighty-second year of his age. John was the Honorable John Stoddard, Esq. who lived at Northampton, and who often, especially in his younger years, served the town as their representative at the great and general court in Boston; and was long head of the county of Hampshire as their chief colonel, and chief judge of the court of common pleas: and he long served his Majesty, and the province of the Massachusetts Bay, as one of His Majesty's council. He was remarkable as a politician, and for his spirit of government; a wise counsellor, an upright and skillful judge, a steady and great friend to the interest of religion. He was a great friend and admirer of Mr. Edwards, and greatly strengthened his hands in the work of the ministry while he lived. A more particular account of the life and character of this truly great man may be seen in the sermon which Mr. Edwards preached and published on the occasion of his death.

Mr. Stoddard's father was Anthony Stoddard, Esq. of Boston, a zealous congregational man. He had five wives, the first of which, Mr. Stoddard's mother, was Mrs. Mary Downing, sister to Sir George Downing, whose other sister married Governor Bradstreet. Mr. Solomon Stoddard was their oldest child.

satisfaction and pleasure in studying it, than the most greedy miser in gathering up handfuls of silver and gold from some new discovered treasure.

Though he made good proficiency in all the arts and sciences, and had an uncommon taste for Natural Philosophy, which he cultivated to the end of his life, with that justness and accuracy of thought which was almost peculiar to him; yet Moral Philosophy or Divinity was his favorite study. In this he early made great progress.

He lived at college near two years after he took his first degree, designing and preparing for the work of the ministry. After which, having passed the prerequisite trials, he was licensed to preach the gospel as a candidate. And being pitched upon, and applied to by a number of ministers in New England, who were instructed to act in behalf of the English Presbyterians at New York, as a fit person to be sent to them, he complied with their request, and went to New York the beginning of August, 1722; and preached there to very good acceptance about eight months. But by reason of the smallness of that society, and some special difficulties that attended it, he did not think they were in a capacity to settle a minister, with a rational prospect of answering the good ends proposed. He therefore left them, the next spring, and retired to his father's house; where he spent the summer in close study. He was indeed earnestly solicited by the people he had been among at New York to return to them again; but for the reason just mentioned, he could not think himself in the way of his duty to gratify them.

In September, 1723, he received his degree of Master of Arts; about which time he had invitations from several congregations to come among them in order to his settlement in the work of the ministry; but being chosen tutor of Yale College the next spring, in the year 1724, being in the twenty-first year of his age, he retired to the college, and attended the business of tutor there above two years.

While he was in this place he was applied to by the people at Northampton, with an invitation to come and settle in the work of the ministry there, with his grandfather Stoddard, who, by reason of his great age, stood in need of assistance. He therefore resigned his tutorship, in September, 1726, and accepted of their invitation; and was ordained in the work of the ministry at Northampton, colleague with his grandfather Stoddard, February 15, 1727, in the twenty-fourth year of his age, where he continued in the work of the ministry till June 22, 1750, twenty-three years and four months.

Between the time of his going to New York and his settlement at Northampton, he formed a number of resolutions, and committed them to writing: the particular time, and special occasion of his making many of them, he has noted in his Diary which he then kept; as well as many other observations and rules, which related to his own exercises and conduct. And as these resolutions, together with the things noted in his Diary, may justly be considered as the foundation and plan of his whole life, it may be proper here to give the reader a taste and idea of them: which will therefore be done in the following extracts.

## PART II   *Containing* EXTRACTS *from his* PRIVATE WRITINGS, *etc.*

### *Section I*   HIS RESOLUTIONS

Being sensible that I am unable to do any thing without God's help, I do humbly intreat Him by His grace to enable me to keep these resolutions, so far as they are agreeable to His will, for Christ's sake.

> *Remember to read over these resolutions once*
> *a week.*

1. Resolved, That I will do whatsoever I think to be most to God's glory, and my own good, profit and pleasure, in the whole of my duration, without any consideration of the time, whether now, or never so many myriads of ages hence. Resolved to do whatever I think to be my duty, and most for the good and advantage of mankind in general. Resolved to do this, whatever difficulties I meet with, how many and how great soever.

2. Resolved, To be continually endeavoring to find out some

new invention and contrivance to promote the fore-mentioned things.

4. Resolved, Never to do any manner of thing, whether in soul or body, less or more, but what tends to the glory of God; nor be, nor suffer it, if I can avoid it.

5. Resolved, Never to lose one moment of time; but improve it the most profitable way I possibly can.

6. Resolved, To live with all my might, while I do live.

7. Resolved, Never to do any thing, which I should be afraid to do, if it were the last hour of my life.

9. Resolved, To think much on all occasions of my own dying, and of the common circumstances which attend death.

11. Resolved, When I think of any theorem in divinity to be solved, immediately to do what I can towards solving it, if circumstances do not hinder.

13. Resolved, To be endeavoring to find out fit objects of charity and liberality.

14. Resolved, Never to do any thing out of revenge.

15. Resolved, Never to suffer the least motions of anger to irrational beings.

17. Resolved, That I will live so as I shall wish I had done when I come to die.

18. Resolved, To live so at all times, as I think is best in my devout frames, and when I have clearest notions of things of the gospel, and another world.

20. Resolved, To maintain the strictest temperance in eating and drinking.

21. Resolved, Never to do any thing, which if I should see in another, I should count a just occasion to despise him for, or to think any way the more meanly of him.

24. Resolved, Whenever I do any conspicuously evil action, to trace it back, till I come to the original cause; and then both carefully endeavor to do so no more, and to fight and pray with all my might against the original of it.

28. Resolved, To study the Scriptures so steadily, constantly and frequently, as that I may find, and plainly perceive myself to grow in the knowledge of the same.

30. Resolved, To strive to my utmost every week to be brought

higher in religion, and to a higher exercise of grace, than I was the week before.

32. Resolved, To be strictly and firmly faithful to my trust, that that in Prov. xx. 6. *a faithful man who can find?* may not be partly fulfilled in me.

33. Resolved, Always to do what I can towards making, maintaining and establishing peace, when it can be without overbalancing detriment in other respects.

34. Resolved, In narrations never to speak any thing but the pure and simple verity.

36. Resolved, Never to speak evil of any, except I have some particular good call for it.

37. Resolved, To inquire every night, as I am going to bed, wherein I have been negligent, what sin I have committed, and wherein I have denied myself: also at the end of every week, month and year.

38. Resolved, Never to speak any thing that is ridiculous, or matter of laughter on the Lord's day.

39. Resolved, Never to do any thing that I so much question the lawfulness of, as that I intend, at the same time, to consider and examine afterwards, whether it be lawful or no: except I as much question the lawfulness of the omission.

41. Resolved, To ask myself at the end of every day, week, month and year, wherein I could possibly in any respect have done better.

42. Resolved, Frequently to renew the dedication of myself to God, which was made at my baptism; which I solemnly renewed, when I was received into the communion of the church; and which I have solemnly re-made this twelfth day of January, 1722–3.

43. Resolved, Never hence-forward, till I die, to act as if I were any way my own, but entirely and altogether God's, agreeable to what is to be found in Saturday, January 12.

46. Resolved, Never to allow the least measure of any fretting uneasiness at my father or mother. Resolved to suffer no effects of it, so much as in the least alteration of speech, or motion of my eye: and to be especially careful of it, with respect to any of our family.

47. Resolved, To endeavor to my utmost to deny whatever is

not most agreeable to a good, and universally sweet and benevolent, quiet, peaceable, contented, easy, compassionate, generous, humble, meek, modest, submissive, obliging, diligent and industrious, charitable, even, patient, moderate, forgiving, sincere temper; and to do at all times what such a temper would lead me to. Examine strictly every week, whether I have done so.

48. Resolved, Constantly, with the utmost niceness and diligence, and the strictest scrutiny, to be looking into the state of my soul, that I may know whether I have truly an interest in Christ or no; that when I come to die, I may not have any negligence respecting this to repent of.

50. Resolved, I will act so as I think I shall judge would have been best, and most prudent, when I come into the future world.

52. I frequently hear persons in old age say how they would live, if they were to live their lives over again: Resolved, that I will live just so as I can think I shall wish I had done, supposing I live to old age.

54. Whenever I hear anything spoken in conversation of any person, if I think it would be praise-worthy in me, Resolved to endeavor to imitate it.

55. Resolved, To endeavor to my utmost to act as I can think I should do, if I had already seen the happiness of heaven, and hell torments.

56. Resolved, Never to give over, nor in the least to slacken my fight with my corruptions, however unsuccessful I may be.

57. Resolved, When I fear misfortunes and adversities, to examine whether I have done my duty, and resolve to do it; and let it be just as Providence orders it, I will as far as I can, be concerned about nothing but my duty and my sin.

62. Resolved, Never to do any thing but duty; and then according to Eph. vi. 6, 7, 8. do it willingly and cheerfully as unto the Lord, and not to man; knowing that whatever good thing any man doth, the same shall he receive of the Lord.

65. Resolved, Very much to exercise myself in this all my life long, viz. with the greatest openness I am capable of, to declare my ways to God, and lay open my soul to him: all my sins, temptations, difficulties, sorrows, fears, hopes, desires, and every thing,

and every circumstance, according to Dr. Manton's twenty-seventh sermon on the 119th Psalm.

67. Resolved, After afflictions, to inquire, what I am the better for them, what good I have got by them, and what I might have got by them.[2]

### Section II   EXTRACTS FROM HIS PRIVATE DIARY

*Saturday, Dec. 22, 1722.*  This day revived by God's Spirit. Affected with the sense of the excellency of holiness. Felt more exercise of love to Christ than usual. Have also felt sensible repentance of sin, because it was committed against so merciful and good a God. This night made the thirty-seventh Resolution.

*Sabbath-Day Night, Dec. 23.* Made the thirty-eighth Resolution.

*Monday, Dec. 24.* Higher thoughts than usual of the excellency of Jesus Christ and His kingdom.

*Wednesday, Jan. 2, 1722–3.* Dull. I find by experience, that let me make resolutions, and do what I will, with never so many inventions, it is all nothing, and to no purpose at all, without the motions of the Spirit of God: for if the Spirit of God should be as much withdrawn from me always, as for the week past, notwithstanding all I do, I should not grow; but should languish, and miserably fade away.—There is no dependence upon myself. It is to no purpose to resolve, except we depend on the grace of God; for if it were not for His mere grace, one might be a very good man one day, and a very wicked one the next.

*Sabbath-Day, Jan. 6.* at night. Much concerned about the improvement of precious time. Intend to live in continual mortification, without ceasing, as long as in this world.

*Tuesday, Jan. 8.* in the morning. Higher thoughts than usual, of the excellency of Christ, and felt an unusual repentance of sin therefrom.

*Wednesday, Jan. 9.* at night. Decayed. I am sometimes apt to

[2] The Resolutions are seventy in number. But part of them are here transcribed, as a specimen of the whole. The number here affixed to them, is that by which they are numbered in the original manuscript; and retained here for the sake of the references made to some of them in the Diary, as the reader will presently see.

think, I have a great deal more of holiness than I have. I find now and then, that abominable corruption which is directly contrary to what I read of eminent Christians.—How deceitful is my heart! I take up a strong resolution, but how soon does it weaken!

*Thursday, Jan. 10.* about noon. Reviving. 'Tis a great dishonor to Christ, in whom I hope I have an interest, to be uneasy at my worldly state and condition. When I see the prosperity of others, and that all things go easy with them; the world is smooth to them, and they are happy in many respects, and very prosperous, or are advanced to much honor etc. to grudge and envy them, or be the least uneasy at it; to wish or long for the same prosperity, and that it would ever be so with me. Wherefore concluded always to rejoice in every one's prosperity, and to expect for myself no happiness of that nature as long as I live; but depend upon afflictions, and betake myself entirely to another happiness.

I think I find myself much more sprightly and healthy, both in body and mind, for my self-denial in eating, drinking and sleeping.

I think it would be advantageous every morning to consider my business and temptations; and what sins I shall be exposed to that day: and to make a resolution how to improve the day, and to avoid those sins. And so at the beginning of every week, month and year.

I never knew before what was meant by not setting our hearts upon these things. 'Tis, not to care about them, to depend upon them, to afflict ourselves much with fears of losing them, nor please ourselves with expectation of obtaining them, or hope of the continuance of them. At night made the forty-first Resolution.

*Saturday, Jan. 12.* in the morning. I have this day solemnly renewed my baptismal covenant and self-dedication, which I renewed when I was received into the communion of the church. I have been before God; and have given myself, all that I am and have to God, so that I am not in any respect my own: I can challenge no right in myself, I can challenge no right in this understanding, this will, these affections that are in me; neither have I any right to this body, or any of its members: no right to this tongue, these hands, nor feet: no right to these senses, these eyes, these ears, this smell or taste. I have given myself clear away, and have not retained any thing as my own. I have been to God this morning, and told Him that I gave myself *wholly* to Him. I have given every power to Him; so that for the future I will challenge no right in myself, in any respect. I have expressly promised Him, and do now promise Almighty God, that by His grace I will not. I have this morning told Him, that I did take Him for my whole portion and felicity, looking on nothing else as any part of my happiness, nor acting as if it were; and His law for the constant rule of my obedience: and would fight with all my might against the world, the flesh and the devil, to the end of my life. And did believe in Jesus Christ, and receive Him as a Prince and a Saviour; and would adhere to the faith and obedience of the gospel, how hazardous and difficult soever the profession and practice of it may be. That I did receive the blessed Spirit as my teacher, sanctifier and only comforter; and cherish all his motions to enlighten, purify, confirm, comfort and assist me. This I have done. And I pray God, for the sake of Christ, to look upon it as a self-dedication; and to receive me now as entirely His own, and deal with me in all respects as such; whether He afflicts me or prospers me, or whatever He pleases to do with me, who am His. Now, henceforth I am not to act in any respect as my own.—I shall act as my own, if I ever make use of any of my powers to any thing that is not to the glory of God, and don't make the glorifying Him my whole and entire business; if I murmur in the least at afflictions; if I grieve at the prosperity of others; if I am any way uncharitable; if I am angry because of injuries; if I revenge: if I do anything, purely to please myself, or if I avoid any thing for the sake of my ease: if I omit any thing because it is great self-denial: if I trust to myself: if I take any of the praise of any good that I do, or rather God does by me; or if I am any way proud.

This day made the forty-second and forty-third Resolutions.

*Monday, Jan. 14.*—The dedication I made of myself to my God, on Saturday last, has been exceeding useful to me. I thought I had a more spiritual insight into the Scripture, reading the eighth chapter to the Romans, than ever in my life before.

Great instances of mortification are deep wounds given to the body of sin, hard blows that make him stagger and reel: we thereby get great ground and footing against him.—While we live without great instances of mortification and self-denial, the old man keeps whereabouts he was; for he is sturdy and obstinate, and will not stir for small blows. After the greatest mortifications, I always find the greatest comfort.

Supposing there was never but one complete Christian, in all respects of a right stamp, having Christianity shining in its true luster, at a time in the world; resolved to act just as I would do, if I strove with all my might to be that one, that should be in my time.

*Tuesday, Jan. 15.* It seemed yesterday, the day before and Saturday, that I should always retain the same resolutions to the same height; but alas, how soon do I decay! O, how weak, how infirm, how unable to do any thing am I! What a poor, inconsistent, what a miserable wretch, without the assistance of God's Spirit! While I stand, I am ready to think I stand in my own strength, and upon my own legs; and I am ready to triumph over my enemies, as if it were I myself that caused them to flee: when alas! I am but a poor infant, upheld by Jesus Christ; who holds me up, and gives me liberty to smile to see my enemies flee, when He drives them before me; and so I laugh, as though I myself did it, when it is only Jesus Christ leads me along, and fights Himself against my enemies. And now the Lord has a little left me, and how weak do I find myself! O, let it teach me to depend less on myself, to be more humble, and to give more of the praise of my ability to Jesus Christ. The heart of man is deceitful above all things, and desperately wicked, who can know it?

*Saturday, Feb. 16.* I do certainly know that I love holiness, such as the gospel requires.

At night. I have been negligent for the month past in these three things; I have not been watchful enough over my appetite in eating and drinking; in rising too late a-mornings; and in not applying myself with application enough to the duty of secret prayer.

*Sabbath-Day, Feb. 17.* near sun-set. Renewedly promised, that I will accept of God, for my whole portion; and that I will be contented, whatever else I am denied. I will not murmur, nor be grieved, whatever prosperity, upon any account, I see others enjoy, and I am denied.

*Saturday, March 2.*—O, how much pleasanter is humility than pride! O, that God would fill me with exceeding great humility, and that he would evermore keep me from all pride! The pleasures of humility are really the most refined, inward and exquisite delights in the world. How hateful is a proud man! How hateful is a worm that lifts up itself with pride! What a foolish, silly, miserable, blind, deceived, poor worm am I, when pride works!

*Wednesday, March 6.* near sun-set. Felt the doctrines of election, free grace, and of our not being able to do any thing without the grace of God; and that holiness is entirely, throughout, the work of God's Spirit, with more pleasure than before.

*Monday Morning, April 1.* I think it best not to allow myself to laugh at the faults, follies and infirmities of others.

*Saturday Night, April 6.*\* This week I found myself so far gone, that it seemed to me, that I should never recover more. Let God of His mercy return unto me, and no more leave me thus to sink and decay! I know, O Lord, that without Thy help, I shall fall innumerable times, notwithstanding all my resolutions, how often soever repeated.

*Saturday Night, April 13.*† I could pray more heartily this night, for the forgiveness of my enemies, than ever before.

*Wednesday, May 1.* forenoon. Last night I came home, after my melancholy parting from New York.

I have always, in every different state of life, I have hitherto been in, thought the troubles and difficulties of that state, to be greater than those of any other that I proposed to be in; and when I have altered with assurance of mending myself, I have still thought the same; yea, that the difficulties of that state, are greater than those of that I left last. Lord, grant that from hence I may learn to withdraw my thoughts, affections, desires and expectations, entirely from the world, and may fix them upon the heavenly state; where there is fulness of joy; where reigns heavenly, sweet, calm and delightful love without alloy; where there are continually the dearest expressions of this love: where there is the enjoyment of the persons loved, without ever parting: where those persons, who appear so lovely in this world, will really be inexpressibly

* Edwards miscalculated these dates as April 7 and 14, respectively [ed.].
† Northampton.

more lovely, and full of love to us. How sweetly will the mutual lovers join together to sing the praises of God and the Lamb! How full will it fill us with joy to think, this enjoyment, these sweet exercises, will never cease or come to an end, but will last to all eternity.

Remember, after journeys, removes, overturnings, and alterations in the state of my life, to reflect and consider, whether therein I have managed the best way possible, respecting my soul? and before such alterations, if foreseen, to resolve how to act.

*Thursday, May 2.*—I think it a very good way to examine dreams every morning when I awake, what are the nature, circumstances, principles and ends of my imaginary actions and passions in them, to discern what are my chief inclinations etc.

*Saturday Night, May 4.* Although I have in some measure subdued a disposition to chide and fret, yet I find a certain inclination, which is not agreeable to Christian sweetness of temper and conversation: either by too much dogmaticalness, too much of the egoism; a disposition to be telling of my own dislike and scorn; and freedom from those that are innocent, yea common infirmities of men; and many other such like things. O that God would help me to discern all the flaws and defects of my temper and conversation, and help me in the difficult work of amending them: and that he would fill me so full of Christianity, that the foundation of all these disagreeable irregularities may be destroyed, and the contrary sweetnesses and beauties may of themselves naturally follow.

*Sabbath-Day, May 5.* in the morning. This day made the forty-seventh Resolution.

*Sabbath-Day, May 12.* I think I find in my heart to be glad from the hopes I have that my eternity is to be spent in spiritual and holy joys, arising from the manifestation of God's love, and the exercise of holiness and a burning love to him.

*Saturday Night, May 18.* I now plainly perceive what great obligations I am under to love and honor my parents. I have great reason to believe, that their counsel and education have been my making; notwithstanding, in the time of it, it seemed to do me so little good. I have good reason to hope that their prayers for me, have been in many things very powerful and prevalent; that God has in many things, taken me under his care and guidance, provision and direction, in answer to their prayers for me. I was never made so sensible of it as now.

*Wednesday, May 22.* in the morning. *Memorandum.* To take special care of these following things; evil speaking, fretting, eating, drinking and sleeping, speaking simple verity, joining in prayer, slightiness in secret prayer, listlessness and negligence and thoughts that cherish sin.

*Saturday, May 25.* in the morning. As I was this morning reading the seventeenth Resolution, it was suggested to me, that if I was now to die, I should wish that I had prayed more that God would make me know my state, whether it be good or bad; and that I had taken more pains to see and narrowly search into this matter. Wherefore, *Mem.* For the future most nicely and diligently to look into our old divines' opinions concerning conversion. Made the forty-eighth Resolution.

*Friday, June 1.* Afternoon. I have abundant cause, O my merciful Father, to love Thee ardently, and greatly to bless and praise Thee, that Thou hast heard me in my earnest request, and hath so answered my prayer for mercy to keep from decay and sinking. O, graciously, of Thy mere goodness, still continue to pity my misery, by reason of my sinfulness. O my dear Redeemer, I commit myself, together with my prayer and thanksgiving into Thine hand.

*Monday. July 1.* Again confirmed by experience of the happy effects of strict temperance, with respect both to body and mind. Resolved for the future to observe rather more of meekness, moderation and temper in disputes.

*Thursday, July 18.* near sun-set. Resolved to endeavor to make sure of that sign the Apostle James gives of a perfect man, Jam. iii. 2. *If any man offend not in word, the same is a perfect man, and able also to bridle the whole body.*

*Monday, July 22.* I see there is danger of my being drawn into transgression by the power of such temptations as a fear of seeming uncivil, and of offending friends. Watch against it.

*Tuesday, July 23.* When I find those groanings which cannot be uttered, the Apostle speaks of; and those soul-breakings, for the longing it hath, the Psalmist speaks of, Psal. cxix. 20. to humor and promote them to the utmost of my power, and be not weary of earnestly endeavoring to vent my desires.

To count it all joy when I have occasion of great self-denial, because then I have a glorious opportunity of giving deadly wounds to the body of sin, and greatly confirming and establishing the new nature: to seek to mortify sin, and increase in holiness: these are the best opportunities, according to *January 14*.

To improve afflictions of all kinds as blessed opportunities of forcibly bearing on in my Christian course, notwithstanding that which is so very apt to discourage me, and to damp the vigor of my mind, and to make me lifeless: also as opportunities of trusting and confiding in God, and getting a habit of that, according to the fifty-seventh Resolution. And as an opportunity of rending my heart off from the world, and setting it upon heaven alone. To improve them as opportunities to repent of, and bewail my sin, and abhor myself. And as a blessed opportunity to exercise patience; to trust in God, and divert my mind from the affliction, by fixing myself in religious exercises. Also, let me comfort myself, that it is the very nature of afflictions to make the heart better; and if I am made better by them, what need I be concerned, however grievous they seem for the present?

*Friday Afternoon, July 26.* To be particularly careful to keep up inviolable, a trust and reliance, ease and entire rest in God in all conditions, according to fifty-seventh Resolution; for this I have found to be wonderfully advantageous to me.

*Monday, July 29.* When I am concerned how I shall perform any thing to public acceptance, to be very careful that I have it very clear to me, that I do what is duty and prudence in the matter.

*Wednesday, July 31.*—Never in the least to seek to hear sarcastical relations of others' faults. Never to give credit to any thing said against others, except there is very plain reason for it; nor to behave in any respect the otherwise for it.

*Wednesday, Aug. 7.* To esteem as some advantage, that the duties of religion are difficult, and that many difficulties are sometimes to be gone through in the way of duty. Religion is the sweeter, and what is gained by labor, is abundantly more precious: as a woman loves her child the better for having brought it forth with travail. And even to Christ Jesus Himself, His mediatorial glory, His victory and triumph, His kingdom which He hath obtained; how much more glorious is it, how much more excellent and precious, for His having wrought it out by such agonies!

*Friday, Aug. 9.*—One thing that may be a good help towards thinking profitably in time of vacation is, when I light on a profitable thought, that I can fix my mind on, to follow it as far as possibly I can to advantage.

*Sabbath-Day,* after meeting, *Aug. 11.* Resolved always to do that which I shall wish I had done when I see others do it. As for instance, sometimes I argue with myself, that such an act of good nature, kindness, forbearance, or forgiveness, etc. is not my duty, because it will have such and such consequences: yet, when I see others do it, then it appears amiable to me, and I wish I had done it; and I see that none of those feared inconveniences follow.

*Tuesday, Aug. 13.* I find it would be very much to advantage, to be thoroughly acquainted with the Scriptures. When I am reading doctrinal books or books of controversy, I can proceed with abundantly more confidence; can see upon what footing and foundation I stand.

*Thursday, Aug. 29.*—The objection my corruptions make against doing whatever my hand finds to do with my might is, that it is a constant mortification. Let this objection by no means ever prevail.

*Monday, Sept. 2.*—There is much folly, when I am quite sure I am in the right, and others are positive in contradicting me, to enter into a vehement or long debate upon it.

*Monday, Sept. 23.* I observe that old men seldom have any advantage of new discoveries; because they are beside a way of thinking, they have been so long used to. Resolved, if ever I live to years, that I will be impartial to hear the reasons of all pretended discoveries, and receive them, if rational, how long soever I have been used to another way of thinking.

*Thursday, Oct. 18.* To follow the example of Mr. *B——* who, though he meets with great difficulties, yet undertakes them with a smiling countenance, as though he thought them but little; and speaks of them as if they were very small.

*Thursday, Nov. 26.* 'Tis a most evil and pernicious practice in meditations on afflictions, to sit ruminating on the aggravations of the affliction, and reckoning up the evil, dark circumstances thereof, and dwelling long on the dark side; it doubles and trebles the affliction. And so when speaking of them to others, to make them as bad as we can, and use our eloquence to set forth our own troubles, and are all the while making new trouble, and feeding and pampering the old; whereas the contrary practice would starve our afflictions. If we dwelt on the light side of things in our thoughts, and extenuated them all that possibly we could, when speaking of them, we should think little of them ourselves; and the affliction would really, in a great measure, vanish away.

*Thursday Night, Dec. 12.* If at any time I am forced to tell others of that wherein I think they are something to blame; for the avoiding the important evil, that would otherwise ensue, not to tell it to them, so that there shall be a probability of their taking it as the effect of little, fretting, angry emotions of mind.

*Dec. 31.* at night. Concluded never to suffer nor express any angry emotions of mind more or less, except the honor of God calls for it, in zeal for Him, or to preserve myself from being trampled on.

*Wednesday, Jan. 1, 1723-4.* Not to spend too much time in thinking even of important and necessary worldly business. To allow everything its proportion of thought, according to its urgency and importance.

*Friday, Jan. 10.* [After having wrote considerable in a short-hand, which he used when he would have what he wrote, effectually concealed from everybody but himself, he notes the following words in round hand], remember to act according to Prov. xii. 23, "A prudent man concealeth knowledge."

*Monday, Feb. 3.* Let everything have the value now, that it will have on a sick-bed: and frequently in my pursuits of whatever kind, let this come into my mind: "how much shall I value this on my death-bed?"

*Wednesday, Feb. 5.* Have not in time past in my prayers, enough insisted upon the glorifying God in the world, and the advancement of the kingdom of Christ, the prosperity of the church and the good of men. Determined that this objection is without weight, viz. That 'tis not likely that God will make great alterations in the whole world, and overturnings in kingdoms and nations, only for the prayers of one obscure person, seeing such things used to be done in answer to the united, earnest prayers of the whole church: and if my prayers should have some influence, it would be but imperceptible and small.

*Thursday, Feb. 6.* More convinced than ever of the usefulness of a free religious conversation. I find by conversing on natural philosophy, I gain knowledge abundantly faster, and see the reasons of things much clearer, than in private study. Wherefore earnestly to seek at all times for religious conversation; for those that I can with profit and delight and freedom so converse with.

*Sabbath-Day, Feb. 23.*—If I act according to my resolution, I shall desire riches no otherwise than as they are helpful to religion. But this I determine, as what is really evident from many parts of Scripture, that to fallen man they have a greater tendency to hurt religion.

*Saturday, May 23.* How it comes about I know not; but I have remarked it hitherto, that at those times when I have read the Scripture most, I have evermore been most lively, and in the best frames.

*Saturday Night, June 6.* This week has been a remarkable week with me with respect to despondencies, fears, perplexities, multitudes of cares and distraction of mind; being the week I came hither to New Haven, in order to entrance upon the office of Tutor of the College. I have now abundant reason to be convinced of the troublesomeness and vexation of the world, and that it never will be another kind of world.

*Tuesday, July 7.* When I am giving the relation of a thing, to abstain from altering either in the matter or manner of speaking, so much, as that if every one afterward should alter as much, it would at last come to be properly false.

*Tuesday, Sept. 2.* By a sparingness in diet, and eating, as much as may be, what is light and easy of digestion, I shall doubtless be able to think clearer, and shall gain time. 1*st*. By lengthening out my life. 2*dly*. Shall need less time for digestion after meals. 3*rdly*. Shall be able to study closer without wrong to my health. 4*thly*.

Shall need less time to sleep. *5thly*. Shall seldomer be troubled
with the headache.

*Sabbath-Day, Nov. 22*. Considering that by-standers always
espy some faults which we don't see ourselves, or at least are not
so fully sensible of: there are many secret workings of corruption
which escape our sight, and others only are sensible of: resolved
therefore, that I will, if I can by any convenient means, learn what
faults others find in me, or what things they see in me, that appear
any way blame-worthy, unlovely or unbecoming.

*Section III*   REFLECTION ON THE FOREGOING EXTRACTS

The foregoing extracts were wrote by Mr. Edwards in the
twentieth and twenty-first years of his age, as appears by the dates.
This being kept in mind, the judicious reader will make proper
allowance for some things, which may appear a little juvenile, or
like a young Christian, as to the matter, or manner of expression;
which would not have been found, had it not have been done in
early life. Which, indeed are no blemishes, the whole being taken
together: as by this, it appears more natural, and the strength of
his resolution, and fervor of mind; and his skill and discerning in
divine things, so seldom found even in old age, are the more
striking. And in this view, we shall be led to admire his conscientious strictness, his zeal and painfulness, his experience and judgment in true religion, at so early an age. For here are not only the
most convincing evidences of sincerity and thorough religion, of
his engaging in a life devoted to God in good earnest, so as to
make religion his only business; but through his great attention
to this matter, he appears to have the judgment and experience of
gray hairs.

This is the beginning of a life so eminently holy and useful as
Mr. Edwards's was. He who became one of the greatest divines in
this age; has had the applause and admiration of America, Britain,
Holland and Germany, for his piety, and great judgment and skill
in divinity; and has been honored above most others in the
Christian world, in this century; in his being made the instrument

of doing so much good: he began his life thus: he entered on a public life with such views, such exercises, such resolutions.

This may serve as a direction and excitement to those who are young, to devote themselves to God in good earnest, and enter on the business of strict and thorough religion without delay: especially those who are looking towards the work of the ministry, as they would take the most direct, the only way to answer the good ends which they profess to seek.

It is to be lamented, that there is so much reason to think, there are so few instances of such early piety in our day. If the Protestant world abounded with young persons of this stamp; with young men, who were preparing for the work of the ministry, with such a temper, such exercises, such resolutions, what a delightful prospect would this afford, of the near approach of happier days, than the church of God has ever yet seen! what pleasing hopes that the great, the merciful Head of the church, was about to send forth laborers, faithful, successful laborers into His harvest; and bless His people with "pastors which shall feed them with knowledge and understanding"!

But if our youth neglect all proper improvement of the mind; are shy of seriousness and strict piety; choose to live strangers to it, and keep at a distance from all appearance of it; are wanton, and given to carnal pleasures; what a gloomy prospect does this afford! If they who enter into the work of the ministry; from a gay, careless, and what may justly be called a vicious life, betake themselves to a little superficial study of divinity, and soon begin to preach; while all the external seriousness and zeal they put on, is only from worldly motives; they being without any inward, experimental acquaintance with spiritual, divine things, and even so much as any taste for true divinity, no wonder if the churches "suck dry breasts"; and there are many ignorant watchmen.

But, as the best comment on the foregoing Resolutions and Diary; and that the reader may have a more particular, full and instructive view of Mr. Edwards's entrance on a religious life, and progress in it, as consisting in the views and exercises of his mind; a brief account thereof is here inserted, which was found among his papers, in his own handwriting: and which, it seems, was wrote near twenty years after, for his own private advantage.

*Section IV*   AN ACCOUNT OF HIS CONVERSION, EXPERIENCES, AND RELIGIOUS EXERCISES, GIVEN BY HIMSELF

I had a variety of concerns and exercises about my soul from my childhood; but had two more remarkable seasons of awakening, before I met with that change, by which I was brought to those new dispositions, and that new sense of things, that I have since had. The first time was when I was a boy, some years before I went to college, at a time of remarkable awakening in my father's congregation. I was then very much affected for many months, and concerned about the things of religion, and my soul's salvation; and was abundant in duties. I used to pray five times a day in secret, and to spend much time in religious talk with other boys; and used to meet with them to pray together. I experienced I know not what kind of delight in religion. My mind was much engaged in it, and had much self-righteous pleasure; and it was my delight to abound in religious duties. I, with some of my school-mates joined together, and built a booth in a swamp, in a very secret and retired place, for a place of prayer. And besides, I had particular secret places of my own in the woods, where I used to retire by myself; and used to be from time to time much affected. My affections seemed to be lively and easily moved, and I seemed to be in my element, when engaged in religious duties. And I am ready to think, many are deceived with such affections, and such a kind of delight, as I then had in religion, and mistake it for grace.

But in process of time, my convictions and affections wore off; and I entirely lost all those affections and delights, and left off secret prayer, at least as to any constant performance of it; and returned like a dog to his vomit, and went on in ways of sin.

Indeed, I was at some times very uneasy, especially towards the latter part of the time of my being at college. 'Till it pleas'd God, in my last year at college, at a time when I was in the midst of many uneasy thoughts about the state of my soul, to seize me with a pleurisy; in which he brought me nigh to the grave, and shook me over the pit of hell.

But yet, it was not long after my recovery, before I fell again into my old ways of sin. But God would not suffer me to go on with any quietness; but I had great and violent inward struggles: 'till after many conflicts with wicked inclinations, and repeated resolutions, and bonds that I laid myself under by a kind of vows to God, I was brought wholly to break off all former wicked ways, and all ways of known outward sin; and to apply myself to seek my salvation, and practice the duties of religion: But without that kind of affection and delight, that I had formerly experienced. My concern now wrought more by inward struggles and conflicts, and self-reflections. I made seeking my salvation the main business of my life. But yet it seems to me, I sought after a miserable manner: Which has made me some times since to question, whether ever it issued in that which was saving; being ready to doubt, whether such miserable seeking was ever succeeded. But yet I was brought to seek salvation, in a manner that I never was before. I felt a spirit to part with all things in the world, for an interest in Christ. My concern continued and prevailed, with many exercising thoughts and inward struggles; but yet it never seemed to be proper to express my concern that I had, by the name of terror.

From my childhood up, my mind had been wont to be full of objections against the doctrine of God's sovereignty, in choosing whom he would to eternal life, and rejecting whom he pleased; leaving them eternally to perish, and be everlastingly tormented in hell. It used to appear like a horrible doctrine to me. But I remember the time very well, when I seemed to be convinced, and fully satisfied, as to this sovereignty of God, and his justice in thus eternally disposing of men, according to his sovereign pleasure. But never could give an account, how, or by what means, I was thus convinced; not in the least imagining, in the time of it, nor a long time after, that there was any extraordinary influence of God's spirit in it; but only that now I saw further, and my reason apprehended the justice and reasonableness of it. However, my mind rested in it; and it put an end to all those cavils and objections, that had 'till then abode with me, all the preceding part of my life. And there has been a wonderful alteration in my mind, with respect to the doctrine of God's sovereignty, from that day to this; so that I scarce ever have found so much as the rising of an objection against God's sovereignty, in the most absolute sense, in showing mercy to whom he will show mercy, and hardening and eternally damning whom he will. God's absolute sovereignty, and justice, with respect to salvation and damnation, is what my mind seems to rest assured of, as much as of any thing that I see with my eyes; at least it is so at times. But I have often times since that first conviction, had quite another kind of sense of God's sovereignty, than I had then. I have often since, not only had a conviction, but a *delightful* conviction. The doctrine of God's sovereignty has very often appeared, an exceeding pleasant, bright and sweet doctrine to me: and absolute sovereignty is what I love to ascribe to God. But my first conviction was not with this.

The first that I remember that ever I found any thing of that sort of inward, sweet delight in God and divine things, that I have lived much in since, was on reading those words, I Tim. i. 17. "Now unto the king eternal, immortal, invisible, the only wise God, be honor and glory for ever and ever, Amen." As I read the words, there came into my soul, and was as it were diffused thro' it, a sense of the glory of the Divine Being; a new sense, quite different from any thing I ever experienced before. Never any words of scripture seemed to me as these words did. I thought with myself, how excellent a being that was; and how happy I should be, if I might enjoy that God, and be wrapt up to God in Heaven, and be as it were swallowed up in Him. I kept saying, and as it were singing over these words of scripture to myself; and went to prayer, to pray to God that I might enjoy him; and prayed in a manner quite different from what I used to do; with a new sort of affection. But it never came into my thought, that there was any thing spiritual, or of a saving nature in this.

From about that time, I began to have a new kind of apprehensions and ideas of Christ, and the work of redemption, and the glorious way of salvation by Him. I had an inward, sweet sense of these things, that at times came into my heart; and my soul was led away in pleasant views and contemplations of them. And my mind was greatly engaged, to spend my time in reading and meditating on Christ; and the beauty and excellency of His person, and the lovely way of salvation, by free grace in Him. I found no books so delightful to me, as those that treated of these subjects. Those words Cant. ii. I. used to be abundantly with me: *I am the Rose of Sharon, the lily of the valleys.* The words seemed to me, sweetly to represent, the loveliness and beauty of Jesus Christ. And the whole Book of Canticles used to be pleasant to me; and I used to be much in reading it, about that time. And found, from time to time, an inward sweetness, that used, as it were, to carry me away in my contemplations; in what I know not how to express otherwise, than by a calm, sweet abstraction of soul from all the concerns of this world; and a kind of vision, or fix'd ideas and imaginations, of being alone in the mountains, or some solitary wilderness, far from all mankind, sweetly conversing with Christ, and wrapt and swallowed up in God. The sense I had of divine things, would often of a sudden as it were, kindle up a sweet burning in my heart; an ardor of my soul, that I know not how to express.

Not long after I first began to experience these things, I gave an account to my father, of some things that had pass'd in my mind. I was pretty much affected by the discourse we had together. And when the discourse was ended, I walked abroad alone, in a solitary place in my father's pasture, for contemplation. And as I was walking there, and looked up on the sky and clouds; there came into my mind, a sweet sense of the glorious majesty and grace of God, that I know not how to express. I seemed to see them both in a sweet conjunction: majesty and meekness join'd together: it was a sweet and gentle, and holy majesty; and also a majestic meekness; an awful sweetness; a high, and great, and holy gentleness.

After this my sense of divine things gradually increased, and became more and more lively, and had more of that inward sweetness. The appearance of every thing was altered: there seem'd to be, as it were, a calm, sweet cast, or appearance of divine glory, in almost every thing. God's excellency, his wisdom, his purity and love, seemed to appear in every thing; in the sun, moon and stars; in the clouds, and blue sky; in the grass, flowers, trees; in the water, and all nature; which used greatly to fix my mind. I often used to sit and view the moon, for a long time; and so in the day time, spent much time in viewing the clouds and sky, to behold the sweet glory of God in these things: in the mean time, singing forth with a low voice, my contemplations of the Creator and Redeemer. And scarce any thing, among all the works of nature, was so sweet to me as thunder and lightning. Formerly, nothing had been so terrible to me. I used to be a person uncommonly terrified with thunder: and it used to strike me with terror, when I saw a thunder-storm rising. But now, on the contrary, it rejoiced me. I felt God at the first appearance of a thunder-storm. And used to take the opportunity at such times to fix myself to view the clouds, and see the lightnings play, and hear the majestic and awful voice of God's thunder: which often times was exceeding entertaining, leading me to sweet contemplations of my great and glorious God. And while I viewed, used to spend my time, as it always seem'd natural to me, to sing or chant forth my meditations; to speak my thoughts in soliloquies, and speak with a singing voice.

I felt then a great satisfaction as to my good estate. But that did not content me. I had vehement longings of soul after God and Christ, and after more holiness; wherewith my heart seemed to be full, and ready to break: which often brought to my mind, the words of the psalmist, Psal. cxix. 28. *My soul breaketh for the longing it hath.* I often felt a mourning and lamenting in my heart, that I had not turned to God sooner, that I might have had more time to grow in grace. My mind was greatly fix'd on divine things; I was almost perpetually in the contemplation of them. Spent most of my time in thinking of divine things, year after year. And used to spend abundance of my time, in walking alone in the woods, and solitary places, for meditation, soliloquy and prayer, and converse with God. And it was always my manner, at such times, to sing forth my contemplations. And was almost constantly in ejaculatory prayer, wherever I was. Prayer seem'd to be natural to me; as the breath, by which the inward burnings of my heart had vent.

The delights which I now felt in things of religion, were of an exceeding different kind, from those forementioned, that I had when I was a boy. They were totally of another kind; and what I then had no more notion or idea of, than one born blind has of pleasant and beautiful colors. They were of a more inward, pure, soul-animating and refreshing nature. Those former delights, never reached the heart; and did not arise from any sight of the divine excellency of the things of God; or any taste of the soul-satisfying, and life-giving good, there is in them.

My sense of divine things seemed gradually to increase, 'till I went to preach at New York; which was about a year and a half after they began. While I was there, I felt them, very sensibly, in a much higher degree, than I had done before. My longings after God and holiness, were much increased. Pure and humble, holy and heavenly Christianity, appeared exceeding amiable to me. I felt in me a burning desire to be in every thing a complete Christian; and conformed to the blessed image of Christ: and that I might live in all things, according to the pure, sweet and blessed rules of the gospel. I had an eager thirsting after progress in these things. My longings after it, put me upon pursuing and pressing after them. It was my continual strife day and night, and constant inquiry, How I should be more holy, and live more holily, and more becoming a child of God, and disciple of Christ. I sought an increase of grace and holiness, and that I might live an holy life, with vastly more earnestness, than ever I sought grace, before I had it. I used to be continually examining myself, and studying and contriving for likely ways and means, how I should live holily, with far greater diligence and earnestness, than ever I pursued any thing in my life: But with too great a dependence on my own strength; which afterwards proved a great damage to me. My experience had not then taught me, as it has done since, my extreme feebleness and impotence, every manner of way; and the innumerable and bottomless depths of secret corruption and deceit, that there was in my heart. However, I went on with my eager pursuit after more holiness; and sweet conformity to Christ.

The Heaven I desired was a heaven of holiness; to be with God, and to spend my eternity in divine love, and holy communion with Christ. My mind was very much taken up with contemplations on heaven, and the enjoyments of those there; and living there in perfect holiness, humility and love. And it used at that time to appear a great part of the happiness of heaven, that there the saints could express their love to Christ. It appear'd to me a great clog and hindrance and burden to me, that what I felt within, I could not express to God, and give vent to, as I desired. The inward ardor of my soul, seem'd to be hindered and pent up, and could not freely flame out as it would. I used often to think, how in heaven, this sweet principle should freely and fully vent and express itself. Heaven appeared to me exceeding delightful as a world of love. It appeared to me, that all happiness consisted in living in pure, humble, heavenly, divine love.

I remember the thoughts I used then to have of holiness. I remember I then said sometimes to myself, I do certainly know that I love holiness, such as the gospel prescribes. It appeared to me, there was nothing in it but what was ravishingly lovely. It appeared to me, to be the highest beauty and amiableness, above all other beauties: that it was a *divine* beauty; far purer than any thing here upon earth; and that every thing else, was like mire, filth and defilement, in comparison of it.

Holiness, as I then wrote down some of my contemplations on it, appeared to me to be of a sweet, pleasant, charming, serene, calm nature. It seemed to me, it brought an inexpressible purity, brightness, peacefulness and ravishment to the soul: and that it made the soul like a field or garden of God, with all manner of pleasant flowers; that is all pleasant, delightful and undisturbed; enjoying a sweet calm, and the gently vivifying beams of the sun. The soul of a true Christian, as I then wrote my meditations, appear'd like such a little white flower, as we see in the spring of the year; low and humble on the ground, opening its bosom, to receive the pleasant beams of the sun's glory; rejoicing as it were, in a calm rapture; diffusing around a sweet fragrancy; standing peacefully and lovingly, in the midst of other flowers round about; all in like manner opening their bosoms, to drink in the light of the sun.

There was no part of creature-holiness, that I then, and at other times, had so great a sense of the loveliness of, as humility, brokenness of heart and poverty of spirit: and there was nothing that I had such a spirit to long for. My heart as it were panted after this, to lie low before God, and in the dust; that I might be nothing, and that God might be all; that I might become as a little child.

While I was there at New York, I sometimes was much affected with reflections on my past life, considering how late it was, before I began to be truly religious; and how wickedly I had lived 'till then: and once so as to weep abundantly, and for a considerable time together.

On January 12, 1722–3. I made a solemn dedication of myself to God, and wrote it down; giving up myself, and all that I had to God; to be for the future in no respect my own; to act as one that had no right to himself, in any respect. And solemnly vowed to take God for my whole portion and felicity; looking on nothing else as any part of my happiness, nor acting as if it were: and his law for the constant rule of my obedience: engaging to fight with all my might, against the world, the flesh and the devil, to the end of my life. But have reason to be infinitely humbled, when I consider, how much I have fail'd of answering my obligation.

I had then abundance of sweet religious conversation in the family where I lived, with Mr. John Smith, and his pious mother. My heart was knit in affection to those, in whom were appearances of true piety; and I could bear the thoughts of no other companions, but such as were holy, and the disciples of the blessed Jesus. I had great longings for the advancement of Christ's kingdom in the world. My secret prayer used to be in great part taken up in praying for it. If I heard the least hint of any thing that happened in any part of the world, that appear'd to me, in some respect or other, to have a favorable aspect on the interest of Christ's kingdom, my soul eagerly catch'd at it; and it would much animate and refresh me. I used to be earnest to read public news-letters, mainly for that end; to see if I could not find some news favorable to the interest of religion in the world.

I very frequently used to retire into a solitary place, on the banks of Hudson's river, at some distance from the city, for contemplation on divine things, and secret converse with God; and had many sweet hours there. Sometimes Mr. Smith and I walked there together, to converse of the things of God; and our conversation used much to turn on the advancement of Christ's kingdom in the world, and the glorious things that God would accomplish for his church in the latter days.

I had then, and at other times, the greatest delight in the holy Scriptures, of any book whatsoever. Often-times in reading it, every word seemed to touch my heart. I felt an harmony between something in my heart, and those sweet and powerful words. I seem'd often to see so much light, exhibited by every sentence, and such a refreshing ravishing food communicated, that I could not get along in reading. Used often-times to dwell long on one sentence, to see the wonders contained in it; and yet almost every sentence seemed to be full of wonders.

I came away from New York in the month of April, 1723, and had a most bitter parting with Madam Smith and her son. My heart seemed to sink within me, at leaving the family and city, where I had enjoyed so many sweet and pleasant days. I went from New York to Weathersfield by water. As I sail'd away, I kept sight of the city as long as I could; and when I was out of sight of it, it would affect me much to look that way, with a kind of melancholy mixed with sweetness. However, that night after this sorrowful parting, I was greatly comforted in God at Westchester, where we went ashore to lodge: and had a pleasant time of it all the voyage to Saybrook. It was sweet to me to think of meeting dear Christians in heaven, where we should never part more. At Saybrook we went ashore to lodge on Saturday, and there kept sabbath; where I had a sweet and refreshing season, walking alone in the fields.

After I came home to Windsor, remained much in a like frame of my mind, as I had been in at New York, but only sometimes felt my heart ready to sink, with the thoughts of my friends at New York. And my refuge and support was in contemplations on the heavenly state; as I find in my diary of May 1, 1723. It was my comfort to think of that state, where there is fulness of joy; where reigns heavenly, sweet, calm and delightful love, without alloy; where there are continually the dearest expressions of this love; where is the enjoyment of the persons loved, without ever parting; where these persons that appear so lovely in this world, will really be inexpressibly more lovely, and full of love to us. And how sweetly will the mutual lovers join together to sing the praises of

God and the Lamb! How full will it fill us with joy, to think, that this enjoyment, these sweet exercises will never cease or come to an end; but will last to all eternity!

Continued much in the same frame in the general, that I had been in at New York, till I went to New Haven, to live there as tutor of the college; having some special seasons of uncommon sweetness: particularly once at Boston, in a journey from Boston, walking out alone in the fields. After I went to New Haven, I sunk in religion; my mind being diverted from my eager and violent pursuits after holiness, by some affairs that greatly perplexed and distracted my mind.

In September, 1725, was taken ill at New Haven; and endeavoring to go home to Windsor, was so ill at the North Village, that I could go no further: where I lay sick for about a quarter of a year. And in this sickness, God was pleased to visit me again with the sweet influences of His spirit. My mind was greatly engaged there on divine, pleasant contemplations, and longings of soul. I observed that those who watched with me, would often be looking out for the morning, and seemed to wish for it. Which brought to my mind those words of the psalmist, which my soul with sweetness made its own language. *My soul waitest for the Lord, more than they that watch for the morning, I say, more than they that watch for the morning.* And when the light of the morning came, and the beams of the sun came in at the windows, it refreshed my soul from one morning to another. It seemed to me to be some image of the sweet light of God's glory.

I remember, about that time, I used greatly to long for the conversion of some that I was concerned with. It seem'd to me, I could gladly honor them, and with delight be a servant to them, and lie at their feet, if they were but truly holy.

But some time after this, I was again greatly diverted in my mind, with some temporal concerns, that exceedingly took up my thoughts, greatly to the wounding of my soul: and went on through various exercises, that it would be tedious to relate, that gave me much more experience of my own heart, than ever I had before.

Since I came to this town,* I have often had sweet complacency

* Northampton.

in God, in views of his glorious perfections, and the excellency of Jesus Christ. God has appeared to me, a glorious and lovely being, chiefly on the account of His holiness. The holiness of God has always appeared to me the most lovely of all His attributes. The doctrines of God's absolute sovereignty, and free grace, in showing mercy to whom He would show mercy; and man's absolute dependence on the operations of God's Holy Spirit, have very often appeared to me as sweet and glorious doctrines. These doctrines have been much my delight. God's sovereignty has ever appeared to me, as great part of His glory. It has often been sweet to me to go to God, and adore Him as a sovereign God, and ask sovereign mercy of Him.

I have loved the doctrines of the gospel: They have been to my soul like green pastures. The gospel has seem'd to me to be the richest treasure; the treasure that I have most desired, and longed that it might dwell richly in me. The way of salvation by Christ, has appeared in a general way, glorious and excellent, and most pleasant and beautiful. It has often seem'd to me, that it would in a great measure spoil heaven, to receive it in any other way. That Text has often been affecting and delightful to me, Isai. xxxii. 2. *A man shall be an hiding place from the wind, and a covert from the tempest etc.*

It has often appear'd sweet to me, to be united to Christ; to have Him for my head, and to be a member of His body: and also to have Christ for my teacher and prophet. I very often think with sweetness and longings and pantings of soul, of being a little child, taking hold of Christ, to be led by Him through the wilderness of this world. That text, Matth. xviii. at the beginning, has often been sweet to me, *Except ye be converted, and become as little children etc.* I love to think of coming to Christ, to receive salvation of Him, poor in spirit, and quite empty of self; humbly exalting Him alone; cut entirely off from my own root, and to grow into, and out of Christ: to have God in Christ to be all in all; and to live by faith on the Son of God, a life of humble, unfeigned confidence in Him. That Scripture has often been sweet to me, Psal. cxv. I. *Not unto us, O Lord, not unto us, but unto Thy name give glory, for Thy mercy, and for Thy truth's sake.* And those words of Christ, Luk. x. 21. *In that hour Jesus rejoiced in spirit, and said, I thank thee,*

*O Father, Lord of heaven and earth, that Thou hast hid these things from the wise and prudent, and hast revealed them unto babes: Even so Father, for so it seemed good in Thy sight.* That sovereignty of God that Christ rejoiced in, seemed to me to be worthy to be rejoiced in; and that rejoicing of Christ, seemed to me to show the excellency of Christ, and the spirit that He was of.

Sometimes only mentioning a single word, causes my heart to burn within me: or only seeing the Name of Christ, or the name of some attribute of God. And God has appeared glorious to me, on account of the Trinity. It has made me have exalting thoughts of God, that he subsists in three persons; Father, Son, and Holy Ghost.

The sweetest joys and delights I have experienced, have not been those that have arisen from a hope of my own good estate; but in a direct view of the glorious things of the gospel. When I enjoy this sweetness, it seems to carry me above the thoughts of my own safe estate. It seems at such times a loss that I cannot bear, to take off my eye from the glorious, pleasant object I behold without me, to turn my eye in upon myself, and my own good estate.

My heart has been much on the advancement of Christ's kingdom in the world. The histories of the past advancement of Christ's kingdom, have been sweet to me. When I have read histories of past ages, the pleasantest thing in all my reading has been, to read of the kingdom of Christ being promoted. And when I have expected in my reading, to come to any such thing, I have lotted* upon it all the way as I read. And my mind has been much entertained and delighted, with the Scripture promises and prophecies, of the future glorious advancement of Christ's kingdom on earth.

I have sometimes had a sense of the excellent fulness of Christ, and His meetness and suitableness as a Saviour; whereby He has appeared to me, far above all, the chief of ten thousands. And His blood and atonement has appeared sweet, and His righteousness sweet; which is always accompanied with an ardency of spirit, and inward strugglings and breathings and groanings, that cannot be uttered, to be emptied of myself, and swallowed up in Christ.

Once, as I rid out into the woods for my health, *Anno* 1737;

---

* That is, counted on it [ed.].

and having lit from my horse in a retired place, as my manner commonly has been, to walk for divine contemplation and prayer; I had a view, that for me was extraordinary, of the glory of the Son of God; as mediator between God and man; and his wonderful, great, full, pure and sweet grace and love, and meek and gentle condescension. This grace, that appear'd to me so calm and sweet, appear'd great above the heavens. The person of Christ appear'd ineffably excellent, with an excellency great enough to swallow up all thought and conception, which continued, as near as I can judge, about an hour; which kept me, the bigger part of the time, in a flood of tears, and weeping aloud. I felt withal, an ardency of soul to be, what I know not otherwise how to express, than to be emptied and annihilated; to lie in the dust, and to be full of Christ alone; to love Him with a holy and pure love; to trust in Him; to live upon Him; to serve and follow Him, and to be totally wrapt up in the fullness of Christ; and to be perfectly sanctified and made pure, with a divine and heavenly purity. I have several other times, had views very much of the same nature, and that have had the same effects.

I have many times had a sense of the glory of the third person in the Trinity, in His office of sanctifier; in His holy operations communicating divine light and life to the soul. God in the communications of His Holy Spirit, has appear'd as an infinite fountain of divine glory and sweetness; being full and sufficient to fill and satisfy the soul: pouring forth itself in sweet communications, like the sun in its glory, sweetly and pleasantly diffusing light and life.

I have sometimes had an affecting sense of the excellency of the word of God, as a word of life; as the light of life; a sweet, excellent, life-giving word: accompanied with a thirsting after that word, that it might dwell richly in my heart.

I have often since I lived in this town, had very affecting views of my own sinfulness and vileness; very frequently so as to hold me in a kind of loud weeping, sometimes for a considerable time together: so that I have often been forced to shut myself up. I have had a vastly greater sense of my own wickedness, and the badness of my heart, since my conversion, than ever I had before.

It has often appeared to me, that if God should mark iniquity against me, I should appear the very worst of all mankind; of all that have been since the beginning of the world to this time: and that I should have by far the lowest place in hell. When others that have come to talk with me about their soul concerns, have expressed the sense they have had of their own wickedness, by saying that it seem'd to them, that they were as bad as the devil himself; I thought their expressions seemed exceeding faint and feeble, to represent my wickedness. I thought I should wonder, that they should content themselves with such expressions as these, if I had any reason to imagine, that their sin bore any proportion to mine. It seemed to me, I should wonder at myself, if I should express *my* wickedness in such feeble terms as they did.

My wickedness, as I am in myself, has long appear'd to me perfectly ineffable, and infinitely swallowing up all thought and imagination; like an infinite deluge, or infinite mountains over my head. I know not how to express better, what my sins appear to me to be, than by heaping infinite upon infinite, and multiplying infinite by infinite. I go about very often, for this many years, with these expressions in my mind, and in my mouth, "Infinite upon infinite. Infinite upon infinite!" When I look into my heart, and take a view of my wickedness, it looks like an abyss infinitely deeper than hell. And it appears to me, that were it not for free grace, exalted and raised up to the infinite height of all the fulness and glory of the great Jehovah, and the arm of His power and grace stretched forth, in all the majesty of His power, and in all the glory of His sovereignty; I should appear sunk down in my sins infinitely below hell itself, far beyond sight of every thing, but the piercing eye of God's grace, that can pierce even down to such a depth, and to the bottom of such an abyss.

And yet, I ben't in the least inclined to think, that I have a greater conviction of sin than ordinary. It seems to me, my conviction of sin is exceeding small, and faint. It appears to me enough to amaze me, that I have no more sense of my sin. I know certainly, that I have very little sense of my sinfulness. That my sins appear to me so great, don't seem to me to be, because I have so much more conviction of sin than other Christians, but because I am so much worse, and have so much more wickedness to be convinced of. When I have had these turns of weeping and crying for my sins, I thought I knew in the time of it, that my repentance was nothing to my sin.

I have greatly longed of late, for a broken heart, and to lie low before God. And when I ask for humility of God, I can't bear the thoughts of being no more humble, than other Christians. It seems to me, that tho' their degrees of humility may be suitable for them; yet it would be a vile self-exaltation in me, not to be the lowest in humility of all mankind. Others speak of their longing to be humbled to the dust. Tho' that may be a proper expression for them, I always think for myself, that I ought to be humbled down below hell. 'Tis an expression that it has long been natural for me to use in prayer to God. I ought to lie infinitely low before God.

It is affecting to me to think, how ignorant I was, when I was a young Christian, of the bottomless, infinite depths of wickedness, pride, hypocrisy and deceit left in my heart.

I have vastly a greater sense, of my universal, exceeding dependence on God's grace and strength, and mere good pleasure, of late, than I used formerly to have; and have experienced more of an abhorrence of my own righteousness. The thought of any comfort or joy, arising in me, on any consideration, or reflection on my own amiableness, or any of my performances or experiences, or any goodness of heart or life, is nauseous and detestable to me. And yet I am greatly afflicted with a proud and self-righteous spirit; much more sensibly, than I used to be formerly. I see that serpent rising and putting forth it's head, continually, everywhere, all around me.

Tho' it seems to me, that in some respects I was a far better Christian, for two or three years after my first conversion, than I am now; and lived in a more constant delight and pleasure: yet of late years, I have had a more full and constant sense of the absolute sovereignty of God, and a delight in that sovereignty; and have had more of a sense of the glory of Christ, as a mediator, as revealed in the gospel. On one Saturday night in particular, had a particular discovery of the excellency of the gospel of Christ, above all other doctrines; so that I could not but say to myself;

"This is my chosen light, my chosen doctrine": and of Christ, "This is my chosen prophet." It appear'd to me to be sweet beyond all expression, to follow Christ, and to be taught and enlighten'd and instructed by Him; to learn of Him, and live to Him.

Another Saturday night, January, 1738–9, had such a sense, how sweet and blessed a thing it was, to walk in the way of duty, to do that which was right and meet to be done, and agreeable to the holy mind of God; that it caused me to break forth into a kind of a loud weeping, which held me some time; so that I was forced to shut myself up, and fasten the doors. I could not but as it were cry out, "How happy are they which do that which is right in the sight of God! They are blessed indeed, they are the happy ones!" I had at the same time, a very affecting sense, how meet and suitable it was that God should govern the world, and order all things according to his own pleasure; and I rejoiced in it, that God reigned, and that his will was done.

## PART III  *Containing a* HISTORY *of his* LIFE *from his Entering on the* WORK *of the* MINISTRY, *unto his* DEATH

*Section I.*  HIS GENERAL MANNER OF LIFE

Mr. Edwards made a secret of his private devotion, and therefore it cannot be particularly known: though there is much evidence, that he was punctual, constant and frequent in secret prayer, and often kept days of fasting and prayer in secret; and set apart time for serious, devout meditations on spiritual and eternal things, as part of his religious exercise in secret. It appears by his Diary that in his youth he determined to attend secret prayer more than twice a day, when circumstances would allow. He was, so far as it can be known, much on his knees in secret, and in devout reading God's word and meditation upon it. And his constant, solemn converse with God in these exercises of secret religion made his face, as it were, to shine before others. His appearance, his countenance, words and whole demeanor (though without anything of affected grimace and sour austerity) was attended with a seriousness, gravity and solemnity, which was the natural genuine indication and expression of a deep, abiding sense of divine things on his mind, and of his living constantly in the fear of God.

Agreeable to his Resolutions, he was very careful and abstemious in eating and drinking; as doubtless it was necessary so great a student, and a person of so delicate and tender a bodily make as he was, should be, in order to be comfortable and useful. When he had, by careful observation, found what kind, and what quantity of diet, best suited his constitution, and rendered him most fit to pursue his work, he was very strict and exact in complying with it; and in this respect *lived by rule;* and herein constantly practiced great self-denial: which he also did in his constant early rising, in order to redeem time for his study. He used himself to rise by four or between four and five in the morning.

Though he was of a tender and delicate constitution, yet few students are capable of close application more hours in a day than he. He commonly spent thirteen hours every day in his study. His most usual diversion in summer was riding on horseback and walking. He would commonly, unless diverted by company, ride two or three miles after dinner to some lonely grove, where he would dismount and walk a while. At which times he generally carried his pen and ink with him, to note any thought that should be suggested, which he chose to retain and pursue, as what promised some light on any important subject. In the winter he was wont almost daily to take an axe and chop wood moderately for the space of half an hour or more.

He had an uncommon thirst for knowledge, in the pursuit of which, he spared no cost nor pains. He read all the books, especially books of divinity, that he could come at, from which he could hope to get any help in his pursuit of knowledge. And in this, he confined not himself to authors of any particular sect or denomination; yea took much pains to come at the books of the most noted writers, who advance a scheme of divinity most contrary to his own principles. But he studied the Bible more than all other books, and more than most other divines do. His uncommon acquaintance with the Bible appears in his sermons, and in most of his publications: and his great pains in studying it are manifest in his manuscript notes upon it; of which a more particular account may be given hereafter. He took his religious principles from the Bible, and not from any human system or body of divinity. Though his principles were *Calvinistic,* yet he called no man father. He thought and judged for himself, and was truly very much of an original. This is evident by what he published in his lifetime, and is yet more so by his Mss. Many volumes of which he has left; and the reader may expect a more particular account of them in the sequel. For reading was not the only method he took to improve his mind; but he did this much by writing; without which, 'tis probable no student can make improvements to the best advantage. Agreeable to Resolution 11th, he applied himself with all his might to find out the truth: he searched for understanding and knowledge, as for silver, and digged for it, as for his treasures. Every thought on any subject, which appeared to him worth pursuing and preserving, he pursued, as far as he then could, with his pen in his hand. Thus he was all his days, like the busy bee, collecting from every opening flower, and storing up a stock of knowledge, which was indeed sweet to him, as the honey and the honey-comb. And as he advanced in years and in knowledge, his pen was more and more employed, and his manuscripts grew much faster on his hands.

He was thought by some, who had but a slight acquaintance with him to be stiff and unsociable; but this was owing to want of better acquaintance. He was not a man of many words indeed, and was somewhat reserved among strangers, and those on whose candor and friendship he did not know he could rely. And this was probably owing to two things. First, the strict guard he set over his tongue from his youth, which appears by his Resolutions, taking great care never to use it in any way that might prove mischievous to any; never to *sin with his tongue;* or to improve it in idle, trivial and impertinent talk, which generally makes up a great part of the conversation of those who are full of words in all companies. He was sensible, that in the multitude of words there wanteth not sin; and therefore refrained his lips, and habituated himself to *think* before he *spoke,* and to propose some good and even in all his words; which led him to be above many others, agreeable to St. James's advice, *slow to speak.* Secondly, this was in part the effect of his bodily constitution. He possessed but a comparative small stock of animal life: his animal spirits were low, and he had not strength of lungs to spare, that would be necessary in order to make him what would be called, an affable, facetious gentleman, in all companies. They who have a great flow of animal spirits, and so can speak with more ease and less expense, may doubtless lawfully practice free conversation in all companies for a lower end (*e.g.,* to please and render themselves acceptable) than he, who has not such a stock to expend upon. It becomes *him* to reserve what he has, for higher and more important service. Besides, the want of animal spirits lays a man under a *natural* inability to that freedom of conversation, at all times, and in whatever company he is; which those of more life naturally go into; and the greatest degree of a sociable disposition, humility and benevolence, will not remove this obstacle.

He was not forward to enter into any dispute among strangers, and in companies where were persons of different sentiments; as he was sensible that such disputes are generally unprofitable, and often sinful and of bad consequence; and he thought he could dispute to the best advantage with his pen in his hand: yet he was always free to give his sentiments on any subject proposed to him; and remove any difficulties or objections offered by way of inquiry, as lying in the way of what he looked upon to be the truth. But how groundless the imputation of *stiff* and *unsociable* was, his known and tried friends best knew. They always found him easy of access, kind and condescending; and though not talkative, yet affable and free. Among such whose candor and friendship he had experienced, he threw off the reserve, and was most open and free; quite patient of contradiction, while the utmost opposition was made to his sentiments, that could be by any plausible arguments or objections. And indeed, he was on all occasions, quite sociable and free with all, who had any special business with him.

In his conduct in his family he practiced that conscientious exactness which was perspicuous in all his ways. He maintained a great esteem and regard for his amiable and excellent consort. Much of the tender and kind was expressed in his conversation with her and conduct towards her. He was wont frequently to admit her into his study, and converse freely with her on matters of religion. And he used commonly to pray with her in his study, at least once a day, unless something extraordinary prevented. The time in which this used to be commonly attended, was just before going to bed, after prayers in the family. As he rose very early himself, he was wont to have his family up in season in the morning; after which, before the family entered on the business of the day, he attended on family prayers. When a chapter in the Bible was read, commonly by candle-light in the winter; upon which he asked his children questions according to their age and capacity; and took occasion to explain some passages in it, or enforce any duty recommended etc. as he thought most proper.

He was careful and thorough in the government of his children; and, as a consequence of this, they reverenced, esteemed and loved him. He took special care to begin his government of them in season. When they first discovered any considerable degree of will and stubbornness, he would attend to them till he had thoroughly subdued them and brought them to submit. And such prudent thorough discipline, exercised with the greatest calmness, and commonly without striking a blow, being repeated once or twice, was generally sufficient for that child; and effectually established his parental authority, and produced a cheerful obedience ever after.

He kept a watchful eye over his children, that he might admonish them of the first wrong step, and direct them in the right way. He took opportunities to treat with them in his study, singly and particularly about their own soul's concerns; and to give them warning, exhortation and direction, as he saw occasion. He took much pains to instruct them in the principles of religion; in which he made use of the *Assembly's Shorter Catechism:* not merely by taking care that they learned it by heart; but by leading them into an understanding of the doctrines therein taught, by asking them questions on each answer, and explaining it to them. His usual time to attend this was on the evening before the Sabbath. And as he believed that the Sabbath or holy time began at sunset the evening before the day, he ordered his family to finish all their secular business by that time, or before; when they were all called

together, and a psalm was sung and prayer attended, as an introduction to the sanctifying the Sabbath. This care and exactness
effectually prevented that intruding on holy time, by attending on
secular business, too common in families where the evening before
the Sabbath is pretended to be observed.

He was a great enemy to young people's unseasonable company-
keeping and frolicking, as he looked upon it as a great means of
corrupting and ruining youth. And he thought the excuse many
parents make for tolerating their children in it (viz. that it is the
custom, and others' children practice it, which renders it difficult,
and even impossible to restrain theirs) was insufficient and frivolous; and manifested a great degree of stupidity, on supposition the
practice was hurtful and pernicious to their souls. And when some
of his children grew up he found no difficulty in restraining them
from this pernicious practice; but they cheerfully complied with
the will of their parents herein. He allowed not his children to be
from home after nine o'clock at night, when they went abroad to
see their friends and companions. Neither were they allowed to sit
up much after that time, in his own house, when any came to make
them a visit. If any gentleman desired acquaintance with his
daughters; after handsomely introducing himself, by properly consulting the parents, he was allowed all proper opportunity for it; a
room and fire, if needed: but must not intrude on the proper hours
of rest and sleep, or the religion and order of the family.

He had a strict and inviolable regard to justice in all his dealings
with his neighbors, and was very careful to provide for things
honest in the sight of all men; so that scarcely a man had any
dealings with him, that was not conscious of his uprightness. He
appeared to have a sacred regard to truth in his words, both in
promises and narrations, agreeable to his Resolutions. This doubtless was one reason why he was not so full of words as many are.
No man feared to rely on his veracity.

He was cautious in choosing his *intimate friends,* and therefore
had not many that might properly be called such. But to them he
showed himself friendly in a peculiar manner. He was indeed a
faithful friend, and able above most others to keep a secret. To
them he discovered himself more than to others, led them into his

views and ends in his conduct in particular instances: by which they had abundant evidence that he well understood human nature; and that his general reservedness, and many particular instances of his conduct, which a stranger might impute to ignorance of men, were really owing to his uncommon knowledge of mankind.

His conversation with his friends was always savory and profitable: in this he was remarkable, and almost singular.—He was not wont to spend his time with them, in scandal, evil-speaking and back-biting, or in foolish jesting, idle chat and telling stories; but his mouth was that of the just, which bringeth forth wisdom, and his lips dispersed knowledge. His tongue was as the pen of a ready writer, while he conversed about important, heavenly, divine things, which his heart was so full of, in such a natural and free manner, as to be most entertaining and instructive: so that none of his friends could enjoy his company without instruction and profit, unless it was by their own fault.

His great benevolence to mankind discovered itself, among other ways, by the uncommon regard he showed to liberality, and charity to the poor and distressed. He was much in recommending this, both in his public discourses and private conversation. He often declared it to be his opinion, that professed Christians, in these days are greatly deficient in this duty; and much more so, than in most other parts of external Christianity. He often observed how much this is spoken of, recommended and encouraged in the holy Scripture, especially in the New Testament. And it was his opinion, that every particular church ought by frequent and liberal contributions, to maintain a public stock, that might be ready for the poor and necessitious members of that church: and that the principal business of deacons is to take care of the poor in the faithful and judicious distribution and improvement of the church's temporals, lodged in their hands. And he did not content himself with only recommending charity to others, but practiced it much himself; though, according to his Master's advice, he took great care to conceal his deeds of charity; by which means doubtless most of his alms-deeds will be unknown till the resurrection, which if known, would prove him to be as great an instance of charity as any that can be produced in this age. This is not mere conjecture, but is evident many ways. He was forward to give on all public occasions of charity, though when it could properly be done, he always concealed the sum given. And some instances of his giving more privately have accidentally come to the knowledge of others, in which his liberality appeared in a very extraordinary degree. One of the instances was this. Upon hearing that a poor obscure man, whom he never saw, or any of his kindred, was by an extraordinary bodily disorder, brought to great straits; he unasked, gave a considerable sum to a friend to be delivered to the distressed person; having first required a promise of him, that he would let neither the person, who was the object of his charity, nor anyone else know by whom it was given. This may serve both as an instance of his extraordinary charity, and of his great care to conceal it.[3]

Mr. Edwards had the most universal character of a *good preacher* of almost any minister in this age. There were but few that heard him, who did not call him a good preacher, however they might dislike his religious principles, and be much offended at the same truths when delivered by others: and most admired him above all that ever they heard. His eminency as a preacher seems to be owing to the following things:

First, The great pains he took in composing his sermons, especially in the first part of his life. As by his early rising, and constant attention to his study, he had more time than most others; so he spent more time in making his sermons. He wrote most of his sermons all out, for near twenty years after he first began to preach; though he did not wholly confine himself to his notes in his delivering them.

Secondly, His great acquaintance with divinity, his study and knowledge of the Bible. His extensive and universal knowledge, and great clearness of thought, enabled him to handle every subject with great judgment and propriety, and to bring out of his treasury things new and old. Every subject he handled was instruc-

---

[3] As both the giver, and the object of his charity are dead, and all the ends of the proposed secrecy are answered; 'tis thought not inconsistent with the above-mentioned promise, to make known the fact, as it is here related.

tive, plain, entertaining and profitable; which was much owing to his being master of the subject, and his great skill to treat it in a most natural, easy and profitable manner. None of his composures were dry speculations, or unmeaning harangues, or words without ideas. When he dwelt on those truths which are much controverted and opposed by many, which was often the case, he would set them in such a natural and easy light, and every sentiment from step to step, would drop from his lips, attended with such clear and striking evidence, both from Scripture and reason, as even to force the assent of every attentive hearer.

Thirdly, His excellency as a preacher was very much the effect of his great acquaintance with his own heart, his inward sense and high relish of divine truths, and the high exercise of true, experimental religion. This gave him a great insight into human nature: he knew what was in man, both the saint and the sinner. This helped him to skill, to lay truth before the mind, so as not only to convince the judgment, but touch the heart and conscience, and enabled him to speak out of the abundance of his heart, what he knew, and testify what he had seen and felt. This gave him a taste and discerning, without which he could not have been able to fill his sermons, as he did, with such striking, affecting sentiments, all suited to solemnize, move and rectify the heart of the hearer. His sermons were well connected, not usually long and commonly a large part taken up in the improvement; which was closely connected with the subject, and consisted in sentiments naturally flowing from it.

But no description of his sermons will give the reader the idea of them, which they have who sat under his preaching, or have even read some of his discourses which are in print. There is a great number now in manuscript, which are probably as worthy the view of the public, and at least tend as much to instruct and quicken Christians, as most that have been published in this century.

His appearance in the desk was with a good grace, and his delivery easy, natural and very solemn. He had not a strong, loud voice; but appeared with such gravity and solemnity, and spake with such distinctness, clearness and precision; his words were so full of ideas, set in such a plain and striking light, that few speakers have been so able to demand the attention of an audience as he. His words often discovered a great degree of inward fervor, without much noise or external emotion, and fell with great weight on the minds of his hearers. He made but little motion of his head or hands in the desk, but spake so as to discover the motion of his own heart, which tended in the most natural and effectual manner to move and affect others.

As he wrote his sermons out at large for many years, and always wrote a considerable part of most of his public discourses; so he carried his notes into the desk with him, and read the most that he had wrote; yet he was not so confined to his notes, when he had wrote at large, but that, if some thoughts were suggested while he was speaking, which did not occur when writing, and appeared to him pertinent and striking, he would deliver them; and that with as great propriety and fluency, and oftener with greater pathos, and attended with a more sensible good effect on his hearers, than all he had wrote.

Though, as has been observed, he was wont to read so considerable a part of what he delivered; yet he was far from thinking this the best way of preaching in general; and looked upon his using his notes so much as he did, [as] a deficiency and infirmity. And in the latter part of his life was inclined to think it had been better, if he had never accustomed himself to use his notes at all. It appeared to him that preaching wholly without notes, agreeable to the custom in most Protestant countries, and what seems evidently to have been the manner of the apostles and primitive ministers of the gospel, was by far the most natural way; and had the greatest tendency on the whole, to answer the end of preaching: and supposed that none who had talents equal to the work of the ministry, was incapable of speaking *memoriter,* if he took suitable pains for this attainment from his youth. He would have the young preacher write all his sermons, or at least most of them, out at large; and instead of reading them to his hearers, take pains to commit them to memory. Which, though it would require a great deal of labor at first, yet would soon become easier by use, and help him to speak more correctly and freely, and be of great service to him all his days.

His prayers were indeed *extempore*. He was the farthest from any appearance of a form, as to his words and manner of expression, of almost any man. He was quite singular and inimitable in this, by any who have not a spirit of real and undissembled devotion. Yet he always expressed himself with decency and propriety. He appeared to have much of the grace and spirit of prayer; to pray with the spirit and with the understanding: and he performed this part of duty much to the acceptance and edification of those who joined with him. He was not wont, in ordinary cases to be long in his prayers: an error which he observed was often hurtful to public and social prayer, as it tends rather to damp than promote true devotion.

He kept himself quite free from worldly cares. He gave himself wholly to the work of the ministry, and entangled not himself with the affairs of this life. He left the particular oversight and direction of the temporal concerns of his family, almost entirely to Mrs. Edwards; who was better able than most of her sex to take the whole care of them on her hands. He was less acquainted with most of his temporal affairs than many of his neighbors; and seldom knew when and by whom his forage for winter was gathered in, or how many milk kine he had; whence his table was furnished, etc.

He did not make it his custom to visit his people in their own houses, unless he was sent for by the sick, or he heard that they were under some special affliction. Instead of visiting from house to house, he used to preach frequently at private meetings in particular neighborhoods; and often call the young people and children to his own house: when he used to pray with them and treat with them in a manner suited to their years and circumstances; and he catechized the children in public every Sabbath in the summer. And he used sometimes to propose questions to particular young persons in writing, for them to answer after a proper time given to them to prepare. In putting out these questions, he endeavored to suit them to the age, genius and abilities of those to whom they were given. His questions were generally such as required but a short answer; and yet could not be answered without a particular knowledge of some historical part of the

Scripture; and therefore led, and even obliged persons to study the Bible.

He did not neglect visiting his people from house to house, because he did not look upon it, in ordinary cases, to be one part of the work of the gospel-minister. But he supposed that ministers should, with respect to this, consult their own talents and circumstances, and visit more or less, according to the degree in which they could hope hereby to promote the great ends of the gospel-ministry. He observed, that some ministers had a talent at entertaining and profiting by occasional visits among their people. They have words at will, and a knack at introducing profitable, religious discourse in a free, natural and, as it were undesigned way. He supposed such had a call to spend a great deal of their time in visiting their people. But he looked on his talents to be quite otherwise. He was not able to enter into a free conversation with every person he met with, and in an easy manner turn it to what topic he pleased, without the help of others, and, as it may be, against their inclination. He therefore found that his visits of this kind must be in a great degree unprofitable. And as he was settled in a great town, it would take up a great part of his time to visit from house to house; which he thought he could spend in his study to much more valuable purposes, and so as much better to promote the great ends of his ministry. For it appeared to him, that he could do the greatest good to souls, and most promote the interest of Christ by preaching and writing, and conversing with persons under religious impressions in his study; where he encouraged all such to repair; where, they might be sure, in ordinary cases, to find him: and to be allowed easy access to him, and where they were treated with all desirable tenderness, kindness and familiarity. In times therefore of the outpouring of God's spirit, and the revival of religion among his people, his study was thronged with persons to lay open their spiritual concerns to him, and seek his advice and direction: whom he received and conversed with, with great freedom and pleasure, and had the best opportunity to deal in the most particular manner with each one.

He was a skilful guide to souls under spiritual difficulties. And was therefore sought unto not only by his own people, but by many who lived scores of miles off. He became such an able guide, partly by his own experimental acquaintance with divine things, and unwearied study of God's word; and partly by his having so much concern with souls under spiritual troubles; for he had not been settled in the work of the ministry many years before the Spirit of God was wonderfully poured out on his people, by which a great concern about their souls became almost universal; and a great number were hopefully the subjects of saving conversion. This was principally in the year 1734; a particular account of which has been wrote by him, entitled, *A Faithful Narrative of the surprising Work of God in the conversion of many Hundred Souls in Northampton.* Which has been printed in England, Germany and America; to which the reader must be referred.

And there was another remarkable time of the outpouring of God's Spirit in the year 1740, and 1741, in which Northampton partook largely; though not exclusive of most other parts of the land. Mr. Edwards in this time had to deal not only with his own people, but with multitudes of others. The hearing that the same things were at Northampton some years before, and the fame Mr. Edwards had for knowledge, piety, and a great acquaintance with experimental religion, naturally led both ministers and people, in almost all parts of New England, to look to him for direction and assistance, in this extraordinary time. Being in this time earnestly solicited by the ministers and people of many places to come and preach among them, he went to many; though he was not able to gratify all who desired him. And his preaching was attended with great success.

And as many of the ministers and people in New England had been unacquainted with such things as then appeared, they were greatly exposed to *run wild,* as it were, and actually did, by the subtle temptations of the devil, taking advantage of the ignorance and wickedness of men's hearts, go into great extremes both as opposers and friends to the work of God. Mr. Edwards was greatly helpful by his direction and assistance against the two opposite extremes, both in conversation, preaching and writing. His publications on this occasion were especially of great and extensive service. Of which it may be proper to give some account here.

The first is a sermon preached at New Haven, Sept. 10, 1741, *on the distinguishing Marks of the Spirit of God, etc.*

In the year 1742, he published a book of five parts, entitled, *Some Thoughts concerning the present Revival of Religion in New England, and the Way in which it ought to be acknowledged and promoted, etc.*

In the year 1746, he published a *Treatise on Religious Affections.* All which might be justly considered by the church of Christ as a voice behind them saying, "This is the way, walk therein." Especially the last-mentioned book, which has been esteemed by many the best that has been wrote on that subject; setting the distinction between true and false religion in the most clear and striking light.

To the same purpose, is *The Life of the Rev. Mr. David Brainerd, with Reflections and Observations thereon;* published by Mr. Edwards in the year 1749.

Mr. Edwards was what by some is called a rigid *Calvinist.* Those doctrines of Calvinism, which have been most objected against, and given the greatest offense, appeared to him as Scriptural, reasonable and important as any; and he thought that to give them up, was in effect to give up all. And therefore he looked upon those who called themselves *Calvinists,* that were for palliating the matter, by, as it were, trimming off the knots of Calvinism, that they might conform it more to the taste of those who are most disposed to object against it, were really giving up and betraying the cause they pretended to espouse; and were paving the way not only to Arminianism, but to Deism. For if these doctrines, in the whole length and breadth of them were relinquished, he did not see, where a man could set his foot down with consistency and safety, short of Deism, or even Atheism itself; or rather universal Skepticism.

He judged that nothing was wanting, but to have these doctrines properly stated and judiciously and well defended, in order to their appearing most agreeable to reason and common sense, as well as the doctrines of revelation; and that this therefore was the only effectual method to convince, or silence and shame the opposers of them. All will be able to satisfy themselves of the truth of this, by reading his Treatise *On Justification,* and his two last books on *The Freedom of the Will,* and *Original Sin.*

In this view of things, he thought it of importance that ministers should be very critical in examining candidates for the ministry, with respect to their *principles,* as well as their religious dispositions and morals. And on this account he met with considerable difficulty and opposition in some instances. His opinion was, that an erroneous or unfaithful minister was likely to do more hurt than good to the church of Christ; and therefore he could not have any hand in introducing a man into the ministry, unless he appeared *sound in the faith,* and manifested to a judgment of charity, a *disposition to be faithful.*

*Section II*   HIS DISMISSION FROM NORTHAMPTON, WITH THE OC-
CASION AND CIRCUMSTANCES OF IT

Mr. Edwards was very happy in the esteem and love of his people for many years, and there was the greatest prospect of his living and dying so. He was the last minister almost in New England that would have been pitched upon to be opposed and renounced by his people. But by what has come to pass with respect to this, we have an instructive lesson on the instability of all human affairs, and the unreasonableness of trusting in man.

In the year 1744, Mr. Edwards was informed that some of the young persons in town, who were members of the church, had books in keeping, which they improved to promote lascivious and obscene discourse among the young people. And upon inquiring, a number of persons were found to testify, that they had heard one and another from time to time talk obscenely; as what they were led to by reading a book or books, which they had among them. Upon which Mr. Edwards thought the brethren of the church ought to look into the matter. And in order to introduce it, he preached a sermon from Heb. xii. 15, 16. "Looking diligently, lest any man fail of the grace of God, lest any root of bitterness springing up trouble you, and thereby many be defiled: lest there be any fornicator, or profane person as Esau," etc. After sermon, he desired the brethren of the church to stay, and told them what information he had got; and proposed whether they thought proper to take any measures to examine into the matter. They with one consent, and much zeal, manifested it to be their opinion, that it ought to be inquired into. And proceeded to choose a number of men to assist their pastor in examining into the affair. Upon which Mr. Edwards appointed the time for their meeting at his house: and then read a catalogue of the names of young persons, whom he desired to come to his house at the same time. Some were the accused, and some witnesses; but it was not then declared of which number any particular person was.

When the names were published, it appeared, that there were but few of the considerable families in town, to which none of the persons named did belong, or were nearly related. Whether this was the occasion of the alteration or not, before the day appointed came, a great number of heads of families altered their minds (yea many condemned what they had done, before they got home to their own houses) and declared, they did not think proper to proceed as they had done; that their children should not be called to an account in such a way for such things, etc. etc.; and the town was suddenly all on a blaze. This strengthened the hands of the accused, and some refused to appear, and others that did appear, behaved unmannerly, and with a great degree of insolence, and contempt of the authority of the church. And little or nothing could be done further in the affair.

This was the occasion of weakening Mr. Edwards's hands in the work of the ministry, especially among the young people; with whom by this means he greatly lost his influence! This seemed in a great measure to put an end to Mr. Edwards's usefulness at Northampton, and doubtless laid a foundation, and will help to account for the surprising events which will by and by be related. To be sure he had no great visible success after this; but the influences of God's spirit were greatly withheld, and security and carnality much increased among them. That great and singular degree of visible religion and good order which had been found among them, soon began gradually to decay: and the youth have since been more wanton and dissolute.

Mr. Stoddard, Mr. Edwards's grandfather and predecessor in

the work of the ministry, was of the opinion, that unconverted persons had a right in the sight of God, or considered as such, to the sacrament of the Lord's Supper; that therefore it was their duty to come to that ordinance, though they knew they had no true goodness, or gospel-holiness. He maintained, that visible Christianity does not consist in a profession or appearance of that wherein true holiness or real Christianity consists. That therefore the profession which persons make in order to be received as visible members of Christ's church, ought not to be such as to express or imply a real compliance with, or consent to the terms of the covenant of grace, or a hearty embracing the gospel. So that they who really reject Jesus Christ, and dislike the gospel-way of salvation in their hearts, and know that this is true of themselves, may make the profession without lying and hypocrisy. Accordingly, he endeavored to form a short profession for persons to make in order to be admitted into the church and come to the sacrament, answerable to this principle. And it took place and was practiced in Northampton; and persons were admitted into the church, and to the sacrament, not under the notion of their being true saints, or that they had any real goodness.

Mr. Stoddard's appearing to maintain this principle made a great noise in the country; and he was opposed as introducing something contrary to the principles and practice of almost all the churches in New England. And the matter was publicly controverted between him and Dr. Increase Mather of Boston. However, through Mr. Stoddard's great influence and ascendance over the people at Northampton, it was introduced there, though not without opposition. And his principles by degrees spread very much among ministers and people in that county, and in other parts of New England; though no church except Northampton publicly and professedly acted upon this principle, by altering the profession that those made, who were admitted to the sacrament, to suit it to such a notion: but required of all who joined to the church a profession of that wherein true Christianity, or real godliness consists. And of late years his opinion that persons who have no real goodness, but are in a Christless state, and know themselves to be so, may make a Christian profession and come to the sacrament, without lying and hypocrisy; and that they have a right, and 'tis their duty so to do, has greatly spread in the country.

Mr. Edwards had some hesitation about this matter when he first settled at Northampton, and afterwards; but did not receive such a degree of conviction, that the admitting persons into the church, who made no pretense to real godliness was wrong, as to prevent his practicing upon it with a good conscience, for some years. But at length his doubts about the matter greatly increased, which put him upon examining it more thoroughly than he had ever before done, by searching the Scripture, and reading and examining such books, as were written to defend the admission of persons to sacraments, without a profession of saving faith. And the result was a full conviction that it was wrong, and, that he could not practice upon it with a good conscience. He was fully convinced that to be a *visible Christian* was to put on the visibility or appearance of a real Christian; that the profession of Christianity was a profession of that, wherein real Christianity consists; was therefore a profession of true respect of Christ, and a hearty embracing the gospel, etc. That therefore no person who rejected Christ in his heart, could make such a profession consistent with truth. And therefore, as the ordinance of the Lord's Supper was instituted for none but visible professing Christians, none but those who are real Christians have a real right in the sight of God to come to that ordinance: and that none ought to be admitted thereto, who do not make a profession of real Christianity, and so cannot be received in a judgment of charity as true friends to Jesus Christ, or real saints.[4]

When Mr. Edwards's sentiments were known, in the spring of the year 1744, it gave great offense, and the town was put into a great ferment: and before he was heard in his own defense, or it was known by many what his principles were, the general cry was to have him dismissed, as what alone would satisfy them. This was

[4] They who have a desire more fully to understand this controversy, and know if it is justly represented here, may do it by reading what Mr. Edwards wrote on this occasion, in order to explain and vindicate his principles; together with the Rev. Mr. Williams's answer, and Mr. Edwards's reply to him. And if they please, they may consult what Dr. Mather, and Mr. Stoddard before wrote on this subject.

evident from the whole tenor of their conduct, as they neglected and opposed the most proper means of calmly considering, and so understanding the matter in dispute, and persisted in a refusal to attend to what Mr. Edwards had to say in defense of his principles. And from beginning to end opposed the measures which had the best tendency to compromise and heal the difficulty; and with much zeal pursued those, which were calculated to make a separation certain and speedy.

Mr. Edwards thought of preaching on the subject, that they might know what were his sentiments, and what were the grounds of them (of both which he was sensible the most of them were quite ignorant) before they took any step for a separation between him and his people. But that he might do nothing to increase the tumult, but on the contrary take all those steps, which he could with a good conscience, that tended to peace, he first proposed the thing to the church's standing committee; supposing that if he entered on the subject publicly with their consent, it would prevent the ill consequences which otherwise he feared would follow. But the most of them would by no means consent to it, but strenuously opposed it. Upon which he gave it over for the present, as what in such circumstances would rather raise a tumult, and blow the fire up to a greater height, than answer the good ends proposed.

Mr. Edwards being sensible that his principles were not understood, and much misrepresented through the country; and finding that his people were in too much of a heat calmly to attend to the matter in controversy then; and were in a disposition even to refuse to hear him preach upon it, proposed to print what he had to say on the point; as this seemed to be the only way left him to have a fair hearing. Accordingly his people consented to put off the calling a council, till what he should write was published. But they manifested great uneasiness in waiting, before it came out of the press. And when it was published, it was read but by very few of them. Mr. Edwards being sensible of this, renewed his proposal to preach upon it, and, at a meeting of the brethren of the church asked their consent in the following terms, "I desire that the brethren would manifest their consent, that I should declare the reasons of my opinion relating to full communion in the church, in lectures appointed for that end: not as an act of authority, or as putting the power of declaring the whole counsel of God out of my hands; but for peace sake, and to prevent occasion of strife." But it passed in the negative.

Mr. Edwards then proposed that it should be left to a few of the neighboring ministers, whether it was not, all things considered, reasonable that he should be heard in this matter from the pulpit, before the affair should be brought to an issue. But this also passed in the negative.

However, he having had the advice of the ministers and messengers of the neighboring churches, who met at Northampton to advise them under their difficulties, proceeded to appoint a lecture, in order to preach on the subject, proposing to do so weekly till he had finished what he had to say. On Monday there was a precinct or society meeting, in which a vote was passed to choose a committee to go to Mr. Edwards, and desire him not to preach lectures on the subject in controversy, according to his declaration and appointment. And accordingly proceeded to choose a committee of three men for this purpose, who waited on him, and did their errand. However, Mr. Edwards thought proper to proceed according to his proposal, and accordingly preached a number of sermons till he had finished what he had to say on the subject. These lectures were very thinly attended by his own people: but great numbers of strangers from the neighboring towns attended them, so many as to make above half the congregation. This was in February and March, 1750.

The calling a decisive council to determine the matter of difference between pastor and people, or rather to dismiss the pastor from his church and people (for the delay of which a great deal of impatience had been publicly manifested), was now more particularly attended to by Mr. Edwards and the church.

Mr. Edwards had before this insisted upon it from time to time, that they were by no means ripe for such a procedure (as they had not yet given him a fair hearing in defense of his cause: which if they would do, perhaps the need of such a council would be superseded). And besides, he thought there was abundant public evidence, that they were not yet in a temper suited to attend on, and be active in such a transaction, as the dissolving of the relation between them and their pastor; which would, as things then stood, probably be the event. He observed, "That it was exceeding unbecoming churches of the Lamb of God to manage their religious affairs of greatest importance in a ferment and tumult, which ought to be managed with great solemnity, deep humiliation, and submission to the awful frowns of heaven, humble dependence on God, and with fervent prayer and supplication to Him. That therefore for them to go about such an affair, in such a manner as they did, would be most unbecoming the gospel, greatly to the dishonor of God and religion, and a way in which a people cannot expect a blessing. That such a great affair as this should be gone about with calm consideration; but that such a temper as the people were then in, was wholly inconsistent with this."

But having used all means which he could think of within his power to bring them to a more calm and charitable temper, and to hear and weigh what he had to say in his own defense, with attention and candor; and finding that nothing prevailed; but rather the tumult and uproar was increased; he consented that a decisive council should be called without any further delay.

But a difficulty attended the choice of a council, which was for some time insuperable. It was agreed that the council should be mutually chosen, one half by the pastor, and the other half by the church: but the people insisted upon it that he should be confined to the county in his choice. Mr. Edwards thought this an unreasonable restraint on him, as it was known that the ministers and churches in that county were almost universally against him in the controversy that divided him and his people, and made the two parties. He indeed did not suppose that the business of the proposed council would be to determine whether his opinion which was the occasion of the difficulty between him and his people, was right or not; or that what they were to judge of, depended upon this. But their business would be—to see and determine whether any possible way could be devised for an accommodation between a pastor and people, and to use their wisdom and endeavor in order to this. And if they found this impracticable, they must determine, whether things were now ripe for a separation; whether what ought in justice to be previous to a separation had already actually been done, so that there was nothing further in justice to be demanded by either of the parties concerned, before a separation should take place. And if he was dismissed by them, it would be their business to set forth to the world in what manner and for what cause he was dismissed: how far he was innocent, and whether he might yet be employed in the work of the ministry, etc. All which were matters of great importance to him, and required upright and impartial judges. And considering the great influence a difference in religious opinions has to prejudice men one against another; and the close connection of the point, in which most of the ministers and churches in the county differed from him, with the matter to be judged of, he did not think they could be reasonably looked upon so impartial judges, as that the matter ought to be wholly left to them. Besides, he thought the case being so new and extraordinary, required the ablest judges in the land. For these, and some other reasons, which he offered, he insisted upon liberty to go out of the county for those members of the proposed council in which he was to have a choice. In this, as was just now said, the people strenuously and obstinately opposed him. They at length agreed to leave the matter to a council consisting of the ministers and messengers of the five neighboring churches: who, after they had met twice upon it, and had the case largely debated before them, were equally divided, and therefore left the matter undetermined.

However, they were all agreed, that Mr. Edwards ought to have liberty to go out of the county for *some* of the council. And at the next church meeting, which was on the 26th of March, Mr. Edwards offered to join with them in calling a council, if they would consent that he should choose *two* of the churches out of the county, in case the council consisted of but *ten* churches. The church however refused to comply with this at one meeting after another repeatedly; and proceeded to warn a church meeting and choose a moderator, in order to act without their pastor.

But, to pass by many particulars, at length at a meeting of the church, warned by their pastor, May 3, they voted their consent to his proposal of going out of the county for two of the churches, that should be applied to. And then they proceeded to make choice of the ten ministers and churches, of which the council should consist. Accordingly, the churches were sent to, and the council convened on the 19th of June. Who, after they had made some fruitless attempts for a composition between the pastor and church, passed a resolve, by the majority of one voice[5] only, to the following purpose: "That 'tis expedient that the pastoral relation between Mr. Edwards and his church be immediately dissolved, if the people still persist in desiring it." And it being publicly put to the people, whether they still insisted on Mr. Edwards's dismission from the pastoral office over them? A great majority (above two hundred against twenty) zealously voted for his dismission. And he was accordingly dismissed June 22, 1750.

The dissenting part of the council, entered their protest against this proceeding, judging that it was too much in a hurry, as they were by no means ripe for a separation, considering the past conduct, and present temper of the people. And some of that part of the council that were active, expressed themselves surprised at the uncommon zeal and engagedness of spirit, publicly manifested by the people in their voting for a dismission; which evidenced to them, and all observing spectators, that they were far from a temper of mind becoming such a solemn and awful transaction, considered in all its circumstances.

Being thus dismissed, he preached his farewell sermon on the first of July, from 2 Cor. 1. 14. The doctrine he observed from the words was this, "Ministers and the people that have been under their care, must meet one another before Christ's tribunal, at the day of judgment." It was a remarkably solemn and affecting discourse, and was published at the desire of some of the hearers.

After Mr. Edwards was dismissed from Northampton, he preached there sometimes occasionally when they had no other preacher to supply the pulpit, till at length a great uneasiness was

[5] One of the churches which Mr. Edwards chose did not see fit to join the council. However, the minister of that church being at Northampton at the sitting of the council, was desired by Mr. Edwards and the church to sit in council and act, which he did. But there being no messenger from the church, the council was not full, and there was a disparity; by which means doubtless, there was *one* vote more for an immediate dismission, than against it.

manifested by many of the people, at his preaching there at all. Upon which, the committee for supplying the pulpit, called the town together, to know their minds with respect to that matter: when they voted that it was not agreeable to their minds, that he should preach among them. Accordingly, when Mr. Edwards was in town, and they had no other minister to preach to them, they carried on public worship among themselves, and without any preaching, rather than to invite Mr. Edwards!

Every one must be sensible that this was a great trial to Mr. Edwards. He had been near twenty-four years among that people; and his labors had been, to all appearance, from time to time greatly blessed among them: and a great number looked on him as their spiritual father, who had been the happy instrument of turning them from darkness to light, and plucking them as brands out of the burning. And they had from time to time professed that they looked upon it as one of their greatest privileges to have such a minister, and manifested their great love and esteem of him, to such a degree; that (as St. Paul says of the Galatians), if it had been possible, they would have plucked out their own eyes, and given them to him. And they had a great interest in *his* heart: he had borne them on his heart and carried them in his bosom for many years; exercising a tender concern and love for them: for their good he was always writing, contriving, laboring; for them he had poured out ten thousand fervent prayers; in their good he had rejoiced as one that findeth great spoil; and they were dear to him above any other people under heaven.

Now to have *this people* turn against him, and thrust him out from among them, in a great tumult and heat, with haste, and a great degree of violence; like the Jews of old stopping their ears and running upon him with furious zeal, not allowing him to defend himself by giving him a fair hearing; and even refusing so much as to hear him preach; many of them surmising and publicly speaking many ill things as to his ends and designs! To have the tables turned so suddenly and the voice so general and loud against him. This surely must come very near to him, and try his spirit. The words of the Psalmist seem applicable to this case, "It was not an enemy that reproached me, then I could have borne it; neither was it he that hated me, that did magnify himself against me, then

I would have hid myself from him. But it was thou—my guide and mine acquaintance. We took sweet counsel together, and walked unto the house of God in company."

Let us therefore now *behold the man!*

The calm and sedateness of his mind; his meekness and humility in great and violent opposition, and injurious treatment; his resolution and steady conduct through all this dark and terrible storm, were truly wonderful, and cannot be set in so beautiful and affecting a light by any description, as they appeared in to his friends, who were eye-witnesses.

Mr. Edwards had a numerous and chargeable family, and little or no income, exclusive of his salary: and considering how far he was advanced in years; the general disposition of people who want a minister, to prefer a young man who has never been settled, to one who has been dismissed from his people; and what misrepresentations were made of his principles through the country, it looked to him not at all probable that he should ever have opportunity to be settled again in the work of the ministry, if he was dismissed from Northampton: and he was not inclined or able to take any other course, or go into any other business to get a living. So that beggary as well as disgrace stared him full in the face, if he persisted in his principles. To be sure, he viewed himself as taking the most direct way to these, according to the natural course of things, by discovering and adhering to his principles, in the situation he then was. For he foresaw all this, before it came upon him; and therefore had the opportunity and the temptation to escape it, by concealing his principles. When he was fixed in his principles, and before they were publicly known, he told some of his friends, that if he discovered and persisted in them, it would most likely issue in his dismission and disgrace; and the ruin of himself and family, as to their temporal interests. He therefore first sat down and counted the cost, and deliberately took up the cross, when it was set before him in its full weight and magnitude; and in direct opposition to all worldly views and motives. And therefore his conduct in these circumstances, was a remarkable exercise and discovery of his conscientiousness; and his readiness to deny himself, and forsake all that he had, to follow Christ.

A man must have a considerable degree of the spirit of a martyr, not to flinch in such a case as this; but go on with the steadfastness and resolution with which he did. He, as it were, put his life in his hand, and ventured on where truth and duty appeared to lead him, unmoved at the threatening dangers on every side.

However, God did not forsake him. As He gave him those inward supports by which he was able in patience to possess his soul, and calmly and courageously row on in the storm, as it were, in the face of boisterous winds, beating hard upon him, and in the midst of gaping waves threatening to swallow him up: so He soon appeared for him, in His providence, even beyond all his expectations. His correspondents and other friends in Scotland, hearing of his dismission, and fearing it might be the means of bringing him into worldly straits, generously contributed a handsome sum, and sent it over to him.

And God did not leave him without tender, valuable friends at Northampton; for a small number of his people who opposed his dismission from the beginning, and some who acted on neither side, who joined with him after his dismission, and adhered to him, under the influence of their great esteem and love of Mr. Edwards, were willing and thought themselves able to maintain him: and insisted upon it that it was his duty to stay among them, as a distinct and separate congregation from the body of the town, who had rejected him.

Mr. Edwards could not see it to be his duty to stay among them, as circumstances were; as this would probably be a means of perpetuating an unhappy division in the town; and there was to him no prospect of doing the good there, which would counterbalance the evil. However, that he might do all he could to satisfy his tender and afflicted friends; and because in the multitude of counsellors there is safety, he consented to ask the advice of an ecclesiastical council. Accordingly, a council was called, and convened at Northampton on the 15th of May, 1751.

The town on this occasion was put into a great tumult and fire. They who were active in Mr. Edwards's dismission supposed, though without any ground, and contrary to truth, that he was contriving and attempting with his friends, again to introduce himself at Northampton. They drew up a remonstrance against their proceedings, and laid it before the council (though they would not acknowledge them to be an ecclesiastical council), containing many heavy, though groundless insinuations and charges against Mr. Edwards, and bitter accusations of the party who had adhered to him: but refused to appear and support any of their charges, or so much as to give the gentlemen of the council any opportunity to confer with them, about the affair depending; though it was diligently fought.

The council having heard what Mr. Edwards, and they who adhered to him, and any others who desired to be heard, had to say, advised, agreeable to Mr. Edwards's judgment and expectation, that he should leave Northampton, and accept of the mission to which he was invited at Stockbridge; of which a more particular account will be given presently.

Many other facts relative to this sorrowful, strange, surprising affair (the most so doubtless of any of the kind, that ever happened in New England; and perhaps, in any part of the Christian world) might be related; but as this more general history of it, may be sufficient to answer the ends proposed, viz. to rectify some gross misrepresentations that have been made of the matter, and discover the great trial Mr. Edwards had herein, 'tis thought best to suppress other particulars. As a proper close to this melancholy story; and to confirm, and further illustrate what has been related, the following letter from Joseph Hawley, Esq. (a gentleman who was well acquainted with, and very active in the transactions of this whole affair, and very much a head and leader in it) to the Rev. Mr. Hall of Sutton, published in a weekly newspaper in Boston, May 19, 1760, is here inserted.

### To the Rev. Mr. HALL of SUTTON

*Northampton, May 9, 1760*

*Rev. Sir,*

I have often wished that every member of the two ecclesiastical councils (that formerly sat in Northampton upon the unhappy differences between our former most worthy and Rev. pastor Mr. Jonathan Edwards and the church here) whereof you was a member; I say, Sir, I have often wished every one of them truly knew my real sense of my own conduct in the affairs that the one and the other of said council are privy to; and as I have long apprehended it to be my duty not only to humble myself before God for what was un-Christian and sinful, in my conduct before said councils, but also to confess my faults to them, and take shame to myself therefor before them. I have often studied with myself in what manner it was practicable for me to do it; and when I understood that you, Sir, and Mr. Eaton were to be at Cold Spring at the time of their late council, I resolved to improve the opportunity fully to open my mind there to you and him thereon; and thought that probably some method might be then thought of, in which my reflections on myself touching the matters above hinted at, might be communicated to most if not all the gentlemen aforesaid, who did not reside in this county: but you know, Sir, how difficult it was for us to converse together by ourselves when at Cold Spring, without giving umbrage to that people; I therefore proposed writing to you upon the matters which I had then opportunity only most summarily to suggest; which you, Sir, signified would be agreeable to you; I therefore now undertake what I then proposed, in which I humbly ask the divine aid; and that I may be made most freely willing fully to confess my sin and guilt to you and the world in those instances which I have reason to suppose fell under your notice, as they were public and notorious transactions, and on account whereof, therefore, you, Sir, and all others who had knowledge thereof, had just cause to be offended at me.

And in the first place Sir, I apprehend that with the church and people of Northampton, I sinned and erred exceedingly in consenting and laboring that there should be so early a dismission of Mr. Edwards from his pastoral relation to us, even upon the supposition that he was really in a mistake in the disputed point: not only because the dispute was upon matters so very disputable in themselves and at the greatest remove from fundamental, but because Mr. Edwards so long had approved himself a most faithful and painful pastor to said church; and also changed his sentiments in that point wholly from a tender regard to what appeared to him to be truth; and had made known his sentiments with great moderation and upon great deliberation, against all wordly motives, and from mere fidelity to his great Master, and a tender regard to the souls of his flock, as we had the highest reason to judge: which considerations now seem to me sufficient; and would (if we had been of a right spirit.) have greatly endeared him to his people, and made us to the last degree, reluctant to parting with him, and disposed us to the exercise of the greater candor, gentleness and moderation: how much of the reverse whereof appeared in us, I need not tell you Sir, who was an eye-witness of our temper and conduct.

And although it does not become me to pronounce decisively on a point so disputable as what was then in dispute; yet I beg leave to say, that I really apprehend that it is of the highest moment to the body of this church, and to me in particular, most solicitously to inquire, whether like the Pharisees and Lawyers in John Baptist's time, we did not reject the council of God against ourselves, in rejecting Mr. Edwards and his doctrine; which was the ground of his dismission. And I humbly conceive that it highly imports us all of this church, most seriously and impartially to examine what that most worthy and able divine, about that time, published in support of the same, whereby he being dead yet speaketh.

But there were three things Sir, especially in my own particular conduct before the first council, which have been justly matter of great grief and much trouble to me almost ever since, viz.

In the first place I confess Sir, that I acted very immodestly and abusively to you, as well as injuriously to the church and myself, when, with much zeal and unbecoming assurance, I moved the council that they would interpose to silence and stop you in an address you was making one morning to the people, wherein you was, if I don't misremember, briefly exhorting them to a tender remembrance of the former affection and harmony that had long subsisted between them and their Rev. Pastor, and the great comfort and profit which they had apprehended that they had received from his ministry; for which Sir, I heartily ask your forgiveness; and I think, that we ought, instead of opposing an exhortation of that nature, to have received it with all-thankfulness.

Another particular of my conduct before that council, which I now apprehend was criminal, and was owing to the want of that tender affection and reverend respect and esteem for Mr. Edwards which he had highly merited of me, was my strenuously opposing the adjournment of the matters submitted to that council, for about two months; for which I declare myself unfeignedly sorry; and I with shame remember, that I did it in a peremptory, decisive, vehement and very immodest manner.

But Sir, the most criminal part of my conduct at that time, that I am conscious of, was my exhibiting to that council a set of arguments in writing, the drift whereof was to prove the reasonableness and necessity of Mr. Edwards's dismission in case no accommodation was then ef-

fected with mutual consent; which tract by clear implication contained
some severe, uncharitable, and if I don't misremember, groundless and
slanderous imputations on Mr. Edwards, and expressed in bitter language; and although the original draft thereof was not done by me, yet
I foolishly and sinfully consented to copy it: and, as agent for the
church, to read it, and deliver it to the council, which I could never
have done, if I had not had a wicked relish for perverse things: which
conduct of mine, I confess was very sinful; am persuaded was highly
provoking to God, and for which I am ashamed, confounded, and have
nothing to answer.

As to the church's remonstrance (as it was called), which their committee preferred to the last of said councils, to all which I was consenting, and in the composing whereof I was very active, as also in bringing
the church to their vote upon it: I would in the first place only observe,
that I don't remember anything in that small part of it which was plainly
discursive of the expediency of Mr. Edwards's resettlement here as pastor
to a part of the church, which was very exceptionable; but as to all the
residue, which was much the greatest part thereof (and I am not certain
that any part was wholly free), it was everywhere larded with un-
christian bitterness, sarcastical and unmannerly insinuations, contained divers direct, grievous and criminal charges and allegations
against Mr. Edwards; which I have since good reason to suppose were
all founded on jealous and uncharitable mistakes, and so were really
gross slanders, also many heavy and reproachful charges upon divers
of Mr. Edwards's adherents, and some severe censures of them all in-
discriminately; all of which (if not wholly false and groundless) yet
were altogether unnecessary, and therefore highly criminal. Indeed I am
fully convinced, that the whole of that composure, excepting the small
part thereof above mentioned, was totally unchristian, a scandalous,
abusive, injurious libel, against Mr. Edwards and his particular friends;
especially the former, and highly provoking and detestable in the sight
of God; for which I am heartily sorry and ashamed; and pray I may
remember it with deep abasement and penitence all my days. Nor do I
now think that the church's conduct in refusing to appear and attend
before that council to support the charges and allegations in said remonstrance against Mr. Edwards and said brethren, which they demanded, was ever vindicated by all the subtle answers that were given
to said demand; nor do I think that our conduct in that instance was
capable of a defense, for it appears to me, that by making charges of
scandalous matters against them before said council, we necessarily so

far gave that council jurisdiction; and I own with sorrow and regret, that I zealously endeavored, that the church should perseveringly refuse to appear before said council for the purpose above said; which I humbly pray God to forgive.

Another part of my conduct, Sir, of which I have long repented, and for which I hereby declare my hearty sorrow, was my obstinate opposition to the last council's having any conference with the church; which said council earnestly and repeatedly moved for, and which the church finally denied (as you know). I think it discovered a great deal of pride and vain sufficiency in the church, and showed them to be very opiniative, especially the chief sticklers, one of whom I own I was, and think it was running a most presumptuous risk, and acting the part of proud scorners, for us to refuse hearing and candidly and seriously considering what that council could say or propose to us; among whom there were divers justly in great reputation for grace and wisdom.

In these instances Sir, of my conduct, and others (to which you was not privy) in the course of that most melancholy contention with Mr. Edwards, wherein I now see that I was very much influenced by vast pride, self-sufficiency, ambition and vanity. I appear to myself vile, and doubtless much more so to others who are more impartial; and do in the review thereof, abhor myself, and repent sorely; and if my own heart condemns me, it behooves me solemnly to remember, that God is greater, and knoweth all things; and I hereby own, Sir, that such treatment of Mr. Edwards, as is herein before mentioned, wherein I was so deeply concerned and active, was particularly and very aggravatedly sinful and ungrateful in me, because I was not only under the common obligations of each individual of the society to him, as to a most able, diligent pastor; but I had also received many instances of his tenderness, goodness and generosity to me, as a young kinsman, whom he was disposed to treat in a most friendly manner.

Indeed, Sir, I must own, that by my conduct in consulting and acting against Mr. Edwards within the time of our most unhappy disputes with him, and especially in and about that abominable remonstrance, I have so far symbolized with Balaam, Ahitophel and Judas, that I am confounded and filled with terror oftentimes when I attend to the most painful similitude.

And I freely confess that on account of my conduct above mentioned, I have the greatest reason to tremble at those most solemn and awful words of our Saviour, Matth. xviii. 6. and those Luke x. at the 16.: and I am most sorely sensible, that nothing but that infinite grace and mercy which saved some of the betrayers and murderers of our blessed Lord, and the persecutors of his martyrs, can pardon me; in which alone I hope for pardon, for the sake of Christ, whose blood (blessed be God) cleanseth from all sin. On the whole, Sir, I am convinced, that I have the greatest reason to say as David, "Have mercy upon me, O God, according to Thy loving kindness, according to the multitude of Thy tender mercies, blot out my transgressions, wash me thoroughly from mine iniquity, and cleanse me from my sin; for I acknowledge my transgressions, and my sin is ever before me: hide Thy face from my sins, and blot out all mine iniquities: create in me a clean heart, O God, and renew a right spirit within me; cast me not away from Thy presence, and take not Thy holy Spirit from me. Restore unto me the joy of Thy salvation, and uphold me with Thy free Spirit."

And I humbly apprehend that it greatly concerns the church of Northampton most seriously to examine whether the many hard speeches, spoken by many particular members against their former pastor, some of which the church really countenanced, and especially those spoken by the church as a body, in that most vile remonstrance, are not so odious and ungodly, as to be utterly uncapable of defense; and whether said church were not guilty of great sin in being so willing and disposed for so slight a cause, to part with so faithful and godly a minister as Mr. Edwards was. And whether ever God will hold us guiltless till we cry to Him for Christ's sake to pardon and save us from that judgment which such ungodly deeds deserve, and publicly humble and take shame to ourselves therefor. And I most heartily wish and pray that the town and church of Northampton would seriously and carefully examine whether they have not abundant cause to judge that they are now lying under great guilt in the sight of God; and whether those of us who were concerned in that most awful contention with Mr. Edwards, can ever more reasonably expect God's favor and blessing, till our eyes are opened, and we become thoroughly convinced that we have greatly provoked the Most High, and been injurious to one of the best of men; and until we shall be thoroughly convinced that we have dreadfully persecuted Christ by persecuting and vexing that just man and servant of Christ; until we shall be humble as in the dust therefor, and till we openly in full terms, and without baulking the matter, confess the same before the world, and most humbly and earnestly seek forgiveness of God, and do what we can to honor the memory of Mr. Edwards, and clear it of all the aspersions which we unjustly cast upon him, since God has been pleased to put it beyond our power to ask his forgiveness. Such terms I am persuaded the great and righteous God will hold us to, and that it will be in vain for us to hope to escape with impunity in any other way. This I am convinced of with regard to myself, and this way I most solemnly propose to take myself (if God in His mercy shall give me opportunity,) that so by making free confession to God and man of my sin and guilt, and publicly taking shame to myself therefor, I may give glory to the God of Israel, and do what in me lies, to clear the memory of that venerable man from the wrongs and injuries I was so active in bringing on his reputation and character; and I thank God that He has been pleased to spare my life and opportunity therefor to this time, and am sorry that I have delayed the affair so long.

Altho' I made the substance of almost all the foregoing reflections in writing, but not exactly in the same manner to Mr. Edwards and the brethren who adhered to him, in Mr. Edwards's life, and before he removed from Stockbridge, and I have reason to believe that he, from his great candor and charity, heartily forgave me and prayed for me: yet because that was not generally known, I look on myself obliged to take further steps; for while I kept silence, my bones waxed old, etc.

For all these my great sins therefore, in the first place, I humbly and most earnestly ask forgiveness of God; next, of the relatives and near friends of Mr. Edwards. I also ask the forgiveness of all those who were called Mr. Edwards's adherents; and of all the members of the ecclesiastical councils above mentioned; and lastly, of all Christian people, who have had any knowledge of the matters above said, or any of them.

I have no desire, Sir, that you should make any secret of this letter; but desire, you would communicate the same to whom you shall judge proper; and I purpose (if God shall give me opportunity) to procure it to be published in some one of the public newspapers; for I can't devise any other way of making known my sentiments of the foregoing matters to all who ought to be acquainted therewith, and therefore I think I ought to do it, whatever remarks I may foresee will be made thereon.

Probably when it comes out, some of my acquaintance will pronounce me quite over-run with vapors; others will be furnished with matter for mirth and pleasantry; others will cursorily pass it over as relating to matters quite stale; but some I am persuaded will rejoice to see me brought to a sense of my sin and duty; and I myself shall be conscious that I have done something of what the nature of the case admits, towards undoing what is, and long has been, to my greatest remorse and trouble that it was ever done.

Sir, I desire that none would entertain a thought from my having spoken respectfully of Mr. Edwards, that I am disaffected to our present pastor; for the very reverse is true; and I have a reverend esteem, real value, and hearty affection for him, and bless God, that He has notwithstanding all our unworthiness, given us one to succeed Mr. Edwards, who (as I have reason to hope) is truly faithful.

I conclude this long letter, by heartily desiring your prayers, that my repentance of my sins above mentioned may be unfeigned and genuine, and such as God in infinite mercy for Christ's sake will accept; and I beg leave to subscribe myself,

Sir, your real, though very unworthy friend,
and obedient servant,
Joseph Hawley

*Section III*   HIS MISSION TO THE INDIANS AT STOCKBRIDGE, ETC.

The Indian mission at Stockbridge (a town in the western part of the province of the Massachusetts Bay, sixty miles from Northampton) being vacant by the death of the late Rev. Mr. Sergeant, the honored and reverend commissioners for Indian affairs, in Boston, who have the care and direction of it, applied to him, as the most suitable person they could think of to betrust with that mission. And he was at the same time invited by the inhabitants of Stockbridge; and being advised by the council, above mentioned, to accept of the invitation, he repaired to Stockbridge, and was introduced and fixed as missionary to the Indians there by an ecclesiastical council called for that purpose, August 8, 1751.

When Mr. Edwards first engaged in the mission, there was a hopeful prospect of its being extensively serviceable, under his care and influence; not only to that tribe of Indians which was settled at Stockbridge, but among the Six Nations: some of whom were coming to Stockbridge to settle, and bring their own, and as many of their neighbors' children as they could get; to be educated and instructed there. For this end, a house for a boarding-school, which was projected by Mr. Sergeant, was erected on a tract of land appropriated to that use by the Indians at Stockbridge: where the Indian children, male and female were to be educated, by being clothed and fed, and instructed by proper persons in useful learning. And the boys to be learned husbandry or mechanic trades, and the girls all sorts of women's work. For the encouragement of which, some generous subscriptions were made both in England and America. And the great and general court of the province of the Massachusetts Bay, did much to promote the affair, and provided lands for the Mohawks to settle on, who should incline to come. And the generous Mr. Hollis, to encourage the thing, ordered twenty-four Indian children to be educated on the same footing, wholly at his cost. Also the society in London, for propagating the gospel among the Indians in and about New England, directed their commissioners in Boston to do considerable towards this design.

But partly by reason of some unhappy differences that took place among those who had the chief management of this affair at Stockbridge, of which a particular account would not be proper in this place; and partly by the war's breaking out between England and France, which is generally very fatal to such affairs among Indians, this hopeful prospect came to nothing.

Mr. Edwards's labors were attended with no remarkable visible success while at Stockbridge: though he performed the business of his mission to the good acceptance of the inhabitants in general, both English and Indians, and of the commissioners, who supported him honorably, and confided very much in his judgment and wisdom in all matters relating to the mission.

Stockbridge proved to Mr. Edwards a more quiet, and, on many accounts, a much more comfortable situation than he was in before. It being so much in one corner of the country, his time was not so much taken up with company, as it was at Northampton, though many of his friends, from almost all parts of the land, often made him pleasant and profitable visits. And he had not so much concern and trouble with other churches as he was obliged to have when at Northampton, by being frequently sought to for advice, and called to assist in ecclesiastical councils. Here therefore he followed his beloved study more closely, and to better purpose than ever. In these six years he doubtless made swifter advances in knowledge than ever before, and added more to his manuscripts than in any six years of his life.

And this was probably as useful a part of his life as any. For in this time he wrote the two last books that have been published by him (of which a more particular account will be given hereafter), by which he has doubtless greatly served the church of Christ, and will be a blessing to many thousands yet unborn.

Thus, after his uprightness and faithfulness had been sufficiently tried at Northampton, his kind Master provided for him a quiet retreat, which was rendered the more sweet by the preceding storm; and where he had a better opportunity to pursue and finish the work God had for him to do.

*Section IV*   HIS BEING MADE PRESIDENT OF NEW JERSEY COLLEGE; HIS SICKNESS AND DEATH

On the 24th of Sept., 1757, the Rev. Mr. Aaron Burr, President of New Jersey College, died.—And at the next meeting of the trustees, Mr. Edwards was chosen his successor. The news of which was quite unexpected, and not a little surprising to him. He looked on himself in many respects so unqualified for that business, that he wondered that gentlemen of so good judgment, and so well acquainted with him, as he knew some of the trustees were, should think of *him* for that place. He had many objections in his own mind against undertaking the business, both from his unfitness, and his particular circumstances; yet could not certainly determine, that it was not his duty to accept. The following extract of a letter which he wrote to the trustees will give the reader a view of his sentiments and exercises on this occasion, as well as of the great designs he was deeply engaged in, and zealously prosecuting.

*Stockbridge, 19th October, 1757*

*Reverend and Honored Gentlemen,*

I was not a little surprised, on receiving the unexpected notice of your having made choice of me to succeed the late president Burr, as the head of Nassau Hall.—I am much in doubt whether I am called to undertake the business, which you have done me the unmerited honor to choose me for—If some regard may be had to my outward comfort, I might mention the many inconveniences and great detriment, which must be sustained, by my removing with my numerous family, so far from all the estate I have in the world (without any prospect of disposing of it, under present circumstances, without losing it, in great part) now when we have scarcely got over the trouble and damage sustained by our removal from Northampton, and have but just begun to have our affairs in a comfortable situation for a subsistence in this place; and the expense I must immediately be at to put myself into circumstance tolerably comporting with the needful support of the honor of the office I am invited to; which will not well consist with my ability.—But this is not my main objection: The chief difficulty in my mind, in the way of accepting this important and arduous office, are these two: First my own defects, unfitting me for such an undertaking, many of which are generally known; besides other, which my own heart is conscious to.—I have a constitution in many respects peculiarly unhappy, attended with flaccid solids, vapid sizzy and scarce fluids and a low tide of spirits; often occasioning a kind of childish weakness and contemptibleness of speech, presence and demeanor; with a disagreeable dulness and stiffness, much unfiting me for conversation, but more especially for the government of a College.—This poorness of constitution makes me shrink at the thoughts of taking upon me, in the decline of life, such a new and great business, attended with such a multiplicity of cares, and requiring such a degree of activity, alertness and spirit of government; especially as succeeding one, so remarkably well qualified in these respects, giving occasion to every one to remark the wide difference. I am also deficient in some parts of learning, particularly in Algebra, and the higher parts of Mathematics and in the Greek Classics; my Greek learning having been chiefly in the New Testament.—The other thing is this; that my engaging in this business, will not well consist, with those views, and that course of employ in my study, which have long engaged, and swallowed up my mind, and been the chief entertainment and delight of my life.—

And here, honored Sirs (emboldened by the testimony, I have now received of your unmerited esteem, to rely on your candor), I will with freedom open myself to you.

My method of study, from my first beginning the work of the ministry, has been very much by writing; applying myself in this way, to improve every important hint; pursuing the clue to my utmost, when anything in reading, meditation or conversation, has been suggested to my mind, that seemed to promise light, in any weighty point.—Thus penning what appeared to me my best thoughts, on innumerable subjects for my own benefit.—The longer I prosecuted my studies in this

method, the more habitual it became, and the more pleasant and profitable I found it.—The further I traveled in this way, the more and
wider the field opened, which has occasioned my laying out many
things, in my mind, to do in this manner, if God should spare my life,
which my heart hath been much upon: particularly many things against
most of the prevailing errors of the present day, which I cannot with
any patience see maintained (to the utter subverting of the gospel of
Christ) with so high a hand, and so long continued a triumph, with so
little control, when it appears so evident to me, that there is truly no
foundation for any of this glorying and insult—I have already published something on one of the main points in dispute between the
Arminians and Calvinists: and have it in view, God willing (as I have
already signified to the public) in like manner to consider all the other
controverted points, and have done much towards a preparation for it
—But besides these, I have had on my mind and heart (which I long
ago began, not with any view to publication) a great work, which I
call a *History of the Work of Redemption,* a Body of Divinity in an
entire new method, being thrown into the form of an history, considering the affair of Christian theology, as the whole of it, in each part,
stands in reference to the great work of redemption by Jesus Christ;
which I suppose is to be the grand design, of all God's designs, and the
summum and ultimum of all the divine operations and decrees; particularly considering all parts of the grand scheme in their historical
order.—The order of their existence, or their being brought forth to
view, in the course of divine dispensations, or the wonderful series of
successive acts and events; beginning from eternity and descending
from thence to the great work and successive dispensations of the infinitely wise God in time, considering the chief events coming to pass
in the church of God, and revolutions in the world of mankind, affecting the state of the church and the affair of redemption, which we have
account of in history or prophecy; 'till at last we come to the general
Resurrection, Last Judgment and consummation of all things; when it
shall be said, *It is done. I am Alpha and Omega, the Beginning and the
End.* Concluding my Work, with the consideration of that perfect state
of things, which shall be finally settled, to last for eternity.—This history will be carried on with regard to all three worlds, heaven, earth
and hell: considering the connected, successive events and alterations,
in each so far as the Scriptures give any light; introducing all parts of
divinity in that order which is most scriptural and most natural: which
is a method which appears to me the most beautiful and entertaining,

wherein every divine doctrine, will appear to greatest advantage in the brightest light, in the most striking manner, showing the admirable contexture and harmony of the whole.

I have also for my own profit and entertainment, done much towards another great work, which I call *the Harmony of the old and New Testament* in three Parts—The first considering the prophecies of the Messiah, His Redemption and Kingdom; the Evidences of their references to the Messiah etc. comparing them all one with another, demonstrating their agreement and true scope and sense; also considering all the various particulars wherein these prophecies have their exact fulfillment; showing the universal, precise, and admirable correspondence between predictions and events. The second part: Considering the types of the Old Testament, showing the evidence of their being intended as representations of the great things of the gospel of Christ: and the agreement of the type with the antitype.—The third and great part, considering the harmony of the Old and New Testament, as to doctrine and precept.—In the course of this work, I find there will be occasion for an explanation of a very great part of the holy scripture; which may, in such a view be explained in a method, which to me seems the most entertaining and profitable, best tending to lead the mind to a view of the true spirit, design, life and soul of the scriptures, as well as to their proper use and improvement.

I have also many other things in hand, in some of which I have made great progress, which I will not trouble you with an account of.—Some of these things, if divine Providence favor I should be willing to attempt a publication of—So far as I myself am able to judge of what talents I have, for benefiting my fellow creatures by word, I think I can write better than I can speak.

My heart is so much in these studies, that I cannot find it in my heart to be willing to put myself into an incapacity to pursue them any more, in the future part of my life, to such a degree as I must, if I undertake to go thro' the same course of employ, in the office of a President, that Mr. Burr, did, instructing in all the languages, and taking the whole care of the instruction of one of the classes in all parts of learning, besides his other labors.—If I should see light to determine me to accept the place offered me, I should be willing to take upon me the work of a President, so far as it consists in the general inspection of the whole society and subservient to the school, as to their order and methods of study and instruction, assisting myself in immediate instruction in the arts and sciences (as discretion should direct and occasion serve, and the state of things require) especially the senior class: and added to all, should be willing to do the whole work of a professor of divinity, in public and private lectures, proposing questions to be answered, and some to be discussed in writing and free conversation, in meetings of graduates and others, appointed in proper seasons for these ends.—It would be now out of my way, to spend time, in a constant teaching of the languages; unless it be the Hebrew tongue, which I should be willing to improve myself in, by instructing others.

On the whole, I am much at a loss, with respect to the way of my duty in this important affair: I am in doubt, whether if I should engage in it, I should not do what both you and I should be sorry for afterwards. Nevertheless, I think the greatness of the affair, and the regard due to so worthy and venerable a body, as that of the Trustees of Nassau Hall, requires my taking the matter into serious consideration: And unless you should appear to be discouraged, by the things which I have now represented, as to any further expectation from me, shall proceed to ask advice, of such as I esteem most wise, friendly and faithful; if after the mind of the Commissioners in Boston is known, it appears that they consent to leave me at liberty, with respect to the business they have employed me in here.

In this suspense he determined to ask the advice of a number of gentlemen in the ministry, on whose judgment and friendship he could rely, and to act accordingly. Who upon his, and his people's desire, met at Stockbridge, Jan. 4, 1758. And having heard Mr. Edwards's representation of the matter, and what his people had to say by way of objection against his removal, determined it was his duty to accept of the invitation to the presidency of the college.

When they published their judgment and advice to Mr. Edwards and his people, he appeared uncommonly moved and affected with it, and fell into tears on the occasion; which was very unusual for him, in the presence of others: and soon after said to the gentlemen, who had given their advice, that it was a matter of wonder to him, that they could so easily, as they appeared to do, get over the objections he had made against his removal, to be the head of a college; which appeared great and weighty to him. But as he thought it his duty to be directed by their advice, he should now endeavor cheerfully to undertake it, believing he was in the way of his duty.

Accordingly, having had, by the application of the trustees of the college, the consent of the commissioners to resign their mission; he girded up his loins, and set off from Stockbridge for Princeton in January. He left his family at Stockbridge, not to be removed till spring. He had two daughters at Princeton, Mrs. Burr, the widow of the late President Burr, and his oldest daughter that was unmarried.

His arrival at Princeton was to the great satisfaction and joy of the college. And indeed all the greatest friends to the college, and to the interest of religion, were highly satisfied and pleased with the appointment of Mr. Edwards to the presidency of that college, and had their hopes and expectations greatly raised hereby. And his correspondents and friends, and well-wishers to the college in Scotland, greatly approved of it.

The corporation met as soon as could be with conveniency, after his arrival in the college, when he was by them fixed in the president's chair.

While at Princeton, before his sickness, he preached in the college-hall from Sabbath to Sabbath, to the great acceptance of the hearers: but did nothing as president, unless it was to give out some questions in divinity to the senior class, to be answered before him; each one having opportunity to study and write what he thought proper upon them. When they came together to answer them, they found so much entertainment and profit by it, especially by the light and instruction Mr. Edwards communicated in what he said upon the questions, when they had delivered what they had to say, that they spoke of it with the greatest satisfaction and wonder.

During this time, Mr. Edwards seemed to enjoy an uncommon degree of the presence of God. He told his daughters, he had had great exercise, concern and fear, relative to his engaging in that business; but since it now appeared, so far as he could see, that he was called of God to that place and work, he did cheerfully devote himself to it, leaving himself and the event with God, to order what seemed to him good.

The smallpox had now become very common in the country, and was then at Princeton, and likely to spread. And as Mr. Edwards had never had it, and inoculation was then practiced with great success in those parts, he proposed to be inoculated, if the physicians should advise to it, and the corporation would give their consent.

Accordingly, by the advice of the physician, and consent of the corporation, he was inoculated February 13. He had it favorably, and it was thought all danger was over: but a secondary fever set in; and by reason of a number of pustules in his throat, the obstruction was such, that the medicines necessary to staunch the fever, could not be administered. It therefore raged till it put an end to his life on the 22d of March, 1758, in the fifty-fifth year of his age.

After he was sensible that he would not survive that sickness, a little before his death, he called his daughter to him, who attended him in his sickness, and addressed her in a few words, which were immediately taken down in writing, as near as could be recollected, and are as follows:

*Dear Lucy,*

It seems to me to be the will of God that I must shortly leave you; therefore give my kindest love to my dear wife, and tell her, that the uncommon union, which has so long subsisted between us, has been of such a nature, as I trust is spiritual, and therefore will continue forever: and I hope she shall be supported under so great a trial, and submit cheerfully to the will of God. And as to my children, you are now like to be left fatherless, which I hope will be an inducement to you all to seek a Father, who will never fail you. And as to my funeral, I would have it to be like Mr. Burr's; and any additional sum of money that might be expected to be laid out that way, I would have it disposed of to charitable uses.[6]

[6] President Burr ordered, on his death bed, that his funeral should not be attended with that pomp and cost, by procuring and giving away a great number of costly mourning-scarfs, etc. and the consumption of a great quantity of spirituous liquors; which is an extravagance that is become too customary in those parts, especially at the funerals of the great and the rich: and that nothing should be expended but what was agreeable to the dictates of Christian decency. And that the sum which must be expended at a modish funeral, over and above the necessary cost of a decent one, should be given to the poor out of his estate.

It is to be wished and hoped, that the laudable example of these two worthy presidents, in which they bear their dying testimony against a practice so unchristian, and of such bad tendency so many ways, may have some good effect.

He said but very little in his sickness; but was an admirable instance of patience and resignation to the last. Just at the close of his life, as some persons, who stood by, and expecting he would breathe his last in a few minutes, were lamenting his death not only as a great frown on the college, but as having a dark aspect on the interest of religion in general; to their surprise, not imagining that he heard, or ever would speak another word, he said, "TRUST IN GOD, AND YE NEED NOT FEAR." These were his last words. And what could have been more suitable to the occasion! And what need of more! In these is as much matter of instruction and support, as if he had wrote a volume. This is the only consolation to his bereaved friends, who are sensible of the loss they, and the church of Christ have sustained in his death; *God is all-sufficient, and still has the care of His church.*

He appeared to have the uninterrupted use of his reason to the last, and died with as much calmness and composure, to all appearance, as that with which one goes to sleep.

The physician who inoculated and constantly attended him in his sickness, has the following words in his letter to Mrs. Edwards on this occasion: "Never did any mortal man more fully and clearly evidence the sincerity of all his professions, by one continued, universal, calm, cheerful resignation and patient submission to the divine will, through every stage of his disease, than he. Not so much as one discontented expression, nor the least appearance of murmuring through the whole. And never did any person expire with more perfect freedom from pain: not so much as one distorted hair, but in the most proper sense of the words, he really fell asleep."

## PART IV *Containing an Account of his* MANUSCRIPTS, *and the* BOOKS *published by him*

### Section I    HIS MANUSCRIPTS

Mr. Edwards has left a great many volumes in manuscript, which he wrote in a miscellaneous way on almost all subjects in divinity; which he did, not with any design they should ever be published in the form in which they are; but for the satisfaction and improvement of his own mind, and that he might retain the thoughts, which appeared to him worth preserving. Some idea of the progress he had made, and the materials he had collected in this way, he gives in the foregoing letter to the Trustees of Nassau-Hall; he has wrote much on the prophecies of the Messiah, Justification, the divinity of Christ and the eternity of hell torments. He wrote a great deal on the Bible, in the same way, by opening his thoughts on particular passages of it, as they occurred to him in reading or meditation; by which he has cast much light on many parts of the Bible, which has escaped other interpreters. And by which his great and painful attention to the Bible, and making it the only rule of his faith, are manifest.

If the public was willing to be at the cost, and publishing books of divinity met with as much encouragement now, as it has sometimes, there might be a number of volumes published from his manuscripts, which would afford a great deal of new light and entertainment to the church of Christ: though they would be more imperfect, than if he himself had prepared them for public view.

As the method he took to have his miscellaneous writings in such order, as to be able with ease to turn to anything he had wrote upon a particular subject, when he had occasion, is perhaps as good as any, if not the best that has been proposed to the public; some account of it will here be given, as what may be of advantage to young students, who have not yet gone into any method, and are disposed to improve their minds by writing.

He *numbered* all his miscellaneous writings. The first thing he wrote is No. 1. the second No. 2. and so on. And when he had occasion to write on any particular subject, he first set down the number, and then wrote the subject in capitals or large character, that it might not escape his eye, when he should have occasion to turn to it. As for instance, if he was going to write on the happiness of angels, and his last No. was 148, he would begin thus— 149. ANGELS, their happiness.—And when he had wrote what he designed at that time on that subject, he would turn to an alphabetical table which he kept, and under the letter A, he would write, Angels, their happiness, if this was not already in his alphabet; and then set down the Number, 149, close at the right hand of it. And if he had occasion to write any new thoughts on this same subject;

if the number of his miscellanies was increased, so that his last number was 261, he would set down the number 262, and then the subject, as before. And when he had done writing for that time, he turn'd to his table, to the word angels; and at the right hand of the Number 149, set down 162. By this means he had no occasion to leave any chasms; but began his next subject where he left off his last. The number of his miscellaneous writings rang'd in this manner, amounts to above 1400. And yet by a table contained on a sheet or two of paper, any thing he wrote can be turned to, at pleasure.

## *Section II*    HIS PUBLICATIONS

Mr. Edwards was greatly esteemed and famed as an author, both in Europe and America. His publications naturally raised in the reader of taste and judgment, an opinion of his greatness and piety. His books met with a good reception in Scotland especially, and procured him great esteem and applause there. A gentleman of note there for his superior genius and talents has the following words concerning Mr. Edwards, in a letter to one of his correspondents in America.

I looked on him as incomparably the greatest divine and philosopher in Britain or her Colonies; and rejoiced that one so eminently qualified for teaching divinity was chosen President of New Jersey College.

And in another letter the same gentleman says,

Ever since I was acquainted with Mr. Edwards's writings, I have looked upon him as the greatest divine this age has produced. And a rev. gentleman lately from Holland, says, That Mr. Edwards's writings, especially on the *Freedom of the Will,* were had in great esteem there: that the professors of the celebrated academy, presented their compliments to President Edwards. Several members of the Classis of Amsterdam gave their thanks, by him, to pious Mr. Edwards, for his just observations on Mr. Brainerd's life; which book was translated in Holland, and was highly approved of by the University of Utrecht——.

A brief Account of what he published is therefore here subjoined.

A Sermon preached at Boston, on I Cor. i. 29, 30, 31. With a Preface by one of the Ministers of Boston.

A Sermon preached at Northampton, in the year 1734, from Math. xvi. 17. entitled, A divine and supernatural Light immediately imparted to the Soul by the Spirit of God.

The narrative which has been mentioned, wrote Nov. 6, 1736. which was first printed in London, and recommended by Dr. Watts, and Dr. Guyse; and had two editions there. And then it had another Edition in Boston, in the year 1738. recommended by four of the senior ministers in Boston. To which were prefixed five Discourses on the following subjects.

I. Justification by Faith alone. II. Pressing into the Kingdom of God. III. Ruth's Resolution. IV. The Justice of God in the Damnation of Sinners. V. The Excellency of Jesus Christ.

Deliver'd at Northampton, chiefly at the time of the wonderful pouring out of the Spirit of God there.

The Discourse on Justification by Faith alone, may be recommended as one of the best things that has been wrote on that Subject; setting this truth in a most plain, Scriptural and convincing light; and as well worthy the careful perusal of all Christians; especially candidates for the ministry. The other Discourses are excellent, having much divinity in them, and tending above most that are published, to awaken the conscience of the sinner, and instruct and quicken the Christian.

A Sermon preached at Enfield, July 8, 1741. entitled, Sinners in the Hands of an angry God. Preached at a time of great awakenings there; and attended with remarkable impressions on many of the hearers.

A Sermon on the distinguishing Marks of a work of the Spirit of God, preached at New Haven, Sept. 10, 1741. from I Job. iv. I. published with great enlargements. This was re-printed in Scotland.

Some thoughts concerning the present revival of religion in New England, and the way in which it ought to be acknowledged and promoted humbly offered to the public, in a treatise on that subject, in five parts. Published in the year 1742. This had a second edition in Scotland.

A Treatise concerning religious Affections. Published in the year 1746. These three last have been mentioned before, with the particular occasion and design of their publication.

A treatise entitled, An humble attempt to promote explicit agreement, and visible union of God's people in extraordinary prayer, for the revival of religion etc. Recommended by five of the principal ministers in Boston. Published in 1747. In which he shows his great acquaintance with Scripture, and his attention to, and good understanding of the prophetic part of it.

An account of the life of the rev. Mr. David Brainerd, minister of the gospel and missionary to the Indians etc. with reflections and observations thereon. Published in the year 1749.

An enquiry into the qualifications for full communion in the visible church. Published in the year 1749. intended as an explanation and vindication of his principles in the matter, which occasioned his dismission from Northampton.

A reply to the rev. Mr. William's answer to the forementioned inquiry. Published in the year 1752.

A Sermon preached at Newark, before the Synod, Sept. 28, 1752. from Jam. ii. 19. entitled, True grace distinguished from the experience of Devils.

A careful and strict inquiry into the modern prevailing notion of that freedom of will, which is supposed to be essential to moral agency etc. Published in the year 1754.

This is justly thought by good judges to be one of the greatest efforts of the human mind, that has appeared, at least, in this century. In which the author shows that force and strength of mind, that judgment, penetration and accuracy of thought, that justly entitles him to the character of one of the greatest geniuses of this age. This treatise doubtless goes further towards settling the main points in controversy between Calvinists and Arminians, than anything that has been wrote: he having herein abundantly demonstrated the chief principles on which Arminians build their whole scheme, to be false and most absurd. Whenever therefore this book comes to be generally attended to, it will doubtless prove fatal to Arminian and Pelagian Principles. This was re-printed in London Anno 1762: and has been introduced by the Rev. T. Clap, President of Yale College, to be recited there by the Students.

The great Christian doctrine of Original Sin defended; evidences of its truth produced and arguments to the contrary answered. Containing, in particular, a reply to the objections and arguings of Dr. John Taylor etc. Published in the year 1758. This was in the press when he died.

Besides these, he published, several Ordination Sermons, and some others, preached upon particular occasions.

# Jonathan Edwards

To come to Andover with a lecture on Jonathan Edwards seems well-nigh an impertinence. Here, where his name has been honored more, if it be possible, than anywhere else in New England, where his life and works have long been familiarly and affectionately studied, where most of his unpublished manuscripts are guarded, there is nothing novel that a lecturer can offer; nor can he expect his knowledge of his theme to compare in thoroughness with that of several of his hearers. Yet the lecturer is reminded that this is a course on Congregationalism, not on unfamiliar Congregationalists; and to treat of the eighteenth century without glancing up, at least for a few moments, at the towering figure of our most original New England theologian, is like shutting out from memory the Presidential Range as one thinks of the White Mountains.

Passing along the sandy road that skirts the edge of the low bluff above the level meadowland, that borders the east bank of the Connecticut River, in the town of South Windsor, one sees by the roadside the site where stood, till the beginning of the nineteenth century, the "plain two-story house"[1] in which Jonathan Edwards was born. Though pleasant farming country, there is little in the immediate surroundings to detain the eye; but the blue

---

[1] See J. A. Stoughton, *Windsor Farmes* (Hartford, 1883), p. 46; H. R. Stiles, *History and Genealogies of Ancient Windsor* (Hartford, 1891), I, 556. The house stood till 1813.

---

From Williston Walker, *Ten New England Leaders* (New York: Silver, Burdett and Company, 1901), pp. 217–263.

hills beyond the river to the westward stretch away into the distance as attractively now as they did then when, if tradition is to be
trusted, Jonathan's autocratic father, the parish minister, warned a
neighbor whose refusal to remove a wide-spreading tree annoyed
him, that if this disrespectful conduct was continued he would not
baptize that contumacious neighbor's child. Behind the house, to
the eastward a few rods, rises a low, tree-covered hill, cutting off
the view in that direction, and affording a retreat to which father
and son were accustomed to withdraw in pleasant weather for
meditation or for prayer.[2] Here at what is now South Windsor,
Timothy Edwards, Jonathan's father, exercised an able, spiritual,
and conspicuously learned ministry from 1694 to his death in
1758.[3] Grandson of William Edwards, an early settler of Hartford, and son of Richard Edwards, a prominent merchant of
Hartford, and of his erratic wife, Elisabeth Tuthill,[4] Timothy
Edwards had graduated with distinction from Harvard College in
1691, and was always a man of marked intellectual power. The
considerable list of boys fitted in his home for college[5] bears
witness to his abilities as a teacher, and the judgment of his congregation that he was a more learned man and a more animated
preacher than his son, Jonathan,[6] reflects the esteem in which he
was held by the people of his charge. His wife, Jonathan's mother,
was a daughter of Solomon Stoddard, of Northampton, the ablest
minister of the Connecticut Valley when the seventeenth century
passed into the eighteenth, and granddaughter of John Warham,
the first pastor of Windsor.

Into this intellectual, strenuous, and yet cheerful home in this
bit of rural New England Jonathan Edwards was born on October
5, 1703. Here he grew up, the fifth among eleven children and the
only brother among ten tall sisters. Here he was fitted for college
in his father's study, and the intellectual sympathy thus begun
between father and son was to be a lifelong bond.

Youthful precocity is by no means an infallible prophecy of

---

[2] Stoughton, pp. 46, 47.
[3] *Ibid., passim.*
[4] See *Colonial Records of Connecticut,* IV, 59; Stoughton, pp. 39, 69.
[5] For some of these names see Stoughton, pp. 77, 78, 101–103.
[6] S. E. Dwight, *Life of Pres. Edwards* (New York, 1830), p. 17.

mature strength, but with Jonathan Edwards the mind received an
early development and manifested a grasp that was little less than
marvelous at an age when most schoolboys are scarcely emerging
from childhood. His observations on nature, notably the well-
known paper on the habits of the spider, apparently written when
Edwards was about the age of twelve; and even more his notes on
the mind, some at least of which seem to have been the immediate
fruit of his reflections upon Locke's famous *Essay,* which he had
read when fourteen, witness to his early intellectual maturity. The
same precocious strength of mind is apparent in his less easily
dated, but youthful, attainment of some of the positions of Berkeley or Malebranche—an attainment that seems to have been due
to an independent development, rather than to acquaintance with
their writings.[7]

Naturally, such a boy went early to college; and we find
Edwards entering Yale in September, 1716, about a month before
the close of his thirteenth year. The institution whose distinguished
graduate he was to become was far enough removed from the
university of the present. Founded in 1701, and therefore only two
years older than Edwards himself, its precarious existence had thus
far been spent at Saybrook; but the question of removal to New
Haven was in heated debate just at the time that Edwards entered,[8]
and a month after the beginning of his freshman year was decided
by the trustees. Their decision in favor of New Haven was un-
popular in the section of the colony in which Edwards' home was
situated; and, before the close of 1716, a considerable portion of
the students of the distracted college had gathered at Wethersfield
under the instruction of two tutors, one, a recent graduate of
Harvard, the other, three years an alumnus of Yale.[9] Of these

[7] *Ibid.,* pp. 22–63, 664–702; G. P. Fisher, *Discussions in History and
Theology* (New York, 1880), pp. 228–232; Alexander V. G. Allen, *Jonathan
Edwards* (Boston, 1889), pp. 3–31; E. C. Smyth, in *Proceedings of the
American Antiquarian Society* for 1895, pp. 212–236; Fisher, *History of
Christian Doctrine* (New York, 1896), pp. 396, 403. H. N. Gardiner, *Jona-
than Edwards: A Retrospect* (Boston, 1901), pp. 115–160.

[8] F. B. Dexter, *Biographical Sketches of the Graduates of Yale College,* I,
159, 160.

[9] Elisha Williams, Harvard, 1711, afterward president of Yale, speaker of
the Connecticut lower house, judge of the Superior Court, and colonel of the
Connecticut troops; and Samuel Smith, Yale, 1713.

emigrating dissenters Edwards was one; and at Wethersfield he
remained till the healing of the division in the early summer of
1719 carried him to New Haven.[10] Here he lived in the newly
erected hall and dormitory, then known distinctively as Yale
College, in a room rented at the moderate rate of twenty shillings a
year; and here, too, he boarded in commons at a charge of five
shillings—83⅓ cents—a week. These prices were in no way exceptionally moderate, nor is there any evidence of which I am
aware that Edwards' student days were not as comfortable from a
pecuniary standpoint as those of any of his position in the com-
monwealth. Here at New Haven he graduated, in September,
1720, at the head of a class of ten, after a course involving little
more than an acquaintance with a few books of Virgil and orations
of Cicero, the Greek Testament, the Psalms in Hebrew, the
elements of logic, Ames' *Theology* and *Cases of Conscience,* and
a smattering of physics, mathematics, geography, and astronomy.[11]
In Edwards' case, however, this course had been greatly supplemented by the reading at Wethersfield of such books as he could
borrow or purchase, and at New Haven by the use of the largest
and best selected library then in Connecticut, which the diligence
of Jeremiah Dummer and of other friends in England had procured for the college. It was doubtless the opportunity afforded by
this library that kept Edwards at New Haven engaged in the study
of theology till the summer of 1722, when, it seems probable, he
was licensed to preach.[12]

Somewhere in this period of study, probably about the time of
his graduation,[13] Edwards passed through the deepest experience
that can come to a human soul, a conscious change in its relations
to God. As John Wesley was a Christian and a minister before he
was "converted," and yet was wrought upon mightily by that
spiritual experience that came to him as he heard Luther's Preface
to the *Commentary on Romans* read in the Moravian Chapel in

[10] See Edwards' letter of March 26, 1719, Dwight, pp. 29, 30.

[11] Dexter, pp. 115, 141–143, 177, 200, 203; Dwight, p. 32.

[12] Hopkins, *Life and Character of the Late Reverend Mr. Jonathan
Edwards* (Boston, 1765; Northampton, 1804), p. 4; Dwight, p. 63.

[13] Dwight, p. 58. He is supposed to have joined the church of which his
father was pastor soon after his graduation.

Aldersgate Street, London, at a quarter before nine on the evening
of May 24, 1738, so Edwards, moved by religious convictions
when a boy and again when in college, yet rebellious against the
absoluteness of the divine sovereignty which his theology and his
philosophy alike demanded, came in an instant to a "sense of the
glory of the divine Being"[14]—to quote his own words—which
thenceforth changed the entire conscious attitude of his soul
toward God. And as Calvin, after the severe struggle involved in
the submission of his will to that of God, made the divine sovereignty the cornerstone of his system, so Edwards now found that
doctrine "exceedingly pleasant, bright, and sweet." But it was not,
as with Calvin, a submission to an infinite authority that was the
central thought of the experience that came to Edwards as he read
the words "Now unto the King eternal, immortal, invisible, the
only wise God, be honor and glory forever and ever, Amen."
Rather it was the high-wrought, mystic conception of the excel-
lence of the God to whom his heart went out in a flood of devotion
that mastered him with an overwhelming sense of the divine
presence and majesty. With true mystic outflowing of affection he
seems to have had relatively little sense of a burden of the guilt of
sin; he was above the plane which makes the question of one's own
interests central. By him sin was felt chiefly in a profoundly
humiliating sense of his own infinite unlikeness to God. But he
longed with all the power of an ardent nature to "enjoy that God,
and be rapt up to him in heaven, and be, as it were, swallowed up
in him forever." And this new apprehension of "the glorious
majesty and grace of God" found poetic satisfaction in enjoyment
of Solomon's Song, in sympathy with external nature, the sky,
clouds, "grass, flowers, trees," or the majesty of the lightning and
the power of the storm.

This new sense of the divine glory, almost a pure intuition of the
majesty, holiness, and power of God, satisfied the mystic and
imaginative side of Edwards' nature, no less than the speculations
which found in all being but the manifestation of spirit, and especially of the potent Spirit of God operating directly on the human
spirit, satisfied the philosophic tendency so strangely joined with

[14] See Hopkins, pp. 24–42; Dwight, pp. 60, 61.

an almost oriental wealth of fancy in this remarkable man. And from both sides of his thinking his theology flowed: rock-ribbed in its speculative logic, in its limitation of the power of human freedom, in its recognition of the immediate agency of God in all events, in its emphasis on the absolute and arbitrary sovereignty of the Creator over his creatures; yet insistent on a "conversion" the chief resultant of which was an affectionate delight in God, and finding the highest Christian experience in a mystical and almost incomprehensible sense of the divine glory manifested to the loving human soul.

This experience, no less than Edwards' belief in the immediacy and power of the operations of the divine Spirit on the soul of man, led him to emphasize a struggling and conscious "conversion," rather than a scarce-observed process of growth, as the normal instead of the occasional method of entrance into the Kingdom of God. This is a view always widely prevalent in times of deep religious quickening. It was preached in early New England by Hooker, Cotton, Shepard, and the founders generally. Wesley and Whitefield taught it. And it was set forth with such persuasiveness by Edwards as an underlying principle of his conception of the religious life as profoundly to affect New England for a century after his death. Emphasizing as it does the great truth of the divine origin of all Christian life, its overemphasis as a necessary law tends to rob baptism of significance, to minimize the covenant relationships of Christian households, and to leave the children of the truest servants of God presumptively outside the Christian fold till consciously touched by the transforming power of the Spirit. Edwards' own son and namesake could write years later: "Though I had, during my father's life, some convictions of sin and danger, yet I have no reason to believe I had any real religion, till some years after his death."[15]

In the power of these thoughts Edwards entered on his first pastoral experience, taking charge of a small Presbyterian church in New York City from August, 1722, to April, 1723—a relation which the congregation would gladly have made permanent. This

[15] Letter of March 30, 1789, Hawksley, *Memoirs of the Rev. Jonathan* ... (London, 1815), p. 255.

practical experience but deepened his previous aspirations and
convictions into a remarkable series of seventy resolutions. Some
are the familiar maxims of earnest men, as "To live with all my
might while I do live"; but more represent the peculiar coloring of
Edwards' religious life, as "Never to do any manner of thing,
whether in soul or body, less or more, but what tends to the glory
of God, nor be, nor suffer it, if I can possibly avoid it."[16]

New York, though pleasant, did not seem to Edwards a hopeful
field for his life work, and in May, 1723, he was back in his
father's house in South Windsor. But other churches speedily
sought his services. North Haven called him in vain in September,
1723; and, in November of that year, he accepted an invitation to
the pastorate at Bolton, a little eastward of his home. Yet, for
some reason now unknown he did not enter upon this ministry,
and June, 1724, found him, instead, in a tutorship at Yale College.[17]

The period was one of great distraction in that much vexed
institution. Without a president since the defection of Rector
Cutler to Episcopacy in 1722, its government and instruction were
in the hands of two young and frequently changed tutors. During
Edwards' incumbency, begun when he was not yet twenty-two, the
work was done with credit to himself and benefit to the college;
and he might have continued in it for several years longer had not
a most attractive invitation come to him from the people of
Northampton to become the colleague of his grandfather, the
venerable Solomon Stoddard. Induced by family ties, drawn by the
prominence of the congregation, then esteemed the largest in Massachusetts outside of Boston, and by that repute for a certain
aristocratic and social charm which Northampton then, as now,
enjoyed, he resigned his tutorship and, on February 15, 1727, was
ordained to the colleague pastorate of the Northampton church.
The death of Stoddard two years later[18] left him in sole charge.

The establishment of these ties was speedily followed by the
formation of others of a more personal character. On July 28,

[16] In full in Dwight, pp. 68–73.
[17] Dexter, pp. 218, 219.
[18] February 11, 1729.

1727, he married Sarah Pierpont, daughter of Rev. James Pierpont of New Haven, and great-granddaughter of Thomas Hooker, the founder of Hartford. Our New England ancestors married early—the bride and groom were seventeen and twenty-four—but Edwards had long been attracted by the character, even more than by the beauty, of the young woman who thus linked her life with his; and his description of her at the age of thirteen is one of the few striking bits of poetic prose which the rather arid literature of eighteenth-century New England produced.[19] Mrs. Edwards was well worthy of his regard. Hers was a nature not only of remarkable susceptibility to religious impression, but of executive force, cheerful courage, social grace, and sweet, womanly leadership.[20] She added cheer to his house, supplemented his shyness and want of small talk, and it was no inapt, though facetious, tribute to her general repute that affirmed "that she had learned a shorter road to heaven than her husband."[21] Devoted to that husband, whose frail health required constant care, administering a large part of the business affairs of the home with cheerful forgetfulness of her own disabilities that he might be free to spend his accustomed thirteen hours daily in his study, or to take his solitary meditative walks and rides,[22] she brought up eight daughters and three sons and bore her full share of labor in the vicissitudes of Edwards' life. Warmly attached to each other, husband and wife were but briefly separated by death, she surviving him less than seven months.[23] Every recollection of Edwards' achievements should also involve a remembrance of the devoted and solicitous care which made much of his work possible.

Edwards' ministry was marked from the first; and it was not

[19] In full in Dwight, pp. 114, 115; Allen, pp. 45, 46.

[20] Sketch by Hopkins in his *Life and Character of the Late Reverend Mr. Jonathan Edwards* (Boston, 1765); see also Dwight, pp. 113–115, 127–131, 171–190; Allen, pp. 44–49.

[21] Allen, pp. 47, 48.

[22] Hopkins, p. 43; Dwight, pp. 110–113. Professor F. B. Dexter informs me that an examination of Edwards' unpublished correspondence shows that he was more of a man of business than his older biographers believed him to be. He certainly left a larger estate than most New England ministers of his time.

[23] Died October 2, 1758.

long before the Northampton pulpit was strongly felt in Massachusetts and Connecticut in a direction largely counter to the religious tendencies of the time. Taken as a whole, no century in American religious history has been so barren as the eighteenth. The fire and enthusiasm of Puritanism had died out on both sides of the Atlantic. In this country the inevitable provincialism of the narrow colonial life, the deadening influence of its hard grapple with the rude forces of nature, and the Indian and Canadian wars rendered each generation less actively religious than its predecessor; and, while New England shone as compared with the spiritual deadness of Old England in the years preceding Wesley, the old fervor and sense of a national mission were gone, conscious conversion, once so common, was unusual, and religion was becoming more formal and external.

Then, too, it seems to be the law of the development of a declining Calvinism everywhere, whether in Switzerland, France, Holland, England, or America, that it passes through three or four stages. Beginning with an intense assertion of divine sovereignty and human inability, it ascribes all to the grace of God, a grace granting common mercies to all men, and special salvatory mercy to the elect. This special grace has its evident illustrations in struggling spiritual births, lives of high consecration, and conscious regeneration. In seasons of intense spiritual feeling, like the Reformation or the Puritan struggle in England, it is easy to ascribe all religious life to the special, selective, irresistible, tranforming power of God. But, in time, the high pressure of the spiritual life of a community or of a nation, which has passed through such a crisis-experience as had the founders of New England, abates. Men desirous of serving God do not feel so evidently the conscious workings of the divine Spirit, and they ask what they can do, not indeed to save themselves—this second stage of Calvinism with no less emphasis than the first asserts that God alone can accomplish salvation by special grace—but what they can do to put themselves in a position where God is more likely to save them. And the answer from the pulpit and in Christian thought is an increased emphasis on the habitual practice of prayer, faithful attendance at church, and the reading of God's Word, not as of themselves salvatory but as "means" by which a man can put himself in a more probable way of salvation. From this the path to the third stage is easy; to the belief that religion is a habit of careful attention to the duties of the house of God and observance of the precepts of the gospel in relation to one's neighbors—a habit possible of attainment by all men, and justifying the confidence that though men cannot render an adequate service to God, yet if each man labors sincerely to do what he can under the impulse of the grace that God sends to all men God will accept his sincere though imperfect obedience as satisfactory. This stage was known in Edwards' day on both sides of the Atlantic as "Arminianism," and it was accompanied by an unstrenuous or negative attitude toward the doctrines which the first stage of Calvinism had made chief. From this position it was an easy transition for some to the fourth stage, in which the essence of the Christian life is made to consist in the practice of morality, and the need of man is represented to be education and culture, not rescue and fundamental transformation. English Puritanism had reached the fourth stage in some of its representatives when Edwards began his ministry; New England had not gone farther than the third as yet, and was chiefly in the second; but an Arminian point of view was rapidly spreading, even among those who would warmly have resented classification as Arminians. Rev. Samuel Phillips of Andover, who was certainly thought a Calvinist, thus expressed a prevalent feeling in 1738:

I can't suppose, that any one . . . who at all Times, faithfully improves the *common Grace* he has, *that is to say,* is diligent in attending on the appointed Means of Grace with a Desire to profit thereby; . . . and in a Word, who walks up to his Light, to the utmost of his Power, shall perish for want of *special* and saving Grace.[24]

Now it was Edwards' great work as a religious leader to be the chief human instrument in turning back the current for over a century in the larger part of New England to the theory of the method of salvation and of man's dependence on God which marked the earlier types of Calvinism. Yet it was not wholly a return. While he emphasized the arbitrary and absolute character

[24] *Orthodox Christian*, 1738, p. 75.

of the divine election as positively as the older Calvinists, and even more strenuously asserted the immediacy of the divine operations in dealing with the human soul, he tried to find place for a real and still existent, if unused and unusable, natural human power to turn to God, and hence a present, as well as an Adamic and racial, responsibility for not so doing.

Edwards' stimulating preaching soon had a marked effect on the little Northampton community of two hundred families.[25] The town was not unfamiliar with religious quickenings. At least five had occurred under the able ministry of Solomon Stoddard. But Edwards' sermons were on themes calculated to stir a community, and especially an isolated rural community. Two sudden deaths in the spring of 1734 excited the concern of the little town—a concern which was deepened by a vague alarm lest the spreading Arminianism which the Northampton pulpit denounced was a token of the withdrawal of God's redemptive mercy from sinful men. And the preacher set forth, in sermons which read with power after a lapse of more than a hundred and sixty years, the complete right of God to deal with his creatures as he saw fit, the enmity of human hearts against God, the terrors of the world to come, and the blessedness of acceptance with God. "I have found," said Edwards, "that no sermons have been more remarkably blessed, than those in which the doctrine of God's absolute sovereignty with regard to the salvation of sinners, and his just liberty with regard to answering the prayers or succeeding the pains of mere natural men, continuing such, have been insisted on." By December, 1734, a movement of spiritual power was manifest in the community which resulted in six months' time in "more than three hundred" conversions. The experience of those wrought upon, in large measure, corresponded to the type of preaching to which they had listened; and Edwards describes it as normally involving three definite stages. Of these the first was an "awful apprehension" of the condition in which men stand by nature, so overwhelming as to produce oftentimes painful physical

[25] Edwards gave a full account of these events in his *Narrative of Surprising Conversions* (1736–1737), S. Austin, ed., *Works of Jonathan Edwards* (Worcester, 1808–1809), III, 9–62, from which the statements in this paragraph are taken.

effects. Next followed, in cases which Edwards believed to be the genuine work of the Spirit of God, a conviction that they justly deserved the divine wrath, not infrequently leading to expressions of wonder that "God has not cast them into hell long ago." And from this valley of humiliation the converts emerged, often suddenly, into "a holy repose of soul in God through Christ, and a secret disposition to fear and love him, and to hope for blessings from him," and into such "a sense of the greatness of his grace" as to lead, in many instances, to laughter, tears, or even to a "sinking" of the physical frame, as if the inward vision of God's glory were too much for mortal spirits to endure.

This type of Christian experience is foreign to the altered and unemotional age in which we live, but it was not peculiar to Edwards' congregation. The Puritan founders of New England had entered the Kingdom of Heaven by the same door; and one finds in the sermons of Hooker or of Shepard the same analysis of the inmost feelings of the sinful human heart, the same sense of the exceeding difficulty and relative infrequency of salvation, and the same consciousness of desert of the divine wrath. It was to appear again not merely in the Great Awakening of 1740–1742, but in the remarkable series of revivals which, beginning in the last decade of the eighteenth century, lasted nearly to the Civil War. But in Edwards' sermons the view of conversion of which this experience is the normal accompaniment is put with a relentlessness of logic and a fertility of imagination that have never been surpassed. We trace his steps as he argues, in terms in which no parent would estimate the misdeeds of his child, that sin is infinite in its guilt because committed against an infinite object.[26] We follow his reasoning with a recoil that amounts to incredulity that such is the latent hatred of the unregenerate human mind that it would kill God if it could.[27] We revolt as we read Edwards' contention that the wicked are useful simply as objects of the destructive wrath of God;[28] as he beholds the unconverted members of the congregation before him withheld for a brief period by the restraining hand

[26] Sermon on Romans 4:5, *Works*, VII, 27, 28.
[27] *Ibid.*, 5:10, *Works*, VII, 168, 175.
[28] Sermon on Ezekiel 15:2–4, *Works*, VIII, 129–150.

of God from the hell into which they are to fall in their appointed time;[29] as he pictures the damned glow in endless burning agony like a spider in the flame;[30] and heightens the happiness of the redeemed by the contrast between the felicities of heaven and the eternal torments of the lost, visible forever to the saints in glory.[31] No wonder one of his congregation was led to suicide and others felt themselves grievously tempted.[32]

Repulsive as this presentation is, it is but fair to Edwards to remember that it seemed to him to be demanded no less by his philosophic principles than by his interpretation of the Bible. And it is merely justice to recall, also, that though the terrors of the law fill a large place in his pulpit utterances, no man of his age pictured more glowingly than Edwards the joys of the redeemed,[33] the blessedness of union with Christ, or the felicities of the knowledge of God. When all deductions have been made from his presentation of Christian truth—and much must be made—he remains a preacher such as few have been of the eternal verities of sin, redemption, holiness, judgment, and enjoyment of God.

It is evidence that this awakening at Northampton was not the effect of Edwards' preaching alone, that a similar stirring took place within a few months throughout that section of Massachusetts and in a number of towns of Connecticut.[34] The news of this then unusual work drew attention to the young Northampton minister, not only from all parts of New England but from across the Atlantic. His sermons and methods brought some enemies, but many friends; and, at the request of the Rev. Drs. Isaac Watts and John Guyse, the leading Congregational ministers of England, Edwards prepared, and these ministers published at London, in 1737, an extended account of the revival.[35]

[29] Sermon on Deuteronomy 32:35, *Works,* VII, 487, 491, 496, 502.
[30] Sermon on Ezekiel 22:14, *Works,* VII, 393.
[31] *Ibid.,* 15:2–4, *Works,* VIII, 141–143.
[32] *Narrative of Surprising Conversions, Works,* III, 77, 78.
[33] E. g., his sermon on John 14:27, *Works,* VIII, 230–247.
[34] *Narrative of Surprising Conversions, Works,* III, 77, 78.
[35] *A Faithful Narrative of the Surprising Work of God in the Conversion of Many Hundred Souls in Northampton and the Neighbouring Towns* (London, 1737). Generally known as the *Narrative of Surprising Conversions.* A briefer account by Edwards had been published at Boston late in 1736.

Known thus far and wide as one whose ministry had been
signally distinguished by dramatic manifestations of spiritual
power, it was natural that when the coming of Whitefield to the
Congregational colonies, in the autumn of 1740, gave the human
impetus to the marvelous religious overturning known as the
"Great Awakening," Edwards should be regarded as the best
American representative of the revival spirit which then had its
most extensive manifestation. The story of that momentous stirring
will be told in the next lecture more fully than our time will permit
today. To Edwards it seemed at first the very dawning of the
millennial age, and the visible manifestation of the divine glory.[36]
It appeared but the repetition, not merely in Edwards' own parish,
but on a scale coextensive with the American colonies, of the
revival of his early ministry. He welcomed the youthful Whitefield
to his pulpit; who, in turn, recorded an approval of the occupants
of the Northampton parsonage in the words: "He is a Son himself,
and hath also a Daughter of *Abraham* for his wife"; and said of
Edwards, "I think I have not seen his Fellow in all *New England*."[37]
Edwards himself preached as an evangelist in many pulpits
besides his own. And when criticism arose and waxed to denuncia-
tion in many quarters as the more radical elements of the movement ran their violent and divisive course, he defended the revival
as a true work of the Spirit of God, which every Christian ought to
favor to the utmost of his power, while deprecating the excesses of
many of the exhorters, in his treatise of 1742, entitled *Some
Thoughts concerning the Present Revival of Religion in New England.*

But though Edwards distrusted, in this volume, the weight laid
by many of the friends of the revival on the bodily effects which so
frequently accompanied the preaching of Whitefield, Tennent,
Parsons, Bellamy, or his own, he nevertheless insisted that they
were oftentimes a real product of the Spirit of God, and he cites in
proof an experience of his wife begun probably near the close of
1738 and reaching its culmination in the revival scenes of 1742. In

[36] *Some Thoughts concerning the Present Revival of Religion in New
England* (Boston, 1742), pp. 96–103.
[37] Whitefield's *Seventh Journal,* pp. 47, 48.

so doing he gave a part of one of the most interesting chapters in mystic biography anywhere recorded[38]—the complement to it being contained in Mrs. Edwards' own account published by Dr. Dwight.[39] It is one which shows how Edwards' thought had in it the germ of a development of his theology fully reached by his disciples as to the extent to which a Christian must be cordially submissive to the divine disposal. Edwards did, indeed, deprecate the statements of converts that they were willing to be damned, if God so chose. "They had not clear and distinct ideas of damnation," he says; "nor does any word in the Bible require such self-denial as this."[40] And he also held that an impenitent man might rightfully pray for God's mercy.[41] But Edwards taught that the essence of virtue is the preference of the glory of God to any personal interests. And the burden of Mrs. Edwards' struggle was this crucial problem of submission. It is illustrative of the wifely devotion of this remarkable woman that the very crises of her trial were her willingness to endure, if necessary, the disapproval of her husband, and to see another more successful than he in his Northampton pulpit, if God so desired. After these battles had been won, it was easy to go on to a sense of readiness to "die on the rack, or at the stake," or "in horror" of soul, rising at last to a willingness to suffer the torments of hell in body and soul "if it be most for the honour of God."[42]

These experiences were accompanied not once, but repeatedly by such a sense of the divine glory that[43]

the Strength of the Body [was] taken away, so as to deprive of all Ability to stand or speak; sometimes the Hands clinch'd, and the Flesh cold, but Senses still remaining;

and the result was

[38] *Thoughts*, pp. 62–78.
[39] Dwight, pp. 171–186.
[40] *Narrative of Surprising Conversions, Works*, III, 37.
[41] Letter of 1741, Dwight, p. 150: "There are very few requests that are proper for an impenitent man, that are not also, in some sense, proper for the godly."
[42] Dwight, p. 182.
[43] *Thoughts*, pp. 63, 76.

all former Troubles and Sorrows of Life forgotten, and all Sorrow and Sighing fled away, excepting Grief for past Sins, and for remaining Corruption . . . a daily sensible doing and suffering every Thing for GOD, . . . eating for GOD, and working for GOD, and sleeping for GOD, and bearing Pain and Trouble for GOD, and doing all as the Service of Love.

What shall we say to these things? Not that they are not the real experiences of sensible men and women, in a period of high-wrought religious feeling. They are; or we must deny the Christian consciousness of Paul, of Bernhard, of Francis. But they are not the experiences of the normal religious life, and to insist on them as such is to make a great mistake.

And Edwards also came to feel that it was in some sense a mistake. When the Great Awakening was over, he published, in the light of that tremendous wave of excitement and its disappointing results, his noblest purely religious exposition, the *Treatise concerning Religious Affections,* of 1746. None but a man of remarkable poise of judgment could have written it. It betrays no reaction against the movement which had so come short of what he hoped. It sees the good and the bad in it; and, rising above the temporary occasion, seeks to answer the question, "What is the Nature of True Religion?"[44]

Edwards,[45] unlike modern psychologists, divided the soul into two "faculties," understanding and affections—the latter including, but not separating, the will and the inclinations. Each faculty is the realm of religion, but that of the affections most of all—that is to say, no religion can be genuine which remains merely a matter of intellectual knowledge of truth without prompting to acts of will and outgoings of emotion.

But to be moved by strong emotions, Edwards perceived, is not necessarily to be religious. This was the mistake that many had made in the recent revival, and it was as great an error, Edwards thought, as the denial that the affections had to do with religion, which reaction from the excesses of the revival had produced in some. That emotion is greatly stirred, or that bodily effects are

[44] *Religious Affections,* Preface.
[45] In this paragraph I have tried to give a brief synopsis of the book.

produced, are no signs that men are truly religious—though Edwards here sticks to his guns and declares that to affirm that bodily effects are not of themselves evidences of religion is not to affirm that true religious emotion may never have bodily effects. Nor are we to trust to a fluent tongue, a ready recollection of Scripture, an "appearance of love," a peculiar sequence of religious experiences, a sense of assurance, a zeal for attending meetings, or an ability to give a well-sounding account of an alleged work of grace, as proving a man a Christian. Rather, true Christian affections involve a "new spiritual sense," which comes not by nature, but by the indwelling power of the Holy Spirit, inducing a new attitude of the heart toward God; an unselfish love for divine things because they are holy; a spiritual enlightenment which leads to a conviction of the certainty of divine truth and a humiliating sense of unworthiness; and a change of disposition which shows itself in love, meekness, tenderness of spirit, producing symmetry of character, increasing longing for spiritual attainments, and a life of Christian conduct in our relations to our fellow-men.

The ideal that Edwards held up is of exceeding loftiness—too high to be made, as he and his followers made it, the test of all Christian discipleship. But it is a noble ideal for a Christian man, and especially for a Christian minister, to hold before himself as that toward the realization of which his Christian life is striving in feeling and animating purpose.

It is as a personal illustration of the *Religious Affections,* I think, that we should view the biographical edition of the diary of his young friend, David Brainerd, the missionary to the Indians, which Edwards published in 1749.[46] Betrothed to Edwards' daughter Jerusha, and dying at Edwards' house, in 1747, at the age of twenty-nine, Brainerd's story has the pathetic interest always attaching to frustrated promise; and his missionary zeal has made his consecration a stimulus to others. But, though one of the most popular of Edwards' books at the time of its publication, his *Life*

[46] "There are two Ways of representing and recommending true Religion and Virtue to the World, which GOD hath made Use of: The one is by Doctrine and Precept; the other is by Instance and Example." *An Account of the Life of the Late Reverend Mr. David Brainerd* (Boston, 1749), Preface.

*of Brainerd* is a distressing volume to read. The morbid, introspective self-examinations and the elevations and depressions of the poor consumptive are but a sorry illustration at best of the noble ideal of the full-rounded, healthful Christian life.

Edwards shared with Brainerd what our generation looks upon as the young sufferer's most winsome trait—his missionary sympathy; but opportunities for manifesting it in a rural New England parish in the middle of the eighteenth century were few. One such came in 1746, when a proposition reached New England from a number of Scotch ministers that Christians unite in a "concert of prayer for the coming of our Lord's kingdom" throughout the earth.[47] Edwards welcomed it eagerly, and, in 1747, published an extensive treatise in furtherance of the suggestion.[48] In the course of this essay he took occasion not only to urge the desirability of united prayer and to answer some objections to union which seem rather absurd to our age, though they were then regarded as real difficulties, but to set forth his interpretation of prophecy and his ardent hope for the speedy coming of a brighter religious day.

Edwards' own personal trials were thickening in the years following the revival at which we have just been glancing. Some of the causes of growing estrangement between him and his Northampton people are patent enough; some are obscure. Two are distinctly in evidence. The first was a case of discipline, apparently of the year 1744, wherein proceedings against a number of young people in his congregation for circulating what he deemed, doubtless truly, impure books, were so managed or mismanaged, as to alienate from him nearly all the young people of the town.[49]

The other evident cause was the controversy over the terms of church membership, which was the ostensible ground of his dismission.[50] In a former lecture some account was given of the rise of the "Halfway Covenant"—that system approved by the second

[47] *Works*, III, 370–372.

[48] *An Humble Attempt to promote Explicit Agreement and Visible Union of God's People in Extraordinary Prayer for the Revival of Religion and the Advancement of Christ's Kingdom on Earth* (Boston, 1747).

[49] Dwight, pp. 299, 300.

[50] Dwight gives a full and documentary account of this controversy, *ibid.*, pp. 300–448.

generation on New England soil, by which the children of church members, though themselves not consciously regenerate, were admitted to sufficient standing in the church to bring their children in turn to baptism, although themselves barred from the Lord's table. Hence the nickname "Halfway Covenant," indicating that those who stood in this relation were members enough to enjoy the privileges of the one sacrament for their children, but not members enough to participate in the other.

This system became general in New England by the beginning of the eighteenth century; but in some places the earlier practice was yet further modified. Some argued that if earnest-minded though unregenerate children of church members were themselves sufficiently church members, by reason of the divine promise, "to be a God unto thee, and to thy seed after thee,"[51] to bring their children in turn to baptism, they were sufficiently members to come to the Lord's Supper. Indeed, it was their duty to come thither, if sincerely desirous of leading a Christian life, for they would find the communion, like prayer and public worship, a means tending to conversion. This view was made popular in the upper Connecticut Valley by the great influence of Edwards' grandfather and predecessor, Solomon Stoddard. Held by him as early as 1679, he did not introduce the practice into the Northampton church till after 1700; but it soon after became the custom in that church and in most of its immediate neighbors.[52] Edwards was settled under it and practiced it for nearly twenty years.

Edwards' own lofty conceptions of the Christian life and his emphasis on conversion as its beginning led him gradually, however, to the conclusion that no church privileges should be given to those not conscious, in some degree, of a work of the Spirit of God in their own souls. He intimated this change of view in his *Religious Affections* of 1746;[53] but it illustrates the spiritual torpor that followed the fever of the Great Awakening, and possibly the alienation between Edwards and his young people, that he waited

[51] Genesis 17:7.
[52] Some account may be found in Walker's *Creeds and Platforms,* pp. 279–282.
[53] Edwards' own statement, in Dwight, p. 314.

from 1744 to December, 1748, for a single candidate for church membership to come forward even under the easy terms of the Northampton church. When an applicant at last appeared he made known his change of opinion, and intended change of practice, temperately and moderately. There was, indeed, a good deal to be said against such a modification as the pastor proposed. His honored grandfather had introduced the existing system; he had been settled, well knowing what it was; he had practiced it. It might be urged that it was a breach of contract for him to abandon it. But, even granting this, one hardly understands the virulence of the opposition which Edwards encountered from those who must almost all have been his spiritual children. One hardly sees sufficient ground for the hostility that led to charges that Edwards planned a Separatist congregation; that refused to hear his arguments; that sought to induce prominent ministers to answer the admirable book which he published in 1749 in defense of his position;[54] that appears in the long wrangle over the composition of the council which should consider his further relations to the Northampton congregation; or in the bitter enmity of some of his kinsfolk in and out of the ministry of the county. Edwards himself once declared that he had little skill in conversation; "he was thought by some . . . to be stiff and unsociable"; he held himself aloof from pastoral calling save in cases of real need;[55] and one can but suspect that he lacked the art of leading men. Honest and conscientious to the core—in this change of practice, as in the case of discipline, he seems to have taken none of the preparatory measures which often make all the difference between success and failure in swaying a democratic body. Stoddard had certainly held his peculiar views for nearly thirty years before they became the practice of his congregation, but such careful nurturing of a desired measure was apparently foreign to Edwards' nature. That the matter was intellectually clear to him was sufficient; it ought to be so to others.

But, however explainable, the fact remains that in this crisis

[54] *An Humble Inquiry into the Rules of the Word of God, concerning the Qualifications Requisite to a compleat Standing and full Communion in the Visible Christian Church* (Boston, 1749).
[55] Hopkins, pp. 44–46, 54.

Edwards had the support of no considerable portion of his congregation, nor did the strong sense of professional unity characteristic of the clergy of the eighteenth century prevent a majority of his neighboring ministers from opposing him. A council of nine churches met on June 19, 1750.[56] That advisory body having decided that Edwards' dismission was necessary if his people still desired it, the Northampton church voted by more than two hundred to twenty-three to dismiss its pastor. That action the council approved by a majority of one on June 22. And the town added what was an insult to the burdens of the deposed pastor by voting, probably in November, 1750, that Edwards should not preach in the community. It is interesting to note that one, at least, of those of Edwards' congregation prominent in procuring his removal, and esteemed by the Northampton pastor his most energetic opponent, Joseph Hawley, Edwards' cousin, and a leading lawyer and politician, afterward not only privately but publicly avowed his regret and repentance for what had been done.[57] And Edwards' contention in the principal subject of this controversy was not without abundant ultimate fruitage. His friends, notably his pupil, Rev. Dr. Joseph Bellamy, carried forward his attack on Stoddardeanism and the Halfway Covenant, with the result that, by the first decade of the nineteenth century, when Edwards had been fifty years in his grave, the system had been generally set aside by the Congregational churches.

Turned out from his pastorate thus, at the age of forty-seven with a family of ten living children,[58] he had to look about for a new charge. His friend, Rev. Dr. John Erskine, suggested a settlement in Scotland, where Erskine was a leader in the church;[59] the people of Canaan, Connecticut, heard him with approval;[60] but

[56] Dwight gives the documents, pp. 398–403; Edwards wrote a most interesting account in letters of July 5, 1750, to Erskine, and of July 1, 1751, to Gillespie, *ibid.*, pp. 405–413, 462–468.

[57] Letter of May 9, 1760, *ibid.*, pp. 421–427. See Edwards' characterization of him, *ibid.*, pp. 410, 411.

[58] Two daughters, however, were married in the year of Edwards' dismission.

[59] Edwards' letter of July 5, 1750, Dwight, p. 412.

[60] Dexter, *Biographical Sketches of the Graduates of Yale College*, I, 219, 220.

the place of his next seven-years sojourn was determined by a two-
fold call that came to him through the efforts of his friend and
pupil, Samuel Hopkins, in December, 1750, from the church in the
little frontier village of Stockbridge to become its minister, and
from the English "Society for the Propagation of the Gospel in
New England," which had grown out of Eliot's labors a century
before, to become its missionary to the Housatonic Indians at the
same place.[61] Thither he and his household removed in the
summer of 1751. But Stockbridge was not without its serious controversies between the new pastor and missionary and those who
were exploiting the Indians for pecuniary advantage; and the chief
of his new foes was a relative of some of his leading opponents in
the Northampton separation. These disputes distressed the first
years of his new settlement, but Edwards' position was so mani-
festly just that, with the support of the commissioners whose missionary agent he was, victory and peace came to him.[62]

Edwards doubtless conscientiously fulfilled his stipulated duty
of preaching to the Indians once a week through an interpreter,[63]
besides ministering to the English-speaking Stockbridge congregation, but he was too settled in scholastic ways to make a successful
missionary. His own judgment of himself he expressed when he
wrote to Erskine, in 1750, that he was "fitted for no other business
but study."[64] And at Stockbridge opportunity came to him, even
amid the distractions of the great military struggle between France
and England in which little Stockbridge was at times a turmoiled
frontier outpost,[65] for studies which produced the four treatises by
which he is best known—his *Careful and Strict Enquiry into the
Modern Prevailing Notions of Freedom of Will*,[66] his "Concern-

---

[61] Dwight, p. 449; see also Hopkins' statement, West, *Sketches of the Life
of the Late Rev. Samuel Hopkins* (Hartford, 1805), pp. 53–57.

[62] For some aspects of this controversy, see Dwight, pp. 450–541.

[63] There is an outline of one of these sermons in Grosart, *Selections from
the Unpublished Writings of Jonathan Edwards* (Edinburgh: Privately
printed, 1865), pp. 191–196.

[64] Dwight, p. 412.

[65] Compare Edwards' letter of April 10, 1756, to McCulloch, Dwight,
p. 555.

[66] First edition, Boston, 1754.

ing the End for which God Created the World," his "Nature of True Virtue,"[67] and his *Great Christian Doctrine of Original Sin Defended.*[68]

This is not the time and place, even if the lecturer possessed the ability, to enter on any thorough criticism, or even on any elaborate exposition, of these works. Viewed simply as feats of intellectual achievement they present the highest reach of the New England mind and have given their author a permanent place among the philosophers of the eighteenth century. Were Edwards' writings subtracted from the literature of colonial New England the residue would embrace little more than the discussions of a narrow and provincial society, aside from the course of the world's affairs. It was Edwards who gave to the thought of eighteenth-century New England about whatever interest and lasting repute it bears in other lands. Edwards' treatises involved no changes in his theology. Rather they were the logical formulation of what he had long taught.

Edwards' volume on the *Will,* usually esteemed his crowning work, was long planned,[69] but was not written till 1753. It was his supreme effort against the Arminianism which had been the horror of his early ministry. Calvinism, in this feature of its strenuous creed, had fallen low. Its contemporary defenders in England, like Watts and Doddridge, had been compelled, as Edwards' son Jonathan phrased it, to "bow in the house of Rimmon, and admit the *Self-Determining Power"* of the will.[70] In the *Discourse* published by Daniel Whitby, rector at the English Salisbury, in 1710, predestination in the Calvinistic sense was widely believed to have received its deathblow; and we may imagine that the arguments therein advanced had often been pressed upon Edwards' attention by his keen-minded kinsman and opponent in Northampton, Joseph Hawley, when the latter was a student in his household.[71] But whatever of local and personal interest there may have been for Edwards in the theme, the general defense of what he deemed the

---

[67] These two treatises were first published at Boston in 1765.
[68] First edition, Boston, 1758.
[69] Dwight, p. 507.
[70] "Improvements in Theology," *ibid.,* p. 614.
[71] *Ibid.,* pp. 410, 411.

truth against widely prevalent error was motive enough to rouse a
man of his temperament to utmost endeavor.

To Edwards' thinking,[72] human freedom signifies no more than
a natural power to act in accordance with the choice of the mind.
With the origin of that choice the will has nothing to do. Man is
free to do as he chooses, but not free to determine in what direction his choice shall lie. His will always moves, and moves freely,
in the line of his strongest inclination, but what that inclination
will be depends on what man deems his highest good. While man
has full natural power to serve God—that is, could freely follow a
choice to serve God if he had such an inclination—he will not
serve God till God reveals himself to man as his highest good and
thus renders obedience to God man's strongest motive. Moral
responsibility lies in his choice, not in the cause of the choice; and
hence a man of evil inclination deserves condemnation, since each
choice is his own act, even though the direction in which the
choices are exercised is not in his control. Man cannot choose
between various choices, nor can his choice originate without some
impelling cause external to the will; but his will acts in the direction in which he desires to move, and is free in the sense that it is
not forced to act counter to its inclination.

In this treatise Edwards took up conceptions essentially re-
sembling those advanced by Hobbes, Locke, and Collins, with
whose religious speculations he had no sympathy; but his use of
these ideas was profoundly original. He appears to have been
acquainted with the writings of Locke only, and his grasp of the
points involved is far surer than that of the English philosopher.
The volume was, till comparatively recent times, in extensive use,
being esteemed by Calvinists generally an unanswerable critique of
the Arminian position. It has met, however, with growing dissent,
and though not often directly opposed of late years, is largely felt
to lie outside the conceptions of modern religious thought; but it
has acceptance still, especially with those who hold a necessitarian
view of the universe, and may be said never to have had a positive

---

[72] In describing Edwards' books I have borrowed some sentences from
my *History of the Congregational Churches in the United States* (New York,
1894), pp. 283–286.

and complete refutation, though suffering a constantly increasing neglect.

The preparation of this treatise on the *Will* was followed by the composition of two smaller essays, probably in 1755[73]—that "Concerning the End for which God Created the World," and that on the "Nature of True Virtue." Of the former investigation into a profound and mysterious theme it may be sufficient to say that Edwards' immediate interpreters, notably his son Jonathan, regarded it as uniting the two heretofore supposedly mutually exclusive explanations of the universe as created either for the happiness of finite beings or as a manifestation of the glory of the Creator. This union Edwards would effect by showing that both results "were the ultimate end of the creation," and that, far from being incompatible, "they are really one and the same thing." The universe in its highest possible state of happiness is the ultimate exhibition of the divine glory.[74]

The second of these treatises—that on the "Nature of True Virtue"—though incomplete, expresses in metaphysical form the feature of the teaching of Edwards that has probably most affected New England thought. He asserted that the elemental principle in virtue is benevolence, or love to intelligent being in proportion to the amount of being which each personality possesses.[75] Other things being equal, the worth of each personality is measured by the amount of being which it has. To use Edwards' illustration, "an *Archangel* must be supposed to have more existence, and to be every way further removed from *nonentity,* than a *worm.*"[76] And the benevolence which constitutes virtue must go out to all in proportion to their value thus measured in the scale of being. Closely connected with this benevolence toward being in general is a feeling of love and attraction toward other beings who are actuated by a similar spirit of benevolence. But any love for being less wide than this, or springing from any motive narrower than general benevolence cannot be true virtue.

[73] Dwight, p. 542.
[74] "Improvements in Theology," Dwight, pp. 613, 614.
[75] "The Nature of True Virtue," *Works,* II, 394–401.
[76] *Ibid.,* p. 401.

This theory profoundly influenced New England theology. Reduced to popular thought, it taught that selfishness is sin, and that disinterested love to God and to one's fellow-men is righteousness. It seemed to furnish a self-evident demonstration of the necessity of a divinely wrought change of heart. It gave a ground also for holding that virtue is identical in its nature in God and man by showing that benevolence toward intelligent personalities in proportion to the amount of being that each possesses leads God, as the Infinite Being in comparison with whom the rest of the universe is infinitesimal, to seek first his own glory, while man, if actuated by the same motive of general benevolence, seeks first the glory of God. Nor was this doctrine less effective in giving a basis for philanthropy. It was no accident that classed Samuel Hopkins, sternest of the pupils of Edwards, or Jonathan Edwards the younger, clearest-minded expounder of the Edwardean system, among the earliest New England opponents of Negro slavery, or drew the earliest missionaries of the American Board from Edwardean ranks. Like the *Treatise concerning Religious Affections,* this essay holds love to be the basal element in piety; but in its banishment of self-interest it left room for the assertion by some of Edwards' successors that no true benevolence could be present till the soul was ready to submit willingly to any disposition of itself which God saw was for the best good of the universe, even if that disposition was the soul's damnation. We have already noted that though Edwards never asserted this necessity, Mrs. Edwards reached this degree of self-renunciation in the revival of 1742.

The fourth important fruit of Edwards' studies was a volume that was passing through the press at the time of his death—that on *Original Sin.* Of all his works none is more ingenious or intellectually acute, but none has met so little acceptance. The subject of original sin, like that of the powers of the will, was one on which the eighteenth-century opponents of the historic Augustinian view were widely supposed to have got much the better of its defenders. Chief among these opponents in popular regard was John Taylor, a Presbyterian Arian minister at Norwich, England, whose *Scripture Doctrine of Original Sin,* of 1738, argued that sorrow, labor, and physical death are consequences to us of

Adam's transgression, but we are in no sense guilty of Adam's sin, our rational powers are in no way disabled, nor are we on account of that sin in any state of natural corruption so as to be now without capacity fully to serve God.

These opinions were reflected in eastern Massachusetts; and, in 1757 and 1758, a lively exchange of pamphlets took place in which Rev. Samuel Webster of Salisbury and Rev. Charles Chauncy of Boston attacked the doctrine of original sin, while Edwards' friend, Rev. Peter Clark of Danvers, and his pupil, Rev. Joseph Bellamy, defended it. Edwards had probably written most of his volume when this American discussion opened; but though he had Taylor primarily in mind, it was doubtless hastened through the press in view of the debate on this side of the Atlantic.[77]

In his volume on original sin Edwards argued, with great wealth of illustration, the innate corruption of mankind at whatever stage of their existence from earliest infancy to old age, with proofs drawn from Scripture and experience. This corruption amounts in all, of whatever age, to utter ruin. It has its root in Adam's sin, and that sin is ours, but not by any Augustinian presence of humanity in Adam.[78] On the contrary, Edwards explained our guilt of that far-off transgression by a curious theory of the preservation of personal or racial continuity—a theory drawn in part from Locke's speculations on Identity and Diversity.[79] That which makes you and me today the same beings that thought or walked or studied yesterday is the constant creative activity of God. God, by a "constitution," or appointment of things, that is "arbitrary" in the sense that it depends on his will alone, sees fit to appoint that the acts and thoughts of the present moment shall be consciously continuous of those of the past; and it is this ever-renewed creation that gives all personal identity to the individual.[80] What is true of each man is also true of the race. God has constituted all men one

[77] Some account of this controversy may be found in my *History of the Congregational Churches*, pp. 273–276.

[78] Here again I borrow from the volume above cited.

[79] Compare Fisher, *History of Christian Doctrine*, p. 403.

[80] See *Original Sin* (1758), pp. 338–346.

with Adam, so that his primal sin is really theirs, and they are viewed as *"Sinners,* truly guilty, and *Children of Wrath* on that *Account."*[81]

Mr. Lecky has characterized this volume as "one of the most revolting books that have ever proceeded from the pen of man."[82] Without at all sharing the severity of his criticism, it may fairly be said to be a work that renders more difficult, if anything, one of the most mysterious problems of religion—the origin and universal pervasiveness of evil.

Our glance at Edwards' principal writings has necessarily been fleeting; but it has sufficed to show that he impressed several principles on the minds of his contemporaries and successors. Teaching that the sinner possesses the natural power, but not the inclination, to do the will of God, he held that a change of disposition, wrought by a conversion through the transforming work of the Spirit of God, was not merely the primary, but the only important, thing in beginning a Christian life. He taught, also, that the essential characteristic of that life was love to God and to his creatures rather than to self, and that there could be no true religious life which did not have its seat in the emotions and will even more than in the intellect. Edwards did not live long enough to work out a full-rounded system. But besides the evident features of his teachings at which we have glanced, he dropped many hints and half-elaborated suggestions which made his work not merely the beginning of a development carried much farther by his followers, but have led to the claim that he was the father of most various tendencies in later New England thought.

Edwards' pastorate at Stockbridge was the harvest-time of his intellectual activity; but it was followed by a brief episode that had the promise of usefulness for him as a former of character and a leader of young men. The death of Rev. Aaron Burr, the husband of Edwards' third daughter, Esther, in September, 1757, left vacant the presidency of Princeton College, which Burr had occupied since 1748. The "College of New Jersey" had been founded,

---

[81] *Ibid.,* p. 355.

[82] *History of the Rise and Influence of the Spirit of Rationalism in Europe* (New York, 1866), I, p. 368; see also Allen, *Jonathan Edwards,* p. 312.

in 1746, as an institution in more hearty sympathy with the revival movement to which Edwards was attached than were Harvard or Yale. Nine of its trustees were graduates of Yale.[83] The college had recently been permitted (1753) by the Connecticut legislature to raise funds in Edwards' native colony by means of a lottery, "for the encouragement of religion and learning," as the act read.[84] It appealed to New England as much as to the Middle States, and represented what was then freshest and most spiritually warmhearted in New England thought. Naturally the trustees looked to Edwards; and, two days after Burr's death, elected him to the vacant presidency.[85]

Edwards hesitated. He wished to complete his *History of the Work of Redemption,* which should set forth his conceptions of theology as a whole.[86] Yet the call was one he felt to be pressing, and with the supporting advice of an ecclesiastical council which met at Stockbridge early in January, 1758, he accepted the appointment. But he was destined to assume the work of the proffered office only to lay it down. Inoculated with smallpox as a protective measure, on February 13, 1758, the disease, usually mild under such circumstances, took an unfavorable turn, and he died at Princeton, March 22, in his fifty-fifth year, leaving his work, from a human point of view, incomplete.

Jonathan Edwards the controversialist, the revival preacher, and the metaphysician is the figure oftenest in our thought. It is necessary that it should be so, for in all these respects he was a leader of men. But as we think of him in these attributes he seems remote. His controversies are over questions in which our age takes languid interest, his denunciatory sermons we read with reluctance, his explanations of the will, of the constitution of the human race, or of the end for which God created the world we admire as feats of intellectual strength; but they do not move our hearts or altogether command the assent of our understandings. The thought I wish to leave with you is rather of the man who walked with God.

[83] Dexter, *Biographical Sketches,* I, 220.
[84] *Colonial Records,* X, 217, 218.
[85] Dwight, p. 565.
[86] Letter to the Trustees of the College of New Jersey, *ibid.,* p. 569.

No stain marred his personal character, no consideration of personal disadvantage swayed him from what he deemed his duty to the truth in the controversy at Northampton which led to his dismission. He was the type of a fearless, patient, loyal scholar. But this steadfast-mindedness was based on more than personal uprightness. To him God was the nearest and truest of friends, as well as the strongest of sovereigns. In his narrative of his religious experience he noted the delight and the strength that he found in the saying of the old Hebrew prophet regarding the Saviour: "A man shall be as an hiding place from the wind, and a covert from the tempest; as rivers of water in a dry place, as the shadow of a great rock in a weary land."[87] Above all his other gifts and acquisitions he had, and he made men feel that he had, a vision of the glory of God that transfigured his life with a beauty of spirit that makes his memory reverenced even more than his endowments of mind are respected.

[87] Isaiah 32:2; see Hopkins, p. 36; Dwight, p. 132.

✪

# The Young Philosopher

It would not have been surprising if a boy educated under such conditions had learned nothing at all; but Edwards seems to have profited from the very freedom which he enjoyed.

Probably the Wethersfield curriculum was similar to that which Rector Pierson had instituted at Saybrook; but it was not quite so medieval in spirit. Elisha Williams, like Samuel Johnson, realized that the philosophers of Europe had not been inactive in the ninety years since the fathers of New England had taken their degrees at Cambridge; and the political pamphlet which he wrote eighteen years later shows a profound admiration for the philosophy of John Locke. Presumably it was he that introduced Locke to his pupil; for in his second year at Wethersfield Edwards read the *Essay concerning Human Understanding,* and derived from it, as he related many years afterwards, a greater pleasure "than the most greedy miser finds, when gathering up handfuls of silver and gold, from some newly discovered treasure."

Stimulated by his reading of Locke, the fourteen-year-old school-boy began on his own account a series of notes on philosophical problems. The first was a definition of "excellency," so long and elaborate that we may suppose it to have been a frequent subject of meditation. He could not have started more appropriately.

He began by defining material beauty; and with the aid of

Reprinted by permission of the author from Henry Bamford Parkes, *Jonathan Edwards: The Fiery Puritan* (New York: Minton, Balch & Company, 1930), pp. 52–65.

several geometrical designs, he satisfied himself that it was all a matter of symmetry; beauty was a harmony in which the details were balanced against each other. "The beautiful shape of flowers, the beauty of the body of man, and of the bodies of other animals"; the pleasures of music, and colors, and sweet tastes and smells: all were derived from harmony. His explanations were inadequate enough; but what interested him was to pass on to spiritual beauty. That too was based on harmony: the harmony of the separate souls with each other and with God, which is called love.

To the young dreamer, walking alone in the fields at Wethersfield, the whole universe was a single harmony, the whole universe was beautiful; and if any of the details seemed ugly, that was because the universe, like a complicated melody, required "a vastly larger view" to comprehend it. For the universe was God's artistic creation; it was God expressing Himself, for His own aesthetic delight. And the beauty of each soul was to participate in the melody of the universe, by loving the universe and God. "A lower kind of love," he said, a love for a woman or a possession, "may be odious, because it hinders, or is contrary to, a higher and a more general. Even as a lower proportion is often a deformity, because it is contrary to a more general proportion."

The boy passed on still further. Why was harmony beautiful? What was the highest good? What was the ultimate reality? To Edwards, exulting in the powers of his mind and in aesthetic delights, it was life itself; life was the highest good; harmony was good because it promoted life, disharmony was ugly because it contradicted life. God was life in excelsis; and the human being was most beautiful and most alive when it loved God, most ugly and nearest to nothingness when it hated Him.

These ideas were new; no other New Englander had ever approached them; the boy Edwards worked them out by himself; and forty years later he was still elaborating them; for after he was converted, his God-intoxication united with the traditional theology of Calvinism to form a new compound.

There were seventy-two notes in all. The schoolboy meditated upon a great variety of philosophical topics. Incidentally—for the fact is not important—he worked out an idealism similar to that of

Berkeley in England; he also anticipated some of the most important suggestions of Hume and Kant; and played with ideas of the relativity of motion and the finiteness of the universe in words which might have been written yesterday. But his central theme was the glory of God, the God whom he had found in sweet sensations and natural beauties, a God who loved Himself and all things living, not the Calvinist God who punished men in hell. There is all the charm of innocence and novelty, and sometimes also an unearthly mystic beauty, about these early notes, which disappeared from the treatises of the theologian.

He took all knowledge as his field; and after reading Newton and Rector Pierson, began a second series of notes on natural science. He was not a scientist: his purpose was to prove the existence of God, not to discover truth. Upon a suggestion or an observation, wholly unproved, he would build the most magnificent fancies. He was a poet, playing with possibilities; he took an exuberant delight in striking out hypotheses, in exercising his mind with logical speculations. Of the scientific skepticism, the need to experiment, the search for proof, he had not a trace. The most memorable passages in these notes are poetic: as when he describes "nothing" as "the same that the sleeping rocks do dream of." Typical of them are memoranda like: "To find out a thousand things by due observation of the Spheroid of the Universe"; and, after discussing the refraction of light rays, "To seek out other strange phenomena, and compare them together, and see what qualities can be made out of them: And if we can discover them, it is probable we may be let into a New World of Philosophy." The sense of wonder is magnificent, worthy of a Leonardo; but it is not science.

He used the Newtonian theory to prove that if the smallest atom were misplaced, the whole universe would, in the course of infinite time, be thrown into confusion; hence it must have had an all-wise designer. This was the core of his speculations.

In the eighteenth century it did not occur to people that the universe might have evolved by accident, or that it was already in confusion.

The scope of his observations was prodigious: the human anatomy, the saltness of the sea, the structure of light waves, the nature of stars and atoms, the cause of lightning, the erosion of valleys, the growth of trees, the content of fogs, the color of the sun's rays when they passed through the leaves of a tree on to the pages of a book—he had new theories to propound about them all.

He proved thus that water could be compressed. The solid earth, according to the second of the ten commandments, rested upon water; obviously that water was compressed. But nobody had actually been able to compress water; that however was merely for lack of power.

He had some remarkable suggestions to offer about planetary influence on human history. The heavenly bodies, he suggested, discharged streams of particles which hit the earth, and caused direct alterations in terrestrial affairs; such alterations must have been stronger before the flood, when the atmosphere of the earth was less disturbed; and the antediluvian patriarchs, being long-lived, had enjoyed special opportunities for observing them scientifically; thus a tradition, handed down by Noah, had probably caused the general opinion that the moon and the planets affected the movement of events.

As the notes increased, and with them his pride in his own intellectual capacity, he began to dream of glory; he would publish a great philosophical treatise, and become famous in Europe. He drew up a scheme for it: it was to have two parts, the first on the mind, the second on the external world. For the treatise on the mind he enumerated fifty-six subjects, covering every branch of psychology. For the treatise on the external world he wrote an introduction, and some preliminary propositions, and notes on "being" and "atoms," and a series of eighty-eight topics to be "written fully about."

On the inside page of the cover of his notebook he wrote down a number of rules to guide him in writing this work. Those in long-hand were naïve but harmless. "Let much modesty be seen in the style," he reminded himself. And "let there be much compliance with the reader's weakness, and according to the rules in the Ladies' Library, Vol. 1, p. 340." He resolved "to be very moderate in the use of terms of art. Let it not look as if I was much read, or was conversant with books, or with the learned world." And he decided that the preface should form part of the body of the work; "then I shall be sure to have it read by every one."

But several of the notes were written in shorthand, in order that they might be illegible to his classmates. Two of these were: "Before I venture to publish in London, to make some experiment in my own country, to play at small games first. That I may gain some experience in writing, first to write letters to some in England and to try my hand in lesser matters before I venture in great." And, "The World will expect more modesty because of my circumstances, in America, young, etc. Let there therefore be a superabundance of modesty and, though perhaps 'twill otherwise be needless, it will wonderfully make way for its reception in the world. Mankind are by nature proud and exceeding envious and evermore jealous of such upstarts, and it exceedingly irritates and affronts them to see them appear in print."

Such self-confidence, from a youth of seventeen in a backward province on the edge of the civilized world, is amazing; almost as amazing as the speculative genius which prompted it.

Meanwhile his attitude to religion was ambiguous. He accepted Christianity; he even began a series of notes on the Bible, and another on theology; but he had not been converted; he had no appreciation of the depravity of man, and the imminence of hellfire; he was, in fact, like most other New Englanders of his day, a nominal believer.

His conversion occurred when he was seventeen years old, in the first of his two years as a graduate student. This event has had such an enormous influence on the future of America that it is necessary to study it carefully; unfortunately the evidence is scanty, and any account of why it happened must be based partly on guesswork.

The dogma of original sin, upon which Christianity is built, is a mythological explanation of the feeling that something is wrong with life in this world. It has reference both to the inner life of the soul and to the external world. Calvinist theology declared that the inner life was corrupted first, by deliberate choice in Adam but by an inevitable inheritance in his descendants, and that God's anger then blasted the external world.

To young Edwards, in the woods of the Connecticut Valley, the world was beautiful. In his last year at college he learned that it was also ugly.

He realized that some day he must die; perhaps he would die quite soon, before he had finished his speculations, before he had published his treatise and earned applause in London. He fell ill with pleurisy, and for a time his life was in danger. He had a delicate constitution and there was no knowing what might happen to him. Sudden death was the commonest of occurrences in New England; strong men went to bed in health, awoke in the night with violent pains, and died in a few hours; doctors were worse than useless; food might easily cause horrible diseases, and worms many feet long were sometimes found inside men's bodies. A myriad accidents might await a young philosopher: Red Indians and Frenchmen descending from the Berkshire Hills, a rattlesnake in the grass or a mettlesome horse, a sudden storm at sea.

Children often died before they were properly alive. This was a very puzzling phenomenon; and Edwards watched their death-pangs with a kind of fascination. The "throat-distemper," apparently what we call diphtheria, descended upon the New England towns, one after another, in the twenties and thirties, and slew the children by scores; entire families were wiped out. The accepted remedy was to beat together mustard, pepper, and the rind of elder bark, and apply it to the nape of the neck; this was supposed to "draw away the malignity." Why, asked Edwards, should innocent creatures endure these dreadful pains? The young man saw their feverish brows, their anguished cries, their tortured expressions, as they passed out of a life which they had scarcely entered. It seemed to him that the children offered up to Moloch in the fire or roasted inside the brazen bull could scarcely have suffered such torments. How could this be reconciled with a God of beauty and all-embracing love?

The theology of his forefathers gave him an explanation: God had given man a law; man had disobeyed God and broken the law; God was therefore angry with man and with the world.

In his own soul there were phenomena equally puzzling. His ambition was to live passionately the life of a philosopher; he wanted to live intensely with his whole being every hour of the day. But his body was weak; he was attacked by headaches; he became tired and dull; he was easily upset by eating wrong foods. His consciousness was beset by alien impulses; desires, not included in the system which he had imposed upon himself, sprang up from his subconsciousness and distracted him; sensuality, which he had banned from the circle of life, became the enemy of life; to Edwards it was not an aid to passionate living, but an encumbrance; he used arithmetic as an anaphrodisiac, but he knew now that there was a devil.

Once more the theology of his forefathers gave him an explanation: the first man had sinned; and hence all his descendants, born in sin, were unable to be perfect and heirs of corruption.

Intellectually convinced, he turned to religion; he abandoned all habits which were considered sinful, and practiced many religious duties. But he took no delight in behaving piously; and he still rebelled against hellfire and predestination.

One day he was reading, from the Book of Timothy, "Now unto the King eternal, immortal, invisible, the only wise God, be honour and glory for ever and ever, Amen." The rhythm of the words, with their slow repetitiveness, like the music of a Catholic mass, threw a spell upon him, and he fell into a trance. There was a God, eternal, immortal, invisible; there was a God, who knew all things, who could do all things; there was a God, beautiful, mighty, majestic; there was a God, matchless in all perfections; there was a God, who was life in excelsis, who was passionate yet immovable. "Oh, if only I might enjoy that God! If only I might be rapt up to Him in heaven, and swallowed up in Him for ever!" he cried. He began chanting to himself, again and again, "Now unto the King eternal, immortal, invisible, the only wise God, be honour and glory." For God was all that he could never be; He was that beauty which filled his dreams; He was that power for which he pined. He had forgotten himself; he thought only of the glory of God.

"It never came into my thought," said Edwards, "that there was any thing spiritual, or of a saving nature in this." Several years afterwards he came to regard it as his conversion. But it violated all the regulations which the theologians had laid down, because it was not caused by fear of hell; so for a long time Edwards was not sure whether he had really been saved.

According to the theologians a necessary preliminary to conversion was to become very heartily terrified of hellfire. The unconverted man was completely depraved; he was not merely sinful; everybody was sinful; the unconverted man was incapable of a single deed or word or thought which was not wicked. For everything not done for the glory of God was wicked; and unconverted men were men who acted to please themselves or to please other people or to benefit the world, and not for God's glory. Consequently it was useless to tell the unconverted man how good God was or how beautiful virtue was; he was unable in his wickedness to appreciate anything good; he must be thoroughly terrified by telling him about the pains of hell; this first stage in the conversion of a sinner was called "legal repentance." When the sinner was thus prepared, God, if He so willed it, gave him His grace; He poured into the sinner's soul the knowledge of Himself and His own perfection; henceforth the sinner, having something good inside him, endeavored to obey God's law, and to act only for the glory of God; he was now capable of "evangelical repentance."

Edwards, however, had scarcely been terrified of hell at all; he had never had any strong sense of sin; he had never felt that he was disobedient to God; he had been dissatisfied with the world, and had had a mystic experience. This difference between what he had actually experienced and what, according to the theologians, he ought to have experienced, caused him much perplexity; even four years later he was still worried about it.

If he had thought about it more deeply, he might have become the greatest figure in the history of American thought; he might have altered the whole of the future history of America.

But, when one considers his environment and the possible alternatives, his acceptance of the Calvinist system is easy to understand: it explained the beauty of the natural world; it explained why men and innocent children lived such miserable lives and were tormented by such horrible diseases; it explained Edwards' dissatisfaction with his own personality. Most other kinds of Christianity would have explained these problems equally well. But for Edwards, in New England, in 1721, the only alternatives were deism and the Anglicanism of the eighteenth century. The deists offered no explanation at all for what puzzled Edwards. They went about saying that God was benevolent; God benevolent, when infant children were allowed to die in torment! The Anglicans—those at least whom Edwards knew—were hardly an improvement. They affirmed that God punished men for their good; but how were infant children benefited by being slain with the throat distemper? It was like justifying a parent who broke the bones of his children, not because they had sinned, but for fear they might sin. They believed in free will, and denied the necessity of conversion; but Edwards had himself experienced conversion, and he knew that it was not his own willing that had caused it, but the grace of God showered upon him from above. Moreover, to be an Anglican meant to deny the wisdom of the founders of New England, to belong to the same confession as royal governors in Boston and persecuting bishops in Great Britain, to increase the subserviency of the New World to the Old; Edwards was becoming patriotic.

So from the spring of 1721 he adopted the Calvinist creed and the Calvinist moral code, and set himself to school his nature to it and to convert other people.

In the course of years he accepted predestination and hellfire, as he accepted the belief in the imminence of the millennium, because they formed part of the theology which corresponded in other ways to his experience. He found for the mystery of hell a new and strange solution, growing out of his old conviction of the beauty of the universe. He explained it by the necessity of contrast. Goodness was impossible without wickedness, beauty without ugliness, and happiness without misery; a universe which contained a maximum of goodness must contain also a maximum of evil; a universe all white would be a universe of gray, and therefore there must also be black. For this reason God, when He made the world, had withdrawn His light from a part of it, in order that He might shine more brightly on the remainder. The world was a drama, a picture, a melody, the most beautiful which God could have made;

and men were puppets whom God elected, as He thought best, for goodness or wickedness. Those elected for goodness, having fought in this world against evil, would in the next be lifted up to an infinite happiness; and looking down out of heaven, they would realize their own ecstasy by contrasting it with the infinite misery of the sinners in the flames of hell. Thus the beauty of the Calvinist universe satisfied the laws worked out by the pantheist schoolboy; it was a harmony in which the details—heaven and hell—were balanced against each other.

❂

# The Life of a New England Minister

The last years of the 1730's are uneventful. There is time to pause, and describe the daily life of the minister of Northampton.

His main occupation is study. At four in the morning he leaves his bed, and lights his single candle; thirteen hours a day he spends poring over the tiny lettering of his volumes of theology, until his eyes, like those of almost all his colleagues, grow astigmatic; he reads always with a pen in his hand, and writes illegible notes which accumulate year by year. His studies, however, are not wholly theological; he devours every book on which he can lay his hands; most of the classics of English literature appear in his reading lists, and a few French books in English translations; he subscribes to an English monthly magazine; and, soon after publication, reads the novels of Fielding and Richardson. His opinion of Fielding is not recorded; but Richardson, whose *Pamela* is advertised, to suit the taste of New England, as likely to "cultivate the Principles of Virtue and Religion in the Minds of the Youth of Both Sexes," and is read all over the country by colonels' daughters and ministers' daughters, wins his strong commendation; Sir Charles Grandison is, in his opinion, "wholly favorable to good morals and purity of character"; when he reads it, he regrets his own inattention to the graces of good writing.

Reprinted by permission of the author from Henry Bamford Parkes, *Jonathan Edwards: The Fiery Puritan* (New York: Minton, Balch & Company, 1930), pp. 124–137.

After dinner, every midday, he rides out for three miles to a lonely grove, where he dismounts and meditates; or in winter he sometimes chops wood for half an hour. In the evening he enjoys an hour's relaxation, when he and his wife smoke their long clay pipes by the fireside and talk with their children. Only by the strictest regularity of life and the most careful attention to diet is the minister, with his sickly constitution, able to spend such long hours in study.

The details of household business he leaves to his wife. Their closest friend describes her as "a most judicious and faithful mistress of a family, habitually industrious, a sound economist, managing her household affairs with diligence and discretion. She is conscientiously careful, that nothing should be wasted or lost; and often, when she herself takes care to save any thing of trifling value, or directs her children or others to do so, or when she sees them waste anything, she repeats the words of our Saviour—'That nothing be lost.'" The minister must sometimes attend to the business of the farm; he writes letters to a friend, arranging for the purchase of sheep, in order that his family may have wool. But his salary is the largest in New England, outside Boston, and is paid with quite unusual regularity; so in general he can leave his farm to the care of his wife and their hired man; and in course of time he becomes more and more aloof and absent-minded.

Nevertheless it is necessary always to exercise the strictest economy. Owing to the depreciation of the currency all New England is in distress; the law courts are crowded with debtors; and the ministers, with their fixed salaries which, even when paid, are usually quite inadequate, are everywhere complaining of their poverty to God, to their parishes, and to the General Assembly. They eat meat once a day; their breakfast and supper consist solely of bread and milk; their only wine is what is left over from communion services; and coffee, chocolate, rum, tobacco, and books are considered as luxuries.

Children come to the minister and his wife with Puritan regularity, one every two years; there are eleven in all; no less than six are born on the Sabbath, thus disproving the old superstition that children born on the Sabbath were conceived on the Sabbath, and, being the fruit of wickedness, should be denied baptism. Mrs. Edwards has the chief care of them: and her dreadful responsibility in bringing into the world yet another sinner worthy of damnation causes her to pray vehemently to God for the conversion of the future babe as soon as she is pregnant. She never speaks angrily to them, and never uses heavy blows; very rarely does she punish them at all. An eyewitness reports that they never quarrel with each other; and that "when their parents come into the room, they all rise instinctively from their seats, and never resume them until their parents are seated; and when either parent is speaking, no matter with whom they have been conversing, they are all immediately silent and attentive."

Mr. Edwards is bowed down by the fear that even one of them may go to hell, and cares infinitely more about their spiritual welfare than about the health of their bodies. Unconverted children, he believes, go to hell like unconverted adults; and it would be a terrible breach of duty not to describe to them the terrors of eternal punishment; how many souls, dying in childhood, he asks, must curse their parents for such false kindness? "As innocent as children seem to be to us," he declares, "yet, if they are out of Christ, they are not so in God's sight, but are young vipers and are infinitely more hateful than vipers; . . . they are naturally very senseless and stupid, being born as the wild ass's colt, and need much to awaken them. Why should we conceal the truth from them?" When his daughters are away from home, he writes them curious solemn letters. To Sarah he says: "You have very weak and infirm health, and I am afraid are always like to have; and it may be, are not to be long-lived; and while you do live, are not like to enjoy so much of the comforts of this life, as others do, by reason of your want of health; and therefore, if you have no better portion, will be miserable indeed." And to Mary, who is visiting friends in Portsmouth: "If you should be taken with any dangerous sickness, that should issue in death, you might probably be in your grave, before we could hear of your danger. But yet, my great concern is not for your health, or temporal welfare, but for the good of your soul." When young Timothy at New York is in danger of smallpox, he tells him: "If I hear that you have escaped—either that you have not been sick, or are restored—though I shall rejoice, and have great cause of thankfulness, yet I shall be concerned for you. If your escape should be followed with carelessness and security, and forgetting the remarkable warning you have had, and God's great mercy in your deliverance, it would in some respects be more awful than sore sickness." Jonathan, at the age of nine, he sends to live among the Indians, in order that he may learn their language, and be able to preach the gospel to them when he is a man.

Nevertheless his family are not miserable. A happy home is the truest proof of Christianity; and Mrs. Edwards and her children all adore him passionately; she can scarcely endure a reprimand from him; and except Pierpont, who is less than eight years old when Mr. Edwards dies, they are all devout Edwardeans, and continue so through life. For he can be indulgent to them; one day he spends four and sixpence on a child's plaything; and Mrs. Edwards buys, for her adornment, a gold locket and chain which costs eleven pounds. When their daughters grow to be sixteen and eighteen, and ministers and Northampton gentlemen come to court them, they are allowed every freedom to become well acquainted.

To his parishioners he is not so human; they love him less and fear him more; he is so absorbed in his studies that, except at times of awakening, they see too little of him. He preaches twice on the Sabbath and once during the week; he also preaches often at private meetings in particular neighborhoods; and he calls the children to his home and prays with them, and also catechizes them every Sabbath. But he is too shy and aloof, and too absorbed in the things of eternity, to indulge with freedom in worldly conversation; he does not mix well; and any attempt to exchange gossip with his neighbors about the crops or the Indians, and twist it round to religion, results only in a lowering of his dignity. "I have a constitution, in many respects peculiarly unhappy," he says, "attended with flaccid solids, vapid, sizzy, and scarce fluids, and a low tide of spirits; often occasioning a kind of childish weakness and contemptibleness of speech, presence, and demeanor, with a disagreeable dullness and stiffness, much unfitting me for conversation." So he never visits his people unless they send for him. They know him as a solitary horseman, riding out every afternoon for communion with God among the trees; and only Colonel Stoddard, perhaps, is intimate with him.

Some of the neighboring ministers, however, know him more closely, and consider him the greatest genius of the age; for he is a faithful and stimulating friend, with a talent for making disciples. A burly loud-voiced aggressive divinity student, named Bellamy, comes in 1738 to study in his house; he remains for eighteen months before being ordained, and is utterly dominated by the more gentle personality of his teacher; they become most intimate friends, and meet often to discuss the problems of theology; Bellamy is so saturated with the ideas of Edwards that his writings would be indistinguishable from his master's but for his more prosaic style. Three years later a young man from Yale, named Hopkins, having heard Edwards preach, rides to Northampton and presents himself at the house, though he is an utter stranger; Edwards is away, but Mrs. Edwards makes him welcome and invites him to stay the winter. He is gloomy and dejected, and spends most of the time alone in his bedchamber. Mrs. Edwards after some days comes to his room and asks if she can help him. The young man replies that he fears he is damned. Mrs. Edwards replies that she has been praying for him, and promises him speedy comfort. He stays in the family until the following autumn, when he becomes a minister. Bellamy and Hopkins are united in their passionate devotion to Edwards and his theology; they are united too in their admiration for the beauty and charm of Mrs. Edwards; her tactful hospitality makes them immediately feel at home, whenever they visit her husband.

For twenty-three years this is the life of the minister of Northampton. For twenty-three years he sits in his study, elucidating the high problems of divinity. The sun rises over the barren table-land of central Massachusetts, and sets beyond the ranges of the Berkshires; the maples put out their leaves in April, and become yellow and scarlet in October; the thunderstorms break over Mount Holyoke, and the moonlight is reflected in the waters of the stately river Connecticut. The pile of notes grows higher, and the outlines of a complete theological system steadily take form and shape.

Behind him is always the framework of the seasons. In the

spring there is sowing of corn and wheat, and the calves and lambs are born; in the summer there is hay-making, and the barns are repaired for harvest; in the autumn the crops are gathered in, the apples are garnered, and the beer and cider are brewed; then the sheep and oxen are slaughtered, and the river freezes over, and the snow prevents all but the most necessary communication with the world outside; and always there are horses to be fed, and cows to be milked, and butter and cheese to be made. Northampton is dominated by the slow rhythms of nature, and any caprice of the powers that govern it may result in famine.

Life, however, is not one round of duty in a single spot. Through New England there is much coming and going of ministers, who ride along the dirt tracks from town to town. They ride to visit each other or to preach in each other's pulpits. They ride to association meetings, where they discuss obstinate heretics and the smallness of their salaries. Sometimes they ride to a council, where ministers and delegates from half a dozen churches meet to arbitrate a quarrel between another minister and his church; they hear how the minister has admitted members and appointed officers without securing the consent of his people, how it is shrewdly suspected that he drinks too much and is overfond of his maid-servant; the minister replies that his efforts to discipline sinners have been ignored, that his people no longer come to meeting, that his salary has not been paid for several years. The council sits all day and through the night, and, if God favors them, have agreed before sunrise on a "result," which may, with God's help, reconcile the parties.

From Northampton Edwards rides almost every year down the valley to New Haven for Yale commencement, or across the hills to the ministers' convention at Boston. Boston is the longer distance and he spends two nights on the journey at the houses of fellow-ministers. As he rides he meditates systematically upon some theological problem; and amid the hum of the grasshoppers and the rustle of apple orchards, he formulates a theory about the happiness of the angels, or the relationship of God the Father to the Holy Ghost; when he has finished, he fastens a piece of paper to some part of his clothing, to remind himself to write down his

conclusion when he comes home. On the morning of the third day
he is soon clattering over the cobblestones of Boston, on his way
to the house of Benjamin Colman or of Thomas Prince, his two
chief friends among the clergy of the town.

Boston is a very gay town. If Edwards were more observant and
less absorbed in divinity, he would see young ladies in scarlet
hoods and great hooped petticoats tripping along the streets to
dances and singing lessons; if he were not so obviously a minister
somebody might put into his hands an advertisement for a dancing
assembly. He passes a pillory, where a cheater is being pelted by
the onlookers; or his way is blocked by a funeral procession of
many carriages, all loaded with mourners, winding its way up to
Cop's Hill burial ground. Sometimes there is a wild animal on
show, a catamount or a leopard, a "tyger-lyon" or a two-headed
foal; or the streets are filled with servants gaping at a distinguished
visitor—Shick Sidi, the Syrian, for example, who has a swarthy
complexion and wears the Turkish costume, and is said not to like
Boston very well. On the Sabbath as he walks down with Dr.
Prince to the Old South Meeting House, he may find the streets all
lined with noisy crowds; they are waiting to see a murderer, under
sentence of death, brought from the prison to the church. And
when he comments on how the Bostonians pollute the Sabbath,
Dr. Prince may reply that the crowd is nothing compared with that
which awaited the pirates in 1726, when a group of men captured
on the high seas by the vigilance of a private citizen were all
condemned to die; when they were brought through the streets to
hear Dr. Benjamin Colman preach their last sermon, says Dr.
Prince, some of them were penitent, but one hardened rascal wore
a nosegay and gallantly ogled the ladies who craned their necks to
see him. If Edwards is in Boston on Guy Fawkes day he sees
troops of children marching round the town, demanding money
from householders, and breaking the windows of those who refuse.
Whenever there is a birthday or a marriage in the British royal
family, there is a festival: all the church bells ring out peal after
peal; the militia parades and is inspected by the Governor; and in
the evening there is a banquet and a ball. Every day of the week
but two there is a newspaper, relating the latest news from Europe,

mixed with a tale of a Negro slave who has hanged himself, or of two Connecticut farmers who have got drunk, fallen through the ice, and been drowned, and followed by an advertisement of a wet nurse or a parcel of slaves to be sold.

But Boston is not congenial to ministers from the Connecticut Valley. Boston is halfway to London, and London, to judge from family traditions, from its heretical books, and from the tales of wicked noblemen and ladies of easy virtue which the Boston newspapers reprint with such willingness, is obviously a very wicked place. So Edwards cares only for talking with the ministers, and turning over the latest importations in the bookshops on Cornhill; and even the ministers' conventions are marred for him by the liberalism of so many of the Harvard graduates who attend them. He accepts these facts, as he accepts everything, as ordained in God's inscrutable providence. But he thanks God that Northampton is less obviously predestined for hell than Boston.

To Boston, on the other hand, with its dignified merchants, its smart shopkeepers and lawyers, he is a provincial, though less round-eyed and easily impressed than most. They despise the westerners; they are people without refinement, who scarcely know how to use forks and knives, who are startled and horrified by the organs in the Episcopalian churches. They have read in the *Courant* about the practice of bundling, which appeals to them as especially crude and ridiculous; modesty out west, they tell each other with decorous sniggers, is measured by bastards. In Boston, of course, there is a double standard of morals, and the favors of lower-class women are not gratuitous.

The few who can appreciate Edwards become his friends. He makes acquaintances among some high political officers, and corresponds regularly with some of the clergy. His first publication is a sermon preached at the public lecture in Boston in 1731. Dr. Colman and his colleague write a preface, in which they explain that "it was with no small difficulty that the author's youth and modesty were prevailed on, to let him appear a preacher in our public lecture, and afterwards to give us a copy of his discourse." And they "heartily rejoice in the special favor of Providence, in bestowing such a rich gift on the happy church of Northampton."

His wife and children, also, visit his Boston friends; and Miss Esther Edwards becomes the close friend of Miss Sally Prince. But probably Edwards is glad when he turns his horse westward, and on the morning of the third day sees the ridge of Holyoke once more loom up to the left and the spire of his own meeting house visible among the trees in front of him.

While the years slip by, his devotion to his religion only grows more ardent. As he contemplates the infinite beauty of God and appreciates it more vividly, he becomes more conscious of his own feeble and fallible humanity. "Often since I lived in this town," he relates, "I have had very affecting views of my sinfulness and vileness; very frequently to such a degree as to hold me in a kind of loud weeping, sometimes for a considerable time together; so that I have often been forced to shut myself up. . . . It has often appeared to me, that if God should mark iniquity against me I should appear the very worst of all mankind; of all that have been since the beginning of the world to this time; and that I should have by far the lowest place in hell. . . . My wickedness, as I am in myself, has long appeared to me perfectly ineffable, and swallowing up all thought and imagination; like an infinite deluge, or mountains over my head. I know not how to express better what my sins appear to me to be, than by heaping infinite upon infinite, and multiplying infinite by infinite. . . . And it appears to me, that were it not for free grace . . . I should appear sunk down in my sins below hell itself. . . . And yet it seems to me that my conviction of sin is exceedingly small and faint."

With a curious reversed pride, not uncommon in the annals of Christianity, he adds that "when I ask for humility I cannot bear the thought of being no more humble than other Christians. It seems to me, that though their degrees of humility may be suitable for them, yet it would be a vile self-exaltation in me, not to be the lowest in humility of all mankind."

He has times of especial fervor. Once, when walking among the trees, he has "a view that for me was extraordinary, of the glory of the Son of God, as Mediator between God and man"; for an hour he is in a flood of tears, weeping aloud, because he longs to be "emptied and annihilated; to lie in the dust, and to be full of Christ alone." And on one Saturday night he "had such a sense, how sweet and blessed a thing it was to walk in the way of duty; to do that which was right and meet to be done, and agreeable to the holy mind of God; that it caused me to break forth into a kind of loud weeping, which held me some time, so that I was forced to shut myself up, and fasten the doors."

But, in spite of his own wickedness and the wickedness of his parish, he still finds in the natural world beyond his doorstep a shadow of God's excellency. In gentle breezes and singing birds, in the lily and the fragrant rose, in the murmur of rivers and in the golden edges of an evening cloud, "in comets, in thunder, in the hovering thunderclouds, in rugged rocks and the brows of mountains," "in that beauteous light with which the world is filled on a clear day," and in the beauty of the human body, he sees emanations of Christ's glory and goodness.

eparation for war, Bisson viewed the *zaibatsu* as vital partners in Japanese
ilitary aggression and the forging of Japanese "fascist-militarist" regime.[77]
 the *New Republic* issue of August 27, 1945, in which the editors, skeptical
 Grew's views on Japan, separately praised Acheson's replacement of Grew
 undersecretary of state, Bisson emphasized Japan's "Imperial clique" and
e *zaibatsu*, who were, in Bisson's words, "responsible equally with the mil-
arists" for the war.[78] For those who held similar views, *zaibatsu* dissolution
as essential to any attempt to reform Japan and create a democratic Japan.
dwin O. Reischauer could well have had Bisson in mind when he wrote,

> Curiously, the American authorities held to the Marxist interpretation that the
> real villain behind Japan's imperialism had been the excessive concentration
> of industrial wealth and power in the hands of the *zaibatsu*, which was thought
> to have necessitated an aggressive foreign policy. Although Japan's prewar his-
> tory scarcely bears out this theory, it led to a remarkable display of socialist
> zeal on the part of MacArthur and his staff.[79]

Bisson's influence is difficult to gauge. He took active part in the occupation with various assignments in Government Section. But he remained only
a marginal participant in the reforms. Any part he may have played in the
eventual *zaibatsu* dissolution effort was minor at most. He is best remembered for his 1954 study of *zaibatsu* dissolution,[80] which remains the leading
study in English. Whether his wartime writings were widely read or had any
influence on those who were planning for the occupation is even more difficult
to determine. What is important—and underlies the emphasis on Bisson and
his views here—is that he represented the extreme end of a spectrum of knowledgeable and articulate members of the American intellectual community
whose views, although not as far to the left as Bisson's, did count. They viewed
the *zaibatsu* primarily in political rather than economic terms. They condemned the *zaibatsu* like other concentrations of corporate wealth as anti-
thetical to the development and growth of democratic institutions. They
believed that *zaibatsu* dissolution like German deconcentration was an essential component of any effort to create democratic institutions in Japan. They
were hostile to private but not public monopoly. They rejected state planning and controls only if not carried out within a "democratic" political structure. However, neither those Japan specialists who may have sided with Bisson
or with Grew were to play a decisive role in presurrender planning. That honor
belongs to the economists.

The Committee on Private Monopolies and Cartels had ignored Japan
completely throughout the discussions of postwar economic policy. Of a total

punitive U.S. occupation policy toward Germany would be,[60] by May 1945 a
consensus of sorts had been reached and a policy statement for the military
commander of the U.S. occupation forces in Germany in the form of a Joint
Chiefs of Staff directive (JCS/1067) had been completed.[61] As determined a
half a year earlier, JCS/1067 included the mandates of paragraph 5, that "no
action will be taken in execution of the reparations program or otherwise
which would tend to support basic living conditions in Germany on a higher
level than that existing in any of the neighboring countries," and of part II,
that "no steps will be taken, a) leading toward the economic rehabilitation
of Germany or, b) designed to maintain or strengthen the German economy"
except as necessary to carry out stated economic objectives that included
"industrial disarmament" in addition to measures to prevent starvation or
"such disease and unrest as would endanger [U.S. occupation] forces." The
directive separately instructed the commander in chief to take measures to
ensure the decartelization and deconcentration of German industry.

Three months later, on August 2, 1945, at Potsdam, President Roosevelt,
Chairman Stalin, and Prime Minister Attlee agreed to a common statement
of occupation objectives. The protocol did not repeat the JCS directive's prohibition against the measures designed to assist German economic recovery
but did provide for German "industrial disarmament" and, needless to say,
the decentralization of the German economy "for the purpose of eliminating the present excessive concentration of economic power as exemplified in
particular by cartels, syndicates, trusts and other monopolistic arrangements."[62] As German economic recovery became a central issue for U.S. policy, deconcentration also became a subject of considerable controversy. At
the outset of occupation, however, no one disagreed that deconcentration
and decartelization should be among the primary American aims.

Agreement on the issue of deconcentration with respect to U.S. policy
toward Germany was not duplicated in the case of Japan. Deconcentration
became official policy for Japan only after intense debate within the Department of State.[63] Opposing the policy was the group of advisors with the greatest claim to expertise on Japan. By 1944 they were led by Joseph C. Grew,[64]
U.S. ambassador to Japan from 1932 until the official rupture of U.S. relations with Japan following the attack on Pearl Harbor, and Eugene Dooman,
who had served under Grew as embassy counselor for four years before the
war. After internment for seven months in Tokyo, Grew, Dooman, and Robert
A. Fearey, Grew's young private secretary, returned to Washington. By 1944
Grew and Dooman had together become leading players within the State
Department in the formulation of postwar U.S. policy toward Japan. Grew
replaced Stanley Hornbeck as director of the Office of Far Eastern Affairs.

of 164 memoranda reviewed by the committee, including a variety of official and staff reports, 32 dealt with Germany, only one, after the war had ended, with Japan.[81] Given the public campaign against international cartels and industrial concentration in Germany, the committee could assume that deconcentration would become an integral feature of U.S. occupation policy toward Germany. But not until 1944, as the end of war in Europe appeared inevitable, did the economist advisors turn their attention to Japan.

George G. Allen's works provided the most detailed English-language studies of the Japanese economy. As noted previously, Allen emphasized the domination of *zaibatsu* firms in banking and commerce, but also the underlying competitiveness of the Japanese market and the lack of effective cartelization prior to the imposition of government controls. However, his views on competition in Japan were ignored by nearly all. In an IDACFE memo dated June 25, 1943, Fearey had noted the "strong competitive rivalries" among *zaibatsu* firms,[82] but he did not emphasize the point in other writings. Nine months later in a lengthy analysis of the *zaibatsu* and the principal arguments for their dissolution, he had come around fully to Grew's point of view, to argue that "no useful purpose would be served by attempting to alter the future structure of industrial structure of ownership and control" in Japan.[83] Nor did anyone justify a policy of deconcentration for Japan based on detailed documentation on levels of concentration in Japanese industries prior to the mid 1930s or the extent of restrictive practices.

The first draft of what became the directive to MacArthur submitted by the State-War-Navy Coordinating Committee (SWNCC/150), titled "Summary of United States Initial Post-Defeat Policy Relating to Japan," drew heavily on U.S. policy directives for occupied Germany. It was far more interventionist and potentially punitive than the Japan specialists were willing to accept. It did not include the ostensibly punishing mandate of JCS/1067 for "industrial disarmament" nor did it prohibit the Supreme Command, Allied Powers (SCAP) from taking any measures to aid Japanese economic recovery, but its drafters had recommended extensive controls over currency, production, and distribution and, echoing JCS/1067, commanded that "no steps [be taken] which would provide a standard of living to the Japanese out of line with that of neighboring states."[84] To restore Japan to its prewar standing as Asia's preeminent industrial power was out of the question. In response, Dooman with the support of General George V. Strong, the War Department representative, objected and arranged for a subcommittee to redraft the document. A provision that the "military government shall encourage the development of democratic organizations in labor, industry, and agriculture, and shall favor a wider distribution of ownership, management and control of the Japanese economic system" was included without elaboration in the second draft (SWNCC 150/2) of August 12, 1945. Japan's surrender on August 14 forced the issue. The only group urging moderation were the Japan specialists. However, by mid August Grew realized that he did not have the confidence and support of Truman's new secretary of state James F. Byrnes. Two days after Japan's surrender, Grew at age 67, resigned as undersecretary and retired from the service. He was replaced immediately by Assistant Secretary Dean Acheson. Grew's recommendation that Dooman be given a prominent role in East Asian policy was ignored. America's leading Japan specialists ceased to have any further official say in U.S. policy toward Japan.

Backed by General John H. Hilldring, who was responsible for the Civil Affairs Department in the War Department, and economist Herbert Feis, special consultant to the secretary of war, Assistant Secretary of War John J. McCloy, who had just returned from Potsdam, insisted that the directive be rewritten. On August 22 the third version was complete. The economic section had been extensively revised to conform to the deconcentration policies adopted for Germany as set out in the Potsdam declaration and adapted in the draft JCS directive. The SWNCC statement now included for the first time explicit direction for "a program for the dissolution of the large industrial and banking combinations which have exercised control over a great part of Japan's trade and industry." On September 6, 1945, President Truman signed the statement, and the conforming JCS directive was issued to MacArthur. Both called for the Japanese to submit "plans for dissolving large Japanese industrial and banking combines, pools, mergers, and semi-official companies and communicate the results of such survey to this Government through the Joint Chiefs of Staff."[85]

The first mention of any need for a deconcentration policy had been in a July 21, 1943, memo authored by Fearey,[86] but, as noted, he had recanted within the year. Except for Fearey and Bisson until mid November 1945, no one had fully made the case for the application of German policy to Japan. And not until the 1946 State-War Mission on Japanese Combines led by Corwin Edwards did anyone ever document the degree of concentration or analyze the extent of restrictive practices. Without supporting data on Japan to justify the application of U.S. deconcentration policies for Germany to Japan, the economists working with the State Department commissioned a separate study. Its author was Eleanor Hadley. A graduate student at Radcliffe who had lived in Japan for two years following her graduation from Mills College in 1938, she had joined the Office of Strategic Services (OSS) as a research analyst. Terrill recruited her in 1944 to provide the missing data. The resulting product was intended as more of a justifying brief to confirm policies previ-

ously agreed to than an objective analysis. Titled "Control of Corporate Organization (Japan)," the memo, dated November 15, 1945,[87] began by noting
the political rather than economic aims of deconcentration. The "dispersion
of ownership, management and control of the Japanese economic system"
was, the memo argued, an "important aspect" of U.S. demilitarization policy in Japan. It continued with eight recommendations that had been decided
upon earlier:

1. Prohibit, for whatever period of time is necessary, transfers of and dealings in private or public securities and other business properties in order
   to prevent the establishment of concealed ownerships.
2. Protect from destruction, and maintain for such disposition as will after
   be determined, all technological information records, files, documents and
   similar data of all large Japanese business firms and trade and research
   associations.
3. Establish a public agency responsible for reorganizing Japanese business
   in accordance with the military and economic objectives of the United
   States. This agency should submit, for approval by the Control Authority,
   plans for liquidating combines and other monopolies and establishing independent operating rules.
4. Establish surveillance over Japanese combines and monopolies, in order
   to assure conformity to the military and economic objectives of the
   United States until satisfactory plans of reorganization have been approved.
   It is to be presumed that in any territory under the jurisdiction of the
   Control Authority which lies outside the boundaries of the main islands
   of Japan, surveillance will be exercised directly over local subsidiary corporations or branch plants to the maximum extent possible; and that within
   the main islands of Japan, such surveillance will be exercised through the
   central office of each combine or monopoly.
5. Dissolve control associations (toseikai). Any necessary public function previously performed by these associations should be transferred to public
   agencies approved and supervised by the Control Authority. These agencies should be staffed by civil service personnel.
6. Terminate and prohibit all Japanese participation, domestic and international, in cartels or other private agreements or arrangements which have
   the effect of restricting production or trade, such as production and sales
   quota agreements, price fixing agreements, agreements providing for
   division of fields of production or market territories, arrangements for
   exclusive or preferential access to technological information in excess of
   the normal monopoly granted by a patent or a trade-mark.

7. Abrogate all legislative or administrative measures which limit free entry of firms into an industry where the purpose or effect of such measures is to foster and strengthen private monopoly. When the Control Authority deems it advisable to maintain or impose restrictions in the public interest, as in the case of public utilities, the restrictions should be administered by a public agency under the supervision of the Control Authority.
8. Make a survey of Japanese combines, pools, mergers and semi-official companies, and communicate the results of such survey to this Government. This survey should serve as a basis or determining refinements in the measures set forth above as well as for the progressive formulation and development of policies to achieve the objective of a wider distribution of ownership, managements and control of the Japanese economic system.

Several of these recommendations were already in the directive to MacArthur, but they still lacked support that Hadley now furnished. The recommendation in item 3 that a public agency be created to direct a dissolution program reflected the proposal to SCAP made a few days previously by the Japanese, as noted below, for a government-sponsored committee to direct the effort. Item 8 in effect repeated MacArthur's response: a request for an expert survey that culminated in the mission of experts led by Corwin Edwards. Of special interest is item 7. The abrogation of all legislative and administrative versions restricting new entry was the most radical proposal. By 1940 legal barriers to new entry created and enforced through rigid licensing requirements constituted, as mentioned, the most effective constraints on competition in prewar Japan. This was the only recommendation ignored by SCAP and Japanese authorities alike. Their failure to implement this proposal in any form had, in hindsight, profound and, especially for the financial services sector of the economy, long-lasting consequences. The arguments of the Japan specialists now refuted and the predilections of the economists affirmed, all that remained was to implement a policy of industrial deconcentration and to enact permanent antitrust legislation.

OCCUPATION PROGRAMS

Fundamental differences defined the form and effectiveness of all policies pursued under American military occupation in Germany and Japan. The most obvious were structural. Divided into four separate zones, Germany was subject to the commands of very different military regimes with often conflicting aims and approaches. Bereft of overseas colonies and territories as well as the northern islands, Japan, in stark contrast, was governed under a unified command with the Americans in complete control. The creation of the Far Eastern Commission comprising representatives of each of the Allied nations made little difference. Its views were generally disregarded unless they coincided with those of scap.

The scope and effect of the postwar purge also profoundly effected policy in the two occupied countries. The extent of the purge in Germany provided the opportunity for new leaders to emerge at almost all levels. Denazification in all four German zones meant the removal of public officials and private citizens from positions of control and influence throughout Germany. Nazi party membership, for more than a decade a prerequisite for most public offices and many positions of leadership in the business community, became upon surrender a ground for internment, a bar to participation in public affairs, and a potential cause for criminal prosecution. Within the first year of occupation in the American zone more than a million and a half Germans, a tenth of the total population in the zone, were screened to determine whether they had participated in Nazi party activities. By the end of May 1946 more than 350,000 Germans had been removed or excluded from office.[88] Pending new elections and the establishment of democratic local and state governments, during the first months of occupation American military officers directly governed the smallest hamlets as well as the largest urban centers within the zone. Occupation legislation in Germany was just that. The "laws" and "ordinances" of the military occupiers were initially drafted, enacted, and enforced without meaningful German participation or acquiescence.

scap ruled indirectly though existing or reformed "demilitarized and democratized" political structures staffed by prewar and wartime officials. Left intact was the basic structure of government. scap thus directed and supervised Japanese officials who at senior levels had begun their careers in the late 1920s or early 1930s. Indirect rule and Japanese acceptance of scap's authority meant that American occupation policies could be formulated as Japanese legislation rather than the victor's military orders. The most forceful commands could even be cast as polite suggestions—General MacArthur's "Dear Mr. Prime Minister" letters come to mind—or as approvals and disapprovals of more routine Japanese administrative decisions. By the same token, incidental suggestions from scap officials were frequently treated as intended commands.[89] Even today the ambivalence between pretense and real consent hinders accurate assessment of the influence of the occupation in all areas of postwar Japanese law. Whether intended as a coercive order or mere suggestion, in either event occupation policies were incorporated in Japanese legislative and administrative enactments.

Accordingly, scap conducted only a limited purge of civilian officials and business leaders. No individual screening of Japanese civilians occurred. Of an estimated 200,000 people removed from official posts, four-fifths were military officers. Fewer than 40,000 Japanese civilian officials were removed from office.[90] Many were colonial officials. Only about 2,200 business leaders were purged and even temporarily excluded from participating in public life.[91] The decision to allow existing Japanese political institutions to function under SCAP direction and to carry out all mandated reforms combined with the more limited purge in Japan ensured a continuity of leadership in government and business. The consequences for antitrust policy in Japan were to be dire.

Any comparison between occupied Germany and Japan must also take into account the differences in the magnitude of the destruction of property and dislocation of people that engulfed both countries in defeat. Unlike Japan, no piece of Germany and no individual German were left untouched by war and defeat. However extensive the destruction of bombs and fire, except for Okinawa there was no invasion of Japan. No city served as an arena for street-to-street combat. And few rural communities suffered directly the war's destructive force.

Finally, a more subtle contrast permeated the two theaters. Despite the respect that American military officers had for the military skills and determination of their German military opponents as soldiers and concern for the acute suffering of German civilians, the horrors of Nazi atrocities were too evident to allow much sympathy for those who had held positions of authority. In Japan, however, the first soldiers who arrived feared the worst. The closer American forces had come to Japan, the more fierce and fanatic the Japanese resistance. Yet upon arrival, American soldiers encountered an unanticipated acquiescence and, as fears on both sides abated, unexpected hospitality. The result for many was a lasting empathy and, as Japan recovered from the war, deepening respect.

Japanese deference to SCAP authority was beguiling, in the fullest sense of the word. For some occupation authorities it confirmed prewar experiences and led them to play more protective roles, encouraging the Japanese to take the initiative in reform programs and acting more as buffers against those who sought to impose what they recognized were ill-fitting American models and approaches. The reforms they supervised thus often reflected proposals made before the war by Japanese scholars and officials who had access to the occupation authorities through official government committees.[92] Not all shared such sanguine views of Japan. Others resisted. They distrusted Japanese suggestions and were as a result much more demanding in their dealings with the officials they worked with, insisting on preconceived notions of the appropriate forms and—usually American-centered—approaches to particular reform programs.

Implementation of the economic reform policies contained in the directives to Eisenhower in Europe[93] and to MacArthur in Japan[94] commenced almost immediately as military occupation began in Germany in the summer of 1945 followed by Japan in autumn. Eisenhower moved quickly. In Order No. 2 of July 5, 1945, he directed the seizure of all I. G. Farben assets in the U.S. zone. Within days a special agency to take control over I. G. Farben was formed within the Office of the Military Governor of the United States. The deconcentration of German industry, at least within the American zone, had begun. A Cartels Division was created along with a separate I. G. Farben Control Office. Both were gradually staffed by lawyers and economists, predominately people who had worked for the Antitrust Division of the Justice Department under Thurman Arnold or his successor. In December 1945, the division was reorganized as the Decartelization Branch, taking over the functions of the Farben Control Office, under the Economic Division headed by Brigadier General William H. Draper, Jr. Draper, a military officer in World War I, had left a prosperous career as an investment banker to rejoin the army during World War II. He became personal confidant and the single most influential advisor to General Lucius B. Clay, Eisenhower's successor as army commander in chief. The Decartelization Branch was initially headed by James S. Martin, a young and ardent antitrust lawyer who had been general counsel as well as instructor at an undergraduate college. From the outset Martin and Draper disagreed about whether deconcentration or economic recovery should receive priority.

The Decartelization Branch initially conducted a series of extensive investigations that culminated in a three-volume work, *Report on German Cartels and Combines.*[95] On the basis of the report the process of deconcentration was to begin. The first step was to enact the necessary military legislation. Disagreement among the Allies, however, stalled initial American efforts to enact a comprehensive decartelization and deconcentration statute applicable in all four zones. The principal dispute focused on the issue of mandatory standards for deconcentration. The United States joined by France and the Soviet Union sought to include standards that would establish a presumption of concentration in the case of enterprises with capacity and employees in excess of a specified size. The presumption could be rebutted by evidence that the concentration was not harmful in fact or that deconcentration would impair technological efficiency. The British objected. They proposed a more flexible, case-by-case, firm-by-firm approach. As in the case of British opposition to American proposals for inclusion of provisions against restrictive business practices in the Havana Charter,[96] deconcentration of German industry did not appeal to either British Tory or Labor leaders. On the one hand, British (as well as American) firms had well-established relations with German industry and had participated actively with German firms in prewar cartels. On the other, British socialists viewed the concentration of both British and German industry as a precondition to effective nationalization, an attitude that complicated later negotiations with respect to the deconcentration of German industry in the Ruhr.[97] Such issues were less ostensibly significant to the French and Soviets than the unwanted notion of any generally applicable legislation and the creation of a single economic administration. As discussions among the four Allies broke down, bilateral negotiations between the United States and British authorities continued over the statute as well as over bizonal economic administration. The result was agreement in September 1946 on a unified economic administration for the two zones. In December 1946 a bizonal economic administration was created, and in February 1947 separate but nearly identical regulations (without mandatory standards) were promulgated simultaneously in the American and British zones.[98] One consequence was to give greater voice in overall economic policy to German officials from various *Land* (state) governments who were appointed to advising councils and commissions.

On the opposite side of the globe, the Japanese made the first move. In early November, an official party proposed the Yasuda Plan, the voluntary dissolution of the four principal *zaibatsu* under the supervision and direction of a Holding Company Liquidation Committee or, as it was eventually called in English, Commission (the HCLC).[99] As defeat had become more and more certain, Japanese civilian officials had also begun to prepare for a postwar occupation. By June 1945 a Special Survey Committee had been formed comprising economists and officials from the Greater East Asian Ministry to plan for postwar reconstruction. Chaired by University of Tokyo economist Takafusa Nakamura, the survey committee reflected the prevailing economic ideologies of its members, a mélange of prewar Marxist-mercantilist notions. Their views were more in tune with Bisson than Grew. They laid the blame for much of Japan's prewar ills on the *zaibatsu* and were nearly as willing as the American occupiers to jettison the conglomerates. As stated in the English translation of their September 1946 report,

> The big industries that had been constructed through the sacrifice of farmers and small-sized businesses, however, consequently had difficulty in finding markets within the country because of the poor purchasing power of the major-

ity of the people, and were compelled to strive to secure export markets while looking to government for large demand due to military expansion. Thus was the foundation built for Japan's progress toward becoming a militaristic and aggressive nation.[100]

With no more empirical support for these and other propositions than their American counterparts, faith not facts dictated their conclusions. They revealingly proposed instead economic planning and government-sponsored collective action by medium and small enterprises[101]—in other words, a Manchurian-styled industrial policy with wartime control associations minus the *zaibatsu* and the military. Japan also had to deal with its loss of colonies to recoup the "monopolistic markets" that had allowed expansion of exports to other markets.[102] The Yasuda Plan, it appears, was not an entirely insincere proposal.

MacArthur responded with SCAP Directive No. 244 on the Dissolution of Holding Companies (November 6, 1945,[103] nine days before the Hadley memorandum was ready for distribution). The directive adopted key features of the Yasuda Plan but also called for "such laws as will eliminate and prevent monopoly and restraint of trade, unreasonable interlocking directorates, undesirable security ownership and assure the segregation of banking from commerce, industry and agriculture as well as provide equal opportunity to firms and individuals to compete in industry, commerce, finance, and agriculture on a democratic basis."[104] With this the dissolution effort commenced.

SCAP meanwhile was in the process of creating a branch similar to the OMGUS Decartelization Branch. The Anti-Trust and Cartels Division was headed initially by James M. Henderson, and from April 1947 by Edward C. Welsh, whose energy and passion for implementation of the occupation antitrust and deconcentration programs matched Martin's. As in Germany, the division was under the Economic and Scientific Section headed first by Raymond C. Kramer and later by Major General William F. Marquart. In addition, the process of enacting legislation under which to implement the American antitrust program had also begun. Faced with the Yasuda Plan, MacArthur requested a mission of antitrust experts to provide advice. The result was the State-War Mission on Japanese Combines led by Edwards.[105] The mission arrived in Japan in January 1946 and remained for two and a half months. Its report was more comprehensive and influential than similar efforts in Germany. Although in some respects a rationalization for programs that had already been determined and were already being implemented, the report provided the directions for both an expansion of *zaibatsu* dissolution and Japan's antitrust statute.

Edwards was too honest an economist not to disclose what he found. He and the other members of the mission did not discover undue concentration in any industry, nor did they find any pattern of effective price fixing or production controls. Nineteen firms deemed prima facie to be *zaibatsu* were identified and studied. None had significantly high market shares.[106] The "strongholds" of *zaibatsu* power, they concluded, were the various linkages with government that had proliferated during the war. Through the control associations, government financial policies, and legally imposed restrictions on entry into banking and insurance, *zaibatsu* firms had been able to gain preferential positions in nearly all of the industries in which they operated. Moreover, as Harry First emphasizes, the Edwards mission decided that among the most serious problems were exclusionary practices by *zaibatsu* firms to restrict access to markets by their competitors as well as new entrants.[107]

The Edwards mission made twenty-one recommendations, most of which simply amplified those made more than six months earlier in the report prepared by Eleanor Hadley. They dealt primarily with *zaibatsu* dissolution (recommendations 1–13). These included detailed provisions for identification of *zaibatsu*-like concentrations of economic power, the elimination of "communities of interest based on family ties," and adequate compensation. The other recommendations (14–21) included the enactment of permanent antitrust legislation and amendment of Japan's patent, company, tax, and inheritance laws. Like the Hadley memo, the Edwards mission report also expressed concern over government restrictions on new entry. Recommendation 14 provided that "all forms of subsidy, legal monopoly and trade barriers" should be systematically reviewed and those without a "demonstrable public purpose" should be terminated. Of special concern were Ministry of Finance controls over financial institutions, which in the mission's view contributed to the *zaibatsus'* ability to prevent the emergence of potential rivals.[108]

On the basis of the recommendation for a general antitrust statute (recommendation 15), the chief of the newly formed Antitrust Legislation Branch of the Anti-Trust and Cartels Division, Posey T. Kime, a two-term Indiana State Court of Appeals judge (1931–38) who subsequently joined the Antitrust Division of the Justice Department, set out to codify the Edwards Mission report.[109] Kime headed the drafting effort for less than a year. The only surviving record of his contribution is a draft dated August 6, 1946. Although rejected by the Japanese and completely rewritten after Kime left Japan in October, several of the basic features of the original draft were incorporated with modifications into the final statute. The draft reflected Kime's consolidation of the principal provisions of the Sherman, Clayton, and Federal Trade Commission Acts, along with additional provisions related to international contract review originating in Edwards' long campaign to eliminate international cartels. They included

1. prohibition of monopolization or attempts to monopolize, with criminal sanctions (section 2);
2. prohibition of agreements in restraint of trade, subject to criminal penalties (section 3);
3. separate prohibition against "unfair methods of competition," without criminal sanctions (section 9);
4. filing and approval requirements for contracts with foreign companies;
5. controls on mergers and acquisitions (section 6); and
6. a private treble damage remedy.

The subsequent versions, it appears, were written by members of the Japanese committee assigned to work with SCAP on the legislation under the supervision of Kime's successor, Lester N. Salwin.[110] Salwin reviewed at least six drafts prepared initially by the Japanese committee, suggesting or demanding changes that he or his superiors considered necessary. Salwin's actual contribution was presumably greater than the paper record might suggest. Salwin's views prevailed in nearly every instance, including the creation of a separate regulatory agency, similar to the Federal Trade Commission, as the exclusive antitrust enforcement authority, instead of a division in the Japanese Ministry of Justice, as preferred by the Japanese drafters.[111] The final version in any event elaborated the basic provisions of the Kime draft.

No one seems to have noted the anomaly of including a separate provision for "unfair methods of competition" in addition to "unreasonable restraints of trade." One of the peculiarities of American law is the concurrent jurisdiction of two separate enforcement agencies by virtue of statutory construction defining the two concepts to cover similar conduct. The Federal Trade Commission has civil enforcement authority to prosecute "unfair methods of competition" under the Federal Trade Commission Act. The Antitrust Division of the Justice Department has civil and criminal enforcement responsibility to prosecute "restraints of trade" under the Sherman Act. Price fixing and output restrictions constitute violations of both. The inclusion of the two in the Japanese statute with a single enforcement authority made little sense. The draft's lack of criminal sanctions for "unfair methods of competition" but inclusion for "unreasonable restraints of trade," for example, is difficult to explain except as a mechanical replication of American law. Japanese courts would later sort out the differences, defining the two concepts in ways that for the sake of coherence would necessarily differ from their American antecedents.

Among the issues that divided the two sides, as in the case of the dispute between the Americans and the British, was the American preference for mandatory or per se prohibition of specified concerted restraints on competition. The Kime draft, for example, had included a mandatory prohibition against a variety of enumerated "joint actions," including price-fixing agreements, output restrictions, territorial allocations, market-access exclusions, boycotts, and tying agreements. He had included common sales agencies, orderly marketing agreements, standardization agreements, certain patent license restrictions, data-sharing agreements, and other listed practices as illegal to the extent they "burden or adversely affect trade" (section 7).[112] The explicit dichotomy between the two categories was eliminated in later drafts, and in the end, apparently without objection by Salwin or others, the mandatory approach was abandoned in favor of language that in effect established a "rule of reason" for all violations.

The Japanese also objected to the inclusion of the provisions related to international contracts and import and export transactions. Representing the requirement of the basic directive, Salwin insisted that international cartels be prohibited,[113] and the provision for international contract filing and approval introduced in the Kime draft was retained. The Japanese successfully negotiated for a single damage provision as well as a limitation on its application to conduct first determined by the administrative enforcement authorities to constitute a violation of the statute.[114] The Japanese draft had added a penalty to the Kime draft, subjecting "unfair methods of competition" to criminal penalties, but this addition was deleted from later drafts.[115] The ban on holding companies does not appear in any early draft and was presumably added at Salwin's suggestion or insistence.[116] The process ended on March 31, 1947—one month after the promulgation of Law No. 56 in Germany—with enactment by the Diet of the Law concerning the Prohibition of Private Monopoly and Preservation of Fair Trade.[117] A year later the Diet passed the companion Trade Association Law.[118]

It took nearly a year as well under extreme SCAP pressure for the Diet to pass the Japanese equivalent to Law No. 56, but in December 1947, the Elimination of Excessive Concentration of Economic Power Law (Law No. 207),[119] which excluded HCLC's authority and expanded the dissolution program, was enacted. To persuade the Japanese Diet to accept the law took considerable SCAP pressure and time. The short-lived Socialist government under Prime Minister Tetsuo Katayama was inclined to agree with labor leaders and the business community in opposing the statute. Like Socialists in Europe, they viewed business concentrations as an inevitable and useful prelude to nationalization. Also, Japanese officials who disagreed with both the Socialists and American reformers were well aware of mounting divisions over the dissolution policy within the American camp.[120] Behind the scenes, they urged delay.

Law No. 207 is generally attributed to recommendations in the Edwards Mission report, which after approval by swncc were adopted by the Far East Commission as official Allied policy as fec 230. The policy called for an extension of the *zaibatsu* dissolution program beyond its initial scope to include all "excessive concentrations of economic power." The original program had been limited. Only 10 *zaibatsu* holding companies were initially designated for liquidation.[121] Under Law 207, the hclc formally designated 257 industrial firms and 68 service corporations. The number was reduced in the months that followed to 131, of which even fewer were actually subjected to dissolution measures as a result of the May 12, 1948, decision to end the effort.

Doubts over the proposal began to circulate. Henderson, a member of the Edwards Mission who remained in Japan to supervise the effort as head of the Anti-Trust and Cartels Division, is said to have expressed concern that the plan was "too extreme and impractical."[122] Even Marquart, the chief of the Economics and Scientific Section, is described as having been "skeptical."[123] The economists in the section persuaded their superiors to accept the plan.[124] Its implementation, however, fell to Welsh, Henderson's replacement. Welsh was committed to the political aims of the dissolution effort. In an interview in 1974 he is quoted as saying that "big and dominant corporations are undemocratic of themselves."[125]

In fact, Law No. 207 closely tracked the U.S. deconcentration statute for Germany, Law No. 56. Of the two statutes, Law No. 56 was on its face considerably more stringent. It began with an absolute prohibition against "excessive concentrations of German economic power, whether within or without Germany and whatever their form or character" (art. I, ¶ 1). Declared to be "excessive concentrations of economic power" were "cartels, combines, syndicates, trusts, associations or any other form of understanding or concerted undertaking" that had the "purpose or effect of restraining, or of fostering monopolistic control of, domestic or international trade or other economic activity" (art. I, ¶ 2). The enforcement authorities were granted broad powers to take whatever actions were deemed necessary to implement the prohibitions (art. IV). The statute did not include any procedural protections. Those required by regulation were cursory (see Reg. No. 1, art. VIII).

The regulations explicitly excluded, for example, any right to an oral, evidentiary hearing (Reg. No. 1, art. VIII, ¶ A). The right to appeal was limited. The regulations also allowed the imposition of criminal penalties for appeals found to have been brought "without good cause and solely for the purposes of delay" (Reg. No. 1, art. VIII, ¶ B). Along with frivolous appeals to delay action, violations, evasions, and attempts to violate or evade the law or "any regulation, order, directive issued thereunder" were all subject to criminal penalties, including imprisonment for a maximum of ten years (Law No. 56, art. VII).

In comparison, Law No. 207 empowered the HCLC to designate "excessive concentrations of economic power," which were defined as "any private enterprise conducted for profit, or combination of such enterprises, which by reason of its relative size in any line or the cumulative power of its position in many lines, restricts competition or impairs the opportunity for others to engage in business independently, in any important segment of business" (art. 3). As Harry First has observed,[126] the statute's "original intent" included particular emphasis on exclusionary practices that prevented or hindered new entry and market access. The Japanese statute also set out in detail the procedural requirements for HCLC investigations, hearings, and decisions (art. 5, 6, 9, 11, 12, 13). Article 6 required HCLC to determine and make public the standards used to define "excessive concentrations of economic power" and detailed the factors that had to be considered. Article 14 allowed appeals from HCLC to the prime minister. Findings of fact had to satisfy a "substantial evidence" test (art. 13), and the effectiveness of any HCLC order was automatically suspended pending the outcome (art. 15). Although the Japanese statute also included criminal penalties for violations, incarceration was limited to three years.

With Welsh in charge, the Anti-Trust and Cartels Division began plans to extend existing dissolution efforts beyond *zaibatsu* firms to include any industrial, commercial, or financial enterprise that met the standards of concentration Welsh had proposed be drafted into Law No. 207. Before Law No. 207 had been promulgated, Welsh had apparently indicated that as many as 5,000 firms might be included. In the end, as indicated above, only 325 companies were actually designated. The number was successively reduced to 131 by mid May 1948.[127]

Much of the controversy in Japan focused on the inclusion of banks and insurance companies in the deconcentration program. They were excluded as a consequence of the program's abrupt termination. Once again, no one seems to have analyzed Japan's financial services industry in terms of competition and the legal barriers to entry imposed under the 1927 Banking Law.

## FROM INDUSTRIAL DISARMAMENT TO ECONOMIC REHABILITATION

As the implementation of Law No. 56 in Germany and efforts to enact Law 207 in Japan continued, the differences between German and Japanese industrial structure and American attitudes toward the two countries began to emerge. For the moment, however, common problems and responses marked the next phase in occupation policy. After a year of occupation, economic conditions had not improved in either Germany or Japan, and the sense of crisis felt by Clay as well as MacArthur over the failure of recovery, severe food shortages, and an American Congress pressing the administration to reduce occupation costs led both commanders to a similar conclusion. Economic recovery had to be made a priority whatever the intent of the initial directives. Within days after arriving in Berlin as Eisenhower's newly appointed deputy commander in April 1945, Clay was writing about the deplorable economic conditions and the need for Washington to rethink its policies. To Secretary of State James F. Byrnes, long a close friend, he wrote, "Conditions in Germany are getting progressively worse and large sections of all important cities have been obliterated. Of course we have a long-range problem in preventing the restoration of Germany's war potential. However, this is not the short range problem as several years will be required to develop even a sustaining economy to provide a bare minimum standard of living. The coming winter months will be most difficult."[128]

A week later Clay repeated his concern to Assistant Secretary of the Army John J. McCloy, who had been instrumental in Clay's selection: "I think that Washington must revise its thinking relative to destruction of Germany's war potential as an immediate problem. The progress of the war has accomplished that and it is my view now (based on general impressions, I must admit) that the industry which remains, with few exceptions, even when restored will suffice barely for a very low minimum living standard in Germany."[129]

As head of the Economic Section, Draper was directly responsible for the administration of OMGUS's economic controls in the American zone. He fully shared Clay's views. By autumn he was proposing massive industrial assistance. His suggestion that the United States provide a billion dollars to finance the purchase of industrial raw materials was not politically feasible in 1946 but was in effect agreed to in 1947 and acted upon in 1948 with the European Recovery Program. Whether German recovery could have occurred earlier had Draper's advice been followed remains a contentious issue.[130]

By the end of 1946 the food crisis in Europe had become critical. In response, President Truman appointed Herbert Hoover to lead a food-relief fact-finding mission. Although Hoover did not make his official reports public until

February and March 1947,[131] the mission itself reflected the shift in priorities taking place in Washington as well as OMGUS. Clay and other OMGUS officials briefed the mission on the occupation economic programs in Berlin in March. Byrnes's speech in Stuttgart in September 1946 marked the reversal. German economic recovery had become the priority Clay and Draper sought.

In the meantime, the deconcentration and decartelization program proceeded. Clay's support was evident. He had pressed the War Department to enlist the support of the State Department to put pressure on the British to accept mandatory provisions for the joint deconcentration legislation being negotiated (Law No. 56 and Ordinance No. 78), without which, he wrote, "We have little hope that a law . . . would really be effective."[132] Earlier, in long letter to McCloy on conditions in Germany, he noted that he had proposed the complete takeover of I. G. Farben with American managers as a "step in the right direction which would do much to convince doubters that we mean business with respect to large German combinations."[133] Nevertheless, the premises of American deconcentration policies had begun to take their toll.

Conceived politically as a component of a disarmament policy, any attempt to implement deconcentration policies fully was bound to produce resistance among those who believed that recovery was the overriding need. Perceptions of the role of cartels and concentration as a source of German industrial and military might had prompted the demand that all cartels and industrial concentrations be dismantled to prevent a resurgence of German military potential. The inexorable conclusion was that economic recovery required some mitigation of these efforts.

Tensions within the American camp surfaced within the year. In May 1947, Martin, the dedicated trustbuster, resigned as chief of the Decartelization Branch, in his words to "make it impossible for those in charge to attribute their delaying tactics to alleged 'feuding' between [Martin] the chief of the Deconcentration Branch and [Draper] the Economic Advisor to the Military Governor."[134] Martin returned to the United States and continued to criticize publicly and privately the lack of commitment to an effective program of deconcentration by Clay and his advisors. The American business community had also begun to raise questions about the program, arguing against any efforts that would, in their view, retard German recovery. The Hoover Mission report also expressed concern that "certain phases" of the program "limit recovery."[135] Members of Congress in response began to voice objections. Their criticisms tracked those of Martin and others who for various reasons favored vigorous implementation of an expansive deconcentration program.

On July 15, 1947, Michigan Democrat George G. Sadowski addressed the

House of Representatives with a long and detailed indictment of American occupation policies.[136] High officials, influenced by their own and others' economic interests, he charged, had subverted U.S. policy. With respect to decartelization, "The Allies have also permitted the Germans to retain their grip on the huge combines. The gigantic Siemens Electrical Trust, Vereinigte Stahlwerke, Mannesmann, I. G. Farben, and so forth are still operating and there is no indication, in spite of our avowed intentions, that they will be effectively decartelized and their equipment delivered as reparations to the German 'victims.'" Sadowski concluded with a demand that the Congress "thoroughly investigate our entire German policy and to see that demilitarization, denazification, decartelization are carried out, and that Germany's war potential is destroyed and that she remain powerless to wage another war."[137] Nine days later he included in the *Congressional Record*[138] an article by Thomas L. Stokes from that morning's *Washington News*. Stokes had voiced "doubts and suspicion" about the "campaign going on in behalf of a strong internal German economy," noting that "anti-Russian feeling and the fears aroused over communism" had found an "outlet in the idea of building up Germany as a bulwark against Russia." Stokes suggested that behind the campaign were the same "powerful economic and financial interests" in the United States that had participated with German firms in international cartels and had been sympathetic toward the Nazi regime before the war. In closing he warned his readers against a revived Germany that was "too strong." The same day, Representative Adolph J. Sabath, an Illinois Democrat, brought to the attention of his colleagues a press release from the Society for the Prevention of World War III, Inc., in his words "an organization composed of Americans with patriotic devotion to the best interests of America, not only today but in the future."[139] The press release included a list of twenty-one purportedly "pro-Nazi and pan-German" industrialists.

In Germany plans to dismantle integrated firms continued to conflict with efforts to promote German economic recovery and the more mundane needs of the occupying forces. The controversy over the Henschel und Sohn firm was typical. Established in 1810 as a gun manufacturer, by the 1920s the company had become Germany's leading producer of locomotives. During the war Henschel plants were converted to produce a variety of heavy military equipment, including Tiger tanks and 88-millimeter guns, but by 1947 the firm had resumed its dominant position in the production of locomotives, controlling more than 70 percent of all of Germany's locomotive-manufacturing facilities and 90 percent of its trolley-bus manufacturing capacity.[140] In September 1947, the Decartelization Branch took aim and began the process of deconcentration. The branch drafted a directive, which was approved by the corresponding Decartelization Branch of the British military government. In October the Economics Division of omgus cleared the matter, but the Trade and Commerce Division voiced concerns on the grounds that Herschel had only one customer, the state-owned railway. In response, General Lucius D. Clay, as military governor, decided that no deconcentration action be taken.[141]

The Henschel decision was one of several[142] that Clay made pursuant to the conclusion that he and Richardson Bronson, newly appointed chief of the Decartelization Branch, had reached to exempt firms in the capital goods and heavy industries from reorganization. The German deconcentration program, at least in the American zone, would focus instead on producers of consumer goods. Bronson announced the new policy to his staff on March 11, 1948. They were, he told them, to concentrate enforcement efforts under Law No. 56 on consumer goods industries. Their reaction was immediate. Nineteen members of the staff signed a statement addressed to Clay criticizing the change and asking for clarification. The news became public. The *New York Times* carried reports on the change in policy by correspondent Delbert Clark.[143] Clay reacted strongly. In a private note to Draper on March 14 he characterized the stories as "another outburst of disloyalty from the same old crowd who want their views accepted."[144] On March 22, Clay confronted the staff and made clear that the decision had been his.[145] Three days later on the floor of the House, Representative Sadowski attacked Clay, Draper, Bronson, and Hawkins by name. He included for the record a copy of the signed memorandum of the nineteen members of Bronson's staff. He concluded with a diatribe against all efforts to foster German recovery. "I shall vote," he said, against the Economic Cooperation Act, which embodied the Marshall Plan, and "this whole evil business."[146]

The controversy over deconcentration policies reached a climax with the appointment by Secretary of the Army Kenneth C. Royall of a committee to study the decartelization and deconcentration program in Germany. Chaired by Garland S. Ferguson, a member of the Federal Trade Commission, the committee conducted a month-long, on-site study from early December 1948. The committee's report[147] was sent to Secretary Royall in mid April 1949. It described the internal controversy and offered a series of recommendations for more effective pursuit of the deconcentration program. By this time Clay had left Germany. In his place the newly appointed Allied high commissioner, John J. McCloy, shifted responsibility for decartelization from the Economic Division to the Legal Division. Implementation of the reduced program quietly continued.

The Ferguson committee report appears to have made little difference in occupation policy or its implementation. By 1949 the focus of American attention had shifted irreversibly, as Sadowski and Stokes had feared, to the need for a strong Germany to counter the perceived threat from the Soviet Union. Containment not deconcentration was in vogue. Interest and responsibility for German antitrust policy also shifted, fortunately, to the Germans themselves. Totally ignored, it appears, by Martin and his colleagues in the Decartelization Branch were the Germans, led by Ludwig Erhard, who seized the moment to provide their country with an authentically German approach to competition policy. The American debate served more as an indictment than an inspiration.

Meanwhile a similar controversy erupted in Japan. On the Pacific side the roles were reversed. As in the case of Germany, the debate over SCAP's deconcentration efforts pitted those who sought significant structural reform of the Japanese economy against political and business leaders who like Clay viewed their commitment as extreme. Unlike Germany, conflict within SCAP was negligible, and the debate on the floors of Congress pitted powerful political leaders against the reformers. The two debates raged simultaneously without any reference of one to the other. Even more remarkably, even today no mention is made of one to the other.

The Japanese "reverse course" had, like that in Germany, originated with concerns over recovery in the first months of the occupation. In Japan the initial issue was not massive industrial assistance but food imports. Members of the Far Eastern Commission had severely criticized MacArthur's urgent requests for food shipments from the United States, arguing that Japan should not be permitted a standard of living higher than that of the Chinese or Russian allies. As a result the first shipments were delayed until April 1946. Similar demands from members of the FEC for reparations to be made by dismantling Japanese industry, along with the recommendation of the Pauley Mission[148] to use the reparations program "to destroy the Zaibatsu,"[149] forced MacArthur to argue that Washington needed to consider the economic role of Japan in Asia and the need for Japan to have the capacity to engage in trade in order to satisfy the economic needs of the region.[150] In MacArthur's first press conference on March 17, 1946, echoing the concerns of the pre-surrender planners he emphasized the need to embark on an economic recovery program with the resumption of international trade as a high priority.[151]

SCAP did not, however, view *zaibatsu* dissolution as a barrier to Japan's recovery. One of the closest advisors to MacArthur was Charles Kades, deputy chief of Government Section. Kades, a lawyer, had been an alternate delegate from the Treasury Department to TNEC in the 1930s and fully supported the dissolution effort. Kades, who is said to have been involved with the drafting of JCS/1067 for Germany,[152] allegedly helped Welsh come up with an acceptable enforcement agency for Law No. 207, suggesting the HCLC could be used.[153] Bisson also gives credit to Kades for having helped persuade MacArthur, at his and Eleanor Hadley's urgings, to support the Edwards Mission recommendations despite the early (summer 1946) doubts of Marquart and other advisors.[154] Whatever the cause, SCAP pressures on the Japanese government to enact both antitrust legislation and a deconcentration statute continued unabated until autumn 1947.

Other Americans were less enthusiastic. In August 1947 Draper was appointed undersecretary of the army. One of his first tasks was to review the situation in Japan. He arrived in Tokyo in September. Among those he met were Marquart and Welsh. His experience with Martin and others responsible for the OMGUS deconcentration program quite fresh, he was dismayed. SCAP was proceeding to do what he had fought so hard in Germany to prevent, what he viewed as a destructive dismantling of Japan's economic infrastructure. Upon Draper's return to Washington, a consensus formed in the newly created Department of Defense. From that moment, from Secretary of Defense James V. Forrestal[155] on down, Washington sought to curtail if not terminate the *zaibatsu* dissolution program.

The public controversy over *zaibatsu* dissolution began with the publication in the December 1, 1947, issue of *Newsweek* of parts of a report by James Lee Kauffman, who was reported to have been asked by Draper to report on SCAP's economic reform program. It appears, however, that the report was initially prepared by Kauffman without any official sanction ostensibly to inform his clients of the climate for investment in Japan.[156] Kauffman was a knowledgeable if biased observer.[157] He had first gone to Japan before World War I as a young Harvard law graduate to teach American law at the Tokyo Imperial University Faculty of Law upon the recommendation of Roscoe Pound, then dean of the Harvard Law School. In Japan he met a former United States consul who, having lost his government position as a result of a change in U.S. administrations, had opted to remain in Japan as a lawyer. They formed a partnership, McIvor and Kauffman—the first firm of American lawyers in Japan. Kauffman practiced law in Japan—permitted at the time—until he returned to the United States in the 1920s. He continued to practice with his Tokyo-based firm from New York until his death in Tokyo in the mid-1960s. At the end of the war, Kauffman was one of the few Americans with long, firsthand experience in prewar Japan. Kauffman's views regarding *zaibatsu* dissolution coincided closely with those held by Grew, Dooman, and the other "Japan hands" in the State Department. They were well aware of the intensity of disdain that Japan's nationalistic bureaucrats and military leaders had for the *zaibatsu* and the more liberal and "internationalist" proclivities of Japan's business establishment. Kauffman no less than Grew regarded the proposed economic reforms as misguided. He made only one visit to Japan during the occupation. He joined a business delegation. In Japan he met with Welsh. Needless to say, he was appalled. Kauffman also saw Takeshi Watanabe, a key liaison official in the Ministry of Finance, to whom he apparently relayed the message that not all Americans agreed with the current dissolution program.[158] Whether Kauffman's study was actually commissioned as stated in the *Newsweek* article or was instead a personal attack, written ostensibly for business clients interested in the climate for investment in Japan but widely distributed, is not clear. What is significant is that among those who received a copy was the newly appointed undersecretary of the army, Brigadier General Draper, who, according to *Newsweek*, having "gained an outstanding reputation as economic advisor to General Clay in Germany, became aware of FEC-230" during a recent visit to Japan.

The *Newsweek* report ignited the same sort of reaction among conservative Republicans that Delbert Clark's communiqués from Berlin provoked among liberal Democrats. After the election in 1946, however, the Republicans were in control. On December 19, 1947, with a copy of FEC 230 in hand, California Senator Knowland denounced the measure as "contrary to American standards of decency and fair play."[159] In January, a much relieved Knowland reported that FEC 230 no longer reflected effective policy. In its stead he said, a new antitrust law, "which is better than our own antitrust laws," had been enacted and promulgated and was in effect.[160]

The *zaibatsu* dissolution program did not end immediately. MacArthur continued to support the effort. But the die was cast. The State and War Departments agreed. The deconcentration program in Japan would have to be restrained in the interest of economic recovery. In February 1948, Undersecretary of State Lovett announced that the dissolution program was under overall review.[161] Lovett's statement was followed by a speech by Secretary of Army Royall on January 6, 1948, in which he emphasized that the aim of American policy in Japan was to build a self-sufficient democracy, "strong enough and stable enough to support itself, and at the same time to serve as a deterrent against any other totalitarian war threats which might hereinafter arise."[162]

A month later George Kennan, director of the State Department's Policy Planning Staff, was sent to Japan to meet with MacArthur. On his agenda were Japan's role in the emerging American containment policy and the closely related issue of economic recovery.[163] A rehabilitated Japan was to play in Asia the role of the revived West Germany in Europe. Once again, American policy in Germany determined the policy toward Japan.

During Kennan's visit, a month before Clay's action in Germany, the War Department cabled SCAP that U.S. support for FEC 230 (Law No. 207) was withdrawn. In March Draper returned to Japan as a member of the mission led by Percey H. Johnson, chairman of the Chemical Bank and Trust Company. Although formally charged with inquiry into Japan's economic problems, the mission made the demise of the dissolution program a priority. Welsh's proposed expansion was doomed. Within the year the HCLC gradually completed its work. On May 12, 1948, the dissolution effort ended. Left intact, however, was the first legislated extension of American antitrust law abroad and the most stringent statute on the globe.

The debates within the two occupation regimes and in the United States over deconcentration policies in Germany and Japan should be understood today not merely as interesting episodes. The messages sent to both Germans and Japanese were to haunt those who sought to establish effective competition policies in the two countries for many years thereafter. The American proponents of forceful deconcentration in Germany and Japan on one extreme viewed occupation policy as an essentially punitive measure designed to prevent either country from ever again having the industrial capacity to engage in war. Even the most benign saw in these policies the means to cure antidemocratic tendencies by eliminating the resurgence of industrialist political influence.[164] The unstated premise of both viewpoints was that antitrust had economically destructive consequences. Antagonists like Clay, Draper, Kauffman, and Knowland accepted these premises. They saw the proponents as ideologues bent on the destruction of the industrial capacity of Germany as well as Japan. Only a few lonely American voices—Edward Levi for one[165]—argued for competition as a condition for economic recovery and growth. They were hardly heard. It is not surprising therefore that the Germans and Japanese listening to the Americans debating American plans for their future should have come away with a fearful sense that competition and antitrust meant industrial debilitation and economic stagnation. Fortunately, fifty years of antitrust in both countries proved the Americans on both sides of the debate wrong.

# 2 / Transformation and Convergence— the German and Japanese Responses

As the American, British, and French governments gradually relinquished sovereignty to a politically reformed German state between 1949 and 1955, Germans also gained control over the development of permanent antitrust legislation. The first step had been the creation of a unified German economic administration, from the outset a paramount aim of the United States—as reflected in article 2, section B, paragraph 14 of the Potsdam protocol. Progress was slow. The Soviet Union refused. The French held back. The British finally agreed in September 1946 but only after prolonged negotiations and mounting economic distress. They had well-founded misgivings that a unified economic zone meant diminution if not an end to their voice in economic policy, particularly with respect to the Ruhr region, which had been exclusively under British control until the bizonal agreement. The French joined at the last moment only after intense pressure and the evident success of the American and British bizonal economic authority. Three separate but almost identical decartelization and deconcentration regulations were now applied throughout the western zones—Law No. 56 in the American zone, Ordinance No. 78 in the British zone, and finally Ordinance No. 98 in the French zone. The three zones fully merged as a new constitution (the Bonn Basic Law) was prepared and national elections were held in 1949 for a government for the newly established Federal Republic of Germany. During the interim, emerging German leaders took the initiative in developing an authentically German antitrust statute.[1]

## GERMAN INITIATIVES

An integral part of the bizonal arrangement had been to work with the economic ministers of each of the German states within the two zones (for the U.S. zone: Bavaria, Württemberg-Baden, and Greater Hesse; for the British zone: Lower Saxony, North-Rhine/Westphalia, and Schleswig-Holstein). An executive committee on economics, Verwaltungsrat für Wirtschaft (vaw), was formed for this purpose to coordinate and implement economic policies between the two zones. By the end of 1948, the committee, renamed the Verwaltung für Wirtschaft (vfw) and under the direction of Ludwig Erhard, had evolved into the most centralized administrative organ for planning and implementing economic policy within occupied Germany. Upon the formation of the Federal Republic in 1949 under the new constitution and its first government, the vfw became the Ministry of Economics, with Erhard its first head.

In July 1946 the vaw undertook the task of drafting a German decartelization law. The task was committed to a group headed by Dr. Paul Josten from the Länderratskommission in Stuttgart, of which Ludwig Erhard, the Bavarian minister of economics, was also a member. Josten had been the head of the Cartel Office in the Ministry of Economics and after 1945 commissioner for price fixing in the Länderrat. He was joined by Walter Bauer and Franz Böhm, both of whom were also members of the Stuttgart commission, in addition to Wilhelm Köppel, Wilhelm Kromphard, Kurt Fischer, and Bernard Pfister. Böhm, a law professor from Freiburg who had been dismissed from his teaching post in the late 1930s because of his public opposition to the Nuremberg laws, provided the intellectual leadership. Along with economists Walter Eucken and Leonard Miksch, Böhm was a founding member of the Freiburg or ordo-liberal school of political economists. Beginning in the mid 1930s, the three had separately begun to develop the idea that competition policy required strong state intervention.[2]

They viewed legislated competition policy in constitutional terms. Social policy was to be subsidiary in a state-fostered competitive market economy.[3] In contrast to the American emphasis on the evils of cartels and concentration, the ordo-liberals articulated in positive terms a persuasive case for competition. Competition, they argued, operated as a more effective alternative to both socialism and the corporate state in generating wealth. They shared the classical liberal commitment to a free economy and rejection of state planning. They refused, however, to be limited to an either/or choice between a laissez-faire policy of nonintervention or a centrally administered economy. The issue was not, in the words of Walter Eucken,[4] "more or less State activity" but the need for a positive state policy to ensure a market form of competition. In other words, they believed that strong state intervention was necessary to create as well as to protect a competitive economic order. They did not reject the need for state intervention to assure social welfare, although they stressed the distributive effects of competition as the gains from efficiency and productivity are passed to the consumer rather than to shareholders or labor. Except for their emphasis on competition and consequent rejection of the idea of the corporate state, their views were otherwise compatible with German social economic policy since Bismarck.[5]

Josten's committee completed and submitted their work to Ludwig Erhard, as director of the vFW, in July 1949. The committee recommended two separate statutes—a Law for the Protection of Competition (Gesetz zur Sicherung des Leistungswettbewerbs) and a Law for a Monopoly Office (Gesetz über das Monopolamt).[6] Together the statutes would bar virtually all anticompetitive agreements (section 7 of the Law for the Protection of Competition) except for those exempted by an independent Monopoly Office (Monopolamt). The linchpin of the proposal was the careful definition of "market power" in economic terms as the capacity to determine (not merely to fix) prices (section 3 of the Law for Protection of Competition). The basic statute also provided for the dissolution of trade and industry associations, concerns, consortia, as well as single enterprises into units without market power. The proposal included additional regulations to prevent the acquisition of market power through consolidation. The proposals—known today as the "Josten drafts"—went too far for the vFW. Its members began to distance themselves from them.[7] Nevertheless, the Josten drafts provided the benchmark—and conceptual framework—for an authentically German competition policy.

Credit for this break with the past must be given in part to the ideological success of the ordo-liberals, particularly Böhm.[8] Their efforts during the early postwar years helped to popularize the idea of competition secured through state intervention to ensure the working of a free-market economy. Erhard was their most influential advocate. He and others who shared the ordo-liberal vision had been engaged during the last years of the war in planning within the government for the postwar period. In this role they gained firsthand knowledge of the pitfalls of state planning.[9] But, as noted before, it is doubtful that they would have risen to positions of such prominence in postwar Germany had it not been for the vacuum in leadership that resulted from the purge.

Erhard's views deserve particular attention. Unlike most American advocates for antitrust, he articulated a compelling argument for the economic benefits of competition. To Erhard competition was a "central pillar" in a just social order—a social market economy—in which the proceeds of economic efficiency would be shared equitably with consumers.[10] "Only as a result of competition," Erhard argued, "shall we liberate those forces which will guarantee that economic progress and improvements in working conditions will not be absorbed in greater profits, private incomes and other benefits, but these benefits will be passed to the consumer."[11] Erhard opposed state planning, *dirigisme,* and other forms of collective public as well as private controls that restricted competition and free prices.[12] Like Eucken and his ordo-liberal colleagues, Erhard considered his vision of the "social market economy" as a much preferred alternative to laissez-faire liberalism, state ownership, and regimes that attempted to combine comprehensive state planning with private enterprise.

The strong public response to the call for a free-market economy, however, may have been less the result of positive persuasion than that of a widely shared aversion to the "coercion economy" of the Third Reich and its continuation until 1948 under the occupation. West German rejection of all manner of collectivism, reinforced by the negative example of East Germany, thus prepared the ground for the embracement of ordo-liberal ideas. The spectacular success of Erhard's daring gamble in 1948 to eliminate rationing and price controls in the combined American and British zones also played a crucial role in winning popular support.[13]

Even then not all were persuaded. The American proposal for Law No. 56 had been made in December 1946. German authorities initially responded by proposing a return to the Weimar policy of approving cartels, subject to carefully defined standards, and policing abuses of concentrated or collective market power. The minister-presidents of the three *Länder* within the American occupation zone petitioned General Clay not to impose Law No. 56 but to allow for an approach that would be consistent with German legal terminology and practice, one that would deal with the abuses of economic power.[14] Many business leaders and lawyers, especially those most closely involved with the cartelized sectors of the economy, reacted similarly to the Josten drafts, viewing them as at best the unnecessary and potentially destructive introduction of American ideas unsuited to the German economic environment. They could point to American concerns that continuation of strong deconcentration and antitrust programs would retard German recovery. Thus they fought, delayed, and eventually weakened the legislation enacted a decade later.[15]

In 1952 the Adenauer government introduced a draft bill for a Law against Restraints of Competition.[16] The bill was the product of extensive effort. It had been preceded by 805 earlier drafts, 472 of which had been sponsored by the Adenauer government.[17] Like the final statute enacted in 1957, the 1952 bill reflected the tensions between two separate approaches. The first, exemplified by the Josten drafts, was to proscribe in general any agreement or concerted action among competitors to gain collective market power enabling them to control— that is, to determine—prices and output. Such agreements were to be defined, prohibited, and subjected to criminal sanctions. The 1952 bill did not go that far. Section 1 of the bill simply invalidated "agreements made by enterprises for a common purpose and resolutions of associations of enterprises" that by restraining competition could affect "production or market conditions." No provision was made for joint or concerted action not constituting an "agreement." Moreover, the bill qualified the proscription with a series of statutory exemptions subject to approval by a new Cartel Authority, a federal agency, as well as cartel authorities to be established by each *Land* government. The exemptions included "structural crisis" cartels formed to alleviate the consequences of temporary declines in sales not caused by "a fundamental change in demand" in order "to prevent the total closing down of plants of the participating enterprises or of considerable parts of such plants" (§ 2), "rationalization cartels" intended "to raise considerably the efficiency of the participating enterprises or to foster considerably the economical operation of the participating enterprises from a technical, managerial, or organizational point of view" (§ 3), joint organizations established to use by-products whose use would be otherwise economically impracticable (§ 4, ¶ 2), and cartels designed to promote foreign trade in cases where competing foreign firms were not subject to German or other antitrust regulation (§ 5).

The second approach reflected the influence of those who preferred a strengthening of the 1923 cartel legislation to allow cartels but to police any abuses. The most visible advocate was Rudolf Isay, a persistent and articulate critic of the Josten drafts as well as the 1952 bill. Isay had been one of the first German lawyers to take an interest in cartel policy, authoring his first book on the private and public law of cartels in 1922. He wrote extensively on the 1923 cartel law and was a prolific proponant of the 1923 approach allowing cartels in principle but subjecting them to approvals and careful monitoring to prevent abuse. Isay had emigrated to Brazil in the wake of the Nuremberg laws but returned to Germany in 1951 at age sixty-six. He quickly joined the debate over the legislation being drafted, serving as advisor to the Bundesband der deutschen Industrie (BDI), the national federation of German industries.[18]

Isay's views were reflected in the 1952 bill by the inclusion of exempt cartels and provisions that empowered the Cartel Authority to police particular market abuses by "market-dominating enterprises" (§ 17). The draft also contained provisions that either invalidated directly or empowered the Cartel Authority to invalidate other restraints, such as vertical price fixing (resale price maintenance agreements) (§ 10).

Also included in the 1952 bill were merger controls (§ 18) and prohibition of specified discriminatory market practices (§§ 13, 15, 16). The primary Cartel Authority was to be a new, quasi-independent Federal Cartel Office under the jurisdiction of the federal minister of economics (§ 40). Exercising more limited authority were the separate regulatory authorities to be organized in each *Land* (§ 36, ¶2). Violations of the statute were subject to administrative fines (§§ 31 through 35), but not criminal penalties. A civil damage remedy (§ 28) was included.

Throughout this period, as federal minister of economics in the Adenauer government, Ludwig Erhard remained the countervailing force behind the law.[19] Concern that a draconian deconcentration program might be imposed as more than interim legislation provided impetus and opportunity. Some argue that Erhard contributed to delay in enactment of the law through a number of tactical mistakes.[20] Nonetheless, Erhard played the pivotal role especially at a time when the conservative government of which he was a member grew less and less enthusiastic about enacting a strong statute in the face of waning Allied influence and resurgent German industry.

Erhard also opposed imposition of protectionist foreign investment and trade controls. Instead he favored forcing German industry to face the challenge of recovery within a context that precluded protective regulatory barriers to entry by foreign competitors. He remained nonetheless quite skeptical about the formation of the European Coal and Steel Community and its expansion into a regional common market as the European Economic Community under the 1957 Treaty of Rome, fearing a political tilt toward corporatism.[21]

ENACTMENT AND IMPLEMENTATION IN GERMANY AND EUROPE

The occupation of Germany ended in the western zones on May 5, 1955, two years before the Law against Restraints of Competition (Gesetz gegen Wettbewerbsbeschränkungen; hereinafter, GWB) was enacted (July 27, 1957) and two and a half years before its effective date (January 1, 1958). Pursuant to German legislation, Law No. 56 as well as its British and French counterparts continued in effect,[22] ensuring the continuity of antitrust in postwar Germany.[23] The 1952 bill, as noted, fell considerably short of the original goals the ordo-liberals as well the Americans had set for German economic policy. Indeed, some regarded the bill and the eventual statute as enacted a victory for those who had proposed a return to the 1923 pattern of cartel licensing and policing.[24] A complete ban on all anticompetitive agreements among competitors was simply not a politically feasible option. The American occupation authorities could nevertheless claim at least two enduring achievements in the field of antitrust—both of which proved to be far more significant than anyone at the time could have anticipated. The least obvious was the extent to which German courts had begun to develop an antitrust jurisprudence based on their enforcement and review of occupation legislation.[25] The other was the proscription against cartels and concentration in the European Coal and Steel Community Treaty of April 1951.

Although the establishment of the European Coal and Steel Community (ECSC), its influence on the creation of a European Community under the 1957 Treaty of Rome, and the gradual evolution to the European Union are outside the purview of this study, the reciprocal influences between German and European antitrust law are too important to ignore. Others have told the story in its full complexity exceptionally well.[26] The basic plot is much easier to relate.

Once the bizonal economic authority was created, the Americans insisted that deconcentration measures be applied to the Ruhr, until then under exclusive British control. The British resisted. Neither the British business community nor the Socialists were keen on American-styled deconcentration measures. The Labor government was especially concerned that the German coal and steel industry would be easier to nationalize if concentrated. British resistance to American demands that decartelization and deconcentration be written into any occupation regulations for the German steel industry indeed might have prevailed had the rejection of the American proposal been a higher priority than the Labor government's preoccupation with nationalization. At least according to Isabel Warner's account, the British insisted to the end that nationalization be a viable option. The Americans conceded on the condition that the decision be left to the German government and that deconcentration measures proceed.

The French, on the other hand, were quite willing to accept the American proposals for deconcentration and decartelization—apparently perceiving these to be detrimental to any future reestablishment of German industrial ascendancy.[27] The French were more concerned about preventing the resurgence of the German steel industry as a basis for German military power. Any measures—especially multinational controls—that promised such preventative effect were acceptable. The French were also interested in ensuring that the German coal and steel industry not be allowed to engage in discriminatory practices that, in their view, had in the past handicapped French heavy industry. With these goals in mind they supported the American efforts.

Finally, the Germans, assuming from 1948 onward greater control over economic policies, had one overriding concern—not to allow control over the German steel industry to pass to others. The negotiated trade-offs produced a willingness on the part of all parties to accept the American proposal. Hence, deconcentration and decartelization measures were drafted into the occupation statute[28] for the Ruhr and ultimately formed the basis for the provisions in the 1951 ECSC Treaty. The basic provisions were much broader than either the Josten drafts or the 1952 bill. Article 65 of the treaty prohibited all agreements, industry association measures, and concerted actions that "directly or indirectly" tended "to prevent, restrict or distort the normal operation of competition within the [coal and steel] common market." Article 66 dealt with "any transaction" that had "the direct or indirect effect of bringing about a concentration" in the industry. Such transactions had to be reported and approved. Article 60 prohibited predatory as well as discriminatory pricing.

While the foundations for the ECSC were being laid from 1946 to 1951, decartelization and deconcentration measures had become a permanent feature of the community's legal framework. These provisions were then carried forward—also influenced by the Havana Charter and the 1953 United Nations Report of the Ad Hoc Committee on Restrictive Practices—as articles 85 and 86 of the Treaty of Rome (since 1999, arts. 81 and 82). Although article 85 parallelled article 65 of the ECSC Treaty, article 86 reflected the influence of German law in its prohibition of abuses by firms "of a dominant position within the Common Market." Whatever the influence or origin, a Europe-wide antitrust regime was created—a regime that has expanded with the development of the European Union to envelop and overshadow in many respects German national law.

Records of the negotiations over the Treaty of Rome were purposely not kept. Thus what factors led to the inclusion of the prohibitions against restrictive business practices of articles 85 and 86 remain uncertain. The most likely explanation may be the sum of the concerns that motivated the French acceptance of the deconcentration and decartelization provisions in the ECSC Treaty, the procompetition policies of Erhard within the Adenauer government and at least some of the German representatives, the example of the ECSC Treaty itself, and perhaps more subtle American influence. The result in any event was to extend both American and ordo-liberal influence beyond German borders as European institutions and competition law have expanded. In 1957, however, few predicted that European competition law would at least in some areas eventually swallow up even the strongest national antitrust regimes.

Two months after the Treaty of Rome was signed, the German parliament finally enacted the GWB. The statute followed the basic pattern set out in the 1952 draft. Two of the major changes were to delete the merger-control provisions and to exclude export cartels not affecting German markets from the scope of the statute altogether. The GWB was in most respects a much more timid piece of antitrust legislation than either the ECSC Treaty or the 1947 antitrust statute enacted in Japan. As enacted the GWB nonetheless represented a significant piece of antitrust legislation, especially for Germany.

Since enactment the GWB has been amended six times, the sixth amendment in 1998.[29] The first,[30] in 1965, expanded the exemption for standardization cartels and introduced a new exemption for "specialization" cartels. It also strengthened the provisions related to abuses by market-dominating enterprises related to vertical price fixing. In 1973 the second amendment[31] represented the first major effort to strengthen the law. It introduced merger-control provisions and a prohibition against concerted conduct. The 1973 amendment also repealed the exemption for resale price maintenance for branded goods, expanded the powers of the cartel authorities to deal with abusive practices by market-dominating enterprises, and broadened the prohibition against discriminatory practices. The third amendment, enacted in 1976, strengthened the merger-control provisions of the statute related to newspapers and other publishers.[32] The fourth amendment, in 1980,[33] expanded the law's merger controls with respect to conglomerates and vertically integrated enterprises and small enterprises. It also strengthened the prohibition against discriminatory practices, limited the exemption for financial institutions and public utilities, and increased the fines for violations. The fifth amendment[34] went into effect on January 1, 1990. It introduced a new exemption for small and medium enterprises to form purchasing cartels, weakened the prohibition against discrimination against dependent enterprises while strengthening the prohibition against discrimination of small enterprises, and expanded the merger-control provisions. Also amended were provisions related to exemptions for transportation, banking, insurance, and public utilities. In addition, the 1990 amendment simplified merger-notification procedures and introduced new procedural rules to protect the confidentiality of business secrets in court proceedings (§ 70[1]). The most recent amendment was enacted in 1998.[35] Designed to harmonize the GWB with European Union law, it was also the most extensive. The amendment brought the GWB into greater conformity with European law in several respects. First, the GWB merger-control provisions were revised to require pre-merger notification in all relevant cases. The definition of merger was expanded to include acquisition of control. Also, investigation procedures, including those involving prohibitions and clearances, now require both publication and explanation. In addition, section 1 was revised to prohibit explicitly anticompetitive agreements and trade association actions as well as concerted practices (*aufeinander abgestimmtes Verhalten*) formerly proscribed under section 25(1). As a result of the 1998 amendments, the GWB for the first time also explicitly prohibits abuses by market-dominating enterprises and unauthorized retail price recommendations. Finally, although a supplementary exemption was added to the general exemption of section 7, the exemptions for rebate, export, and import cartels were repealed. The expanding role of European competition law has indeed been one of the most significant influences on antitrust policy in Germany.

## REFORM, RESURGENCE, AND THE SECOND AMERICAN IMPETUS IN JAPAN

The Japanese contrast could hardly have been greater. Dominated by Marxist and mercantilist theoreticians, in the late 1940s and early 1950s the community of Japanese academic economists had no place for liberals or ordo-liberals. SCAP's reliance on Japanese government officials to enact and implement its reform programs helped consolidate, rather than destroy, the pattern of cooperation between business and government that had developed during the war. No longer challenged either by the military or by independent political interests, those who had close involvement with the wartime economic controls and had developed intimate personal connections with the *zaibatsu* executives and middle managers were in a position to dominate Japan's postwar policies even more effectively than before. Upon them were thrust the SCAP-inspired procompetition policies. As noted in two seminal studies— one by one of Japan's most distinguished economists and the other by an equally prominent American political scientist—the infrastructure of the postwar government-business relationship was framed during these years.[36] Instead of undoing these relationships, occupation policies helped to cement them by removing any effective challenge from the outside and by, simultaneously, reinforcing bureaucratic governance.[37]

Nobusuke Kishi was Japan's counterpart to Ludwig Erhard. Kishi began his career in 1920 as an official in what was then the Ministry of Agriculture and Commerce. He became a leader of the "new" or "revisionist" bureaucrats, who like their counterparts within the military were critical of corruption they deemed endemic in parliamentary politics and the social ills they associated with liberal capitalism and big business.[38] In the mid 1930s, Kishi held a leading civilian post in Manchuria and, as noted, was instrumental in developing an "industrial policy" for the territory that included the preferential treatment for the Nissan (Aikawa) *zaibatsu* as a means to offset the political and economic influence of the old business establishment. In 1939 he had risen to the highest career post in the Ministry of Commerce and Industry as its vice-minister. From 1941 through 1944, Kishi served in the Tojo cabinet as minister of munitions, the wartime ministry established in place of the Ministry of Commerce and Industry to improve Japanese mobilization. Purged, tried, and convicted as a war criminal, Kishi nevertheless remained a powerful force. Upon his release from prison in 1948, he entered politics. First elected to the House of Representatives in 1953 as a member of the Liberal Party (Jiyūtō), within two years he had become the secretary-general of the Japan Democratic Party (Nihon Minshūtō). In 1955 Kishi helped to engineer the merger of the two conservative parties into the existing and still ruling Liberal Democratic Party. He served as prime minister between 1957 and 1960, ironically overlapping with Ludwig Erhard's tenure as chancellor. Throughout his career, Kishi was a forceful advocate of Japan's postwar industrial policies and Japan's most powerful critic of the occupation's legacy of competition law. Now in leadership positions, his protégés in the Ministry of Commerce and Industry—reestablished as the Ministry of International Trade and Industry (MITI) in 1952—became the principal institutional proponents of Japan's postwar "industrial policy."

Led by Kishi and his cohorts, an effort in Japan to dismantle the occupation's antitrust measures commenced even before they had been fully assembled. As noted, *zaibatsu* dissolution under occupation economic policy had received priority, as exemplified by the 1947 Deconcentration Law.[39] With the termination of the deconcentration effort, emphasis shifted to the long-term antitrust program in the form of the Antimonopoly Law, which had been enacted at the end of March 1947. Stronger opposition delayed the passage of the Trade Association Law,[40] which was finally promulgated in July 1948. By then, SCAP had given up on the deconcentration effort, leaving the banking and insurance industries untouched. In 1949, the first significant amendment to the Antimonopoly Law weakened some important provisions of the statute, but the changes were generally considered necessary—such as the elimination of the requirement for prior approval for all international agreements—or represented in retrospect only a modest retreat. The endeavors to weaken the new antitrust legislation gained momentum, however, as the occupation ended on April 30, 1952. Almost immediately, the Japanese government repealed the prohibition against use of *zaibatsu* names and substantially amended the Trade Association Law. Related legislation drastically reduced the number of FTC personnel. Then in September 1953 the Diet enacted a sweeping revision[41] of the Antimonopoly Law. With the Adenauer government's 1952 bill as model for the cartel exemptions,[42] the principal changes were as follows:

1. Exemptions for recession (*fukyō*) and rationalization (*gōrika*) cartels.
2. Redefinition of "unfair methods of competition" under the new rubric "unfair business practices."
3. Procedures for authorized resale price maintenance.
4. Further easing of the restrictions on intercorporate shareholding, interlocking directorates, and mergers.
5. Repeal of article 4, prohibiting specific restraints of trade; article 5, outlawing control organizations; and article 8, empowering the FTC to restructure enterprises to preclude undue disparities in bargaining power.

Despite these changes and the implicit rejection of the procompetition policies of the occupation reforms, the basic framework of antitrust enforcement remained intact. Some of the provisions of the original statute that did remain would hardly have been tolerated for their intrusive reach even in the United States. The law continued to include the unique prohibition of all holding companies, the international contract-screening requirement, shareholding restrictions for financial institutions, and the first merger controls, including pre-merger review requirements, of any antitrust legislation.

The enactment of the 1953 amendments and the decade of limited enforcement that followed represented the high-water mark of effective opposition to procompetition policies. From 1955 to 1960 special statutes were then enacted to provide further cartel exemptions for a variety of products and industries, beginning with the 1952 Export and Import Transactions Law to permit voluntary export and import cartels. Special authorization for restrictive activities by small and medium-sized businesses, fertilizer producers, sake producers and sellers, port transport firms, and fishery companies followed. These measures substantially expanded the exemptions previously available under the 1947 law and the companion exemption statute. Subsequent legislation in the 1950s broadened the exempted categories to include electronics and machinery, coal mining, metals, and textiles. By 1970 more than twenty-two separate cartel exemptions had been created under the Antimonopoly Law and ten special statutes.[43]

Left intact were the general prohibitions of the original statute against unreasonable restraints of trade, private monopolization, and unfair methods of competition (reworded as unfair business practices). The review procedures for international agreements with the specific prescription against the inclusion of either unreasonable restraints on trade or unfair business practices, in addition to the prohibition against holding companies, restrictions on shareholding and interlocking directorates, and merger controls also remained. Nor were the penalties for violations reduced. Thus aside from the expansion of exempted cartels and relaxation of authorization procedures for resale price maintenance of branded goods, the amendments left in place the general proscriptions while deleting more specific prohibitions. On its face the statute remained nearly as severe as before insofar as the remaining provisions could be construed to cover most of the deleted prohibitions. For example, article 19 of the 1947 law stated, "No entrepreneur shall employ unfair methods of competition," such methods defined in article 2 as any one of the following practices:

1. unwarranted refusal to receive from or to supply to other entrepreneurs commodities, funds, and other economic benefits;
2. supplying commodities, funds, and other economic benefits at unduly low prices;
3. supplying commodities, funds, and other economic benefits at unduly discriminatory prices;
4. unreasonably inducing or coercing customers of a competitor to deal with oneself by offering benefits or threatening disadvantages;
5. trading with another party on condition that said party shall, without good cause, refuse acceptance of supply of commodities, funds, and other economic benefits from a competitor of oneself; and
6. supplying commodities, funds, and other economic benefits to another party on such conditions that shall unduly restrain transactions between said party and his suppliers of commodities, funds, and other economic benefits or customers or that shall unduly restrain relations between said party and his competitors, or on condition that the appointment of officers (hereafter referring to directors, unlimited partners who are executives, auditors, or persons similar thereto, manager or chief of the main or branch office) of the company of said party shall be subject to prior approval on part of oneself.

A further subparagraph provided for the inclusion of other practices that might be found to be "contrary to the public interest" and so designated by the FTC under its rule-making powers provided for in articles 71 and 72.

The 1953 amendments also substituted the term "unfair business practices" for "unfair methods of competition" and defined them more broadly as

1. unduly discriminating against other entrepreneurs;
2. dealing at unfair prices;

3. unreasonably inducing or coercing customers of a competitor to deal with oneself;
4. trading with another party on such conditions as will restrict unjustly the business activities of said party;
5. dealing with another party by unwarranted use of one's bargaining position; and
6. unjustly interfering with a transaction between an entrepreneur who competes in Japan with oneself or with the company of which oneself is a stockholder or an officer and his customers; or, in case such an entrepreneur is a company, unjustly inducing instigative or coercive means on stockholders against the interest of such a company or an officer of such a company to act.

To be considered illegal, however, the conduct must have been designated in advance by the FTC as an unfair business practice that "endangers fair competition." Pursuant to the authority of current article 2(9), the FTC almost immediately issued a General Designation of Unfair Business Practices, which expanded the original provisions. The 1953 general designation was amended, without any significant change in substance, in 1982.[44] The number of FTC personnel remained constant after the postoccupation cutback, and the number of decisions by the agency declined to a handful.

That the 1953 amendments did not go further than they did can be explained in part by concern over American criticism. Also to be factored in was Prime Minister Shigeru Yoshida's deep distrust of Kishi and other economic bureaucrats. He managed to keep them at bay. This check was removed with Yoshida's resignation as prime minister in 1954, followed by the election of Ichirō Hatoyama as new prime minister and the 1955 merger of the conservative parties into the Liberal Democratic Party, all of which Kishi helped to stage-manage. Equally symbolic of the shift in power and new direction of Japanese antitrust policy, but more substantial, was the elimination of all but a formal vestige of FTC authority to police the increasing list of special statutory exemptions to the Antimonopoly Law, as exemplified by the transfer in 1955 of the authority to approve or disapprove export and import cartels under the Export and Import Transactions Law from the FTC to MITI.[45] After the 1953 amendments, the most significant test of the durability of antitrust in Japan came in the late 1950s, amid the first significant slowdown in the Japanese economy since the Korean War. Simultaneously, Japan faced the first major demands for liberalization of its trade and investment policy as the postwar trade restrictions in Europe were removed. The response of business leaders, officials in the economic ministries, and the cabinet now led by Kishi was predictable. In October 1957 the latter appointed a special committee to study additional revisions to reduce even further the Antimonopoly Law's constraints on cartels and concentration.

"It is a condition of our economy," Prime Minister Kishi told commission members at their first meeting, "to fall into the bad habit of excessive competition."[46] To correct this "bad habit" and to meet the threat of international competition through rationalization of Japanese industry, the Antimonopoly Law was to be reviewed for possible revision. The committee, dominated by industry leaders, issued its report in February 1958. It proposed a series of major changes with a telling introduction: although credit was to be given antitrust legislation for its contribution to postwar economic recovery and democratization, the committee found it "difficult to say" that antitrust policies "necessarily contributed to the smooth operations of our nation's economy."[47]

On the basis of the committee's proposals, a bill was quickly drafted and introduced into the Diet in September. As noted in the case of the statute authorizing voluntary export and import cartels, legislation enacted after 1955 by and large gave MITI rather than the FTC the authority to approve exemptions to the Antimonopoly Law. Nonetheless, the FTC retained its authority under the 1947 statute to approve rationalization and recession cartels, mergers, and exemptions to the shareholding restrictions. The 1958 bill simply extended the pattern introduced in 1955. The main features were (1) substantial easing of the standards and procedures for approving recession cartels, (2) broadening of the scope of permitted rationalization cartels, (3) recognition of mergers for purposes of "rationalization," and (4) a variety of critical changes in FTC procedures. Under the bill the FTC would have also effectively lost any such claims as an independent agency by virtue of a requirement that the agency "listen" to the opinions of the competent economic ministries before taking any corrective actions or granting or denying approvals.[48] In a remarkable show of support for antitrust policy as well as political influence, consumer groups, labor unions, agricultural organizations, small and medium-sized business groups, and an increasing number of neoclassical economists and legal scholars with expertise in American and German antitrust law rallied and killed the measure in committee.[49]

The economic ministries led by MITI next attempted to achieve a similar result through the most ambitious special-exemption measure proposed— the Designated Industries Promotion Special Measures bill (*Tokutei sangyō shinkō rinji sochi hōan*). The bill was designed to permit certain industries, particularly automobile, petroleum, and specialty steel manufacturers, to achieve legally greater concentration and restrictive specialization. However, the envisioned level of governmental intervention and supervision, especially by MITI, was too great for the industries concerned, and the combined opposition of industrial, consumer, and other groups prevented the enactment of the bill. It finally died in 1963 after having been introduced three times in the Diet in vain.[50] Thus ended the last frontal assault on the Antimonopoly Law in the postwar period.

In the early 1960s only one option was left to those who sought to avoid the constraints of the Antimonopoly Law: evasion through extralegal support for private restrictive practices. MITI's influence had waxed and waned along with that of Kishi and his coterie of ex-bureaucrats. The era of quiescence was to be relatively short. Antitrust in Japan was about to revive.

During the period between 1953 and 1963 the average annual increase in gross private investment in producers' durables was a stunning 19.8 percent.[51] Yet this was not a period of significant cartelization or concentration, although the number both of exempt cartels and of mergers increased rapidly toward the end of the decade. We should accept at face value Kishi's statement to the 1958 commission on antitrust revision: extensive interfirm rivalry was indeed a predominant feature of Japan's economy.

The Korean War had provided a long-needed catalyst for Japanese economic recovery. With procurement orders to support the war effort and demand by Japanese industrial consumers (coupled with the closure of Japan to foreign imports and investment as the principal means to enforce a policy of import substitution and export promotion), Japanese manufacturing and competition expanded. New entry characterized nearly all segments of Japanese industry. New entrants challenged incumbent manufacturers of integrated steel, automobile, electronics, and pharmaceuticals. Even in retailing unprecedented levels of competition resulted from the less layered distribution systems being introduced by new large-scale manufacturers of consumer goods and the emergence of "super" retail stores.

Given concomitant expansion of capacity, the relative decrease in demand in the early and mid 1960s caused considerable concern to businesses forced to reduce prices despite high fixed costs and government officials who desired both growth and stability. For both, Japan's antitrust legislation was a serious obstacle. Unable to weaken the statute further through action in the Diet, they resorted to the existing exemptions and what are euphemistically referred to as "guidance cartels." From the appointment of the special commission to the defeat of the Designated Industries Promotion bill, these developments have been described extensively elsewhere,[52] but no study fully analyzes either the relationship of the Diet defeat of MITI's recommendations to the increasingly frequent resort to evasion of antitrust statute through administrative guidance or the essential weakness of the position taken by MITI and other proponents of anticompetition policies that these episodes reveal. MITI's influence within the ruling LDP and the cabinet was manifest in the fact that these bills were introduced in the Diet, but their defeat calls into question the often expressed view that de facto or de jure MITI determined the economic policies for Japan. Coincident with the trend toward evasion by administrative guidance was a surge in antitrust enforcement activity.

In the eight years between 1962 and 1970 the FTC moved against more illegal cartels than in the previous sixteen years combined. In fact, more FTC decisions were handed down against illegal cartels in the six years between 1962 and 1968 than in the first six years of antitrust enforcement under the occupation. This expanded enforcement effort continued unabated into the mid 1970s. And, as in Germany, for the first time since enactment, amendments to the law significantly expanded its reach and effective enforcement.

Proponents of a strong antitrust policy—including a growing band of antitrust economists and legal scholars—ceased fighting rearguard actions and took the initiative during the third decade of antitrust in Japan. The timing was not coincidental. In the early 1970s Japan faced the most serious economic and political crises of the postwar era. In August 1971 President Richard Nixon announced the end of the Bretton Woods accord. Henceforth the United States would not maintain fixed exchange rates. Within a month the yen rose against the U.S. dollar by 30 percent, immediately making Japanese exports significantly more expensive in all foreign markets. Within two years the first oil embargo by the Organization of Petroleum-Exporting Countries (OPEC) resulted in Japan's most severe postwar recession. In 1974 wholesale prices increased by 40 percent and consumer prices by 30 percent. Political crisis came next. Public allegations of massive corruption over the course of several years finally forced the resignation of Prime Minister Kakuhei Tanaka in early December 1974. Taking advantage of public concern over inflation as well as the political turmoil that followed Tanaka's resignation, the FTC began to play an activist role, culminating in a campaign initiated in 1974 by Chairman Toshihide Takahashi to strengthen the Antimonopoly Law.[53] The result was enactment of the 1977 amendments, the first legislation to strengthen antitrust policy since enactment of the Trade Association Law in 1948. The amendments are best known for the addition of new substantive provisions on "monopoly conditions" (*dokusen-teki jōtai*) to deal with firms with monopoly power, which included a return to the FTC of explicit power to order dissolution of cartels.

The most important changes in practice were new or strengthened sanctions. Fines were increased tenfold, and a new provision empowered the FTC to levy a surcharge on cartel proceeds (*kachōkin*). Again German law provided a model. The provision represented a modified version of the GWB cartel-proceeds fine (*Mehrerlös*). The surcharge in particular corrected what many observers, such as Hokkaido University Professor Kenji Sanekata,[54] considered the greatest weakness in the law: the difficulty of penalizing cartels without resort to criminal sanctions.

The willingness of the FTC to challenge evasion of antitrust policy, even when the firms involved had strong support within MITI or other economic ministries, was evident long before the 1977 amendments. In 1966 investigation was begun into the practice of maintenance of television resale prices by Sony and Matsushita.[55] The investigation, which revealed extensive domestic price-fixing arrangements among all of Japan's leading electronics manufacturers, led to a new FTC action.[56] Almost simultaneously, the FTC attempted, albeit unsuccessfully, to prevent the merger of Yawata and Fuji Steel. Although the effort failed, the FTC still managed to extract some concessions in exchange for the final consent decision that permitted formation of the New Japan Steel Corporation[57] and thus succeeded in dramatizing the existence of antitrust constraints in merger cases. Moreover, no merger of equivalent magnitude was ever again attempted.

Following these efforts, in a series of decisions in 1972, the FTC held Japan's leading synthetic textile manufacturers guilty of illegal price fixing and output restrictions (1972 *Synthetic Fiber* case).[58] A year earlier, the FTC had commenced a series of actions that would prove to be the most important antitrust enforcement proceedings of the first half century of antitrust in Japan. In 1971 the agency charged Japan's Petroleum Federation and major domestic petroleum companies with collusive output and price restrictions imposed with the overt support of MITI officials. After conclusion of the administrative proceedings leading to "recommendation decisions" (*kankoku shinketsu*) in 1974,[59] the FTC took the unprecedented step of filing criminal referrals against the offenders. The procuracy followed suit with indictments, and after lengthy trials, the Tokyo High Court held in two separate cases in September 1980 that the "guidance cartels" at issue were illegal and imposed criminal sanctions for price fixing.[60] (The defendants were acquitted in the output restriction case for lack of criminal intent.)

The Tokyo High Court decisions, which were subsequently upheld by the Supreme Court of Japan,[61] confirmed for the first time the incapacity of MITI officials to legitimate through "administrative guidance" an otherwise illegal cartel. In two earlier decisions involving Tōyō Rayon and Noda Soy Sauce,[62] the FTC had held guidance cartels illegal; but since the respondents in those cases had not appealed, the oil cartel cases were the first opportunity the courts had to decide the issue. The decisions gave new life to the criminal provisions of the Antimonopoly Law. How often they would be used in the future was open to question, but the risk for parties participating in a cartel became much greater than anyone could have predicted even in the mid 1970s.

From the perspective of the 1960s or even the early 1970s, antitrust in Japan appeared weak and ineffectual. To speak of antitrust policy or the FTC as having any role in framing Japan's economic policies seemed rarified at best. Notwithstanding these perceptions, closer analysis shows that antitrust policy actually played an expanding role throughout the 1960s. The number of cartels may have proliferated, but they remained subject to scrutiny and, in the case of "guidance cartels," direct attack. Thus the ability of participants to withdraw from a cartel or to cheat was maximized and the effectiveness of cartels over any length of time curtailed. Beginning in 1966 as indicated in figure 1, the number of exempt cartels began to decrease markedly.

Few in the United States, however, noticed the fundamental change that had occurred in Japanese antitrust policy in the 1960s. Instead, as the annual deficits in U.S. trade of manufactured goods with Japan continued to reach new heights, the legacy of industrial policy remained the paramount issue for those Americans concerned with Japan. Nontariff barriers to foreign goods were increasingly viewed as the causes of chronic trade imbalances. Japanese government actions and prevailing business practices, it was argued, had effectively prevented access by foreign firms to Japanese consumer and industrial markets.[63] Some argued in addition that profits from widespread cartelization in Japanese domestic markets enabled Japanese firms to subsidize exports.[64] Such concerns led to a noticeable shift in U.S. trade policy. In response to political demands for action, efforts to increase U.S. exports to Japan replaced a decades-old emphasis on Japanese export restraints. By the late 1980s the need to strengthen Japanese antitrust reinforcement had become a major component of the package of economic reforms the American government urged Japan to undertake.

With the new leverage of article 301 of the Omnibus Trade and Competitiveness Act of 1988, in 1989 the Bush administration initiated a new series of trade negotiations with Japan to reduce perceived structural barriers to imports and foreign investment. Antitrust reform was high on the proposed agenda. The American side viewed the failure of effective antitrust enforcement as one of the main causes of various anticompetitive and exclusionary practices that made entry by foreign firms into the Japanese market difficult. Many in Japan welcomed the American focus on the need for stronger antitrust enforcement. U.S. trade negotiations provided a useful political catalyst to renew efforts by Japanese antitrust authorities to strengthen the Antimonopoly

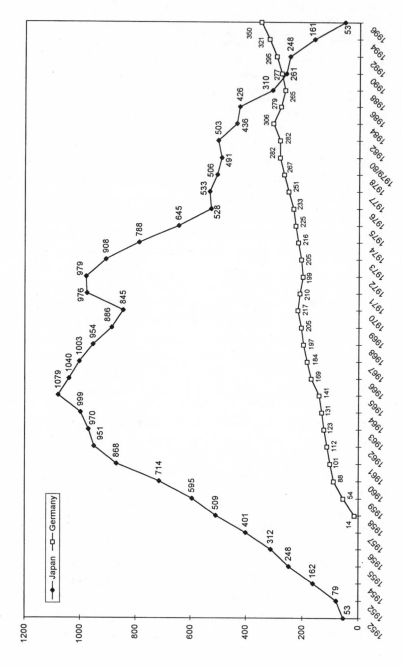

FIG. 1. Exempt Cartels under Japanese Law, 1953–96 and German Law, 1958–96 (SOURCE: FCO and FTC Annual Reports 1950–97)

Law. This coincidence of pressures led to more rigorous antitrust enforcement and a continuing process of antitrust reform. As detailed below, the Japanese government acted in response to this second American impetus to increase antitrust enforcement staff, penalties, and most recently repeal a majority of all legal cartel exemptions, including export and import cartels. Although significant, these reforms represent a continuation of the resurgence of antitrust enforcement that had begun in the mid 1960s. Except for a brief period following the oil shocks of the early 1970s, the number of exempt cartels declined steadily along with a less dramatic but still significant increase in enforcement actions. By the early 1990s, fewer legally exempt cartels were in force in Japan than Germany.

The only amendments enacted since the 1950s to ease the stringent prohibitions of the Antimonopoly Law were the 1997 and 1998 structured controls amendments that allow the formation of holding companies under article 9 subject to specified constraints to prevent "excessive concentration of economic power" and ease shareholding restrictions. Japan still remains the only country to regulate holding companies directly. For good or ill, since the 1960s antitrust policy and enforcement in Germany and Japan have tended to converge. More detailed comparison is necessary, however, to fully appreciate the extent of such convergence as well as the significant differences that remain in the coverage and enforcement of the two statutes.

# PART 2

# ANTITRUST REGULATION
# AND ITS ENFORCEMENT
# IN GERMANY AND JAPAN

An understanding of the basic similarities and differences in the substantive principles and rules of law is a prerequisite for any meaningful comparative analysis. Equally important, however, is an appreciation of the institutions and procedures for enforcement. Legal rules have very little real life apart from their enforcement. The words of codes and statutes, even the decisional pronouncements of judges, must be applied to have any effect. Enforcement is a more complex subject than some may think. Even the simplest aspect if probed proves to be multifaceted. To begin with, who enforces matters greatly. Those who control the enforcement process in effect control the law and its viability. Identifying who actually enforces the law can be difficult, however, especially in systems of multiple means and processes for enforcement.

To a significant degree the forms of relief and penalties determine who enforces a particular legal rule. In the case of torts (delicts) or other civil (private law) damage actions, private parties take the initiative and control the process. The greater the number of potential plaintiffs, the more certain and expansive the law's enforcement will be. Similarly, to confine the sanction to an administrative or criminal penalty empowers officials—administrative or prosecutorial as the case may be—allowing them to control. Judges have the last official word in cases of formal enforcement at least to the extent that judicial review is an option. Even if no appeal is be taken, as is usually the case, the expectation of the outcome of judicial review based on past decisions— bargaining, as some say, in the "shadow of the law"—in effect empowers judges as law enforcers. Law enforcement is not, however, confined to formal proceedings. Social sanctions also come into play, empowering peers and the community who select among the legal rules they value in penalizing offenders.

Procedures also matter. In evaluating German and Japanese antitrust enforcement processes, we need to keep in mind the intrinsic tensions among the basic aims of all administrative processes—accuracy, efficiency, and fairness. Seldom are they compatible. Procedures designed to promote any one of these basic goals inexorably diminish one or both of the others. Ultimately objectives must be weighed and a balance struck. The policies at stake, the influence of the participants, and, above all, the values of the enforcement officials as well as the community in which they operate determine the priorities of one over the others. The procedural framework for antitrust enforcement in Germany and Japan reflects disparate considerations and the distinctive features of their political, legal, and social environments.

Law enforcement is, however, rarely analyzed as closely and carefully as it deserves. Far more is written about the rules and principles of law than the ways in which either are given effect and meaning. Antitrust law in Germany and Japan is no exception. Considerably less has been written on enforcement than almost any other aspect of German or Japanese antitrust law. The following chapters are intended to fill this gap and thereby, it is hoped, to provide a more accurate and deeper understanding of antitrust in the two countries during the past half century. We necessarily begin with the rules.

# 3 / Prohibitions and Approvals

The principal substantive provisions of the GWB, as amended, continue to be found in the five chapters of part 1 of the statute comprising sections 1 through 31. They include a single provision covering all horizontal restraints. The GWB now prohibits in one section (§ 1) agreements among enterprises, trade-association decisions, and concerted practices that prevent, restrict, or distort competition. As noted previously the new section 1 incorporates the prohibition of concerted practices that was added by amendment in 1973 as section 25(1). As amended, the GWB will continue to distinguish between horizontal and vertical restraints, unlike article 85(1) of the Rome Treaty. Accordingly, resale price maintenance is expressly prohibited under section 14 (former § 15). Nonbinding retail price recommendations to branded goods are allowed, however, under section 23 (former § 38a). The enforcement authorities may continue to prohibit anticompetitive exclusive dealing and tying arrangements under section 16 (former § 18) as well as inappropriate license restrictions under sections 17 and 18 (former §§ 20, 21). Boycotts and refusals to deal are covered under section 21 (former § 26[1]). Abuses of market power—in the language of the statute, abuses by "market-dominating enterprises" or *marktbeherrschende Unternehmen*—are prohibited under sections 19 and 20 (former §§ 22[4] and 26[2] and [3]). A "market-dominating enterprise" continues to be defined as an enterprise not subject to substantial competition or with a "superior market position" in relation to competitors. A "superior market position" is determined by a cluster of factors: turnover; assets; access to capital, suppliers, and customers; and barriers to entry. Any enterprise with a market share of one-third or more is presumed to be market dominating. Two or three enterprises with a combined market share of 50 percent or above or up to five firms that control two-thirds or more of the market are also presumed to be "market-dominating" (§ 19 [3]). The 1998 amendment eliminated the turnover requirements of former section 22(3).

Chapter 7 provides for control over mergers, acquisitions, and consolidations (*Zusammenschuß*) in sections 35 through 43 (former §§ 23, 24). Former section 24b established an independent Monopoly Commission (Monopolkommission) in Cologne. The commission's organization and functions are detailed in sections 44 through 47. It supplements the role of the Federal Cartel Office (Bundeskartellamt, FCO)—in Berlin until 1999, thereafter in Bonn—in merger control through collecting and reporting information on concentration and issuing opinions on policy. The Monopoly Commission does not exercise any policing or enforcement powers. These remain with the FCO.

Exempted under sections 2 through 8 (both old and new) are a variety of agreements that come within the ambit of section 1. They can be divided into three procedural categories, beginning with the most stringent: agreements that require express approval, often referred to as "approval cartels" (*Erlaubniskarlelle*); agreements that require notification and do not become effective for three months to allow review and objection or "opposition" (*Widerspruchskartelle*); and those that become effective upon filing but are also subject to review and opposition by the enforcement authorities, so-called notification cartels (*Anmeldungskartelle*).

The 1990 amendment added section 5c (current § 4[2]), an exemption for purchasing cartels (*Einkaufskooperationen*) intended to increase the efficiency of small and medium enterprises. The provision as enacted did not require notification as proposed in the government's original bill.[1] The provision for notification was deleted in the Bundestag to spare small firms the costs and other burdens of registration, and current section 9 continues to exempt such cartels from any notification requirement. The 1990 amendment thus in effect introduced a fourth category of exempt cartels that are defined to be outside the scope of the basic prohibition of section 1 of the GWB for which no notification is necessary.

For a brief period the notification requirement of section 9(2) was not applied to export cartels not affecting German markets. This was the result of the Federal Supreme Court's 1973 decision in the *Oil Field Pipe* case (*Ölfeldrohre*),[2] which held that under section 98(2) export cartels having no effect on German markets were beyond the scope of the GWB. The 1980 amendment added a provision to section 98(2) expressly applying the statute (and thus the notification requirement) to all export cartels exempted under section 6(1) insofar as any party (including corporations) to the cartel agreement "resides" in Germany. Export and import cartels were repealed under the 1998 amendment.

Exempted subject to approval are "structural crisis" or recession cartels (*Strukturkrisenkartelle*) under section 6 (former § 4) and special emergency cartels that require approval by the federal minister of economics rather than the Federal Cartel Office under section 8 (*Gemeinwohlkartelle*). Subject to notification and objection procedures with a three-month delay to become effective (§ 9) are agreements for standardized terms and conditions of trade, excluding price, under section 2 (*Konditionenkartelle*); agreements for specialization by the parties to achieve efficiency (*Spezialisierungskartelle*) under section 3 (former § 5a[1]); and agreements for cooperation among small and medium enterprises to promote efficiency under section 4 (former § 5b) (*Kooperationskartelle*).

Agreements for uniform standards and component parts to promote efficiency (*Normen- und Typenkartelle*) under section 2 (former § 5[1]) have been made subject to opposition procedures, but those standardizing methods for the specification of services and calculating costs for bids (*Angebotsschema-Kartelle*) continue to need only to be filed.

Other exclusions and exemptions include the exemptions under section 15 for resale price maintenance (otherwise invalidated under section 14) for books and other publications (subject to FCO prohibition under section 15[3] and under section 17(3) for restrictive licenses of industrial property rights and know-how (prohibited under section 17[1] if not approved). Sections 8 through 31 (former §§ 99–105) exclude from the jurisdictional scope of the GWB a variety of specific industries and public institutions subject to regulation under separate statutes, such as banking, insurance, and agriculture, but with qualification. Deregulation and privatization measures have required significant amendments to these exemptions. For example, the 1998 amendment deleted transportation and public utilities. Finally, the provisions of chapter 4 operate as a type of exemption by permitting trade and professional associations to establish rules governing competition (*Wettbewerbsregeln*) subject to registration and consequent FCO review.

The procedures for approvals, filing of notifications, and the FCO's generally applicable powers in overseeing these exemptions are contained in sections 9 through 13. The *Land* authorities are competent to grant approvals or review notification cartels that do not affect markets outside of the *Land*. The remaining provisions of part 1 deal with sanctions: private damage actions and injunctive relief (§ 34, former § 35), administrative prohibition orders (§ 32, former § 37a), administrative sanctions (§ 34, former §§ 38 and 39). The organization and general powers of the FCO and *Land* enforcement authorities are covered in part 2 (§§ 48–53, former §§ 44–50). Administrative proceedings and judicial appeals are treated in part 3 (§§ 54–96, former §§ 55–96). A new part 4 was added in 1998 for government procurement contracts (§§ 97–129). The scope of the GWB including jurisdictive law is covered in part 5, section 130 (former § 98). Finally, section 131, also in part 5, contains the necessary transitional provisions as the 1998 amendment became effective.

As a result of the 1998 amendment, GWB has become a much more tidily organized statute. Provisions construed to have been out of place have been rearranged. Moreover, the authorities now exercise an array of specific powers subject to various procedural requirements that are no longer set out throughout the substantive sections of the statute.

The GWB as enacted proscribed anticompetitive conduct either by invalidating or nullifying restrictive agreements or resolutions or by expressly prohibiting restrictive conduct. Section 1, for example, declared that anticompetitive agreements and resolutions for a common purpose were ineffective (*unwirksam*), and sections 20 and 21 similarly invalidated restrictive licenses of industrial property and know-how. In contrast, section 15 provided that agreements or resolutions restricting one party's freedom to set prices or the terms of trade were null and void (*nichtig*), and the GWB subjected concerted conduct (§ 25), abuses of market power (§ 22 [5]), and discriminatory conduct, including refusals to deal (§ 26), to express prohibition (*Verbot*). The powers of the enforcement authorities paralleled this structure: they had the power either to declare the agreements or resolutions ineffective or to prohibit the conduct. (see, for example, former §§ 12, 17, 18 22[5], and 24[2]). The only agreements subject to nullification, however, were those covered by former section 15. This requirement foreclosed any possible argument that they could be exempted by the FCO or other enforcement authority.[3] The current statute as noted, now expressly prohibits all proscribed anticompetitive conduct, thus simplifying the statute.

The consequences of ineffectiveness or nullification depended upon the application of general civil law principles, particularly section 139 of the German Civil Code (*Bürgerliches Gesetzbuch* or BGB), which provides that nullification presumptively invalidates the entire contract (juristic act), a provision that can be significant.[4] The distinction was also important at least in theory in determining whether a damage action can be considered a violation. Otherwise, the same sanctions applied whenever a party was found to "disregard" (*Hinwegsetzen*) either the ineffectiveness or nullity of an agreement or resolution or violating a prohibition (see former § 38[1] 1 and 8). The 1998 amendment has eliminated these issues.

The GWB continues to set out the procedural requirements for three types of enforcement proceedings. Two are detailed in chapter 2: ordinary administrative proceedings (*Verwaltungsverfahren*) and civil court actions (*bürgerliche Rechsstreitigkeiten*) in which a violation of the GWB is at issue (§§ 87–91) The third proceeding applies to violations of the GWB treated as *Ordnungswidrigkeiten*. This is a term usually translated into English as "administrative offenses."[5] They are governed, unless otherwise provided in the GWB, by the separate *Gesetz über Ordnungswidrigkeiten* (OWIG)[6] and are thereby subject to administrative fines (*Bußgeld*), not criminal penalties. The GWB also provides for private injunctive relief and damage actions (current § 33). Although the GWB provides for only ordinary, not treble or, as some have proposed,[7] double damages, the enforcement authorities are empowered to levy an excess charge (*Mehrerlös*, officialy translated as "skimming-off additional proceeds") for amounts derived from illegal acts (current § 34, added in 1980, as § 37b). Section 38(4) allows the charge to exceed the 1 million DM maximum fine by treble the amount of any illegal gains. Despite proposals in the late 1970s to add criminal penalties for certain violations, discussed subsequently in detail, violations of the GWB are not subject to criminal sanctions. A recent amendment to the German Criminal Code, however, separately makes bid rigging a crime.[8]

## THE JAPANESE ANTIMONOPOLY LAW

As enacted, the Antimonopoly Law reflects its exclusively American origins. Combining, as described in chapter 1, features of the U.S. Sherman, Clayton, and Federal Trade Commission acts, the statute contains broadly worded general and specific prohibitions that go well beyond even the reach of American legislation. Unlike American legislation, however, the Japanese statute depends more on administrative than judicial interpretation. Thus the statute gives Japanese enforcement authorities wide latitude in applying the law.

Despite extensive amendments in 1949 and 1953, the basic statute remained intact. The 1977 amendment added several new provisions and, to some extent, restored in new guise earlier deletions. All but the most recent of the amendments since 1977 strengthened the statute, particularly its penalties.

In 1997, as noted, the statute's prohibition of holding companies (art. 9) was revised to allow holding companies that do not exert an "excessive concentration of power over other enterprises." And in 1998 the shareholding restrictions were eased.

The statute's basic general prohibitions cover "private monopolization" (*shiteki dokusen*) and "unreasonable restraints of trade" (*futō na torihiki seigen*) both prohibited in article 3. In addition, the statute prohibits "unfair business practices" (*fukōsei na torihiki hōhō*) in article 19. Both private monopolization and unreasonable restraints of trade, but not unfair business practices, are subject to criminal sanctions, an anomaly explained by the origins of the former in the U.S. Sherman Act and the latter, the U.S. Federal Trade Commission Act. The 1977 amendments also empower the Japanese FTC to take remedial measures, including dissolution and divorcement, against enterprises in a "state of monopoly" (*dokusen-teki jōtai*) (arts. 8–4), but as yet there has been no enforcement of this provision.

International transactions are regulated under a general prohibition that forbids any Japanese entrepreneur from entering international agreements containing either unreasonable restraints of trade or unfair business practices (art. 6[1]) and, until 1997, a filing requirement (art. 6[2]) originally intended to prevent Japanese participation in international cartels.[9] In practice the FTC used its review authority principally to protect Japanese firms from overreaching foreign licensors of intellectual property rights. One consequence of its repeal in 1997 will be to postpone any antitrust challenge of licensing restrictions and thereby to make more uncertain their legality at the time of the conclusion of the contract.

Article 8 incorporates the main prohibitions of the 1948 Trade Association Law, prohibiting trade associations from restricting competition, barring new entry, or engaging in unfair business practices. The FTC has also issued special guidelines for trade associations.[10]

Other provisions of the Antimonopoly Law attempt to preserve a competitive economic structure by prohibiting holding companies that (since 1997) create excessive concentration of power over other enterprises (art. 9) and regulating corporate shareholding (arts. 9[2], 10, and 11), interlocking directorates (art. 13), and mergers (art. 16). A provision requiring disclosure and justification of parallel price increases (art. 18[2]) was added in 1977.

Japanese antitrust law is commonly characterized by its exemptions. The product of conscious borrowing from the 1952 government draft of the GWB, as noted, since 1953 FTC- approved "recession" (*fukyō*) and "rationalization" (*gōrika*) cartels have been exempted under articles 24(3) and 24(4). Other provisions of the statute itself exempt the exercise of intellectual and industrial property rights (art. 23), natural monopolies (art. 21), regulated industries under special legislation (art. 22), and cooperatives (art. 24). Unlike German law, the majority of exempt cartels are the product of separate special legislation rather than the Antimonopoly Law itself. As noted in chapter 2 the list was substantial, but as in Germany the most significant, at least in number, have been cartels for exports and medium and small businesses. As noted previously, many cartel exemptions under special legislation were abolished or modified to eliminate their anticompetitive effects under omnibus legislation enacted in 1998.

Articles 27 through 44 relate to the organization and powers of the FTC, the exclusive enforcement agency. The procedures for enforcement actions are detailed in articles 45 through 76. The FTC has issued supplementary regulations that, as described subsequently, closely track GWB procedures. Judicial review is covered in articles 77 through 88(2).

The statutory remedies and sanctions for antitrust violations include single-damage actions based on FTC findings (arts. 25 and 26), criminal penalties (arts. 89 through 95[3]), court-ordered dissolution of trade associations (art. 95[4]), administrative fines (arts. 97 and 98), and most important, since 1977, the power of the FTC to surcharge entrepreneurs for profits resulting from unreasonable restraints of trade (article 7[2]).

Most of the postoccupation amendments to the Antimonopoly Law— whether weakening or strengthening Japanese competition policy—have had close identity with developments in German law. The most notable were the 1953 amendments, which reflected provisions in the GWB bill then being considered by the West German parliament. The most important addition of the 1977 amendments—the cartel profit surcharge—was also an innovation derived from German *Mehrerlös*. A significant difference has emerged in the 1990s as Japan continues to reduce the number of exempt cartels in law and practice, while in Germany they have increased on both counts.

A COMPARATIVE SUMMARY

*Monopoly Power*

The Japanese Antimonopoly Law begins in article 3 by prohibiting private monopolization—a direct borrowing from the U.S. Sherman Antitrust Act's proscription of monopoly and attempts to monopolize—and subjecting such monopolies to criminal sanctions. Article 2(5) defines "private monopolization" as "such business activities, by which any entrepreneur, individually or by combination or conspiracy with other entrepreneurs, or

TABLE I. Comparison of the Scope of the GWB and the Antimonopoly and Fair Trade Law

| | GWB | | Antimonopoly Law |
|---|---|---|---|
| | Former | Current | |
| **1. Horizontal restraints** | | | |
| Cartel agreements | §1 | §1 | The latter part of art.3 |
| Concerted action by competitors not subject to agreement | §25 (1) | | Included in the latter part of art.3 |
| **2. Vertical restraints** | | | |
| Resale price maintenance | §15 | §§14, 15 | Arts. 19, 26 |
| | | | General Designation No. 12 |
| Restrictions on terms and conditions of business | §15, 18 | §§14, 16 | Arts. 19, 6 |
| | | | General Designation No. 13 |
| Tying arrangements (and other license restrictions) | §§18, 20, 21 | §§17, 18 | Arts. 19, 6 |
| | | | General Designation No. 10 (See the Guideline for International License Agreements) |
| Exclusive dealing | §18 | §16 | Arts. 19, 6 |
| | | | General Designation No. 11 |
| **3. Other abuses** | | | |
| Boycotts and refusals to deal | §26 | §§20, 21 | Arts 19, 6, 8 |
| | | | General Designation Nos. 1 and 2 |
| Discriminatory practices | §26 (2, 3) | §20 | Arts. 19, 6,8 |
| | | | General Designation Nos. 3,4, and 5 |
| Excessive or unreasonably low prices (predatory pricing) | §§22 (4), 2 (in case of market-dominating enterprises) | §§20 (4) 2, 19 (4) 2, 3 | Arts. 19, 6 |
| | | | General Designation No. 6 |

| | | | |
|---|---|---|---|
| Unfair inducement to competitors' customers | §22 (4) (in case of market-dominating enterprises) | §19 (4) | Arts. 19, 6; General Designation Nos. 8,9 |
| Interference with appointment of officers | none | | Arts. 19, 6; General Designation No. 14 (v) |
| Abuse of dominant bargaining position | §22 (4) | §19 (4) | Arts. 19, 6; General Designation No. 14 |
| Interference with business activities of competitor | None | | Arts. 19, 6; General Designation No. 15 |
| Internal disruption of competing company | None | | Arts. 19, 6; General Designation No. 16 |
| *4. Structural Controls* | | | |
| Monopolization | None | | Art. 3, the former part of art. 8–4 |
| Merger, acquisitions, and consolidations | §§23, 24b | §§35–43 | Arts. 15, 16 |
| Holding companies | None | | Art. 9 (prohibition) |
| Shareholding restrictions | None | | Arts. 9-2, 10, 11, 14 |
| Interlocking directorates and officerships | None | | Art. 13 |
| *5. Other* | | | |
| Review of restrictive licenses | §§20, 21 | §§17, 18 | Art. 6(2) (international only) |
| Review of international agreements | None | | Art. 6(2) |
| Parallel price increases (reporting) | None | | Art. 18-2 |
| Review of association competition rules | §§28–39 | §§24–27 | None (trade associations generally regulated under art. 8) (Premium and Representation Law, art. 10) |
| Nullification | §15 | §§1, 14, 17, 18 | Arts. 3, 8, 19 |

by any other manner, excludes or controls the business activities of other entrepreneurs, thereby causing, contrary to the public interest, a substantial restraint of competition in any particular field of trade." To the extent that the provision is intended to deal with conduct that is intended to create or has the effect of creating monopoly power, then the only German parallel to this provision of Japanese (and U.S.) law is found in the GWB's provision dealing with abuses of a market-dominating position and concentration control. However, as a criminal prohibition or as a means to deal with firms that have by past, presumptively legal conduct acquired market or monopoly power, the prohibition has no counterpart in German law. Unlike the United States and subsequently, at least in statutory form, Japan, neither German nor European antitrust law attempts to restructure firms with existing market power. The approach of both, as indicated below, is to prevent abuses and, more recently through merger controls, the acquisition of monopoly power (or more accurately a "market-dominating position"). Although potentially a source of considerable divergence, in practice the Japanese prohibition of "private monopoly" and the 1977 grant of powers to deal with enterprises that are deemed to be in a "state of monopoly" have become increasingly extraneous. Only nine formal enforcement actions have been brought against private monopolization,[11] seven of which were successful. Two can only be considered aberrations in which the FTC stretched the concept of private monopolization to its farthest limits to deal with the quite separate problems of resale price maintenance[12] and consolidation.[13] To the extent that the facts are reported, the remaining cases correspond more closely to the German notion of "abuse" of a market-dominating position.[14] As explained in chapter 2, the lack of specific divestiture powers was one of the reasons given for the apparent failure of the FTC to use the prohibition against private monopolization more aggressively to require divestiture of firms that appeared to have monopoly power. Thus the 1977 amendment included the grant of powers to the FTC to deal with firms found to be in a "state of monopoly." Japanese practice has not differed from German law: the FTC has not acted in any case to date to correct a state of monopoly. One explanation is that no enterprise in Japan has yet satisfied the requirements of the provision.

### Horizontal Restraints

The second proscription of article 3 of the Antimonopoly Law prohibits "entrepreneurs" (*eigyōsha*) from engaging in any unreasonable restraint of trade, which in article 2(6) is defined to include any mutual restriction of business activities by "concerted action" causing a substantial restraint of competition in a particular field of trade contrary to the public interest. Although formal agreements need not be proven, the FTC and the courts consider that at least circumstantial evidence of agreement is necessary.[15] Parallel conduct is not sufficient.[16] The definition specifically refers to price fixing, output and supply restrictions, and limitations on technology, facilities, and customers or other trading parties. As in the case of private monopolization, violations are subject to criminal sanctions. The prohibition against unreasonable restraints on trade applies to international agreements under article 6 and trade associations under article 8.

In comparison, section 1 of the GWB, as amended, prohibits "[a]greements between competing undertakings, decisions by associations of undertakings and concerted practices which have as their object or effect the prevention, restriction or distortion of competition." The only significant difference in coverage between the provisions is the GWB's explicit inclusion of potential competition in determining the effect of a restriction.

From the perspective of U.S. antitrust law, the language of article 2(6) would not limit the prohibition of article 3 to horizontal restraints, but the Tokyo High Court in the 1953 *Asahi Newspaper case*[17] construed the language "concerted acts" as used in the subsequently deleted article 4 to apply only to agreements among competitors.[18] Despite suggestions that the question should be posed again, the FTC has followed this construction of "concerted acts" in all subsequent article 3 cases. The German Federal Supreme Court, on the other hand, early viewed GWB section 1 to encompass a requirements contract between a producer-wholesaler and retail tradesman insofar as the challenged agreement eliminated the producer as a potential competitor.[19]

## Vertical Restraints and Abuse of Dominant Market Position

The proscription against unfair business practices of articles 19, 6, and 8 has become the workhorse of the Antimonopoly Law. As defined in article 2(9), an unfair business practice is an act within any of the following categories, as designated by the FTC, that endangers fair competition:

1. unreasonable discrimination,
2. unreasonable pricing,
3. unreasonably inducing or causing customers of a competition to deal with oneself,
4. dealing with another party on conditions that unreasonably restrict its business,

5. unreasonable use of one's bargaining position in dealing with another party, and

6. unreasonably interfering in transactions between a competing entrepreneur in Japan or a company of which one is a shareholder or an officer of the company to act against its interest.

In 1953 the FTC issued a General Designation of Unfair Business Practices (FTC Notification No. 11, 1953) and since then twenty nine designations for specific industries. Beginning in 1996 the FTC reviewed and either abolished or significantly modified all specific industry designations.[20] The 1953 General Designation comprised twelve broadly worded items that covered nearly every conceivable type of anticompetitive restriction including refusals to deal, price discrimination, predatory or other unfair pricing practices, customer and supplies restrictions, tying arrangements, and abuses of a dominant bargaining position. In April 1982, the agency revised the General Designation, expanding the number of categories to sixteen items.[21] The principal contribution of the 1982 revision was to define somewhat more precisely the prohibited conduct as reflected in commission decisions since 1953. The types of conduct actually subject to FTC enforcement, however, have been far more limited. They include, first and foremost, resale price maintenance, except as authorized under article 24(2), and exclusive dealing. The array of other practices remains subject to potential enforcement.

The language of both the 1953 and 1982 General Designation is sufficiently broad to envelop all of the more specific proscriptions of the GWB, including various vertical restraints and abuses. Resale price maintenance, tying agreements, exclusive dealing, and customer restrictions covered under items 11, 12, and 13 of the 1982 General Designation (7 and 8 of the 1953 General Designation) are dealt with under sections 15 and 18 of the GWB. Similarly, items 1 through 10 of the 1982 General Designation (items 1 through 6 of the 1953 General Designation) are generous enough to apply to refusals to deal, discriminatory practices, and other abuses proscribed under current sections 10 and 21 (former §§ 25, 26) of the GWB. The 1982 General Designation also reflects the direct influence of German law in its introduction of an item explicitly covering abuses of a dominant bargaining position that corresponds to the provisions of section 19 (former § 22) of the GWB. The principal differences between Japanese and German law in these areas are less in coverage than enforcement. The breadth of the general principles of the General Designation permits the FTC and the courts in Japan to exercise significantly greater latitude in applying the statute than that available to German authorities.

## Merger and Concentration Control

As in other areas, the 1949 and 1953 amendments diluted the concentration-control provisions of Japanese law, but they did not undo them. The 1947 statute was the only legislation to contain an outright prohibition against holding companies, a requirement for FTC approval for corporate acquisition of shares in other corporations, limitations on share acquisitions by financial companies, restrictions on interlocking directorates, and a requirement for prior notification and approval for all mergers—which would be denied unless specific public interest criteria are met. These provisions complemented the basic prohibition against private monopolization of article 3, and except for the prohibition of holding companies, have been revised only slightly. The shareholding restrictions, for instance, have been eased by making the prohibition apply only to large firms and by increasing the financial company limitation to a 10 (as opposed to 5) percent interest. Mergers were made subject to prohibition procedures instead of prior approvals, but all corporate mergers and acquisitions regardless of size still have to be reported to the FTC. Among the most significant changes was the 1949 amendment of the pivotal term "competition" to exclude potential competition; moreover, mergers were no longer to be disallowed if they did not satisfy a strictly defined public interest test: they could be precluded only if they resulted in a "substantial [actual] restraint of competition." Still the Japanese statute as amended remains broader and much stronger than the GWB.

As enacted, the GWB contained no effective means to prevent undesirable concentration. The only foray into that area of regulation was the disclosure requirement of former sections 23 and 24 under which the parties concerned had to notify the authorities of mergers, defined broadly to include acquisitions of assets, shares, joint ventures, and management contracts. The authorities' only remedial power was to hold public hearings if, as a consequence of the merger, the consolidated enterprises would dominate the market. Not until the 1973 amendments was the FCO empowered to prohibit undesirable concentration, and even then only if such concentration resulted in a 20 percent or greater share of the market in a specific type of goods or services. Only in the event of such market share or if any one of the participating firms had 10,000 or more employees or a turnover that equaled or exceeded DM 500 million or assets valued at DM 1,000 million or more was there any reporting requirement. The 1998 amendments that became effective in 1999 made significant changes in the consolidation control provisions. As amended, section 39 requires that the FCO be notified of all mergers if during the year preceding the consolidation the participating enterprises had a combined turnover of at least DM one billion (U.S. $278 million), with several exemptions and modifications (§ 35) On the face of the statute, the German disclosure requirement continues to remain considerably less stringent than its Japanese counterpart.

The decision by the Council of the European Community in December 1989 to adopt the Regulation on the Control of Concentrations between Undertakings[22] marked a decisive change in European competition law with significant consequences for German and other national merger-control regimes. The regulation gives the European Commission exclusive jurisdiction over mergers with a "European Community dimension." This term of art is further defined to extend the commission's jurisdiction to mergers in which the parties have a combined worldwide turnover of at least ECU 5 billion (U.S. $5 billion) and the aggregate EC-wide turnover is greater than ECU 250 million. One consequence has been to confine the FCO merger-control authorities to relatively minor and purely "national" mergers. Under current section 35 (3) German merger control is preempted in cases where European merger controls apply

## Enforcement: An Overview

Anyone reasonably familiar with either German or Japanese competition policy over the past half century is likely to respond to the conclusion that Japanese law is broader in coverage than the GWB by quickly noting that statutory language provides an extremely limited and imperfect point of comparison. How the two statutes have actually been enforced, most will agree, is the critical question. A caveat must be added. Formal enforcement statistics alone provide an inadequate guide.[23] The question to be asked is to what extent have the two antitrust regimes contributed to a more competitive economy. The answer requires an analysis that takes into account both the differences in the two statutory regimes and the industrial structure and government regulations that affect new entry, firm rivalry, and the opportunities for the acquisition of monopoly power. Also, differences in the levels of formal enforcement need to be assessed in relation to the role and effectiveness of extralegal social controls.

Weak enforcement rather than weak statutory language has long been viewed as the major defect in Japanese competition policy. No one in either Germany or Japan has undertaken a thorough analysis of antitrust enforcement under either of the two statutes, much less a systematic comparison.

A simple statistical comparison of West German and Japanese enforcement is meaningless. First, as indicated above, none of the statutory provisions of the two statutes are identical. Many of the proscriptions of the GWB are treated in the Japanese statute under the more inclusive prohibition of "unfair business practices" in article 19 (as well as articles 6 and 8). Even in the one instance in which provisions of the two laws seem to have the closest resemblance—the proscription of cartel agreements and concerted acts under section 1 of the GWB and articles 3, 6, and 8 of the Antimonopoly Law—their coverage differs with respect to potential competition and vertical agreements. Moreover, in both countries the statistics published by the enforcement authorities are arranged by statutory provision and not by the factual content of the violation. As a result, it is impossible to make exact comparisons. Some apples are necessarily counted as oranges.

Nor are the enforcement mechanisms available to the authorities or their policies the same. As detailed in chapter 4, Japanese enforcement proceedings are subject to considerably greater procedural requirements. Moreover, the enforcement authorities in both systems resort in most cases to informal enforcement measures in the form of cautionary-warnings or agreements to discontinue the alleged violation that may be not included in published statistics.

A review of the statistics on enforcement does, however, suggest several conclusions. First, despite the greater apparent number of cases handled by the German authorities, there has not been significantly greater enforcement of the GWB, at least by the FCO, than of the Japanese Antimonopoly Law—especially, as indicated in table 2 (for even years only), in the area of illegal cartels. For example, between 1958 and 1996 the FCO handled a total of 4,717 cases under GWB section 1 (agreements and trade association decisions) and 47 cases under GWB section 25(1) (concerted action). In only 533 cases, however, was a violation formally determined to have been committed and a fine levied. In 696 cases the violation had ceased and proceedings were terminated. The *Land* authorities dealt with more cases—8,190 under GWB sections 1 and 25(1), of which 3,295 resulted in a formal determination that a violation had been committed and a fine. In 650 the proceedings were discontinued after the violation ceased. As noted in table 2, in 1978 the *Land* authorities found a violation and issued a fine in 2,559 cases. Excluding this aberration—the highest number in any other year was 92 in 1988—the *Land* authorities still handled and found violations in nearly twice as many cases as the FCO. In contrast, during the same period between 1958 and 1996, the Japanese FTC issued formal recommendation, consent, and contested decisions involving restraints of trade in 270 cases under article 3 and 407 under article 8, for a total of 677 cases. The cartel enforcement activity of the FTC was thus comparable to that of the FCO. The cases handled by the *Land* authorities are said

TABLE 2. Formal FCO and FTC Enforcement Actions
against Horizontal Restraints of Competition 1948–1996
(GWB §§1 and 25 [1]; AML arts. 3 [latter part] and art. 8)

| Year | FCO* (Land *Authorities*) | FTC** |
|------|---------------------------|-------|
| 1948 | NA | 2 |
|  | NA | 25 |
| 1952 | NA | 5 |
| 1954 | NA | 1 (1) |
| 1956 | NA | 3 (2) |
| 1958 | 0 (37) | 2 (2) |
| 1960 | 0 (23) | 1 (1) |
| 1962 | 0 (4) | 10 (10) |
| 1964 | 0 (0) | 29 (20) |
| 1966 | 2 (1) | 15 (15) |
| 1968 | 2 (1) | 28 (22) |
| 1970 | 1 (12) | 43 (40) |
| 1972 | 2 (21) | 21 (11) |
| 1974 | 7 (6) | 42 (11) |
| 1976 | 28 (34) | 20 (6) |
| 1978 | 7 (2,559) | 3 (2) |
| 1979/80 | 44 (123) | 12 (8) |
| 1982 | 5 (36) | 12 (7) |
| 1984 | 4 (50) | 9 (5) |
| 1986 | 1 (19) | 4 (1) |
| 1988 | 9 (92) | 5 (0) |
| 1990 | 9 (34) | 11 (7) |
| 1992 | 1 (72) | 34 (11) |
| 1994 | 3 (15) | 21 (14) |
| 1996 | 4 (37) | 23 (8) |

SOURCES: FCO Annual Reports, 1958–96; FTC Annual Report (1997), Appendix, pp. 40–41.
*Figures for Germany represent only final fine decisions. Numbers in parentheses are *Land* decisions.
**Figures for Japan include all formal decisions (recommendation, consent, and contested). Numbers in parentheses are trade association violations of article 8.

to be minor, with little if any effect beyond local markets,[24] and appear to be more typical of the types of cases the Japanese FTC routinely handles by administrative guidance.

Equally revealing are the figures related to cartel exemptions. Here, too, the initial impression that Japanese authorities have been much more permissive is deceptive. It is true that from 1958 to 1980 the total number of exempt cartels under Japanese law greatly exceeded that in Germany. In the period up to 1980, the maximum number of exempt cartels in any one year in Germany was 282. In Japan at no time since March 1958 were fewer than 401 cartels exempt in any one year, with a peak of 1,079 cartels exempted in 1966. As noted previously, most of the exempt cartels in Japan were authorized under special legislation for the protection of small and medium-sized business and in primary and related industries, such as fisheries and fertilizer. In Germany there are also exemptions for agriculture and other primary industries under the GWB, but they are treated as exclusions from the scope of the statute under section 100 rather than as authorized cartels. Export cartels were also been outside the scope of the GWB and thus not counted until 1980. Such cartels are not included in the statistics. The exemption for rationalization cartels to aid small and medium enterprises under GWB section 5b was not added until 1973. A similar purchasing cartel for small and medium enterprises was not added until 1990.

The contrast in the number of export cartels under the GWB and the export cartel exemptions under the Japanese Export and Import Transactions Law reflects a more complex set of factors. First, the Japanese figures are misleading in that they include as separate cartels what is essentially one transaction. For example, an export cartel covering a particular product may be the subject of agreements among manufacturers or decisions by exporters and exporter associations, requiring, say, four separate approvals and hence included in the statistics as four separate cartels listed under exempt export cartels. Also, prior to 1981, as noted above, the parties to an export cartel that the parties deemed not to affect domestic West German markets were not subject to the GWB under section 98(1) and thus needed no exemption. In 1980 section 98(1) was amended, however, to require filing of all export cartel agreements regardless of their domestic effect. As noted, this provision was deleted in 1998. Japanese law, on the other hand, required MITI approval and FTC filing for all export cartels regardless of their effect within Japan. In fact, most Japanese export cartels are believed to have had no effect within Japan and therefore would not have been subject to filing requirements in West Germany before 1980.

The influence of European competition law also has to be taken into account in comparing German and Japanese exempt cartels. The prevention of private arrangements and other nongovernmental constraints on the free movement of goods within the European Common Market has been the primary emphasis of European competition policy. Thus any arrangements for market division or other restraints on competition that would impede competition and the free flow of goods among the member states—whether or not such arrangements might have any effect within a single member's market—come within the purview of European competition law enforcement. Because European markets absorb the majority of German exports,[25] most general export cartels under the GWB were subject to European prohibitions. No supervisory antitrust authority restricted the Japanese exemption.

At least through the 1970s the Japanese authorities, especially MITI and other economic ministries, also apparently gave greater encouragement to the formation of cartels in general than German authorities did. One may also question whether for exemptions that require filing and review by MITI or other ministries, as in the case of export and import cartels, these authorities scrutinized the cartels as carefully as the FCO or the FTC might have to determine whether the statutory standards were satisfied—in the case of export or import cartels, whether they had an effect on Japanese markets. One seldom noted reason for the more permissive attitude of Japanese officials is related to the use of cartels, including export and import cartels, as a vehicle for domestic regulation of business.[26]

Stated bluntly, in addition to control over foreign exchange, government oversight of exports and imports has made available to Japan's economic ministries an array of carrots and sticks useful as indirect sanctions in the regulation of the domestic economy. In cooperation with trade associations the Japanese ministries made fairly extensive use of voluntary export and import cartels as one means of controlling resources, the withholding of which from a firm or group of firms served as a sanction. In addition, export cartels often reflected a Japanese response to pressures from foreign governments, especially the United States, against dumping or voluntary export restraints as exemplified in automobile exports, pressures that the German government has not faced to the same degree.

Finally, in the case of Germany, the principal governmental authority for approval or prohibition of an exemption has been the FCO or in some instances *Land* authorities. Only in the case of emergency cartels under GWB section 8 does the federal minister of economics have the authority to approve an exemption. In Japan, on the other hand, the role of the FTC has been in most instances limited. A statute may have granted it extensive authority for oversight, but such formal legal power has been generally illusory in practice. It has been more in keeping with realities to construe a requirement to file with the FTC any exempt agreement approved by MITI or other economic ministries as a mere record-keeping device. Only where a statute provides for FTC approval is Japanese law comparable to German law. If the consequence of such an institutional arrangement has been an increase in the number of exemptions, it may have made little difference whether the FTC or MITI was the more permissive in terms of economic effect. However, as seen in the Kishi cabinet's attempt to amend the Antimonopoly Law in 1958, the commission did exert a restraining influence. Nor, as noted previously, did MITI's or any other economic ministry's support for cartels in itself establish an exemption. The arrangements had to comply with statutory requirements, including reporting to the FTC. In practice, behind-the-scenes negotiations with FTC staff often took place to preclude potential public objections in any case that could be perceived to restrict competition significantly within Japan. The decrease in the number of authorized export cartels since 1966 is at least in part a reflection of FTC persuasion.

To assess accurately the level of enforcement by the FTC in comparison with the FCO between 1958 and 1998, it is necessary to examine exemptions that are at least roughly similar in content and similarly subject to approval by the respective enforcement agencies. The exemptions for recession and rationalization cartels under the Antimonopoly Law are the two most important. They are comparable to those available under the GWB. Here, too, the Japanese experience does not significantly differ from the German.

Section 6 (former § 4) of the GWB permits the FCO to approve cartel agreements "in the event of a decline in sales caused by a lasting change in demand . . . provided that the agreement or resolution is necessary to systematically adjust capacity to demand, and the arrangement takes into account the conditions of competition in the economics sectors concerned the public welfare."

So-called *Strukturkrisen* or recession cartels under this provision are permitted within a narrower range of circumstances than recession (*fukyō*) cartels under article 24(3) of the Japanese statute. The latter provides for similar approval by the FTC "where there exists extreme disequilibrium of supply and demand for particular goods" when (1) "the price of the goods is below the average cost of production and a considerable part of the enterprise in the business concerned may eventually be forced to discontinue production," and (2) "it is difficult to overcome such circumstances by the rationalization of individual enterprises."

Unlike the practice in Germany, a recession cartel in Japan may be permitted in cases of overproduction. This difference explains why the FCO has denied each of the six applications for exemption under section 6, while the FTC has approved exemptions in similar cases far more frequently. Yet in Japan, except for 1966 when there were sixteen exempt recession cartels in effect and 1972 when there were nine, there have rarely been more than two recession cartels in effect in any single year. Moreover, the requirements were deemed stringent enough by MITI and others in 1958 to require amendments in light of the broader scope for an exemption under Japanese law. The FTC has been significantly more lenient than the FCO.

Section 5, (former §§ 5, 5a, and 5b) of the GWB provides for various types of rationalization cartels (*Rationalisierungskartelle*). The comparable exemption is subsumed under the more inclusive provision of article 24(4) of the Japanese statute. Despite some differences in language, the scope of the rationalization exemptions is quite similar under the more inclusive provision of article 24(4) of the Japanese statute. Article 24(4) of the Japanese statute exempts, subject to FTC approval, "concerted acts by producers . . . when particularly necessary to promote technical improvements, improve quality, reduce costs, increase efficiency or promote any other enterprise rationalization." FTC approval is to be denied, however, if the arrangement (1) "endangers customer interests," (2) risks "destroying the interest of the general consumer and of related entrepreneurs," (3) is "unjustly discriminatory," (4) "unreasonably restricts participation or withdrawal," or (5) "unduly concentrates the production of specific products to particular entrepreneurs."

The German statute provides in contrast for a general rationalization exemption in section 5(1) as well as more specific exemptions for price-fixing and joint-purchase and -selling arrangements under section 5(2). The 1998 amendment eliminated the division of production or service—so-called specialization cartels—under former section 5a, and rationalization cartels for small and medium-scale businesses under former section 5b. The general provision of section 5(1) allows cartels, subject to FCO approval, "which serve to rationalize economic activities . . . provided they are a suitable means of substantially, increasing the efficiency of productivity of the participating enterprises in technical, economic, or organizational respects and of thereby improving the satisfaction of demand." Section 5(2) sets a more stringent standard for price-fixing or joint-purchase or -sale arrangements by limiting approval to cases in which the rationalization objectives cannot be met by any other means. The standards for specialization cartels and small and medium-scale business cartels under former section 5b were much more lenient. Such cartels were subject to notification rather than approval procedures and could be denied only if competition was substantially impaired. As we have seen in comparing other provisions of the two statutes, the language of the Japanese statute can be read to define more narrowly the permissible limits of the exemption. Again we are left with a question of enforcement.

In comparison to the 4–13 rationalization cartels in effect in Japan each year from 1952 to 1974, no rationalization cartels under former section 5(2) or 5(3) were approved by the FCO. Nonetheless, numerous cartels were formed under sections 5a and 5b.

All caveats taken into account, the data on the exempt cartels under Japanese and German law over the past five decades reveal a surprising convergence (see figure 1). The number of exempt cartels in effect under German law has steadily increased. By 1990 as many exempt cartels were in force in Germany as in Japan. The peak of cartel activity for Japan was reached three decades ago. Except for the two-year period between 1971 and 1973, following the "Nixon" shock ending the era of fixed exchange rates, since 1966 the number of exempt cartels in Japan has fallen quite dramatically, especially between 1973 and 1976 immediately after the first OPEC oil embargo. Although the number in both countries is now small, in 1997 Germany had seven times as many formally exempt cartels as Japan. In both countries these tend to be arrangements among small and medium enterprises for "rationalization" and stability. Any differences are likely to be found in distribution. Japanese wholesale markets appear to be more extensively subject to exempt cartel and cartel-like arrangements (such as cooperatives) than those in Germany. This difference can be explained by geographic differences, as well as by the influence of the European Common Market and competition law. Unlike Japanese, German wholesalers are unable for both reasons to preclude competition from outside Germany. Equally if not more significant have been recent legislative actions. In Germany the 1990 amendment introduced a new small and medium enterprise-purchasing cartel exemption.

However, in 1998 the exemptions for rebate, export, and import cartels were eliminated. Japan also moved dramatically in this direction under the 1998 omnibus legislation that repealed or significantly modified the majority of all special cartel exemptions, including export and import cartels.

A similar pattern of convergence but with notable differences in context and consequences is evident with respect to mergers and other forms of corporate consolidation. The Japanese statute was the first in the world to provide for premerger notification and review, applicable to all mergers and acquisitions of assets. On the other hand, only since 1973 has the GWB required reporting and approval—but only for significant mergers and consolidations. The filing requirements under both statutes, as noted above, cover a broad set of consolidation arrangements. Moreover, as noted, since 1989 mergers and other consolidations among the largest enterprises that affect the European Union have been subject to the exclusive jurisdiction of the European Commission.

As in the case of exempt cartels, the number of significant mergers in Germany has steadily increased. Far fewer major mergers have occurred in Japan, and the number has also been relatively constant, except for minor fluctuations corresponding to economic conditions (figure 2).

A narrow focus on the number of mergers and consolidations the authorities have barred under the two statutes might lead some to conclude that German merger controls are more effective. Unless one counts the *Yawata–Fuji Steel Merger* case, which resulted in a consent decision after considerable political pressure on the FTC, no merger has been prohibited by the FTC. In contrast, in Germany through 1980 there were 35 instances of a prohibited merger.[27] In both countries considerable negotiation and informal adjustment takes place. The Japanese authorities appear superficially to be less stringent.

A more accurate assessment challenges such views. Japanese industrial structure, firm organization, and societal values make any form of enterprise consolidation quite difficult and thus equally exceptional. Until the 1980s hardly any consolidation occurred in Japan that would even have had to be reported to the German authorities. Very few of even the largest of the mergers reported to the FTC would have been subject to notification requirements under the GWB. The Japanese statistics (see figure 2) are based on the capitalization of the consolidated firms. In Germany the reporting requirements are based on annual turnover. Very few if any of the reporting Japanese firms had a combined turnover that would have required notification under the GWB standards. For example, of the 367 reported Japanese mergers resulting in a consolidated enterprise with a capitalization of at least ¥5 billion (U.S. $41.5 million) in 1996 only 103 had a capitalization of more than ¥10 billion (U.S. $83 million). Very few of these merging enterprises would have satisfied the German reporting requirement of a combined turnover during the preceding year of at least DM 500 million (U.S. $278 million in the past, now one billion). In fact, since 1980 there were fewer than 50 mergers that even the Japanese authorities considered significant.[28]

Two factors help to explain the relatively low incidence of mergers in Japan. Although in both countries small and medium firms tend to be family firms, in Japan the prevalence of adult adoption enables continuity of a family firm. Thus less incentive exists for acquisition of family firms upon the death of the founders. In the case of larger firms, the communitarian aspects of bureaucratic organizations in Japan are even more pronounced. Permanent employment without lateral entry or exit creates stability and cohesion. Large

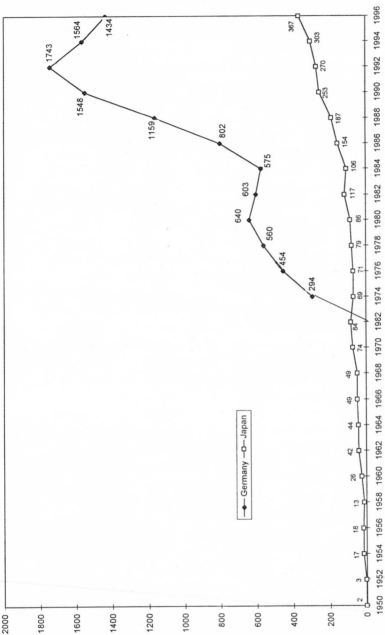

FIG. 2. Mergers and Acquisitions Reported to the Federal Cartel Office and the Fair Trade Commission, 1950–96

*Germany:* Total number of proposed consolidations reported for review (limited under GWB § 23 to enterprises with a combined annual turnover during the year preceding the proposed consolidation of at least 500 million DM [U.S. $278 million]

*Japan:* Included her are the number of reports for mergers that resulted in consolidated enterprises with a capitalization of at least 5 billion yen (U.S. $41.5 million)

SOURCES: FCO Annual Report (1997), p. 156; *Fifty–Year History,* vol. 2, pp. 400–3.

Japanese enterprises become in effect closed communities characterized by distinctive corporate cultures. As a result the merger of large enterprises entails formidable long-term barriers to the successful integration of personnel as well as reductions in costs through employee discharges or layoffs. Mergers among larger businesses are therefore rare except in cases of distress. These cultural and institutional differences help to explain why mergers have not posed as serious a problem for competition policy in Japan as in Germany.

Taking into consideration statutory language, the extent of informal enforcement, and differences in context, the statistics on enforcement do not reveal substantial differences between Germany and Japan. In no area of antitrust control does a statistical comparison indicate that Japan is today more permissive of anticompetitive practices. In both Germany and Japan antitrust enforcement has been used first and foremost to prevent price fixing and output restrictions among competitors. In neither country has antitrust law been solely a means to ensure competitive markets to enhance economic efficiency. Antitrust in Germany and antitrust controls in Japan have been used to protect smaller and less efficient firms against their larger and more efficient rivals.

With respect to both cartel exemptions and mergers, the differences between German and Japanese antitrust law are telling. The Japanese patterns correspond more to cyclical needs—with more exemptions granted along with more vigorous enforcement to prevent unauthorized practices during periods of overcapacity or reduced demand—than do the German patterns. In contrast, the number of exemptions and permitted mergers has increased with linear consistency in Germany. The number of exempt cartels in Germany, as indicated in figure 1, is now higher than in Japan, and the number of significant consolidations several times greater (see figure 2). The structure of the German economy has seemed to become gradually more rigid and less competitive. The justification that cartels are the "children of distress" (*Kinder der Not*) thus seems today far less applicable to Germany than Japan.

# 4 / Processes and Procedures

The processes of antitrust enforcement in both Germany and Japan involve similarly constituted enforcement agencies with similar research, policy-making, and policing functions. In both, but more so in Germany, the policing task involves a variety of reporting, reviewing, and approval procedures as a means to control anticompetitive conduct. Nonetheless, the investigation and prosecution of antitrust violations—including violations of reporting and approval requirements—remain the principal function of the enforcement agencies. Antitrust enforcement in both countries thus involves a familiar series of procedural steps activated by complaint or agency concern over suspect conduct or by application for approvals. Agency review or investigation, with formal or informal adjudication, and possibly judicial review complete the process.

Despite the similarities in function, there has been little convergence in process. Antitrust enforcement procedures in the two countries differ in significant respects. Surprising perhaps to those who might anticipate a greater degree of discretion and informality in Japan, German not Japanese antitrust enforcement is characterized by a relative lack of procedural requirements—particularly the separation of investigatory and prosecutorial functions—as well as by broad prosecutorial discretion enjoyed by the enforcement authorities. The patterns set under the occupation deconcentration legislation, exemplified by the lack of procedural requirements in Law No. 56 in occupied Germany in contrast to the detailed provisions of Law No. 207 in Japan, prevails today. In comparison to German law, Japanese antitrust enforcement procedures are exceptional for their detail and formality. Unlike other administrative processes, antitrust procedures track quite closely their American antecedents, and American standards for procedural due process continue to influence Japanese procedural requirements. A noteworthy difference that does confirm conventional wisdom is the greater resort in Germany to the courts to challenge FCO actions. Predictably in Japan fewer formal actions are brought and far fewer cases are appealed.

A specialized independent or quasi-independent agency is responsible for antitrust enforcement in both Germany and Japan. Both countries have adapted an American-styled enforcement agency to a ministerial cabinet system. For Germany, the creation of the FCO as a quasi-independent enforcement agency was an autonomous German decision. Enforcement of antitrust policy was to be insulated to the extent possible from those responsible for implementing general economic policies without sacrificing the principle of executive accountability to parliament through a ministerial cabinet. Japan had little choice. As described in chapter 1, the Japanese drafters of the law preferred to create an antitrust enforcement authority within the Ministry of Justice following the example of the Antitrust Division in the U.S. Department of Justice, but the American occupation authorities insisted on an independent agency. Japan's only fully autonomous decision was whether to reorganize or to dismantle the FTC once occupation ended. That the FTC survived as an independent agency may perhaps reflect the persuasive force of similar policy concerns, but only in combination with the political effort needed to transform an institutional status quo and residual concern over potential criticism from the United States. To appreciate the process of antitrust enforcement, we need to carefully examine both agencies, their organization, and their powers. Of particular concern is the influence on effective antitrust enforcement of institutional features common to both.

## THE GERMAN FEDERAL CARTEL OFFICE
## AND LAND CARTEL AUTHORITIES

The FCO, until 1999 in Berlin and thereafter in Bonn, is the primary but not exclusive antitrust enforcement agency for the German Federal Republic. Each *Land* shares some responsibility for enforcement in cases that affect only local markets. The FCO exercised exclusive authority in the following cases prior to 1999: approvals for *Strukturkrisen* cartels and export and import cartels (§ 44[1]1a), oversight over permissible resale price maintenance for publications and nonbinding resale price recommendations (*unverbindliche Preisempfehlungen*) for trademarked goods (*Markenwaren*) (§ 44[1]1b), disallowing unauthorized mergers except when approved by the federal minister of economics (§ 44[1]1c), and enforcement actions involving antitrust violations by the Federal Postal Service and the Federal Railway (§ 44[1]1e). The FCO continues to exercise all other enforcement powers under the GWB where the effects of the conduct in question extend beyond the jurisdiction of one *Land* (current § 48[2], former § 44[1]1d). In all other cases the competent authority, as determined by state law in each of Germany's sixteen *Land* (including the five *Länder* created upon unification in 1990), has concurrent jurisdiction. In addition, the GWB gives the federal minister of economics the authority to approve emergency cartels under section 8 and to override FCO decisions to prohibit mergers, currently under section 36 (see former §§ 24 and 44[2]; current § 42). The authority of the FCO has also been increasingly shared or supplanted by the European competition enforcement authorities in Brussels.

As a semi-independent regulatory agency (§ 51[1] 1) within the Federal Ministry of Economics, the FCO is subject to binding general directives (*allgemeine Weisungen*), which, under the express provisions of section 52 (former § 49), must be published in the *Federal Gazette* (*Bundesanzeiger*) by the federal minister of economics. Former section 48 was also construed to give the economics minister the authority to issue similarly binding but not necessarily published directives in specific cases (*Einzelweisungen*).[1] Given the discretion of the FCO over whether to prosecute a particular case,[2] the potential scope of this authority was quite broad. It appears likely that the new section 48, which refers to the ministry as a cartel authority, will be similarly construed. Despite the potential for tension and conflict this dual status produces,[3] intervention by the economics minister has been rare. The FCO has not pressed for complete autonomy. The power to issue directives has been used only five times—none since 1980—in the form of four general directives[4] and only one specific directive.[5] Past FCO presidents have rejected as unnecessary suggestions that the office be made a completely separate agency similar to the United States Federal Trade Commission.[6] Some still argue for complete FCO autonomy.[7] The tension is considered unavoidable under German constitutional requirements for executive accountability (German Constitution article 87[3]) and the quasi-judicial functions of the FCO.[8] The directives of the minister of economics must conform to the mandates of the GWB, but ministerial directives are not binding on the courts.[9]

The *Land* authorities generally lack the autonomy of the FCO. They are in most instances simply sections of the *Land* economics ministries (*Landeswirtschaftsministerium*) with the ministry acting as the "official authority" under section 48. Most have a small staff of three to nine people, who also handle other consumer-protection cases.[10] Despite the constraints of limited

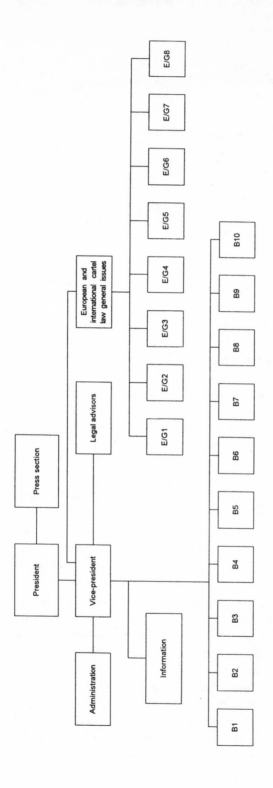

(Legend on facing page)

FIG. 3. Federal Cartel Office

*FIG. 3 LEGEND:*

E/G 1: Harmonization of cartel practice
E/G 2: General questions, public relations
E/G 3: European cartel law
E/G 4: General and European merger control
E/G 5: International competition questions
E/G 6: Cartels
E/G 7: Market domination

*Beschlußabteilung*

B1: Nonmetalic minerals (excluding fertilizers), asbestos goods, abrasives, true ceramics, glass and glassware, lumber, plywood and other wood products, constructions and real estate

B2: Leather, leather goods, footwear, textile, clothing, food products, agriculture and forestry, horticulture and viticulture, fishing and hunting; also condition cartels and recommendations

B3: Chemical products (except photochemicals), fertilizer, plastics and plastic products, rubber products

B4: Machine tools, precision and optical instruments, watches, music instruments, toys, gymnastic and sport equipment, jewelry, containers, and photochemical equipment

B5: Coal, iron and steel, nonprecious metals, metal semimanufactures, steel abrasive and cold-rolling mill and other steel-manufacturing products, streetcars, ships, iron, sheet and metalware; also license contracts, inquiries by public authorities

B6: Printing products, tobacco products, public photocopy, performing arts, film industry, copyrighted products

B7: Aircraft and motor vehicles locomotive and railroad cars, electronic goods, office data-processing equipment and telecommunications

B8: Mining (except coal), petroleum, nuclear fuel, banking and securities, and energy-related utilities

B9: Wholesale, retail and other dealers, tourism, transportation, commercial and industry inquiries

B10: Pulp and paper, paper and cardboard goods, advertising and other auxiliary commercial trades, health care, independent trades, free professions, insurance (including social insurance)

resources, a few are relatively active.[11] Their caseloads generally exceed that of the FCO. Although subject to the political demands of the *Land* governments, they are also constrained by the direct or indirect guidance of the FCO[12] as well as judicial review. Given the novelty of antitrust and the continuing process of privatization and economic restructuring, it is not surprising that there has been very little antitrust enforcement in the five *Länder* of the former Democratic Republic of Germany.

## Organization

The FCO is organized into ten *Beschlußabteilungen* or decisional divisions, each of which has jurisdiction over designated industries and, to some degree, enforcement of particular provisions of the GWB (fig. 3). *Beschlußabteilung* 5, for example, is responsible for oversight of the iron and steel and other metals-related industries and has principal enforcement responsibility for license agreements and resale price recommendations. The *Beschlußabteilungen* are thus the critical sections of the FCO in that they handle all approval, policing, and prosecutional functions. All administrative actions or orders (*Verfügungen*) are "collegial" decisions—that is, they are made by a panel of at least three people (§ 51[3]) appointed by the director of the division. In deciding a particular case, the panel acts independently. There is, however, no separation of functions. The same individuals who investigated a case and urged its prosecution may sit on the panel to decide whether a violation was committed and to levy a fine.[13] The section directors are senior officials, and many if not most remain in the post for extended periods. Four of the current directors have each held the post for at least ten years.[14] One has been a division director for more than twenty years, serving as head of two separate divisions for about ten years in each. The directors thus acquire extensive expertise and knowledge about the industries subject to the section's jurisdiction as well as about the leading executives and managers in the industries.

In addition to the *Beschlußabteilungen* are several administrative posts or divisions such as the press officer and administrative section, as well as reference sections that provide technical expertise and advice on particular enforcement areas, such as mergers, cartels, market power, international competition, antitrust regulation for the European Union, and other matters.

### Personnel

The FCO is relatively small. In 1997 the staff totaled only 231. Two-fifths have basic degrees or additional qualifications in law or economics. The majority are law trained, especially those assigned to the *Beschlußabteilungen*.[15] Section 51 (4) of the GWB provides that the chair of each panel deciding a case should have the qualification of a judge. In other words, the chair must have completed at least three and a half years of study in law and have passed the two state examinations with two years of practical training as *Referendar* with a civil court, criminal court or public prosecutor, administrative office, and law office for a minimum of three months each.[16] (Most professors of law at German universities are similarly qualified.[17]) The other members have at least the qualifications for higher civil service—that is, they must have completed university requirements in law, economics, finance, or social science and have passed the civil service examination. Those qualified as judges automatically qualify.[18] All personnel are civil servants with lifetime appointments (GWB § 51[4]).

The president of the FCO is a pivotal position although its duties are nowhere defined in the GWB. The GWB refers to the president in only two provisions. The first requires consent by the president for any decision ordering inspection or "verification" of books and documents (*Prüfung*) (§ 59[7]), but not for disclosure of information (§ 59[6]) or searches (§ 59[4]). Under section 90(2) the president is empowered to appoint a member of the office to represent it in any civil litigation arising under the GWB to ensure that the views of the office are presented. Nonetheless, the president exercises significant if subtle influence on the office, guiding the direction of antitrust enforcement. German success owes much to the intellectual stature and commitment of Eberhard Günther, who served as president during the first two decades of the office (1958–76). Appointed from the staff of the Economics Ministry, Günther had played a central role within the government in drafting the GWB and was the personal choice of Federal Economics Minister Ludwig Erhard.[19] Günther was succeeded by Wolfgang Kartte, who also played a major role in the development of German antitrust law. Kartte served as president of the FCO from 1976 through 1993. Dieter Wolf is the current president.

*Powers and Duties*

The GWB assigns reporting, policing, and prosecuting functions to the FCO and the *Land* enforcement authorities. With respect to the first, the FCO is obligated under section 53 of the GWB to prepare for publication a formal report (*Tätigkeitsbericht*) on the status of antitrust enforcement and recent developments. The report was originally prepared annually but, since the 1981 amendments, it has been issued every other year on a rotating basis with the Monopoly Commission's biannual report (§ 44[1]). The report must include details on all mergers reported under section 39 and any general directives issued by the federal minister of economics. In fact, it includes much more. It is one of the most valuable sources of information available on the enforcement of the GWB and the views of the FCO. It includes complete enforcement statistics for both the FCO and the *Land* authorities as well as the principal details of enforcement proceedings, exemptions, and recent court decisions.

Included among the policing responsibilities of the FCO and *Land* authorities are review and, if appropriate, objection to notification cartels and, in the case of the FCO, reported mergers; the denial of applications for cartel exemptions that require approval; and general oversight over unreported mergers, abuses of market power, refusals to deal and other illegal discriminatory conduct, and prohibited horizontal and vertical restraints. To perform these tasks fully would require that the FCO and *Land* authorities police the entire economy, obviously an impossible effort even without limited personnel. Thus while the authorities may act on their own initiative—and do so in many major cases—most violations apparently come to their attention as a result of complaints by third parties. This seems to reflect a greater willingness on the local level by German enforcement authorities than American agencies to prosecute violations that injure particular private interests without necessarily causing broader public harm. Such a result follows from the notion that many of the provisions of the GWB are designed more to protect competitors and the parties to the anticompetitive transaction than consumers in general. This point is discussed in greater detail in the discussion on damage actions in chapter 5. In practice most complaints are dealt with informally. Facts are checked and, where violations are thought to exist, the party or parties involved are asked to cease the prohibited conduct. In the majority of cases agreement is forthcoming, terminating the case.

Prior to 1999 the formal powers of the authorities in policing violations parallelled the dichotomy between invalidification or nullification of agreements and resolutions and express prohibition of illegal conduct. Former section 12(1) and (3), for example, empowered the authorities "to declare the agreements and resolutions" for notification cartels "to be ineffective" if they involved an abuse of market power or violated West German treaty obligations. By expressly prohibiting anticompetitive cartel agreements and trade association decisions, the 1998 amendment eliminated the need for the authority to declare them invalid. Section 12 thus currently empowers the FCO to direct a party to cease prohibited actions, to modify offending agreements and decisions, and to issue specific prohibition orders.

One of the most interesting provisions of the GWB is section 32. Added in 1973, 25 section 37a this section gives the FCO and *Land* authorities general authority to issue orders prohibiting (*untersagen*) the implementation of agreements or resolutions invalidated or nullified under former sections 1, 15, 20(1), 21,100(1)3, and 103(2) and conduct prohibited under sections 25, 26 and 38(1). The only significant proscriptions not covered by section 37a were illegal mergers, trade association and professional organization competition rules, and illegal use of market power (former § 22[4])—for which, however, the authorities have specific enforcement powers under the provisions of the GWB related thereto (see, e.g., former §§ 22[5], 24[7], and 31).

On its face section 37a seemed redundant. The provisions of the statute either invalidating agreements (e.g., former § 1) or prohibiting certain conduct (e.g., former § 26) were effective without further administrative action;[20] thus a prohibition order issued under section 37a in effect restated existing prohibitions. The underlying purpose of the section was not to supplement the enforcement powers of the authorities but rather to permit a formal determination of whether a specific agreement or conduct violated the GWB outside of proceedings to levy a fine. As explained in detail below, the GWB separates proceedings in which an administrative fine (*Bußgeld*) is to be levied from ordinarily administrative proceedings involving other determinations—for example, the denial of approval of a cartel exemption. Until the addition of section 37a in 1973, an administrative fine proceeding was the only venue available to the authorities (and the parties) to obtain a formal decision about whether conduct or agreements not covered by specific provisions for approval or review (as in the case of exemptions, mergers, and competition rules) violated the GWB. As discussed below, fine proceedings are subject to stricter procedural requirements as well as to exculpatory defenses unrelated to whether the agreement or conduct in question in fact constitutes a violation.[21] The scope of section 37a (current § 32) was said to be and is now expressly restricted to prohibited acts. The issuing authority is in theory not authorized to order any positive action, and the prohibition must be directed to specific offending conduct.[22] But such theoretical restrictions may still mean little in practice. By rephrasing the order to prohibit all but the desired conduct, the authorities can effectively order positive action on the part of a respondent. For example, in at least one case the cartel authorities were able to require specific price reductions under this section by "prohibiting" higher prices.[23] Thus far it has been used in only ten to twenty cases a year, the majority of which involve discriminatory market practices under section 20 (former § 26[2]).

## THE JAPANESE FAIR TRADE COMMISSION

With the United States Federal Trade Commission in mind, the drafters of Japan's antitrust statute provided for the Japanese FTC as an independent and exclusive antitrust enforcement agency. The Japanese and American drafters were not inclined to duplicate fully the American system with its dual enforcement agencies. The Americans, as noted, rejected the Japanese proposal to locate the antitrust enforcement authority within the Ministry of Justice. No one suggested placing antitrust enforcement with Japan's economics ministry—MITI—and paid scant if any attention to the anomaly of an independent administrative agency in the context of Japan's parliamentary system and the postwar constitution's mandate of executive accountability to the Diet. Nor does it appear that any thought was given to the idea of a semi-independent authority such as the FCO within a ministry to reconcile legislative supremacy with the need for independent authority for enforcement. In this respect the Japanese FTC was not unique. It was only one of many regulatory boards and commissions established under the occupation.[24] However, unlike almost all of the others, which were quietly reconstituted as bureaus or sections within various ministries as Japan regained full sovereignty,[25] the FTC has endured as an independent agency, although located as a matter of form under the prime minister's office.

As a result of this independent status, the FTC is not subject to direct ministerial or cabinet controls as in the case of the FCO. On the other hand, the agency has not had the political advantages of a cabinet-level spokesman or the protection of a politically powerful minister or ministry. In Germany the FCO has never suffered from a hostile minister like Kishi, but neither has the FTC had the benefits of a supportive minister like Erhard. A minister is better able to influence the cabinet and in some instances to mobilize public opinion, an important factor in both systems. Moreover, it can be argued that the FTC's formal independence may have facilitated a greater degree of indirect controls hidden from public scrutiny. Informal "directives" from the minister of finance or MITI need not be published in the official gazette as in the case of formal directives in Germany.

Executive influence on the FTC has taken several forms. First, its annual budget and the size of its staff are set annually by the Ministry of Finance and the cabinet. Also, criminal prosecution is ultimately subject to the discretion of the procuracy within the Ministry of Justice.[26] Third and most important, the composition of the commission is a matter of political appointment.

The Antimonopoly Law initially provided for a seven-member commission with a chairman and six commissioners (art. 29[1]). The 1953 amendments reduced the number to five Each is formally appointed by the prime minister with consent of both houses of the Diet (art. 29[2]). The chairman's appointment is distinguished by imperial confirmation (art. 29[3]). The statutory term of office is five years, but, following a pattern shared with the Japanese Supreme Court and other elite public agencies, most commissioners serve for a shorter period since most are in their sixties when appointed and retirement is compulsory at age sixty-five.[27] On average, commissioners serve for less than four years.

The first appointments followed more of an American pattern. The majority were appointed from the private sector.[28] The first chairman, Kikumatsu Nakagawa, was the former president of the Industrial Bank of Japan and later president of Daidō Steel. The others included a banker, two lawyers, a former law professor, and a justice of the Great Court of Cassation, Masatoshi Yokota, who later succeeded Nakagawa as chairman. Only one of the first commissioners had been a career bureaucrat, a former director of the Price Agency and member of the Economic Stabilization Board. Since the first commission, no one from the private sector has been appointed to the commission.[29] Dominating the commission has been a plurality of retired officials from the Ministry of Finance and its affiliated agencies, such as the Bank of Japan and the National Tax Agency. Eleven of the fifteen chairmen who have served between 1947 and 1997 spent their careers with the ministry or an affiliated institution. Four were former vice-ministers of the Ministry of Finance, the highest career post in the ministry. Three were former directors of the National Tax Bureau, two were retired officials from the Bank of Japan, and two had held high posts in the Ministry of Finance. Of the forty-two commissioners, thirteen spent their earlier careers in the Ministry of Finance or an affiliated agency. Ten were former procurators. Nine were former MCI or MITI officials. The remainder were former FTC staff(5), diplomats (2), or other former government officials or politicians (4).[30] Except for the few former FTC personnel, in stark contrast to the German experience, no commissioner has had any background or experience in antitrust prior to appointment. Article 29(2) requires only that the members of the FTC have a background in law or economics. Since nearly all of Japan's higher civil servants are law faculty graduates, this requirement is easily met.

As might be expected, the attitudes of the commissioners influence the enforcement activity of the staff. In the early 1980s, for example, the FTC staff showed renewed interest in more vigorous antitrust enforcement to prevent anticompetitive practices by financial institutions.[31] The personal contacts of many of the commissioners with the Ministry of Finance made any action against financial institutions a matter of delicacy. For three decades no formal decisions were issued involving financial institutions. Antitrust enforcement against banking practices was left largely to private civil actions without direct FTC involvement.[32]

Unlike the president of the FCO, the chairman of the FTC has rarely played a significant public role in the development of Japanese antitrust policy. But like the heads of other governmental organs in Japan, the chairman's potential for influence can be significant. Given the commissioners' desire for consensus within the government and the agency together with the capacity to rally strong public support for antitrust enforcement, the chairman has been in a position to lead the FTC into new areas of concern. Toshide Takahashi, who served as chair from 1971 to 1976, exemplifies the potential of the office for an activist role—at least during periods of turmoil within the ruling Liberal Democratic Party. These years constituted the pivotal moment for Japanese antitrust; the press characterized them as the "Takahashi era."[33] None of Takahashi's successors, however, have pursued a similar public role.

## Organization

Unlike the FCO, the FTC is organized principally, as indicated in figure 4, into functional units. The agency's chief administrative officer or secretary-general (*jimu sōchō*, prior to June 1996; *jimu kyoku chō*), whose functions combine many of those of both the president and vice-president of the FCO, is subject to the five-member commission. The units below the General Secretariat were reorganized in June 1996. The central administrative staff (*kanbō*) and separate office of five hearing officers (*shinpankan*) responsible to the secretary-general remain without significant change except for the transfer to the *kanbō* of the International Section (*kokusai-ka*), as noted below. Four previous principal functional divisions (*kyoku* or *bu*) were consolidated in 1996 into two departments (*kyoku*)—Economic and Trade Practices (*keizai torihiki kyoku*) and Investigations—both of which have both policy-making and enforcement functions. The regional offices were also consolidated. Currently five regional offices serve Hokkaido (Sapporo), Tohoku (Sendai), central Japan (Nagoya), southwestern Japan (Osaka), Kyushu (Fukuoka). Prior to 1966, separate offices served the island of Shikoku and the Chūkoku area surrounding Hiroshima. In 1996 the regional office in Osaka for the Kinki region was expanded to include administrative responsibility for these districts with branch offices in Hiroshima and the city of Takamatsu on Shikoku island. These regional offices make the Japanese FTC more accessible than the single FCO in Berlin or Bonn. Since they do not share the jurisdictional restrictions of the *Land* cartel authorities under German federalism, the FTC and its regional offices are more accessible than the FCO and potentially provide Japan more comprehensive and uniform enforcement.

The Economics and Trade Practices Department is responsible for coordinating Japan's antitrust policies with other economic and regulatory legislation, for research on business trends and economic conditions, and for reviewing reports and issuing the various approvals required by the FTC under the Antimonopoly Law. It played a major role in the early 1970s in drafting and negotiating the agency's proposals for antitrust reform, culminating in the enactment of the 1977 amendments. Until June 1996 it was subdivided into five sections. It currently has four sections directly under its supervision. The first is an administrative office (*sōmu-ka*). The second is the Coordination Section (*chōseika*), which reviews and advises the cabinet, the Diet, and concerned ministries with respect to proposed economic legislation and administrative regulations that may affect Japanese antitrust policy. Such review was carried out by the former Laws and Regulation investigators (*hōreichōsa-ka*). An example was its advice to the government regarding proposed research

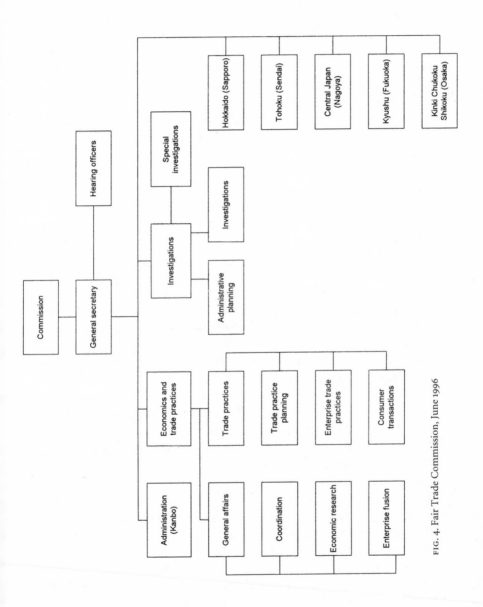

FIG. 4. Fair Trade Commission, June 1996

section legislation to aid small retailers from the competitive onslaught of large discount chains, which restricted new entry into the retail market.[34] The Coordination Section also advises the commission on applications for approvals exempting cartels from domestic antitrust law under the variety of special statutes or provisions of the Antimonopoly Law itself (e.g., depression and rationalization cartels). The former Industry Research Office (*sangyō-chōsa-shitsu*) of the section received reports on parallel price increases and supervised monopolistic situations.

The third departmental unit, the Economic Research Section (*keizai chōsa-ka*; prior to 1996 the *chōsa-ka*), conducts most of the research on business trends. In addition this section conducts the investigations necessary for determining what industries are in a "state of monopoly" under the 1977 amendments. Also directly under the Economics and Trade Practice Department is the Enterprise Fusion Section (*kigyō-ketsugō-ka*), which deals primarily with the reports and approvals required under the law relating to intercorporate shareholding, mergers, and interlocking directorates.

In 1996 the previously separate Trade Practices Division (*torihiki-bu*) was reorganized under the combined Economic and Trade Practices Department. Since 1996 the division has been subdivided into three sections: the Trade Practice Planning Section (*torihiki-kikaku-ka*), the Enterprise Trade Practices Section (*kigyō-torihiki-ka*), and the Consumer Transactions Section (*shōhi-torihiki-ka*). Each of these sections is further subdivided into separate offices (*shitsu*). For example, the section's Trade Practices Research Office (*torihiki-chōsa-shitsu*) has taken over the responsibilities for almost all of the research and investigatory and enforcement functions related to trade associations, including formation-reporting requirements and approvals for exemptions, previously handled by the former Trade Association Section (*dantai-ka*).

Until 1996 research and enforcement with respect to the Law Prohibiting Delayed Payments for Subcontractors[35] and the Unfair Premiums and Misleading Representations Prevention Law[36] as well as the prohibition of unfair business practices under article 19 were handled by three sections. The Distribution Policy Office (*ryūtsū-taisaku-shitsu*) conducted research and reviewed marketing practices. The Trade Practice Section (*torihiki-ka*) was in charge of developing regulations and guidelines relating to unfair business practices, thus overlapping with the International and Trade Association sections of the Economic Department. The Subcontract Section (*shitauke-ka*) had similar responsibility with respect to the Law Prohibiting Delayed Payments for Subcontractors. Since 1996 these functions have been divided among the three new sections of the newly organized Trade Practices Division. For example, the responsibilities of the division's Consumer

Transactions Section includes enforcement of the Unfair Premium and Unfair Representation Prevention Law.

The Investigation Department (*shinsa-kyoku;* formerly the *shinsa-bu*) is the prosecutorial arm of the FTC. It conducts all preliminary investigations related to particular violations of the Antimonopoly Law and related legislation. Until 1996 the department was divided like the German *Beschlußabteilungen,* into four numbered divisions by industry. These functions have been reassigned to three investigation chiefs (*shinasa-chō*) and a separate Special Investigation Division (*tokubetsu shina-bu*).

The International Section, as noted, is currently a unit under the *kanbō.* The section continues to be responsible for the development of policy with respect to the extraterritorial application and effect of Japanese antitrust policy as well as for domestic violations arising out of international agreements. Between 1947 and 1997 the International Section also reviewed all international contracts filed under article 6(2).

*Personnel*

Textbook descriptions of the organization and functions of governmental agencies rarely convey their realities or dynamics. In the case of the Japanese FTC, few factors are as critical to an understanding of both its role and its limitations as the size and actual functions of its staff. As with most bureaucracies, the FTC staff's actual role is far greater than implied from its formal powers.

Staff advice is by necessity decisive in most instances. Staff recommendations are generally followed. The commissioners simply do not have the time personally to carry out all of the agency's functions. There is also a significant deference to the expertise of staff personnel and a sense that any significant errors are unlikely because of the procedural limitations and protections of the investigation and hearing process. Rare is the case in which staff advice for a commission action is not followed. The effectiveness of the agency is directly proportional to the size, competence, and activity of the staff.

Formal decisions by the FTC represent only a small fraction of all cases actually resolved. Illustrative is FTC review of international agreements under article 6(2). Between 1953 and 1997 only eight formal FTC decisions were handed down, none since 1972. Prior to 1992, when new rules to reduce the number were issued, the International Section reviewed between four and five thousand contracts and recommended modification in three to four hundred instances.[37] Between 1992 and 1997 the agency reviewed about eight hundred international agreements a year.[38] In 1997 the requirement of article 6(2) for FTC review was repealed.

The FTC has grown steadily since the mid 1970s (table 3). The largest increase was in 1947–48, when it grew from 284 to 327. Once Japan regained full sovereignty in 1952, the staff was reduced to 241 and remained at roughly this level until 1964. Since then incremental annual increases have increased the staff to its present number. In 1997 the agency had a staff of more than 550. Staff personnel are distributed more or less evenly among the various department sections; the largest are the Investigation Department and the Internal Affairs Section of the General Affairs Office. Understaffing has been especially acute in the district offices. The Osaka office, for instance, had a staff of seventeen when it opened in 1949, but only fifteen from 1952 through 1964 and twenty-two from 1970 through 1976.

Although not totally incapacitated even during the lean years of the 1950s, the lack of personnel precluded any attempt to implement fully even the most critical provisions of the law. With only a dozen or so staff, the International Section could hardly review effectively the several thousand international agreements filed with the commission under article 6(2). Consequently, the FTC has issued guidelines, such as those for international contracts and, more recently, mergers, to indicate how it will enforce particular provisions in the context of its reviewing powers.

The composition of the staff also deserves attention. Japanese civil servants are selected by merit on the basis of a rigorous public examination (kōmuin shiken). Candidates are ranked by comparative result, and most of those at the top of the list vie for appointment by one of the prestigious economic ministries. Were the test results and rankings available, one could determine how new entrants rank various government agencies over a period of time by charting which agencies the highest ranked candidates selected. Unfortunately for our purposes, the scores are strictly confidential. It is generally thought, however, that the FTC was not a favored agency, and staff morale was not high during the 1950s and early 1960s. Presumably, in the intervening years employee status and morale have both risen.

There has also been a tendency to exchange personnel with the economic ministries, especially MITI and the Ministry of Finance, for two-year terms to supplement the expertise of their staffs. Other important sources of temporarily assigned personnel are the procuracy (kensatsukan) and the career judiciary.

The only individuals with legal training and experience beyond the more rarified university curricula are the five hundred or so annual graduates of Japan's elite Legal Training and Research Institute who comprise the career judiciary, the procuracy, and the private bar. Consequently, the FTC has relied

TABLE 3.  Federal Cartel Office and Fair Trade Commission
Personnel and Budgets, 1948–1996

| | Personnel | | Budget (in thousands) | |
| Year | FCO | FTC | FCO | FTC |
| --- | --- | --- | --- | --- |
| 1948 | NA | 327 | NA | 35,914 (U.S. $299) |
| 1954 | NA | 237 | NA | 94,961 (791) |
| 1958 | 127 | 237 | 1,247 (U.S. $692.8) | 108,051 (900) |
| 1980 | 237 | 422 | 13,359 (7,420) | 2,393,247 (19,943) |
| 1982 | 232 | 425 | 14,453 (8,030) | 2,659,514 (22,162) |
| 1984 | 228 | 431 | 14,425 (8,010) | 2,799,830 (23,331) |
| 1986 | 228 | 436 | 15,428 (8,570) | 3,018,665 (25,155) |
| 1988 | 227 | 445 | 16,665 (9,260) | 3,248,967 (27,074) |
| 1990 | 244 | 474 | 17,777 (9,880) | 3,758,887 (31,324) |
| 1992 | 245 | 484 | 20,292 (11,270) | 4,406,727 (36,722) |
| 1994 | 244 | 520 | 21,731 (12,070) | 5,244,397 (43,703) |
| 1996 | 233 | 534 | 20,986 (11,660) | 5,381,953 (44,849) |

NOTE: Figures for the FCO from data provided author by the FCO. Figures for the FTC from *Fifty-Year History*, pp. 98–103. All U.S. dollar figures are based on approximate current exchange rates of 1.8 DM and 120 yen per one U.S. dollar.

heavily on procurators and to a lesser extent judges for specialized legal expertise, particularly in relation to investigations and hearings. Recently the FTC has been able to attract younger lawyers (*bengoshi*) who spend a few years with the agency before entering or returning to private practice.

The professional expertise of procurators—Japan's only government attorneys—and judges is, however, in those areas of Japanese law that have remained the most strongly influenced by continental models. As a result, FTC procedures, especially for investigations and formal hearings, parallel the Japanese criminal process and tend to reflect German rather than American patterns. Despite the obvious statutory analogies to U.S. FTC proceedings, American-styled administrative procedures are exceptional. One example of the differences in approach is the deference given the trustworthiness of the investigatory process. In Japan the role of the procurator in determining guilt in a criminal case equals if not exceeds that of the court, as evidenced by a consistent conviction rate of 99 percent[39] Japanese prosecutors do not usually prosecute unless they are themselves convinced of the guilt of the accused and are also confident that they have sufficient evidence to ensure conviction. This is not to say that the trial (conducted without a jury) is a mere formality. Judicial determination of guilt provides a critical safeguard and helps to ensure the continued diligence and credibility of procuratorial investigations. Nonetheless, in effect it is only a supplementary process. It is important to keep in mind that in Japan procurators have the same educational background as judges. Both are career officials. Japanese judges, like their continental counterparts, do not have special claim to greater deference, integrity, or public trust than the procurators. Their roles should not be viewed with an Anglo-American bias that favors judges.

*Powers and Duties*

In addition to general investigatory and advisory functions, the FTC wields a significant array of statutory powers. The most important are its specific enforcement powers, subject in all cases to formal enforcement proceedings.

In the case of violations of the article 3 prohibitions of private monopolization and unreasonable restraints of trade, the FTC is expressly empowered to issue cease and desist orders, to require the transfer of any part or all of the business of the offending entrepreneur, or "to take any other measures necessary to eliminate" the violation (art. 7). The agency exercises similar powers to correct illegal practices by trade associations (art. 8-2), violations of the prohibition against holding companies, and the restrictions on corporate and individual shareholding, interlocking directorates, and mergers (art. 17-2). In the case of unfair business practices, however, its powers are limited to cease and desist orders. As noted, the authority to order divorcement or dissolution of firms in a "monopoly situation" was added in 1977 (art. 8-4).

In practice the FTC has not construed its powers broadly. FTC decisions are regularly couched in terms of cease and desist orders and often include the requirement that the offending party report to the agency what remedial measures were taken. Occasionally they include an order to make public disclosure of these measures. Nonetheless, in fashioning effective remedial measures the agency seems quite timid, especially to American lawyers, who would naturally construe the open-ended language of "to take any measures necessary" of articles 7, 8-2, 17-2, and 20 as an allusion to the equity power of the courts to fashion appropriate remedies. Such notions are quite alien, however, to Japanese and European notions of judicial power. Despite the recognized American source of the Japanese statute, the FTC exercises its powers in keeping with continental views. During the debate over the 1977 amendments, the Ministry of Justice reportedly questioned the validity of the dissolution power in article 8-4, arguing that such orders would violate shareholder rights under the commercial code.[40]

The Antimonopoly Law contains a variety of reporting requirements. In all but one instance these are coupled with express authority for the FTC to institute formal proceedings for remedial action if a violation is found or statutory standards are not met. The sole exception is the reporting requirement for parallel price increases under article 18-2(2). Although the FTC may act if a violation is found, this is primarily a disclosure provision. Reports to the FTC have been mandated in the following instances:

1. international agreements under article 6(2) and (3) (repealed in 1997);
2. trade association formation, change in the formation report, and trade association dissolution under article 6 (2), (3), and (4);
3. annual shareholding reports by nonfinancial domestic companies with total assets in excess of 2 billion yen, and all nonfinancial foreign companies covering ownership of shares in other domestic companies in its own name or in the name of a trustee, under article 10(2);
4. where an officer or employee of a domestic company is an officer in a competitive domestic company and either company has total assets in excess of 2 billion yen, under article 13(3);
5. shareholding by natural persons or unincorporated associations in two or more domestic companies in competition in Japan, if the holdings include more than 10 percent of the total amount of outstanding stock in any one of the companies, under article 14(2);
6. prior to all mergers and consolidations under article 15;
7. all resale price maintenance agreements authorized under article 24-2(6); and
8. parallel price increases as described above.

Most of the special-exemption statutes required reports to the FTC and by implication, if not express language, permitted the FTC to review and institute enforcement proceedings if any nonexempt violations of the Antimonopoly Law were found.

Finally, formal FTC approvals are required in several instances. Prior FTC approval is necessary for financial companies to acquire an equity interest in Japanese domestic companies above 5 percent of the company's total outstanding shares (art. 11[1]). Both recession and rationalization cartels require prior FTC approval (arts. 24-3 and 24-4), and resale price maintenance is authorized only for trademarked goods specifically designated by the commission (art. 24-2[1]).

ENFORCEMENT PROCEEDINGS

*Germany*

The GWB expressly distinguishes among three types of enforcement proceedings. The first are formal administrative proceedings (*Verwaltungsverfahren*) governed by sections 54 through 80. These provisions apply to all formal actions (*Verfügungen*) by the FCO and *Land* authorities except for proceedings for fines under section 81–86 (formerly § 38). They thereby cover all decisions with respect to the approval or denial of cartel exemptions and mergers as well as other approvals. They also apply to determinations of whether other agreements and conduct conform to the GWB either under specific provisions, such as a declaration that an industrial property license is ineffective under sections 17 and 18 (former §§ 20, 21) or the general grant of authority to issue prohibition orders under section 32 (§37a).[41] Also covered are excess profits charges under section 37b.[42]

The second type of proceeding involves fines under section 81 (formerly § 38). Section 81 provides that specified violations of the GWB constitute *Ordnungswidrigkeiten,* or "administrative offenses." Sections 81 through 86 of the GWB apply to such fine proceedings, but they do not include detailed procedures. Rather, to the extent not covered by the GWB, the proceedings are governed by the OWIG, particularly sections 38 through 47.

Until 1973, the determination of whether a violation had been committed could only be made in the context of a fine proceeding (*Bußgeldverfahren*) subject to defenses, such as lack of negligent or willful conduct, that were not applicable in ordinary administrative proceedings (*Verwaltungsverfahren*). This led, as noted, to the introduction in 1973 of the special administrative prohibition order under section 37a (current §32) to permit the authorities greater procedural flexibility, but it has been used only rarely. The Japanese FTC enjoys greater choice. Based on an American model, the Japanese statute as enacted provided the FTC with power to fashion suitable remedies for a violation without necessarily imposing a sanction (although the provision has not been construed or used in the Japanese context as broadly as in the United States).

Finally, sections 87 through 90 apply to private civil actions (*bürgerliche Rechtsstreitigkeiten*) arising under the GWB or out of cartel agreements or resolutions. Such litigation includes private actions brought under section 33 (former § 35) for damages or injunctive relief as well as other civil suits brought under the GWB, such as those related to withdrawal from cartel agreements for cause under section 13 (repealed in 1998) or admission to trade or professional associations under section 20(6) (former §27).[43]

Both formal administrative and fine proceedings are considered quasi-judicial in nature.[44] The enforcement authorities have broad discretion to initiate such proceedings, and there is an inevitable combination of prosecutorial and judicial functions. Before the commencement of any proceedings, the authorities have the power to conduct investigations and require disclosure of information. They are not neutral judges of the matter before them, but rather have already collected information that has led to formal proceedings.[45]

German practice replicates to some extent the pervasive Japanese preference for resolving antitrust (and other disputes) before the start of the formal process. The GWB does not provide for any formal determination that a violation has been committed on the basis of an admission or agreement of the respondent. In practice, as indicated in the statistics, the majority of cases are settled by agreement and not subject to formal decision. Most cases arising under the GWB and subject to action by the enforcement authorities do begin with at least a formal "commencement" of a proceeding in the sense that documents are duly numbered and filed and subsequently included in the statistical count. Throughout the investigatory process, opportunity exists for a negotiated settlement. The German authorities no less than their Japanese (and American) counterparts attempt to reach an informal, voluntary settlement. Not only do the authorities provide informal opinions and advice,[46] they also use the threat of a formal action to induce compliance. A factor missing in both Japanese and American antitrust practice is the role of the *Beschlußabteilung* directors. Because of their distinctive longevity in office, they are able over the course of years to become very well informed about the industries and particular firms under their jurisdiction and to get to know and deal with many of the managers. Their knowledge and familiarity with the industry and executives facilitate communication and administrative informality. FCO statistics, for example, indicate that such informal administrative enforcement—what in Japan is referred to as "administrative guidance" (*gyōsei shidō*)—is as common to German antitrust enforcement, although perhaps not quite as frequent, as to Japan'. The FCO takes very few formal actions. Most enforcement actions are dismissed on the grounds that the violation has ceased. In other words, the filing of a complaint and response by the FCO is generally sufficient to induce an end to the offending conduct. This is equivalent to the Japanese FTC's use of cautions and warnings, explained below.

The German statistics provide a more accurate measure of enforcement than the Japanese reports, the latter reflecting only a portion of the cases with which the FTC has actually dealt (or, in the case of outside complaints, settled before any FTC action). For this reason German and Japanese statistics on enforcement actions must be qualified for meaningful comparison.

Under section 54(1) of the GWB the authorities—in the case of the FCO, the appropriate *Beschlußabteilung*—commence administrative proceedings either upon complaint (or application in the case of an approval) or their own initiative. No formal decision is necessary,[47] and the authorities have broad discretion not to proceed even though there may be evidence of a violation.[48] Such discretion is limited only when action by the authorities is stated in mandatory terms in the GWB, such as by use of the term "shall" (*ist* or *hat*) in sections 11 and 26 (4). As in English, use of the verb "may" or "can" (*kann*) signals discretion.[49]

The decisions on the parties allowed or required to participate in the proceedings is only partially subject to discretion. Section 54(2) requires that applicants (§ 54[2]1), "the cartel, enterprise, or trade or professional association against whom the proceedings are directed" (§ 54[2]2), *shall* participate; Section 54(2)3, however, permits the enforcement authorities to invite any person or association whose "interests are significantly affected by the decision" ("*deren Interessen durch die Entscheidung erheblich berührt werden*") to participate as a party upon petition. This provision is construed broadly to include consumers and others with an economic or legal interest in the outcome. Felix Stark, a former director in the FCO, notes that the provision enables the authorities to allow broad public representation, especially in the case of approval cartels.[50] He also notes that in the 1952 bill such participation would have been restricted to those whose "legal interests" would be affected (§ 43[2] of the 1952 government bill) as in ordinary administrative proceedings (§ 65 of the Administrative Court Law).[51] Thus the GWB permits significantly greater participation than other administrative proceedings in Germany.

Third parties may also have an opportunity to present evidence and opinions under section 56(2) by invitation of the enforcement authorities. Section 56(2) speaks of "representatives of the economic groups affected by the proceedings" ("*Vertreter der von dem Verfahren berührten Wirtschaftskreise*") and has been construed to include trade unions, business organizations, and consumer groups.[52] As in the case of those allowed to participate as parties under section 54(2)–3 the authorities have the discretion to hear them, but they do not have a right to be heard.[53] Nor do they enjoy the cluster of procedural rights of formal parties to the proceedings. The courts do provide some measure of control. They can review FCO decision's under section 70 to exclude parties. In such cases the courts will determine if the parties were qualified and the authorities exceeded their discretion.[54]

The most important procedural rights that attach to party status are the right to an oral hearing and the right to extensive judicial review. The

German concept of due process (*rechtliches Gehör*, perhaps better translated as a "right to a legal hearing") is significantly less inclusive of procedural safeguards than the conceptual counterpart in American administrative law. Consequently, hearings conducted either under the provisions of the GWB governing ordinary proceedings or under the OWIG for administrative fine proceedings fall short of American procedural requirements, although in both instances they are subject to considerably greater procedural protections for the parties than available for ordinary administrative actions in Germany. Any negative judgment should be reserved. These contrasts in German (and Japanese) administrative practice stem in large part from distinctly different approaches in the judicial process and, more important, the role of the courts, which generally engage in *de novo* review of administrative actions, rather than from differences in fundamental notions of justice or less sensitivity to the fairness of the process or concern for the trustworthiness of the result.

Both ordinary and fine proceedings, as noted previously, are described as quasi-judicial inasmuch as they are subject to many of the procedural constraints of either the civil or criminal process. But the emphasis on the dominant and investigative role of the judge as opposed to the notion of judge-as-umpire in an adversary contest between the parties, coupled with the status of the procuracy as theoretically an equally neutral public servant, tends to mute concern over the effective neutrality of the administrative officials who decide. Moreover, the lack of discovery in German civil procedure similarly reduces any emphasis on full disclosure to the parties by the administrative officials. Consequently, elements now taken for granted in a judicialized administrative proceeding in the United States are missing in Germany (and, to a lesser extent, Japan). In the instance of German antitrust enforcement, they include the following.

First, again as previously noted, there is no separation of functions in either ordinary or fine proceedings. A member of the *Beschlußabteilung* who conducts an investigation that leads to an enforcement action may well sit on the panel to decide the case—for example, whether an approval should be revoked or a prohibition order issued. Moreover, the investigator could participate subsequently to decide whether a fine should be levied. The combination of functions is criticized by some as contrary to the judicial nature of the proceedings.[55] Such concern has not been sufficient, however, to result in amendment or, as in Japan, judicially imposed reform.

Second, the right to be heard must be significantly qualified. Except in the case of ordinary administrative proceedings involving abuse of market power under section 19 and those conducted under the aegis of the federal minister of economics under the merger control provisions, all hearings can be held *in camera* at the discretion of the authorities (§ 56[1]).[56] Even in the two instances for which the GWB mandates a public hearing, hearings may be closed if national security or trade secrets may be endangered (§ 56 [3]). More critical, neither the GWB, the OWIG, nor the constitution (art. 103) requires that the parties have access to all materials available to the decision maker in deciding a case. Under generally applicable requirements of administrative procedure as well as construction of section 56(1), the authorities are obliged to disclose no more than a summary of any written statements made by other participants,[57] they are subject to no constitutional or statutory duty to give the respondents or other parties access to all of the material in their files.[58] Consequently, in reaching a decision the deciding panel may rely on evidence provided to the parties in summary form only and thus not subject to full cross-examination.

Finally, the GWB does not provide for adversarial presentation of witnesses or expert testimony. To the extent permitted, this is done at the discretion of the authorities. Instead, the GWB empowers the enforcement authorities "to conduct all necessary investigations and take all required evidence" and to subpoena witnesses and experts (§ 57), complementing the investigatory powers of section 59, which, as noted, deals with the right to compel disclosures from the respondents, not third parties.

Academic commentary differentiating administrative fine proceedings from ordinary administrative proceedings, as discussed in relation to disclosures of information under section 59 (former § 46), does not indicate any significant procedural differences between the two. If any exist, they are difficult to discern. The potential bias and resulting unfairness of those who investigate a case also deciding it applies, as noted, to both types of proceedings. In either case, fewer qualifications of the respondent's right to be heard apply. As amended in 1968, section 55 of the OWIG makes applicable the hearing requirements of sections 163a(1) and 136a (with modifications) of the Code of Criminal Procedure.[59] These provisions grant the respondent the basic right to be heard in an oral proceeding and limit to some extent the right of the panel to use as evidence material not subject to examination or obtained by illegal means. Also, it appears that under the OWIG the respondent has the right to call witnesses and experts.[60] These are, however, purely statutory rights.

In a decision of December 1, 1966, in the *Konkurrenzfiliale* case,[61] the Federal Supreme Court dismissed objections by a respondent that denial of an oral hearing under section 55 of the OWIG prior to the 1968 revision was unconstitutional. At the time section 55 merely provided for a right to petition the appropriate court for an oral hearing, which was to be granted when deemed necessary.[62] The Federal Supreme Court held that this determination was made within the nonreviewable discretion of the *Kammergericht* and also that no constitutional right to a hearing before the FCO (or apparently other administrative agencies) existed. The due process provision of article 103 of the German Constitution, the court reasoned, citing a series of precedents, applies only to court actions.[63] Reinforcing this conclusion was the respondent's opportunity on appeal to challenge any evidence used in the administrative proceeding and to introduce more in a *de novo* trial on the facts. As the court recognized, a *de novo* determination on appeal removes a major need for judicialized procedures in an administrative hearing.[64] There is room for doubt, however, whether intensive judicial review substitutes for procedural protection in the first instance. Although it is clear from the decisions of German courts that conclusions reached by the administrative enforcement authorities are not accepted without question, the inevitable deference to the expertise of the administrative agency places the respondent at a distinct disadvantage on appeal. That this is not a major issue in Germany probably results from the practice of the enforcement authorities giving respondents the fullest opportunity feasible to present their cases without necessarily accepting their legal "right" to such protection. Such practice is evidenced in part by the length of the proceedings. Three decades ago Eberhard Günther estimated that administrative proceedings before the FCO took two to three years on average.[65] No data are available on the duration of formal *Land* proceedings,[66] but authorities estimate that the average case takes from four months to a year to complete.[67]

## Japan

The Japanese Antimonopoly Law also distinguishes between two separate types of formal enforcement actions. Separate procedures apply in proceedings to levy a cartel profits surcharge (*kachōkin*). All other proceedings, whether to determine if an offense has been committed or to levy an administrative fine, are governed by the statutory provisions of articles 45 through 70-2 and the FTC's 1953 Regulations on Investigations and Hearings.[68]

As might be expected, FTC procedures as set out in the statute follow an American pattern. The FTC's 1953 Regulations on Investigations and Hearings, however, borrowed freely from the 1952 GWB draft. Also apparent is the influence on the regulations and practice of procurators and judges (more familiar with Japan's predominately German-based criminal procedure), who were and continue to be temporarily assigned to the FTC. Consequently, in many respects Japanese proceedings in practice resemble German rather than

American examples. A notable exception, described below, is the continuing emphasis on separation of functions in formal adjudications.

The Japanese process as described graphically in figure 5, comprises four distinct phases. Very few cases move through all four. The vast majority are settled informally during the initial phase.

*Phase One: Initial Review and Disposition.* Japanese enforcement actions begin with a report of a suspected violation from outside the agency or by agency personnel. The most frequent are complaints lodged by people adversely affected by an alleged violation. Article 45(1) of the Antimonopoly Law provides that "any person" may report a violation to the FTC and request that appropriate measures be taken. Article 45(4) empowers the agency to initiate investigations on its own authority (*shokken tanchi*) when, for example, the staff becomes aware of a possible violation through trade journals, newspapers, or other sources. In addition, notice of a suspected violation may also be filed by another government agency. The largest number of complaints filed in a single year was 108,213 in 1980, as a result of a well-organized protest by retailers over resale price maintenance by milk producers. In most years the number has ranged from 1,000 to 2,000 complaints. The lowest number filed was 55 in 1966. Fewer cases have been initiated by the FTC's staff. The number decreased from a peak of 172 in 1948 to 0 in 1959. Since the mid 1970s roughly 10 percent of the FTC's caseload has been initiated by the staff. Since 1951 no outside agency has reported a case to the FTC.

Official accounts of complaints and reported violations are misleading, however. Informal contacts with members of the FTC's staff are not usually included in the official statistics unless they led to formal action. Yet a telephone call or visit to an FTC office to discuss a violation can be as effective in many cases as a formal complaint even though no formal action is taken. A complaint may be filed, but if the parties are able to reach a settlement themselves, it is usually withdrawn and unreported. In such instances, the allegation of an antitrust violation and threat of FTC action is sufficient to induce settlement of a dispute. To the extent that the alleged offense is not considered to be significant or has been appropriately settled, the FTC staff often let the parties resolve the issue without any formal action. In other cases, the FTC officials may become more actively involved. They may counsel or subtly suggest that the matter be settled or dropped for a variety of reasons, including limited resources and the nature of the alleged offense. Such dispositions constitute a large proportion of the FTC's caseload. Most cases in fact end with at most an initial review by the staff in the First Investigation Division with no action, a dismissal (*uchikiri*) for lack of evidence, the death of the respondent, a finding of no violation, or at most a "caution" (*chūi*) or "warn-

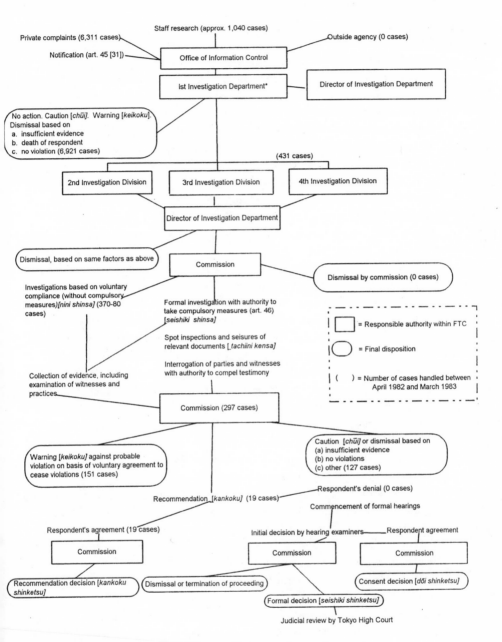

FIG. 5. Process of Japanese antitrust enforcement

*Since June 1996, cases are assigned at this point to either the special or regular investigation division
SOURCE: Hideto Ishida

117

ing" (*keikoku*) after a promise that any suspected violation will cease. In effect, the respondent admits that the activities were at least of questionable legality and agrees to discontinue them. Until the 1990s under U.S. pressure for greater "transparency", few, if any, cautions or warnings at least at this stage were ever made public. Since the early 1990s, all warnings have been made public. As a result, "warnings" have acquired a formal status. Presumably an informal substitute, not subject to public disclosure, is now being used.

To the extent that the staff wishes or is willing to pursue the case further, one of the other three investigation divisions will take charge of the now formal "preliminary investigation" (*yobi shinsa*). The staff conducting the investigation do not, however, have any authority to compel witnesses to testify or to obtain documentary evidence. Again, however, the process usually ends here with no action, dismissal, or agreement by a cooperative respondent to cease the violation.

As noted, the preliminary investigation concludes what in most instances is the determinative stage of FTC proceedings. The vast majority of cases do not proceed beyond this point even if the investigators decide that a violation has been committed. A decision to go forward is generally reached by weighing the time and effort necessary to prosecute against the seriousness of the offense. In most cases, however, no decision is necessary. If there has been a violation, usually sufficient evidence will be developed during the preliminary investigation and a negotiated resolution will be reached with the offender. As indicated in figure 5, 151 of the 297 cases subject to FTC action after investigation in 1982 ended in a warning. If not, the commission—in almost all cases, accepting the staff recommendation—will usually decide to proceed directly to a recommendation decision, explained below, or to initiate a formal investigation (*seishiki shinsa*).

The staff may also recommend that a formal investigation be initiated if, before any direct contact is made disclosing that an investigation is under way, there is little prospect of a cooperative attitude. Only the commissioners' commencement of a formal investigation empowers the investigating staff to obtain evidence under the provisions of article 46. The commissioners then must decide by formal action whether or not to go further and authorize a formal investigation.

*Phase Two: Formal Investigations.* Formal investigations are initiated by the commissioners upon written recommendation by the director of the Investigation Bureau. The recommendation must include an evaluation of the immediacy of the violation and a brief summary of the facts and applicable law (FTC Investigation and Hearings Regs. § 9).

The statute appears to obligate the FTC to undertake an investigation in response to complaints (art. 45[2]). Rarely, if ever, would a complainant insist on further investigation of a case that the staff does not wish to prosecute. The complainant would have no recourse in any event beyond persuasion. At least three attempts have been made to require the FTC to act. Each failed. The courts consistently held that the agency had discretion not to proceed.[69]

The usual reason given for not prosecuting the case is that the investigation did not uncover sufficient facts to support a formal charge, but this rationale is not always accurate. The staff may have decided for the variety of reasons explained above not to proceed despite evidence of a violation.

If the commissioners decide to proceed with the case, they appoint the principal investigators from the appropriate section of the department (art. 46[2]) and authorize them to take whatever measures under article 46(1) of the Antimonopoly Law may be necessary (FTC Investigation and Hearings Regs. § 9[2]). Again at this point the staff and the respondent may agree to terminate the proceedings with a caution or warning. Otherwise the investigation proceeds or the case is dismissed.

Article 46(1) lists the FTC's basic investigatory powers. Acting through the principal investigators, the FTC—that is, the investigating staff—is expressly empowered first to summon and question "interested parties" (*jiken kankeinin*) and "witnesses" (*sankōnin*). The term "interested parties" is generally understood to refer to the entrepreneurs charged with a violation—if juristic persons, their officers and employees. "Witnesses" include those adversely affected by the violation and others who may have information concerning the violation that is considered necessary for the investigation.[70] The FTC may also require experts (*kanteinin*) to give their testimony.

An order requiring interested parties and witnesses to appear (*shutto meireisho*) is to contain the witness's name, the subject of the testimony, the time and place of the interrogation, and the applicable penalties in the event of any failure to appear (FTC Investigation and Hearings Regs. § 10[2]). As in Germany, after the witness has been questioned or has made a statement, the investigator transcribes the testimony in a formal "protocol of testimony" (*shinjin chōsho* or *kyōjutsu chōsho*), which is read by the witness who then signs it (affixes a seal), affirming that the contents are a true and accurate account of the testimony or statement given (FTC Investigation and Hearings Regs. § 12). The party being questioned has the right to refuse to affirm the contents of the protocol. The procedure is nearly identical to that followed in criminal investigations. Witnesses do not take an oath or make similar affirmation attesting to the truth of their statements, since oaths and affirmations are used almost exclusively for testimony before a judge in court. There is provision for oaths in formal hearings in article 53-2, but this is exceptional.

The protocol is admissible in the formal hearings and not infrequently forms the basis for findings that a violation has been committed.[71] Affirmation of the accuracy of the protocol is not required in the case of expert testimony (see FTC Investigation and Hearings Regs. § 13).

Although formal procedural protections pale in comparison with the substantive limits of the FTC's investigative powers, FTC regulations do provide for appeals against measures taken by the investigators. Section 17-2 of the FTC Investigation and Hearings Regulations, added in 1962, provides that a party may appeal to the commissioners against actions by the investigators. As noted below, the commissioners' decision on such an appeal is also subject to judicial review.

The most important provision of article 46, however, is the authority to conduct a warrantless search and seizure under subsection (iv). That a primary purpose of initiating formal investigations is to permit such searches is a reasonable inference from the prevalence of searches once formal investigatory authorization is granted.

*Phase Three: Recommendation Decisions and Adjudicatory Hearings.* At the end of the formal investigation of a case, the investigators report their findings and opinions to the commissioners. The report sets forth the nature and "incipiency" of the violation, a summary of the investigation, a synopsis of the facts found, the applicable provisions of the relevant statute, and the investigators' opinion as to what actions, if any, the commissioners should take (FTC Investigation and Hearings Regs. § 18[2]). If a violation is found, in practice the report includes a draft recommendation for the commissioners to issue. In many but not all cases, the commissioners follow the investigators' advice and issue the recommendation as drafted.

The recommendation includes a recitation of the facts, usually identical to the report, the applicable statutory provisions and the remedial measures the respondent is to take (art. 48; FTC Investigation and Hearings Regs. § 20). The respondent is given a fixed period of time to accept or refuse (FTC Investigation and Hearings Regs. § 20[1]). If the respondent accepts, the commissioners issue the recommendation as a legally binding decision with respect to the remedial measures. If the respondent refuses to proceed further, the commissioners must initiate further proceedings by sending the respondent notice of the decision to commence formal hearings (*shimpan tetsuzuki kaishi kettei sho*) (art. 49). This notice—somewhat misleadingly translated as "complaint"—contains a synopsis of the case, which is in practice the statement of facts from the recommendation. It is signed or sealed by each of the participating commissioners and the chairman (art. 50). The particulars as to the time and place of the initial hearing session, the period for answers to be submitted, and the warning that a trial decision may be handed down at the conclusion of the hearings is attached (FTC Investigation and Hearings Regs. § 22).

The hearings follow the format of a Japanese trial. They are adversarial. The investigators open and present the case against the respondent based on the investigation (art. 51-3; FTC Investigation and Hearings Regs. §§ 29, 41, 42, 44, 58). Witnesses, including experts may be called and are sworn as evidence is presented subject to criminal procedures and probations (art. 53-2; FTC Investigation and Hearings Regs. §§ 46, 51, 56). Also following Japanese judicial practice, FTC hearings often take more than a year, with many intermediate sessions. The hearings close with a final statement by the respondent.

They are conducted in most instances by three hearing examiners appointed by the commissioners from among the five examiners attached to the General Affairs Office (art. 35[2]). The 1947 statute provided only for hearings before the commissioners. The present system of trial examiners (art. 51-2) was added in 1949. Hearings may still be conducted by the commissioners—the chairman and no fewer than two commissioners (art. 34; FTC Investigation and Hearings Regs. §25). But, since 1953 at least, apparently there have been only four such cases. Although, as noted, the commissioners ordinarily appoint three examiners, only one is required (FTC Investigation and Hearings Regs. § 26). The 1977 amendments added a provision that gives respondents in most cases the right to present their case directly before the commissioners (art. 53-2-2). Taking this step may significantly increase the burden of formal hearings and further delay decisions.

There is also the rather unusual statutory provision that hearing examiners must have legal as well as economic expertise and may be lawyers engaged in private practice as well as procurators and other graduates of the Legal Training and Research Institute (art. 35[3][4]). Although in the early years many hearing examiners and some investigators were procurators or judges, few are today. As noted previously, judges and procurators had a significant influence on the procedures followed.

Indicative of American influence, formal FTC hearings are also subject to an array of procedural safeguards unusual for other Japanese or German administrative proceedings. FTC regulations guarantee the independence of the hearing examiner (FTC Investigations and Hearings Reg. § 27[2]). By regulation since 1953 (FTC Investigation and Hearings Reg. § 26[2]) and by statute since 1977, no hearing examiner may preside in a case he investigated. In addition to separation of functions to ensure the neutrality of the hearing examiner, the respondent has an array of express procedural rights. These include, unlike Germany, the rights to counsel, to submit supporting evidence, to have the FTC subpoena witnesses and experts to testify on its behalf and to inspect business premises, and to confront and cross-examine adverse witnesses (art. 52; FTC Investigation and Hearings Regs. §§ 44–60). Testimony by witnesses and experts are subject to the evidentiary restrictions imposed in criminal actions (art. 53-2). Unless closed in the public interest—in one case defined to include potential disclosure of business secrets—all hearings are to be public (art. 52-3). A stenographic record of the proceedings must be kept (art. 53[2]). The respondent has a statutory right to inspect and duplicate the record, which includes all documents prepared in one course of proceedings and evidence submitted to the courts upon review (art. 69).[72] Finally, actions taken by the hearing examiners are subject to appeals to the commissioners and if affirmed, review by the courts (FTC Investigation and Hearings Regs. §§ 61-2, 62).

In the most important judicial decision on antitrust enforcement procedures, the Tokyo High Court overturned an FTC decision on the grounds that a participating commissioner had been involved with the investigation and prosecution of the case as a member of the FTC staff prior to his appointment.[73] As a result, the court held the neutrality of the commissioners was sacrificed and the decision could not stand. Although the decision applies only to Japanese antitrust enforcement, it is the strongest statement of the requirement for a separation of functions in Japanese administrative law. The decision explicitly reflected the incorporation of American procedural guarantees into Japanese antitrust law.

These procedural requirements reflect in part the concerns of the draftsmen of the 1947 statute and thus American influences. However, each of the subsequent amendments of the Antimonopoly Law has added to the original safeguards. That no other Japanese administrative proceeding is by statute subject to so detailed and extensive a set of procedural constraints suggests, at least, that concern for procedural safeguards in administrative law can be as great in Japan as elsewhere when the agency involved is essentially regulatory and adversarial rather than promotional. But here too American analogies can mislead. They are justified on grounds of fairness and their contributions to the accuracy of the decisional process. Neither the Japanese government nor the courts, however, have insisted on similar procedural niceties for other administrative proceedings. These restrictions seem to have been motivated and successfully imposed more to encumber the process and make the expenditure of resources by the agency in handling a case more costly than out of any widely held perception that they are required by considerations of justice or due process.

Third-party intervention is also permitted but, at least in terms of the statute, only if considered necessary by the FTC acting on its own authority and discretion rather than by right (art. 59) or, if the third party is a governmental organ (art. 60), subject to commission approval. Apparently the agency has never caused a third party to intervene, but there is at least one instance where a municipality participated by intervention.[74]

*Phase Four: Consent Decisions and Final Contested Decisions.* At any time after the notice of the decision to commence formal hearings has been served but before the FTC has entered a trial decision, the respondent may agree to a consent decision. This is done by submitting a written statement in which the findings of fact and application of law contained in the notice are admitted and a plan for carrying out remedial measures is detailed (art. 53-3). Obviously, the latter may be subject to intense negotiation between the respondent and agency staff, and thus a consent decision will reflect to some extent the influence of adverse publicity arising out of the hearings as well as the anticipated outcome of the proceedings. The option of a consent decision is foreclosed, however, once the commissioners issue the final decision.

If the commissioners have heard the case, the participating members are to begin preparing their decision immediately after the respondent's trial statements. No deadlines are set, however. If hearing examiners have presided, they are required to draft a decision "initial" or "draft" (*shinketsuan*) and submit it with the record to the commissioners within thirty days after the hearings have ended (FTC Investigation and Hearings Regs. § 66). A certified copy is also sent to the respondent, who has two weeks to file a written protest (*igi*) with the commissioners for review (FTC Investigation and Hearings Regs. § 68).

The commissioners then review the hearing examiners' decision and any protests. The statute is silent about the actions the commissioners may take except to provide for them to order that remedial measures be taken if a violation is found (see art. 54). By regulation, however, the commissioners may enter a contested final decision identical to the initial hearing examiners' decision, modify the initial decision, conduct additional hearings before the commissioners, or remand the case back to one hearing examiner for additional hearings (FTC Investigation and Hearings Regs. § 69). There is also an implied power simply to terminate further proceedings. In most past cases the commissioners have entered a decision with little if any change to the initial decision. The commission has also remanded[75] and terminated[76] several cases. The 1977 amendments enacted into statute the prior FTC practice of limiting its findings to evidence presented during the hearing unless unchallenged or commonly known (art. 54-3).

In form, FTC decisions (recommendations, consent, and final) are in writing and must be signed or sealed by the chair and the participating commissioners. They contain a statement of facts, summary of the evidence, application of the law, the holding and measures the respondent is to take, and the grounds for the decision (art. 57[1]). Minority and dissenting opinions may be attached (57[2]), as in the *Tōbu Railways* case,[77] but such an instance is rare. The vast majority of decisions have been unanimous. The commissioners frequently enter decisions that contain a far more abbreviated explanation of reasons than the initial hearing examiners' decision. Nor are the facts of the case as completely described as they could be.[78] In these respects the commissioners' decisions follow the example of Japanese Supreme Court decisions, which seldom involve more than a response to specific arguments made on appeal. One must review the lower court decisions for full explanation of the facts found and complete statement of the case.

An FTC decision comes into force when a certified copy is served on the respondent (art. 58). Although the respondent is to begin taking all remedial measures immediately upon receipt, the decision is not final in the procedural sense until the thirty-day period for appeal to the courts has elapsed. As explained in greater detail below, unless appealed, all FTC decisions have the same effect as a final court judgment.

*Negotiation and Compromise.* Paralleling the formal FTC procedures for enforcement is, as detailed, an informal, private process through which, in fact, most cases are resolved. At every stage in the formal process, but especially before the issuance of the recommendation, antitrust enforcement in Japan involves negotiation and often a delicate compromise. The possibility that a specific case might embroil the agency in political controversy—as well as limitations of manpower and other resources, not to mention the legal restraints on its enforcement powers—make compromise a necessity.

As described in detail in chapter 5, until recently publicity has been the primary source of FTC leverage. Successful private damage actions have been only a theoretical possibility; only a handful of actions have ever been brought, and until 1996 in no case were the plaintiffs able to prove damages. Criminal actions were equally remote until the oil cartel cases and for nearly two decades thereafter.

The advantages of unpublicized compromise remain in most cases mutual. In a particular instance, however, either side may decide that it holds the strong hand and is willing to devote the time and resources to proceed with a formal action. It will thus refuse a negotiated resolution except on its own terms. Under these circumstances the case usually proceeds to the next stage in the process.

Once the commissioners issue a recommendation, the case becomes public and the stakes increase, but the same process of negotiation may continue in forming the final order. A formal recommendation also may reflect the compromise worked out during prior negotiations. In fact whenever a party agrees to a recommendation, outside observers may reasonably conclude that the decision reflects some points of compromise, particularly with respect to the remedial measures to be taken. Afterward, however, the respondent has the choice of either agreeing to take the recommended measures or forcing the commissioners to institute formal hearings. Then the choice is between a consent decision or a final decision, and the statutory constraints increase. At each point there is less room for compromise since the measures the FTC requires the party to take are public, but the FTC may still concede some points.

As a result of these factors the vast majority of all cases end in warnings, and those that result in formal action have been in the form of recommendation decisions. Between 1947 and 1996, out of a total 1,010 decisions, 784 were recommendation decisions. There were only 82 contested final decisions after formal hearings during the entire period, and 27 of these were entered before 1953. Since 1952, use of consent decisions has been even more rare, with only 42 of the total 115 consent decisions having been entered after 1952 as compared to 55 contested final decisions.

### DISCLOSURE OF INFORMATION

Whether by means of criminal or administrative proceedings, or even private civil actions, for the enforcement of law to be effective, the enforcer must have access to as accurate and complete information as possible with respect to nonconforming conduct. Thus any study of the enforcement of a regulatory scheme must necessarily treat the methods by which the regulators obtain the information essential to enforcement and the scope of their legal authority to compel its disclosure.

There is, however, an inevitable tension in any legal order that serves also in part to protect against arbitrary and oppressive governance between the demands of effective law enforcement and the restrictions on the scope and coercive means of governmental supervision over private citizens. Procedural and evidentiary safeguards that necessitate proof of wrongdoing before any sanction can be applied place an even greater burden on the law enforcer to obtain information. So, too, the effective enforcement of legal restrictions on government power itself requires access to information. The rule of law thus increases the need for courts, prosecutors, and other law enforcers to compel submission of relevant evidence by recalcitrant parties. The greater the safeguards against arbitrary government, the greater the need for the means to coerce disclosure of information.

Consequently, the legal framework for compulsory disclosures of information in any one area of the law, such as antitrust, has broader meaning for the legal and political system. At least in the case of Germany and Japan the law reflects choices made with respect to the proper scope of government intervention not only in the private economic sector but also in the everyday affairs of their citizens.

## GERMANY

The GWB empowers the antitrust authorities to compel disclosure of information under several disparate provisions. There are the usual disclosure requirements related to exemptions and approvals sought by a party from the FCO or local authorities. Section 9, for example, provides for disclosures prior to approval for a cartel exemption under sections 2 through 4, and under section 39(5) in the case of mergers, acquisitions, and other consolidations. The basic grant of information-gathering power, however, is set out in section 59 (former §46). This provision authorizes the FCO and local enforcement officials (1) to require submissions or information pertaining to the business[79] of an enterprise or association, (2) to search business premises and to inspect and examine the business documents and records of an enterprise or association, and (3) to require trade and professional associations to disclose bylaws and resolutions and the numbers and names of members.

The exercise of the authority granted under section 59 is subject to a variety of substantive and procedural constraints that limit its general utility in practice. First, no provision in the GWB, including section 59, is construed to give German antitrust authorities general fact-finding authority. Prior to the 1998 amendment, then section 46 was located under the general provisions governing the FCO and local authorities. Some argued that the section was more properly located with the provisions for administrative proceedings, as explained below, to be used in connection with section 57 (former § 54), which enables enforcement officials to conduct "all investigations and obtain all evidence necessary" in administrative enforcement proceedings.[80] These suggestions were heeded. The 1998 amendment places section 59 within a new Chapter I on "Administrative Proceedings" in Part III on "Procedure."

The introductory language to section 59 (*"Soweit es zur Erfüllung der in diesem Gesetz der Kartellbehörde übertragenen Aufgaben erforderlich ist"*) restricts the authorities to information "necessary" to enforcement of the statute. Given this limitation, as emphasized by the Federal Supreme Court in its 1960 decision in the *Vereidigte Buchprüfer* case,[81] section 59 authorizes compulsory disclosure only with respect to specific statutory provisions providing for oversight by the authorities.[82] As restated by the Stuttgart High Court, "The cartel authorities have the power to compel disclosures of information (*Auskunftsbefugnisse*) under § 46, subsec. 3, sent. 1 [current § 59(3)] GWB only to the extent 'necessary' to fulfill their enforcement responsibilities under the GWB. Consequently, no inquiry is permitted that serves only to clarify general economic matters."[83]

No general "right of inquiry" (*Enquete-Recht*)—that is, a right to information apart from a concrete investigatory purpose—is available to the cartel authorities.[84] In effect, section 59 denies the authorities whatever broader powers to compel disclosure of information they might have enjoyed otherwise under existing legislation.[85] As a result, the authorities must justify any formal demand for disclosure as necessary to the enforcement of a specified provision of the GWB in the context of a formal enforcement proceeding.[86]

Despite considerable debate,[87] it is generally conceded that section 59 is to be used solely in connection with administrative proceedings in conjunction with section 57 and does not extend to evidentiary demands in fine proceedings.[88] The principal court decision was the 1960 *Vereidigte Buchprüfer* case. The case involved an appeal from a disclosure demand made by the FCO in the context of a fine proceeding. As noted below, the Federal Supreme Court held that the appeal was in effect an impermissible interlocutory appeal. The respondent must wait, the court stated, until the final decision in the proceedings to appeal. The opinion proceeded to note that disclosure demands in such proceedings should be based on the provisions of the OWIG (§§ 35–47), not on section 46 (current § 59) of the GWB.[89] Although this was apparently the first and last instance of the Federal Cartel Office's use of the section in a fine proceeding,[90] at least one lower court has specifically denied similar use of the section by *Land* authorities.[91]

The distinction between investigations in administrative proceedings and in fine proceedings seems more theoretical than practical. What begins as a purely administrative investigation may lead ultimately to a decision to levy a fine.[92] The discussion on the use of section 46 (current § 59) in fine proceedings appears even more rarified given the permissive use of the information acquired in administrative proceedings in a fine proceeding[93] and the lack of any significant distinction between the scope of the enforcement authorities investigatory powers under the GWB and the OWIG, especially OWIG section 46. The OWIG does make applicable the principal procedural requirements a criminal investigation by the procuracy,[94] but section 59 of the GWB itself contains similar limitations.

Subsections 4 through 7 of GWB section 59 detail the formal procedural prerequisites for searches, inspections, and disclosure demands. A judicial warrant issued by a local court (*Amtsgericht*) is necessary for a search (§ 59[4]). Although theoretically the warrant can be appealed, it may be issued in an *ex parte* proceeding and permits a valid search despite protests.[95] Either a formal decision in writing (*Einzelverfügung*) by the federal minister of economics or highest *Land* authority or a collegial ruling (*Beschluß*) of the FCO signed by the president is required under section 59(6) and (7) for disclosure orders and demands to inspect books and records.[96] In each case the legal grounds (*Rechtsgrundlage*), object (*Gegenstand*), and purpose (*Zweck*) for the disclosure or inspection must be given. In other words, the investigation must explain the relevance of the information sought to a specific statutory provision.[97]

These prerequisites are coupled with the requirement that the disclosure order take the form of a written interrogatory,[98] each question then being subject to justification by the authorities that the answer relates to the ground, object, and purpose set forth in the decision or ruling.[99] The respondent may refuse to answer any question that does not meet the tests of necessity and relevance.[100]

Refusal to reply to the antitrust authorities may also be based on section 59(5), which provides for the right to silence based on potential incrimination or claims of privileged information. Under this provision a party may refuse to give information that might subject the party or a relative within the scope of section 383(1) through (3) of the Code of Civil Procedure (ZPO) to the risk of either criminal prosecution or the application of administrative sanctions.[101] Nor may disclosures be compelled where the information was obtained in the context of a privileged relationship under section 383 of the ZPO. This privilege extends to lawyers, accountants, and tax advisors,[102] and enforcement officials have been very critical of the use of attorneys to prevent adverse disclosures.[103] Whether these protections apply equally to individuals and corporate entities remains subject to dispute, however.[104]

How seriously such restrictions affect the ability of German antitrust enforcers to obtain information is not clear. No enforcement system short of terror or continuous supervision can overcome such obstacles as the failure to keep records or their destruction. The effect of the restrictions on the investigatory powers of the German authorities is evident, however, in lower court decisions upholding objections to disclosure demands,[105] in the resort to surprise search and seizures, and, perhaps most telling, in the use of informal, noncompulsory requests for information.

One scholar[106] has estimated that 90 percent of all the information obtained by the FCO is produced as a result of voluntary responses to informal letters of request. In an insightful look into this practice, another commentator[107] notes that the authorities are willing to accept less complete and probably less accurate information through such voluntary submissions rather than attempting to comply with the requirements of section 59. Acquiescence is not purely voluntary. The authorities have section 59 on which to fall back. For the party being questioned, the desire to maintain cordial relations with the enforcement authorities, the lack of sanctions for incomplete or inaccurate answers, the knowledge that section 59 can always be invoked, and thus in some cases the hope that a cooperative attitude will forestall broader compulsory investigation are factors that promote a positive response.[108]

## Japan

One of the most revealing contrasts between German and Japanese antitrust enforcement is the dearth of any discussion in Japan on the ability of the FTC (or a private party) to require disclosure of information during the course of a formal enforcement action. Only as Japanese enterprises and individuals became involved in American antitrust and other suits in the United States, it seems, did the problems of discovery and administrative investigative power begin to surface as an issue in Japan.[109]

The German legal limitations on disclosure are exacerbated in Japan. That few have addressed this problem can be first explained by the unique regulatory position of the FTC. The economic ministries with their diffuse programs to promote Japanese industry, unlike the FTC, need not rely on legal means of coercion to obtain information. It flows with relative ease from those such authorities aid.[110] There is also the lingering governmental hostility to private litigation. This is manifested by the disinclination on the part of governmental officials or those who exercise political power in Japan to ease the private litigants' burden by placing discovery powers in their hands.[111] Consequently, Japan has left undeveloped even the limited disclosure powers available in Germany.

The Antimonopoly Law on its face would appear to give the FTC adequate means of forcing disclosure. Coincidentally parallel to the GWB the principal provision is article 46, the first paragraph of which provides:

> The Fair Trade Commission may, in order to conduct necessary investigations with regard to a case, take such measures as mentioned in each of the following subparagraphs:

(i) to summon and question persons connected with a case, or witnesses, or cause thereto submit their views or reports;

(ii) to summon experts and cause them to give expert testimony;

(iii) to order persons holding books of account, documents, and other materials to submit the same, and retain such submitted matters;

(iv) to enter any place of business or other necessary place and inspect the state of business operations, books of account, and other materials.

Subparagraph (iii) empowers the FTC "to order persons holding books of account, documents, or other materials" to submit them to the agency and to retain them. Read into the statute is the requirement that the requested materials are necessary for the investigation[112] a narrow construction from an American perspective. The 1977 amendment replaced the prior term *rinken suru* (to conduct a spot inspection) with *tachi-iri* (to enter) and added the following paragraph to article 46: "The authority to take disciplinary actions pursuant to the provisions of paragraph (1) above shall not be construed as granted for a criminal investigation."

The purpose of these changes was to insulate the FTC from the search warrant and other procedural requirements of articles 53 and 35 of the Constitution.[113] Current constitutional interpretation limits these provisos to criminal investigations. Administrative searches are considered exempt. Consequently, inspections conducted at the investigatory stage by the FTC— as opposed to investigations by the procuracy or the FTC in the context of a criminal proceeding—are thought not to require judicially supervised warrants. This interpretation apparently rests largely on prewar continental concepts of the distinctive nature of administrative law. Thus the language of article 46 as amended was intended to affirm the administrative nature of the FTC's exercise of investigatory powers. Doubts as to the validity of this distinction are expressed, however.[114]

More potent limitations than constitutional constraints blunt the effectiveness of the FTC's investigatory powers. One consequence of the close personal contact between the bureaucracy and business is an apparent difficulty in preventing leaks of pending investigations and especially searches to the firms and individuals concerned. In 1973, for example, the FTC conducted a spot inspection of oil companies operating in Japan. It is generally believed, however, that many of the firms involved had several hours' prior notice, and at least the opportunity to destroy or hide damaging documents. (Nonetheless, as described below, sufficient evidence was obtained to convict the firms and various executives of criminal violations.) Perhaps the most serious legal obsta-

PROCESSES AND PROCEDURES

cles to effective investigation are the narrow limits of the FTC's subpoena power and the lack of any meaningful sanctions to enforce FTC orders. Spot searches enable the agency to uncover only what the investigators themselves can find. Reliance on searches and seizures thus seems to reflect the inability of the agency to force the parties being investigated to submit vital documents. There are at least two causes for this inability. First, the broad-gauged subpoenas of American administrative practice are not acceptable under Japanese law. The FTC must describe with specificity the documents and other materials being requested. Spot searches are often used simply to uncover information concerning the existence of particular documents in the possession of a party in order to permit the FTC later to order their submission. Nor apparently has there been any attempt by the agency to require certain records be kept that could be used in an investigation.

Second, the FTC can do very little if the party responds that the requested materials are missing or simply that it doesn't know anything about them. Since courts in Japan (as in other civil law jurisdictions) do not have general contempt powers or any analog (as in Germany), the only means of enforcement is through the formal criminal process, with the government having to prove that the party had failed to produce materials actually in its possession.

The limitations on the FTC's ability to get at necessary evidence was illustrated vividly several years ago at a conference in New York City on Japanese antitrust law. An official from the Japanese FTC bridled when the disclosure power of the agency was questioned. He proceeded to read article 46. When then asked what happens when a firm refuses to comply with an FTC order for documents or other information, with the excuse that the documents are lost or that they cannot be found, the official admitted, "In that case, of course, we can do nothing."

## JUDICIAL REVIEW AND THE ROLE OF THE COURTS

The formal legal framework for judicial review and other means of judicial participation in antitrust enforcement is unexpectedly similar in Germany and Japan. The contrasts in practice—especially differences in the frequency of appeals and resort to other forms of judicial relief—tend to overshadow the similarities in structure and judicial construction of antitrust law in both countries.

In judicial review of antitrust cases, Japan often departs from traditional continental patterns, as a result of American influence on both the postwar constitution and the Antimonopoly Law. So too in this area, however, does

131

Germany. Where Japan differs from American practice, however, it adheres primarily to a German model. Paradoxically, despite formal similarities, in no other area of antitrust enforcement is the contrast between Germany and Japan greater. Whereas German courts have played a pivotal role in the development of German antitrust law, their Japanese counterparts have exerted only sporadic influence. Simply in terms of numbers, German courts hear nearly as many antitrust appeals in an average year as Japanese courts have decided in the past fifty years.

## Germany

One of the distinguishing features of continental European legal systems is the historical separation of administrative courts from the ordinary judiciary and the corollary development of other special courts. Throughout Europe the structure of the judiciary as a whole reflects the dichotomy between public and private law.[115] The German administrative court structure generally parallels the four-tiered hierarchy of local courts (*Amtsgerichte*), district courts (*Landgerichte*), high courts (*Oberlandesgerichte*), and at the apex, the Federal Supreme Court (*Bundesgerichtshof*) of the ordinary judiciary. (There is no administrative court equivalent to the local *Amtsgericht.*) Since 1945 the administrative courts have had jurisdiction over all public law disputes except for cases subject by statute to the jurisdiction of other courts.[116] Such exceptions include constitutional cases, heard by the special Constitutional Court (*Verfassungsgericht*); tax appeals, subject to the fiscal courts (*Finanzgerichte*); labor disputes, subject to special labor courts (*Arbeitsgerichte*); suits against the government under welfare and social legislation, subject to the social courts (*Sozialgerichte*); and antitrust cases.

As described in chapter 2, the drafters of the GWB attempted to provide a degree of judicial specialization over antitrust matters by concentrating all first appeals (*Beschwerde*), involving issues of fact and law, in the ordinary high courts at the site of the relevant enforcement authority.[117] Had the administrative courts retained jurisdiction over appeals from administrative decisions, a potential for conflict would have existed in the construction of various provisions of the law between the administrative courts hearing the appeals and the ordinary courts deciding damage actions. Consequently, the provisions of section 63(4) for first appeals in general and of section 83(1) for first appeals from administrative fine decisions give the high court at the site of the *Land* authorities[118] exclusive jurisdiction over actions brought against them under the GWB. Under these provisions the high court or *Kammergericht* in Berlin has had exclusive jurisdiction over first appeals from actions by the

FCO. From 1999 the high court in Dusseldorf is the court that will hear such appeals. Second appeals (*Rechtsbeschwerde*), which are solely on points of law from high court decisions, are heard by the special antitrust panel (*Kartellsenat*) of the Federal Supreme Court (GWB § 74). The attempt at concentration is undercut somewhat in that the ordinary district courts have exclusive jurisdiction as courts of first instance over civil disputes, and even the local courts may play an important role in the development of judicial construction of the GWB through review of petitions by the enforcement authorities for search warrants under section 59(4) and provisions of the OWIG that apply to administrative fine proceedings.[119] Their decisions are subject to review on appeal up to the Federal Supreme Court, removing the potential for significant conflicts that would exist were the administrative courts competent to hear administrative appeals.

The exceptional competence of the regular courts over antitrust suits and the application generally of rules of civil procedure to the proceedings do not free judicial review of antitrust decisions from the influence of administrative court practices and procedures. The provisions of the GWB on appeals are read in light of concepts developed in the context of the administrative court system that prescribe both the scope of judicial review and the nature of judicial relief.

Unknown in German practice are the assortment of special writs developed by English courts for judicial control over executive powers.[120] Rather, from the mid nineteenth century, German scholars articulated a set of general abstractions to provide a conceptual basis for administrative judiciary to ensure the proper application of the law[121] and to protect the citizen from illegal official measures.[122] The concept of an "administrative act" (*Verwaltungsakt*) served as the conceptual linchpin. Defined variously by German scholars,[123] the term encompasses measures taken in a particular case by public officials in the public law sphere with some legal consequence.[124] In general only administrative acts are reviewable[125] or enforceable.[126] Consequently, defining whether a particular action constitutes an administrative act subsumes many of the underlying "standing," "case and controversy," and reviewability issues in American law.

The typical administrative act is a formal administrative order (*Verfügung*), which includes decisions (*Entscheidungen*) and decrees (*Beschluß*).[127] Thus the language of section 63(1) of the GWB is read in terms of the traditional limitations on judicial review. It provides that a first appeal (*Beschwerde*) is permitted against all orders (*Verfügungen*) of the Cartel Authority. The language of one Federal Supreme Court decision suggests that not only "orders" but also other "sovereign measures" (*hoheitliche Maßnahme*) of the authorities are reviewable under section 63(1) in light of the requirements of article 19(4)[128] of the Constitution. Scholars also criticize the restrictions imposed by traditional theory.[129] Nonetheless, the courts adhere to the requirement that the action reviewed constitute an administrative act (leaving room for debate whether the term "order" in section 63[1] is coextensive or narrower than "administrative act").[130] Such informal actions as requests for information by the FCO are not considered subject to review by direct appeal.[131] Even more formal measures, such as calling a public hearing on a proposed merger, are not reviewable.[132]

Intertwined with the notion of administrative acts are the available forms of judicial relief or "remedies" of German administrative law. As codified today in the Code of Administrative Courts (VwGO), they include principally the action for revocation (or rescission) of an administrative act (*Anfechtungsklage*) and the action for issuance of an administrative act (*Verpflichtungsklage*) of section 42.[133] Section 43 of the VwGO also provides for a declaratory action (*Feststellungsklage*) as to the existence or nonexistence of a legal relationship and the nullity of an administrative act. Section 63 of the GWB echoes this catalog of actions, except that no provision is made for a more general declaratory action.[134] The provision of section 63(1), quoted above, for appeals from orders by the enforcement authorities is considered to refer to an *Anfechtungsklage,* while the right to a *Verpflichtungsklage* arises from section 63(3): "A first appeal is also permitted from the failure of the Cartel Authority to issue an order applied for, to which the applicant claims to have a right."[135] Despite some discussion over the need for broader forms of relief,[136] there is little evidence that these two actions do not adequately cover the spectrum of appellants' needs, given the initial restrictions relevant in the requirement and definition of an administrative act.

As noted, implicit in the definition of administrative acts is a limitation on who is entitled to relief. Under generally accepted views of "standing," only a party whose "interest" is affected by the administrative measure is entitled to legal protection (*Rechtsschutzbedürfnis*) and satisfies the requirements for an appeal (*Klagebefugnis*).[137] These requirements cannot be satisfied unless the measure constitutes an administrative act in the first place, since it would otherwise not have a "legal" consequence. In addition, the party challenging the measure must be the object of the act. Section 63(2) essentially restates this requirement in providing for appeals only by parties to enforcement proceedings: "First appeals may be filed by parties in proceedings before the Cartel Authority (§ 54[2] and [3])."

In addition, section 67 provides:

(1) Parties to the proceedings before the appellate court shall be:

1. the appellant;
2. the Cartel Authority against whose decision the appeal is made;
3. persons and associations of persons whose interests are substantially affected by the decision and who, upon application, have been admitted to the proceedings by the Cartel Authority.

(2) If the appeal is against a decision of a supreme *Land* authority, the Federal Cartel Office shall also be a party.

Excluded under these provisions are persons invited to comment but not participate as a party. Potential applicants under sections 63(3) and 67 are also subject to the general requirement that they have the requisite legal interest to seek relief from the administrative action (or failure to take action) subject to the appeal.[138] Under section 67, however, parties whose real, but not necessarily legal, interests are affected may participate in the appellate proceedings although not as the appellant. The provision creates an exception to the general rule.[139]

Ordinarily, the filing of an appeal generally suspends the effectiveness of the appealed administrative action.[140] The GWB adopts a more restrictive approach in section 64(1) by providing that an appeal suspends the effect of listed orders only. This list covers revocation, withdrawal, or modification of approvals for exempt cartels and mergers and orders invalidating agreements and resolutions or prohibiting certain conduct. Not included are initial approvals for exempt cartels. Under section 65 the authorities are empowered to override the suspensive effect of section 64(1) if found to be required by the "public interest" or the predominant interest of a party. The appellate court may again suspend the effect of the order if (1) the conditions for its issuance no longer exist, (2) its legality is subject to serious question, or (3) its enforcement would result in undue hardship for the respondent (appellant) and is not required by an overriding public interest (§ 65[3]). These conditions must also be met for the appellate court to suspend the affect of an order not listed in section 64(1). The 1980 amendments gave the enforcement authorities similar authority to issue suspensive orders (current § 65(3), former § 63a[3]).

The limitations on access to judicial review should not be misconstrued as an unreasonable restriction on the role of the courts or on judicial oversight (either by administrative or ordinary courts) of administrative actions. The limitations on reviewability reflect in part the need to restrict the cases that the courts must hear to protect the efficiency of both the judicial and administrative processes. This need is arguably greater in Germany than in the United States, in that German judges generally scrutinize administrative actions on appeal more intensively than do American judges. As noted, a first appeal involves a *de novo* trial of the facts and law. The GWB also expressly permits the court to hear new facts and evidence not presented in the administrative proceeding (§ 63[1]2). Section 70 gives the court extensive authority to conduct an independent, supplemental investigation of the facts underlying an appealed order or failure to take action. Although at least one case holds that this provision does not permit the court to initiate an investigation in lieu of or as a substitute for an administrative investigation,[141] the judges are to decide on the basis of their "independent conclusions reached from the entire record of the proceedings." Only the evaluations of the economy made by the FCO or federal minister of economics under sections 4, (repealed in 1998), 8, and 42 are beyond separate reappraisal by the courts (§ 71[5]2).

The procedural protections perhaps justifiably absent in administrative proceedings become critical in such intensive review. Consequently, the GWB provides that no judicial decision can be based on facts or evidence on which the parties did not have the opportunity to comment (§ 71[1]). The parties have access to the files of the court, and the court cannot rely on records in the files of the administrative authorities unless the parties have been given access to them (§ 72[2]).

A second appeal on issues of law (*Rechtsbeschwerde*) to the Federal Supreme Court is provided for in sections 74 through 76. The second appeal may be taken only where the high court has granted leave to appeal. Under section 74, leave to appeal is to be given in cases where a legal issue of "fundamental importance" is presented or a decision of the Federal Supreme Court is necessary for the development of the law or uniform construction and application. A second appeal is only permitted as a matter of right under section 74(4) for any one of the following procedural defects: illegal composition of the high court, participation by a judge who should be excluded as a matter of law or on grounds of prejudice, denial of the right to be heard, violation of the right to legal representation of a party under the law, violation of the right to a public trial, or failure of the appellate court to give reasons for the decision. A party may appeal a decision denying leave to appeal to the Federal Supreme Court (section 75). Thus the Supreme Court ultimately decides what issues should be decided except where the party has an appeal of right for one of the listed procedural defects or the high court grants leave to appeal. The Federal Supreme Court must adjudicate the appeal in either instance.

Finally, to ensure expertise, appeals are heard by the special antitrust panel (or *Senat*[142]) of the court.

## Japan

Although basically similar to American practice, judicial review of Japanese FTC decisions involves several problems unique to Japan. These must be understood at the outset. The postwar Japanese constitution attempted to superimpose the powers and prerogatives of an American-styled judiciary onto a continental-based system. Under the constitution the judiciary is an independent, coequal branch of government in which the "whole judicial power" is vested (including explicitly the power of judicial review). Special courts outside the ordinary judiciary, such as the prewar Administrative Court (*gyōsei saibansho*), were abolished and their reestablishment prohibited. Nor may any executive agency be given final judicial power or any private citizen denied access to court. Although Japanese courts have adopted some of the protective restrictions of American judicial powers, such as a "case and controversy" requirement, they do not exercise broad equity powers or, as noted, contempt power. Also, much of the prewar German jurisprudence that limited direct appeals from administrative actions remains intact. In effect the Japanese judiciary retains the most restrictive features of prewar Germany and the United States without the broader remedial powers of either.

In terms of organization, the Japanese judicial system comprises four levels and five types of courts. At the apex is the Supreme Court (*saikō saibansho*), in Tokyo. Fifteen politically appointed justices constitute the full court, or Grand Bench, and there are three petty benches of five justices each. With few exceptions, the Supreme Court exercises only appellate jurisdiction for *jōkoku* appeals (a second appeal on matters of law based on the German *Rechtsbeschwerde*).

Below the Supreme Court are eight high courts (*kōto saibansho*), in Tokyo, Osaka, Nagoya, Hiroshima, Fukuoka, Sendai, Sapporo, and Takamatsu. The high courts have jurisdiction in three types of cases: *kōso* appeals or first appeals from district court judgments that, as in the case of Germany, involve a *de novo* finding of the facts; *jōkoku* appeals where *kōso* appeal was heard by a district court (only in civil cases); and *kokoku* appeals in appeals from court rulings or administrative decisions. The high courts usually sit in three-judge panels.

The 52 district courts (*chihō saibansho*) with their 203 branches are the primary courts of first instance. They do exercise appellate jurisdiction in civil cases tried in summary courts (*kan'i saibansho*). At the same level are an equal number of family courts (*katei saibansho*) with exclusive original jurisdiction over disputes involving divorce, adoption, and succession and criminal actions involving minors. The summary courts are the lowest courts in the judicial hierarchy, with jurisdiction only in cases where the amount in controversy does not exceed ¥ 900,000 (approximately U.S.$ 6,500) and minor criminal offenses.

The Japanese courts have both an enforcement and a reviewing role in antitrust cases. Even in cases where there has been no FTC enforcement action, as explained in more detail in chapter 5, the courts may determine the validity of contracts alleged to be in violation of the Antimonopoly Law[143] and entertain regular tort actions for antitrust violations.[144] Civil contract and tort actions also provide a means for indirect review of FTC actions.

Although the separate system for review of administrative actions by a special administrative court in Japan—there was only one—patterned on the German model was abolished under the postwar constitution, the distinction between administrative and ordinary suits and much of the conceptual trappings of German administrative law have remained. Occupation reformers paid scant attention to the problem of reconciling significantly different notions of judicial review.[145] The 1948 Administrative Case Litigation Special Regulations Law,[146] which provided special procedural rules for administrative cases, neglected the basic issue of restrictive judicial review and soon proved to be inadequate in dealing with narrow technical issues. In 1962 the Diet enacted the Administrative Case Litigation Law,[147] the current statute governing administrative cases. It provides for four types of administrative suits or *kōkoku* appeals (*kōkoku sōsho*) based on the German *Beschwerde*:[148] actions for the revocation of dispositions (*shobun no torikeshi no uttae*), actions for the revocation of administrative decisions and rulings (*saiketsu no torikeshi no uttae*), declaratory actions for the affirmation of the illegality of not acting or "forbearance" (*fusakui no ihō kakunin no uttae*), and declaratory actions for the affirmation of nullity (*mukō kakunin no uttae*). No action exists enabling the courts to require an affirmative undertaking by an administrative agency similar to the *Verpflichtungsklage*. The usual form of an administrative appeal from an FTC decision is a *kōkoku* appeal seeking judicial revocation of the decision.

Appeals from FTC decisions differ from appeals from almost all other administrative agencies in two respects. First, the Tokyo High Court has exclusive jurisdiction (art. 86). Second, article 80 of the Antimonopoly Law provides that findings of fact by the FTC, if supported by substantial evidence, are binding on the court in an appeal (art. 80). Both features of FTC appeals reflect the influence of American administrative organization and procedures. The Tokyo High Court has exclusive jurisdiction over appeals from decisions by the Patent Office, the Marine Disasters Board of Inquiry, and the Radio Regulatory Council, all of which were established as agencies with quasi-judicial decision-making authority. The substantial evidence rule is a similar anomaly in the Japanese system. With the exception of the three agency decisions to which this American-derived innovation applies,[149] administrative decisions in Japan as in Germany are subject to *de novo* fact finding by courts as, indeed, are the judgments of courts of first instance on appeal. Particularly troublesome in recent cases has been the conundrum of reconciling the limitation on full judicial review resulting from the substantial evidence rule with the constitutional guarantee of access to court, which in the Japanese context can be persuasively argued to include the right to a *de novo* trial. The courts have responded by noting that FTC findings, although binding on appeal in the case of consent and contested final decisions, remain subject to full *de novo* review in damage actions and partial review on direct appeal even under the rule.

The courts have in effect given appellants ample opportunity to challenge FTC findings through close scrutiny of all evidence submitted during the FTC proceedings. The 1977 amendments reduced even further whatever significance the rule may have had by permitting the introduction of new evidence that the commission failed to take into consideration "without good cause" or was not possible to present during FTC hearings without gross negligence on the part of the submitting party (art. 81).

Few FTC decisions are appealed. Of the eighty-two formal or contested decisions entered between 1947 and March 1996, only twenty-nine were appealed.[150] Of these only five were reversed in part and remanded for further proceedings.[151] In the remainder the FTC decision was upheld.[152] Even fewer cases, ten in total, have been appealed further to the Supreme Court.[153] In that forum the FTC has yet to lose a case.

An additional issue has been whether all three types of decisions are appealable. Ordinarily, a respondent would not challenge a recommendation or consent decision to which it consented. Nonetheless, this issue was faced in six companion appeals decided by the Third Petty Bench of the Supreme Court of April 4, 1978.

The cases involved the 1974 recommendation decision against Idemitsu Kōsan K.K. and eleven other Japanese oil refiners and sellers[154] for fixing the price of petroleum products in November 1973. The twelve respondents agreed in the decision to terminate price controls, to inform all customers and the

FTC of the measures taken in doing so, and also to keep the FTC informed annually about prices, sales, and inventories. In an unprecedented subsequent action the FTC filed criminal referrals based on the decision with the Tokyo High Court Procurator's Office pursuant to article 73 of the Antimonopoly Law. The criminal referrals were actually filed on February 19, 1978, only four days after the recommendation was accepted by the respondents, the papers having been finalized on the day of their acceptance (Feb. 15).[155] As explained in chapter 5, a formal FTC referral is a prerequisite for any criminal prosecution under the statute. Simultaneously, a separate referral was filed against the Petroleum Federation (Sekiyu Renmei) for output restrictions on the basis of a companion recommendation decision.[156]

Six of the respondent firms[157] then appealed the recommendation decision, challenging it on various procedural grounds. Underlying their appeals was the unarticulated charge that they had been misled by the FTC in accepting the recommendation in that they understood that no further action would be brought if the recommendations were carried out. The Tokyo High court rejected the appeal on the merits and dismissed the respondents' claim for revocation of the FTC decision.[158] On jōkoku appeal the Supreme Court upheld the dismissal on the ground that, inasmuch as the findings as to the existence of the violation in the recommendation decision were not formally adjudicated, there was no basis for the appeal.[159]

The Supreme Court's decision can best be understood in light of the generally restrictive standards for direct review of administrative actions in Japan. As noted above, the concept of judicial power is construed narrowly despite the American origins of the postwar constitution. Japanese judges and scholars read into the requirement of a "legal dispute" (hōritsu jō no funsō) for a justiciable case under article 3 of the Court Organization Law[160] the "legal interest" notion derived from prewar German theory including the prerequisite of "an administrative act" in addition to a requirement analogous to the American case and controversy doctrine.[161] The result is that appeals are permitted only from formal administrative dispositions that have direct legal effect on the rights or duties of the appellant. Consequently, appeals by third parties to whom FTC decisions are not directed are considered not to have standing to appeal.[162] Nor may appeals be taken from nonbinding, informal actions by administrative officials.[163] The court reasoned that since the fact of a violation is not itself a necessary element in a recommendation decision or, at least, is not expressly admitted by the respondents but is included simply as a means of clarifying the remedial measures they agree to take, the findings are not judicially reviewable under articles 80, 81, and 82(i).

Recommendation decisions do provide a basis for damage actions under articles 25 and 26. The Supreme Court confirmed in the oil company appeals that the findings in recommendation decisions have *res judicata* effect, but they are not conclusive and therefore remain rebuttable in damage actions.[164] Consequently, as noted, even in recommendation decisions, FTC findings of fact are indirectly reviewable.

# 5 / Remedies and Sanctions

A perceived failure of enforcement was a major theme in discussion of antitrust policy in both Germany and Japan during the 1970s and 1980s. German critics charged that antitrust violations were increasingly being viewed as a *Kavaliersdelikt*, a peccadillo, not deserving much more than a slap on the wrist.[1] In Japan, on the other hand, the 1947 antitrust statute seemed to many to be little more than an abandoned remnant of occupation reforms.[2] Such concerns led to proposals and ultimately repeated legislative action since the mid 1970s to reinforce the available sanctions of both the GWB and the Japanese Antimonopoly Law.

With respect to remedies and sanctions the amendments, especially in the 1970s, were remarkably similar. The 1973 legislation in Germany expanded and the 1977 amendments in Japan added new statutory surcharges to prevent offenders from profiting from illegal cartels. Both increased tenfold the maximum statutory fines. The debates that preceded these amendments continue, especially in Japan. The points raised then and now bring into clearer focus not only the role of penalties in coercing compliance with substantive legal standards, but also the limits of law as defined by the available penalties. Examination of the sanctions and remedies of German and Japanese antitrust law thus yields insights beyond antitrust enforcement. It highlights features of the German and Japanese legal systems that are often obscured by emphasis on substantive law and raises fundamental questions about the nature and role of sanctions in all legal orders.

Both the German and Japanese antitrust statutes set forth an impressive array of penalties and sanctions against antitrust violations. They include administrative fines, private damage actions, and, in the case of Japan, criminal penalties. In practice, however, their effectiveness as deterrents remains questionable. The doubts relate in large part to limitations inherent in individual types of penalties. Features of both legal systems also contribute. Compensating at least in part for the weakness of formal sanctions is the deterrent effect of adverse publicity and the didactic role antitrust enforcement has played in both countries.

The principal formal sanctions under both statutes are administrative fines (of which the most significant is an administratively determined surcharge to recapture the proceeds of illegal conduct). The surcharge was expanded in Germany by the 1980 amendment of the GWB and introduced in Japan by the 1977 amendment of the Antimonopoly Law. Both statutes also provide for civil (nontreble) damage actions. Judicial construction of the GWB and difficulties of proof in both German and Japanese law have diminished (in the Federal Republic) or precluded (in Japan) the efficacy of damage actions as a deterrent. Finally, the Japanese statute provides for criminal penalties, although, to anticipate subsequent discussion, there have been few significant criminal prosecutions. German law differs in not subjecting antitrust violations as such to criminal sanctions, although by recent amendment the German Criminal Code now makes bid rigging a crime.[3] Rather, antitrust violations are treated as *Ordnungswidrigkeiten,* administrative or regulatory offenses. As such they are subject to administrative fine proceedings but not criminal actions.

The concept of an equity power to fashion nonstatutory remedies in order to provide effective relief is alien to both German and Japanese notions of judicial and administrative authority. Beccaria's eighteenth-century maxims *nullum crimen sine lege* and *nulla poena sine legem* have long been incorporated as fundamental constitutional principles in civil law systems, including Germany's and Japan's.[4] All remedies and sanctions must have specific statutory basis. Consequently, the antitrust enforcement authorities in both Germany and Japan are restricted to the limited remedial authority and sanctions delineated by statute. The Antimonopoly Law explicitly empowers the enforcement authorities "to take any other measures necessary to eliminate acts in violation" of various prohibitions,[5] but this language is not construed to give the authorities the breadth of remedial authority that a corresponding grant of equity powers would give an American administrative agency.

Nor do courts in either country have general contempt power. In the case of the Federal Republic there is an apparent but little used analog,[6] but not in Japan. A violation of a court or administrative order may be subject by statute in specific instances to criminal penalty, but, as explained in detail below, criminal sanctions present a variety of special obstacles. Consequently, Germany and Japan have shared a common weakness in antitrust enforcement—the lack of extensive legal sanctions—with a common result: administrative fines, especially the illegal proceeds surcharge, have become the most frequently used statutory sanctions. Education and adverse publicity, however, may be the most effective actual deterrents.

### GENERAL REMEDIAL POWERS

Unlike the GWB, the Japanese antitrust statute provides for open-ended remedial powers rather than fines as the primary enforcement mechanism. The Antimonopoly Law expressly grants the FTC broad powers to order all corrective actions necessary to eliminate violations. These are contained in a cluster of provisions added by amendment in 1949 in relation to specific prohibitions. Article 7, for example, gives the FTC the authority to order a party in violation of the proscriptions against private monopolization and unreasonable restraints of trade in article 3 to cease and desist the violation, to report corrective measures taken, to transfer part of a violating firm's business, and to take "any other measures necessary to eliminate such acts in violation." An innovation of the 1977 amendments, article 8-4, gives the agency additional authority to order divestiture and other structural changes to deal with monopoly power. Article 20 contains a similar provision with respect to unfair business practices, and since 1977 the FTC has had the authority to delete clauses constituting an unfair business practice from contracts. Article 8-2 provides for similar measures to remedy violations by trade associations as well as authority to dissolve an offending association. Under article 17-2(1) companies and juridical persons in violation of the proscriptions against excessive or illegal intercorporate shareholding and illegal mergers may be required to file reports, dispose of any stock held in violation of the statute, transfer a part of the offending company's business, and take other necessary measures to eliminate the violation. Article 17-2(2) grants the FTC similar authority to correct illegal interlocking directorates and officerships, and article 18 permits the FTC to bring a civil action (in the Tokyo High Court) to have illegal holding companies or mergers declared null and void. These powers have been more restricted in practice, however, than they appear on the face of the statute.

First, the scope of FTC orders is narrow. Mandated remedial measures in a decision are considered legally binding only with respect to the violations set out in the facts of the decision. If the decision refers to an illegal price-fixing agreement concluded on, say, March 31, 2000, and orders the respondents to eliminate that violation, it would not necessarily apply to an identical agreement concluded the next day. Thus the FTC has been forced to bring consecutive actions against the same respondents to eliminate what was in technical legal terms a series of separate agreements to fix prices but to the businessman simply a single price-fixing arrangement formally confirmed after each successive FTC decision.[7]

A second limitation is that without effective sanctions to enforce compliance, the FTC is left with little other than adverse publicity to ensure its orders are followed. Apparently, the FTC has never attempted to impose a criminal fine for violation of an order. In addition to criminal fines, the statute provides for administrative fines for failure to comply with FTC decisions[8] and court injunctions,[9] but the amounts are fixed at levels that do not operate as a deterrent. Since 1977 the maximum fine under article 97 has been ¥500,000 (approximately U.S. $4,167 at current rates), an increase from ¥50,000 (U.S. $417). The maximum fine under article 98 has similarly remained ¥300,000 (U.S. $2,500), an increase from ¥30,000 (U.S. $250). Rarely if ever invoked, these provisions do not offer an effective substitute for contempt. This failure of those who drafted the law to appreciate the underlying deficiency caused by the lack of contempt power in the Japanese legal system is best revealed in their provision for judicial injunctive relief.

With American models in mind, the drafters of the 1947 statute empowered the Tokyo High Court to issue, upon application by the FTC, a temporary injunction against acts suspected to be in violation of the law when found to be a matter of urgent necessity.[10] Such a provision makes little technical sense in the Japanese legal system. Court injunctions are used in the United States to obtain the sanction of contempt. Because the contempt sanction is not available for the enforcement of administrative orders, a judicial order is necessary. As in the United States, an order by the FTC itself is as legally binding as a court order. Unlike the United States, however, in Japan no contempt power is available to enforce either. Thus the function of a court injunction in the United States to enable enforcement by the threat of contempt does not apply in Japan.

Requiring the FTC to seek court action does have two advantages. First, it gives the respondent an opportunity to defend before a neutral forum. Second, resort to the court for injunctive relief enables the agency to trigger public response by publicizing its concern and that of the court over a particular violation. Thus as one might expect, its use has been infrequent, limited to major cases with substantial political impact—five cases involving the newspaper industry[11] and the *Yawata-Fuji Steel Merger* case.[12] In construing the urgent necessity requirement, the courts have held that it relates to a situation in which "fair competition is . . . extremely endangered and it would be impossible to eliminate the violation following normal procedures."[13]

The GWB as enacted provided that in the case of willful violations, the fine of DM 100,000 (approximately U.S. $25,000 at the prevailing exchange rate in 1958) could be increased by a surcharge equal to three times any "excess proceeds" (*Mehrerlös*) realized as a result of the violation.[14] In cases of negligent violations the surcharge was double the amount of such illegal proceeds to be added to the maximum fine of DM 30,000. The provision was patterned after section 6 of the OWIG (since 1968, section 17[4]).[15] The 1973 amendments abolished the distinction between willful and negligent violations, setting a uniform treble surcharge and retaining the DM 100,000 maximum fine.[16] GWB section 38(4) (currently § 34[3]) was revised further in 1980 to permit the authorities to calculate the amount realized from illegal conduct on the basis of estimates, and a new provision—section 37b—was added to provide for a similar treble levy on gains realized in cases of willful or negligent violations of prohibition orders against abuses of market power, generally under section 22(5) or specifically in the case of public utilities under section 103(6). In contrast to the illegal proceeds surcharge under section 38(4), which was levied in the context of an administrative fine proceeding subject to the procedural controls of sections 81 through 85 of the GWB and sections 38 through 47 of the OWIG, the surcharge under section 37b was determined in an ordinary administrative proceeding[17] subject to the more lax procedures of sections 51 through 80 of the GWB. The 1998 amendment combined the two surcharge provisions in a new section 34 and thereby eliminated their distinctions. As a penalty the treble surcharge of illegal proceeds of the GWB has obvious if superficial similarity to treble damages under American antitrust laws, as several German commentators have observed.[18] Because of the practical shortcomings of an administratively determined surcharge as opposed to damage actions, however, they do not share functional similarity as an effective sanction. The problem lies in the proof of the amount of illegal proceeds in Germany or damages in the United States. To meet the legal requirements of proof in either case is a difficult and extremely costly task.[19] This effort in a private damage action is made by private attorneys where the costs are borne by their clients and the result is a diffusion of both the required legal manpower and at least the initial costs. Such diffusion of cost and effort is not possible for an administrative penalty. Instead, public enforcement agencies, such as the FCO, already short of personnel, must assemble all necessary data without the scope of discovery available in private litigation in the United States. For this reason the FCO prefers a fixed fine with a high maximum without the attendant problems of proof to the more flexible and potentially higher surcharge.[20] As former FCO vice president Helmut Gutzler remarked, the FCO would have to have a computer and enormous data banks for the surcharge provisions to operate effectively.[21]

The delineation of excess proceeds as construed by the courts is reasonably clear—the difference between revenues actually realized and the amounts that would have been earned had there been no violation.[22] The courts pointedly note that it is a surcharge on illegal revenues, not "profits."[23] As the appellate court for Berlin (the *Kammergericht*) stated in one of the first decisions on the surcharge,[24] it is to be calculated, in the context of a horizontal restriction of output, by subtracting the market price from the cartel price.[25] Such formulations gloss over the central issues: how to construct the "market price" and how to prove how much was actually realized as a result of the violation. In this area any hopes for the kind of certainty customarily (if not constitutionally) required[26] in the case of administrative and criminal fines under German law become illusory. One consequence is the permissive language added in 1980 to permit calculations based on estimates.[27] There is, however, no fixed, legally required method for such calculation, as there is in Japan.[28] Methods that have been used include price comparisons immediately before and during the effective term of a cartel[29] and examination of the price levels of the same or similar products in comparable markets in an attempt to establish a hypothetical market price.[30] No method is considered entirely satisfactory.[31]

Finally, as a consequence of the problems associated with the illegal proceeds surcharge, the FCO has made use of the excess proceeds surcharge provision of GWB section 38(4) in relatively few instances. Between 1968 and 1977, for example, out of 171 administrative fine proceedings, only 26 involved the surcharge.[32] The amounts collected, however, have not been negligible. During this period the surcharge reaped more than DM 110 million (U.S. $61 million at current exchange rates).[33] As indicated in table 4, the sum of all fines levied under section 37a from 1980 through 1996 totaled DM 476.54 million (U.S. $265 million).

In Japan a similar surcharge has proved to be the most severe antitrust sanction. Added, as noted, in 1977, article 7-2 of the Antimonopoly Law enables the FTC to levy a surcharge (*kachōkin*) on the proceeds from an illegal restraint of trade. Until 1977 the statute contained no sanction against illegal cartels other than criminal penalties, minor administrative fines, and dam-

TABLE 4. Antitrust Fines in Germany and Japan, 1980–1996

| Year | Number of cases | | Total amount of fines (in millions) | | | |
|---|---|---|---|---|---|---|
| | Germany | Japan | German* | | Japan** | |
| | | | DM | (U.S.$) | Yen | (U.S.$) |
| 1980 | 56 (137) | 12 | 5.95 | (3.3) | 1,331.0 | (11.09) |
| 1981 | 14 (64) | 6 | 5.76 | (3.2) | 3,730.0 | (31.08) |
| 1982 | 7 (43) | 8 | 12.30 | (6.8) | 483.54 | (4.03) |
| 1983 | 57 (116) | 10 | 57.32 | (31.84) | 1,492.57 | (12.44) |
| 1984 | 8 (53) | 2 | 0.38 | (0.21) | 353.10 | (2.94) |
| 1985 | 11 (43) | 4 | 0.40 | (0.22) | 407.47 | (3.40) |
| 1986 | 4 (35) | 4 | 0.10 | (0.05) | 275.54 | (2.30) |
| 1987 | 3 (39) | 6 | 11.37 | (6.32) | 147.58 | (1.23) |
| 1988 | 13 (98) | 3 | 25.87 | (14.37) | 418.99 | (3.49) |
| 1989 | 68 (52) | 6 | 254.21 | (141.23) | 803.49 | (6.70) |
| 1990 | 12 (44) | 11 | 5.65 | (3.14) | 12,562.14 | (104.68) |
| 1991 | 16 (38) | 10 | 42.74 | (23.74) | 1,971.69 | (16.43) |
| 1992 | 1 (83) | 17 | 3.26 | (1.81) | 2,681.57 | (22.35) |
| 1993 | 10 (80) | 22 | 15.60 | (8.67) | 3,553.21 | (29.61) |
| 1994 | 5 (37) | 26 | 8.23 | (4.57) | 568.29 | (4.74) |
| 1995 | 10 (80) | 24 | 7.84 | (4.35) | 6,446.40 | (53.72) |
| 1996 | 5 (37) | 14 | 19.56 | (10.86) | 7,486.16 | (62.38) |

*Figures for Germany include all fines levied under GWB § 37a by the FCO (figures for *Land* authorities in parentheses). Source: FCO, July 1997.
**Figures for Japan include only surcharge (*kachōkin*) cases. Source: *Fifty-Year History*, p. 386.

age actions, all of which were allowed to atrophy at least before the oil cartel cases. As a result, little incentive to comply with the statute existed until the FTC brought an enforcement action. Even then, in many instances illegal activity could continue with relative impunity.

The Japanese surcharge, like the German counterpart on which it was modeled, is essentially a means to recover the economic gains from illegal cartels. It is levied against entrepreneurs or, under article 8-3, trade associations and their members, for price-fixing or output restrictions that increase the price for goods or services in violation of the prohibitions of articles 3 and 8(1) against unreasonable restraints of trade and of article 6 against international agreements containing unreasonable restraints of trade.[34]

Unlike German law, the statute as supplemented by the cabinet order for its enforcement details the method of computing the surcharge. The formula is complex. Under article 7–2(1), the surcharge is based on the "turnover" or average profit as defined by cabinet order for the period during which the restraint of competition has continued. Until amendment in 1991, the resulting amount was first multiplied by separate ratios for manufacturers, wholesalers, retailers, or "general" business and then reduced by half. Any surcharge of less than ¥200,000 was excused. The 1991 amendment limited the period for the calculation to a maximum of three years, created two new categories—large-scale-firms and small-scale firms—with separate ratios for each—6 percent for large-scale firms (including manufacturers), 3 percent for small-scale firms, 2 percent for large-scale retailers, and 1 percent for both large-and small-scale wholesalers. The resulting amount is no longer reduced by half, thereby doubling the surcharge levied. Surcharges of ¥500,000 or less are excused.

A supplementary cabinet order sets out the method for calculating "turnovers" as the total price of goods delivered or services supplied for the period of the cartel agreement.[35] The result is a fixed if complex formula that gives Japanese law at least an appearance of certainty and fairness.

The 1977 amendments also provided in a new article 48-2 for a separate administrative proceeding to levy the surcharge. Consequently, like the Germans the Japanese now have a bifurcated set of enforcement procedures—one to determine the fact of a violation and to order remedial measures, another to levy the excess proceeds surcharge. Unlike the German administrative fine proceedings, the Japanese surcharge procedures are reasonably efficient and at least procedurally protective. Article 48–2 enables the FTC to calculate the surcharge and then to notify the respondent of the amount, the basis for its calculation, and the illegal activity on which it is based.[36] The notice also includes the deadline for payment. The respondents have the rights to receive prior notice of an FTC decision to issue a surcharge order, to submit evidence, and to present their case.[37] Only after the order is issued do respondents have a right to a hearing.[38] The procedures for the surcharge hearing are the same as those for adjudication of a violation in a contested decision.[39]

A final procedural issue of interest is the language of article 7-2 apparently requiring the FTC to levy the surcharge whenever there has been an illegal price cartel or output cartel affecting price. The mandatory language of the statute is exceptional for any Japanese regulatory penalty and appears to remove any discretion on the part of the FTC over whether to initiate a surcharge proceeding.[40] In practice the FTC appears to have complied. The surcharge has been levied in all relevant cartel cases. Of the ten cases involving violation of article 3 or article 8(1)(i) decided in 1979, final surcharge orders were issued in all but three by the end of March 1981.[41] A surcharge proceeding is premised, however, on an FTC finding of a relevant violation[42] with a statute of limitations provision of three years after the violation ceased (or within one year after a formal decision).[43] One of the most difficult issues in a surcharge proceeding is to determine the duration of the violation.[44] Presumably, the party can contest the fact of the violation in the context of a hearing on the surcharge. The proviso to article 48-w2 requires that where formal hearings on the violation have begun, no surcharge order be issued until after the proceedings are completed—that is a final decision is entered.[45]

The need to include detailed provisions for collection of the surcharge exemplifies the fundamental weakness of civil enforcement in Japan, even when an administrative agency is involved. Article 64–2 provides first that if the respondent fails to pay by the designated deadline, it is to be sent a reminder (¶ 1) and the FTC may collect an additional charge (¶ 2). Upon continued failure to pay, the agency can resort to the collection powers of the National Tax Collection Law[46] (¶ 4) and acquire a lien on the respondent's property superior to all claims except for national and local taxes (¶ 5).

As in the case of the illegal proceeds levy under the GWB, the Japanese surcharge has already generated a significant amount in fines. From 1980 through 1996 there were 185 cases for a total of nearly ¥45 billion (U.S. $375 million) (see table 4). One half of the total (¥22.7 billion) was levied since the 1991 amendment.

PRIVATE DAMAGE ACTIONS AND OTHER PRIVATE LAW SANCTIONS

Three kinds of civil sanctions for antitrust violations are possible under the GWB.[47] Section 33 (former § 35) provides, first, for a private damage action without the trebled penalty of American law. Second, the section also permits private suits for injunctive relief. Finally, the invalidity of acts in violation of the GWB can be asserted both as a defense to a contract action as well as in a suit for a declaratory judgment.[48] In fact, civil sanctions are rarely used. Complete figures on the total number of all private suits brought under the GWB are apparently not available. Few cases are reported. The principal compilation of German antitrust decisions, by the periodical *Wirtschaft und Wettbewerb* (*WuW*), included only seventy-four private actions alleging violations of the GWB during the first two decades after the GWB became effective (1958–78).[49] Of these only thirty-two were brought under article 35, nineteen for injunctive relief, only eleven for damages. This compares to at least twenty-two private actions in which the validity of a contract was the principal issue. In six of these the issue was raised as a defense. The remedy sought in other cases was not reported. Presumably most also involved the validity of a contract or agreement. Whether or not the few cases reported reflect accurately a general dearth of civil actions, few if any observers consider private actions to provide a meaningful mechanism for antitrust enforcement.[50]

Procedural or "process" barriers are not the major cause of the paucity of civil actions. Unlike in Japan, access to the courts has not been a problem in the Federal Republic. Despite recent concerns over delay, the disposition of both trials and appeals remains relatively swift.[51] Of the first-instance civil actions under the GWB reported in *Wirtschaft und Wettbewerb*, seventeen cases were decided less than two years but more than one year after the alleged violation occurred. In twenty-three the interval from the date of the violation to a decision was less than a year but more than six months. At least eight cases were tried within six months. No case took longer than four years from the date of the violation to try, and several took only one month.[52] Lack of discovery and the consequent difficulty in proving damages (as well as the violation) is a substantial hurdle,[53] but it is difficult to say that this is any more serious than the costs to American litigants in prosecuting or defending an antitrust action[54] or the difficulties imposed by American rules of evidence, with which, lacking jury trials, the Germans are fortunate not to have to cope.[55] Unlike American and Japanese litigation (but like the United Kingdom and most other common law jurisdictions), however, the unsuccessful plaintiff as well as defendant becomes liable for all costs incurred by both sides, including reasonable attorneys' fees.[56] Nor is the contingent fee permissible. Consequently, there is little incentive for the prospective plaintiffs to pursue a case they have any likelihood of losing, and they must be able to finance the litigation from the start. The relative lack of success of most plaintiffs makes this a risky venture. Of the first-instance cases surveyed, less than half were successful. Moreover, when awarded, the amount of damages tends to be quite small.[57]

The factor that seems best to explain the relative ineffectiveness of damage suits and injunctive relief as a sanction is their restriction to a limited class of violations. Section 33 is construed within the context of section 823(2) of the Civil Code (*Bürgerliches Gesetzbuch*, or BGB).[58] Under this provision a claim for compensation for injury caused by violation of a statute depends upon whether the injured interests were intended to be violated.[59] Each statute or statutory provision is thus subject to classification as a "protective statute" (*Schutzgesetz*) or "protective provision" (*Schutzvorschrift*) with the party or interest as the "protected object" (*Schutzobjekt*).[60] Such classification requires a determination of legislative intent: whether the statute or provision "serves for the protection of the general public interest alone or is designed wholly or in part, for the protection of an individual interest from violation of the prescribed norm."[61] In the case of the GWB the legislative intent was thought to be clear. Most commentators agreed that only those provisions with an express prohibition (*Verbot*) or mandate (*Gebot*) had the "protective" purpose necessary for a damage action or injunctive relief under former section 35.[62] Subject to similar analysis are violations of administrative and court orders. Orders expressly prohibiting or mandating certain conduct give rise to both damage actions and injunctive relief under section 33 by those within the intended scope of protection.[63]

This construction limited private suits under former section 35 to violations of sections 14, 25, and 26.[64] Under the view that an express prohibition or mandate was required for civil sanctions to apply, violations of provisions or administrative declarations phrased in terms of the invalidity or nullity of agreements were not subject to either private damage actions or injunctive relief. Consequently, no private action under section 35 could be brought against violations of sections 1 or 15, the principal provisions against horizontal restraints or abuses of market power under section 22. Until 1975 both the principal commentaries[65] and cases[66] gave support to this view. There was, however, dissent, particularly with respect to section 1.[67]

Not only did such construction exclude the most important violations from the reach of private law sanctions under section 35, it also created the anomaly that certain conduct, such as "concerted practices" under section 25(1), were subject to private damage suits and injunctions only if *not* subject to formal agreement. Once formalized in a contract, such conduct would violate section 1 as a horizontal restraint or section 15 as a vertical restraint and thus be excluded from the scope of section 35. Doubts as to whether this result accurately reflected the legislative intent were increased by the fact that section 25(1) was added to the GWB in 1973 in response to the Federal Supreme Court decision in the *Teerfarben* case[68] to ensure that the lack of proof of a formal contractual undertaking would not lead to easy evasion of section 1.[69] Such anomalies were inexorable, however, given the awkward scheme followed in the GWB, on the one hand simply invalidating agreements and contractual arrangements but making the performance of such involved agreements subject to an administrative fine, while on the other hand prohibiting noncontractual conduct outright. Other than possible concern over abstract notions of freedom of contract and party autonomy, there seems little reason to penalize the former less severely. Moreover, the evidence of any real legislative intent to do so is sparse at best.

The Federal Supreme Court threw open the issue of whether a damage action can be brought against formalized horizontal and vertical restraints in its decision of April 4, 1975, in the *Krankenhauszusatzversicherung* case.[70]

The case involved a suit by several private health insurance firms against two public hospital insurance plans (with some ten million members) and four private insurers who had agreed to a common special insurance program for cases of higher risk, to the disadvantage of competitors who were not included. The plaintiffs alleged violations of section 1 of the Law against Unfair Competition[71] as well as sections 1 and 26(2) of the GWB. The court decided the case solely on the grounds of section 1 of the GWB, holding that at least *competitors* came within the protected scope of section 1 and could thus obtain injunctive relief or damages under section 35. The case caused considerable controversy and attempts to limit its application.[72] It was generally interpreted to limit the protective reach of section 1 to competitors,[73] or possibly a contract party[74] who can show injury as a result of an agreement proscribed under section 1. Suppliers or direct buyers, much less the ultimate consumers who suffer from the effects of an illegal cartel, are still not considered within the protected category.[75] Ultimately, however, as Professor Fritz Rittner has noted,[76] it is left to judges to decide what interests are protected, and the *Krankenhauszusatzversicherung* case leaves them with a somewhat greater margin for a flexible response to the issue. Nonetheless, the decision has not altogether removed the barriers to more effective resort to article 35 as a sanction. The 1998 amendment eliminates most of these problems. By combining former sections 1 and 25 into a single new section 1 and expressly prohibiting the covered actions and conduct, it significantly expanded the availability of damage actions.

A second potential limitation on the efficacy of damage actions is the necessity of proving fault (negligence or intentional conduct) on the part of the defendant. Proof of fault along with proof of injury and causality is required in damage actions but not (except in terms of standing) for injunctive relief.[77] Yet from the cases surveyed there does not appear to be any significant difference between resort to injunctions and damage claims.

At least brief mention should be made of the third type of civil sanction. Agreements that violated GWB sections 1 and 15 were made either invalid or void by the express language of the statute. Moreover, as noted previously, the enforcement authorities had express authority to issue declarations of the invalidity or nullity of offending agreements. Such agreements plus those expressly prohibited were therefore subject to either judicial declaration or the defense to a contract enforcement action that they were invalid or void under generally applicable provisions of German civil law—that is, sections 134 and 139 of the BGB.[78] Exercised infrequently and only in unusual circumstances, this remedy might not be considered generally effective or meaningful as a sanction. From the lower court decisions reviewed it appears that few parties to cartel agreements brought contract actions to invalidate agreements under section 1. The remedy was equally seldom used in cases subject to section 15 (currently § 16).

A dearth of litigation, however, does not mean that the sanction was totally ineffective. The parties to such agreements may have accepted their invalidity without going to court.

In conclusion, despite the changes made in 1998, without the incentive of treble or even, as proposed in the 1970s by Professor Steindorff,[79] double damages, which are not available under the German system, civil sanctions under the GWB are still not likely to provide a significant deterrent to antitrust violations.

In no area is the contrast between German and Japanese experience in antitrust enforcement greater than with respect to private enforcement actions. In theory Japanese law is considerably more permissive of damage actions. Actions brought under the Japanese statute as opposed to tort actions under the Civil Code require an FTC decision as a prerequisite. The Antimonopoly Law sets out the basis for a claim for damages in article 25:

1. Any entrepreneur who has effected private monopolization or an unreasonable restraint of trade or who has employed an unfair business practice is liable for compensation to persons injured thereby.
2. No entrepreneur may be exempted from the liability prescribed in the preceding paragraph by proving the non-existence of willfulness or negligence on its part.

Because of the second paragraph, article 25 is construed simply to provide for strict liability for damages caused by a violation.[80] Ordinary but high standards for proof of damages and causation must be met by the plaintiff.[81] Damage actions under article 25 are also limited to violations by entrepreneurs, which as defined in article 2(1)[82] excludes trade associations.[83]

Article 26 also restricts the application of the statutory damage action to instances in which the FTC has entered a final recommendation, consent, or contested decision or a final surcharge order under article 54-2(1). Consequently, no damage action can be maintained *under the statute* without prior formal action by the FTC. The findings in the decision, however, do not bind the courts in a damage action under article 25. This accords with the effect given to final court judgments since, at least at present, collateral estoppel is not recognized in Japanese law.[84] However, the FTC's findings do constitute prima facie evidence of the violation.[85]

The view that an ordinary tort action under article 709 of the Civil Code can be brought without a final FTC decision, thus permitting damage actions against trade associations, was long widely held among Japanese antitrust and civil law scholars.[86] In 1981 the first judicial decision so holding was handed down in a tort action against the Sekiyu Renmei, the petroleum industry association, and individual petroleum firms for price fixing in 1973.[87] The Tsuruoka Branch of the Yamagata District Court held that an ordinary tort action under article 709 of the Civil Code could be brought. In 1985 the Akita Branch of the Sendai High Court affirmed the decision. On appeal the Supreme Court agreed. In its decision of December 8, 1989,[88] the Second Petty Bench confirmed that a civil action for compensatory damages could be brought for antitrust violations constituting a delict (tort) under the Civil Code notwithstanding the lack of an FTC decision. Proof of negligence or willful conduct is required in a civil code tort action as opposed to strict liability under the statute.[89]

The difficulties faced by plaintiffs in proving damages seem to explain best why so few damage actions are brought. Until the mid 1990s there had been only a half dozen damage suits in Japan. Of the reported cases, two were settled by compromise[90] and another for lack of the requisite FTC decision.[91] The others were dismissed for failure to prove damages.[92] The first reported decision in which the plaintiffs were successful was handed down in 1996.

The first significant damage action was the 1977 case of *Ōkawa v. Matsushita Denki Sangyō K.K.*[93] The action arose out of a 1971 consent decision against Matsushita Electric Industrial Company for resale price maintenance. The case involved two principal legal issues: whether consumers had standing to bring a damage action under articles 25 and 26 of the Antimonopoly Law, and the scope of review of the FTC's findings. The Tokyo High Court held first that consumers do have standing. Thus a broader spectrum of damage actions are possible in Japan than in Germany, at least at present, although the reverse seems to be the case, as noted, for direct appeals from administrative actions. On the second issue the court refused to apply the substantial evidence rule to damage actions. The consent decision was held to provide prima facie evidence of the violation but not to bind the court. The court nonetheless affirmed the findings that there had been a violation. In the end, however, the plaintiffs lost. They failed to meet the requirements for proof of the amount of damage sustained as a result of the violation. They could not show what the retail price of color television receivers would have been had the defendant not engaged in illegal resale price maintenance.

Because of the failure to prove damages, the courts dismissed three damage actions brought in the wake of the *oil cartel* cases.[94] The first two were brought in the Tokyo High Court under articles 25 and 26. One of these was settled,[95] but the plaintiffs lost the other in a 1981 decision.[96] The plaintiffs won on the principal legal issue whether legitimate administrative guidance by MITI was a defense, but the high court dismissed the action for failure to prove damages.[97] In 1987 the Supreme Court (First Petty Bench) affirmed the decision.[98]

The problems of proof are not insurmountable. A 1996 Tokyo district court awarded more than ¥18 million (approximately U.S. $150,000) in damages for a trade association boycott of a toy maker.[99] The FTC had refused to take action in the case. Nonetheless, the combination of institutional barriers and the limited available relief severely restricts the potential of private civil actions as an antitrust remedy. In response to increased public concern over the hurdles that confront potential antitrust plaintiffs, both MITI and the FTC recently appointed advisory committees to explore possible legislative action to expand civil antitrust remedies.[100]

Additional institutional barriers to litigation, such as delay and costs, the lack of the treble damage incentive, and a possible reluctance on the part of business enterprises to sue as a result of complex and close interrelationships even with their competitors, also work to preclude effective use of the damage action as either remedy or penalty in antitrust enforcement. With slightly fewer than 2,600 judges and 17,000 trial lawyers in Japan[101] compared to more than 22,000 judges and 76,000 lawyers in the Federal Republic,[102] litigation is a far slower and much more costly affair in Japan. The Yamagata District Court (Tsuruoka) tort action was typical. It took more than seven years from the time of both the violation and filing. With appeals it lasted another eight years. Because most actions are brought under articles 25 and 26 and thus are based on an FTC decision, they take even longer from the date of the violation. In comparison, adjudication in Germany is swift.

As to the private law consequences of antitrust violations, it should be noted first that contracts and other juristic acts (hōritsu kōi) that violate public law are not necessarily invalid under Japanese law. As articulated by the Supreme Court, upholding contracts entered without prior approval in violation of the 1949 Foreign Exchange and Foreign Trade Control Law,[103] the test is whether the proscription involved is merely regulatory (torishimari hōki) or mandatory (kyōkō hōki).[104] Whether or not an antitrust violation renders contracts or other juristic acts invalid, and if so, to what extent the act is void or only voidable, has long been an issue of some dispute.[105]

The 1977 Supreme Court decision in K. K. Miyagawa v. Gifu Shōkō Shinyō Kumiai[106] provides a partial answer. The case declared invalid a condition in a loan agreement that the borrower maintain a low-interest deposit equal to the borrowed amount as security. The court held that this violated article 19 as an unfair business practice under item 10 of the FTC's 1953 General

Designation of Unfair Business Practices,[107] which proscribes taking unfair advantage of a superior bargaining position. On the issue of the validity of the contract provision, the court reversed the decision of the Nagoya High Court. The Supreme Court held[108] that the provision was not invalid either as a violation of the Antimonopoly Law or under the public policy provision of the Civil Code (article 90), but rather held it to be unenforceable to the extent it violated the Interest Rate Restriction Law.[109] Unfair business practices in violation of article 19 are not per se invalid, the court stated.[110] Since only the FTC is authorized to take remedial measures, not the courts, the court continued, it would be improper for the courts to invalidate contracts and other juristic acts for antitrust violations.[111] The opinion did not foreclose completely, however, the possibility that the gravity of the violation and the consequences of invalidating a contract could dictate a different result in different circumstances. The court thus opted for an idea first suggested by Professor Ienobu Fukumitsu that the nature of the antitrust offense and consequences of invalidating the contract should be weighed.[112] The net result is that the law in this area remains uncertain and does not promote preventive self-enforcement.

## CRIMINAL VERSUS ADMINISTRATIVE SANCTIONS

On the face of the two antitrust statutes, the most salient difference in sanctions is that German law uses administrative fines instead of criminal penalties. This difference was long of little significance in practice because of the dearth of criminal actions in Japan. The debate in the late 1970s over the criminalization of German antitrust law illustrates the special limitations imposed by German criminal procedure on the use of criminal sanctions to enforce regulatory measures. The Japanese experience points both to general hurdles that restrict their use as well as to public responses that promote their potential efficacy in the antitrust context.

No violation of the GWB as such is punishable as a criminal offense. Instead, as noted previously, the GWB lists a series of particular violations deemed regulatory infractions (*Ordnungswidrigkeiten*) and subject to fines levied pursuant to the OWIG. The introduction of criminal sanctions has nonetheless long been an issue. The Josten drafts relied principally on criminal sanctions.[113] In 1972 a special commission appointed by the Federal Ministry of Justice[114] recommended that horizontal price-fixing and other agreements or concerted action violative of sections 1 and 25(1) of the GWB be treated as criminal offenses.[115] The recommendation was not adopted. The ensuing debate revealed that lack of criminal penalties reflects not only the apparent wishes of the government—particularly the Federal Ministry of Economics, which rejected the 1972 recommendation—but also most antitrust scholars, practitioners, and, perhaps most important, the antitrust enforcement authorities themselves.[116] The opposition reflected several concerns.

Foremost were the practical procedural advantages in applying administrative sanctions under the OWiG, or perhaps more accurately the *disadvantages* of resort to the criminal process under German law. Of central concern was the narrow discretion of the prosecutor in deciding whether or not to prosecute a particular case. Under what is termed the *Legalitätsprinzip*, the "legality" principle of mandatory prosecution, the procuracy must prosecute all persons who, after investigation, are found to have committed all but minor criminal offenses.[117] As a further check on discretion, not only can prosecution be activated by private complaint,[118] but also victims have a right of petition for a court order requiring prosecution upon judicial finding of sufficient evidence.[119] Despite some margin for what amounts to a discretionary decision by the prosecutor not to prosecute,[120] in effect German law shifts prosecutorial discretion from the state to private persons in cases where the evidence of guilt is sufficient for conviction. Nor does the career judiciary in Germany enjoy the traditional flexibility and room for maneuver (i.e., discretion) of common law judges prior to the imposition of guidelines for mandatory sentencing.[121] The prosecutor files the charge and the court determines guilt. Neither has significant discretion, except for sentencing once guilt is proven.

As in other civil law systems, all prosecutions in Germany and Japan require an evidentiary adjudication of guilt. There is no guilty plea enabling the court to avoid adjudicating the issue of guilt based on corroborative evidence even in cases where the accused may confess. Plea bargaining as practiced in the United States is not possible. Once the prosecution begins, however, a somewhat analogous process of negotiation involving the accused offender, the prosecutor, and the judge has become more common, particularly in cases involving "white-collar" crimes.[122] The offense and thus the applicable sanctions may thus be subject to negotiated settlement. However, such "bargaining" involves the active participation of judges during the course of prosecution.

One consequence is obvious: criminal law-enforcement authorities are unable or less likely to select cases to prosecute based on policy considerations—ranging from their concern over the seriousness of the offense or the development of judicial construction of the law to circumstances related to the commission of the offense or the offender.[123] Questions of efficiency also arise. The prosecutor loses the freedom to decide how to allocate resources. If all cases must be prosecuted, prosecutorial efforts are necessarily more diffused than if concentration on particular cases were permitted.[124] The problem is exacerbated by the fact that in 1996 there were only 6,117 public prosecutors in the Federal Republic.[125]

In contrast, under the so-called *Opportunitätsprinzip*, provided for in section 47 of the OWIG, administrative authorities exercise broad prosecutorial discretion over which violations are actually prosecuted. The advantages of such discretion account largely for the strong preference displayed by antitrust enforcement officials for noncriminal sanctions.[126] Because of the economic issues involved, they argue, discretion over prosecution is essential to the development of sound antitrust policy.

A second consideration, however, is the difference in expertise involved. The German procuracy deals exclusively with criminal actions. In civil and administrative cases the government is represented by private counsel or qualified lawyers from a particular agency.[127] Therefore, it is said, the procuracy necessarily lacks exposure to the problems and issues involved in economic regulation, especially those that underlie antitrust actions.[128] This expertise is particularly critical at the investigative stage of a case, which for criminal offenses is left largely to the police.[129]

Another objection to criminal penalties is the greater delay involved in criminal cases compared to proceedings under the OWIG.[130] At least one study provides support for this assertion. Despite the extraordinary efficiency of the German criminal process,[131] the investigation of most economic crimes appears to take at least as long as, if not longer than, an entire administrative proceeding under the GWB.[132]

Closely related to concerns over the adverse consequences of introducing the *Legalitätsprinzip* to antitrust enforcement were objections based on the necessary imprecision in any legal definition of illegal anticompetitive conduct. The limitations on prosecutorial discretion in German law grow out of and reinforce the view that norms enforced by criminal sanctions should be unambiguous and subject to uniform prosecution. In German constitutional terms, as noted above, no act may be subject to a criminal penalty unless its illegality is described in clear and certain terms by statute before the act has been committed. German antitrust specialists have argued that such concepts as "concerted conduct," "restriction of competition for a common purpose," "abuse of market power," or "anticompetitive considerations" lack such certainty.[133] The fear was also expressed that the courts would impose rigid definitions of these terms in order to meet these constitutional requirements[134] and that judges would be reluctant to impose criminal sanctions.[135]

In the background lurks a conceptual distinction between criminal offenses and infractions of regulatory statutes introduced at the turn of the century.[136] Although not reflected in any statutory dichotomy until the postwar period, the notion that conduct violative of regulatory statutes or administrative regulations is by nature conceptually distinguishable from criminal code offenses provided the jurisprudential foundation in 1945 for introducing the concept *Ordnungswidrigkeiten* as a separate category of unlawfulness.[137] Although today few German scholars fully accept the validity of the argument that there is an inherent conceptual difference in the nature of regulatory as opposed to criminal offenses, the distinction persists out of recognition that various features of the German criminal process, as discussed above, are inappropriate in dealing with particular types of unlawful conduct.

Although perhaps flawed as an exercise of conceptual jurisprudence, the traditional justification for the dichotomy does contain an important sociological insight. Apart from the penalties imposed, the procedures followed, or who initiates and controls the process, a criminal action can also be distinguished from both civil and administrative proceedings by the social stigma that attaches to the offender. Indeed, this may be the factor that determines the efficacy of criminal sanctions. Neither the threat nor the imposition of the penalty itself has much effect if the offender is free from any stigma of having committed the offense or having been involved in a criminal proceeding. Consequently, before any conduct is deemed "criminal," social consensus on both sociological and ethical grounds, it can be argued, should confirm that the stigma is justified. Otherwise, the process will be difficult to invoke, and a conviction will be difficult to sustain, by those who have discretion (complainants, prosecutors, or judges, or any combination thereof). To invoke the criminal process without consensus that the penalty suits the wrong committed will tend to erode the legitimacy of the criminal process and the capacity of the label "criminal" to carry any stigma.

Consensus is all the more necessary in a pluralistic society such as Germany where the discretion of the prosecutor and judge is narrowly prescribed and there is no trial by jury. The lack of any intervening discretionary check against prosecution forces the German legislator to consider with care the potential scope of any criminal proscription, as evidenced in German constitutional requirements. This need is all the greater if a significant portion of the community condones, if not encourages, the conduct in question. To the extent legislators are accountable to the public politically, they must be sensitive to community attitudes toward the wrongfulness of the conduct proscribed. The ultimate issue, therefore, is the extent to which society views the conduct or acts in question to be morally or socially reprehensible. As perceived in the traditional conceptual dichotomy between administrative and criminal offenses in Germany, there does or should exist a qualitative difference between criminal conduct and other unlawful behavior. This distinction is better defined, however, in terms of community values and attitudes rather than jurisprudential conceptualizations. It has been stated in terms of the "ethical" content of the offense.[138] One would be hard-pressed to find a better example than antitrust.

The GWB, as noted, reflected a series of political compromises. As a matter of political reality, the statute could not have been enacted with the criminal sanctions that had been provided in the original Josten draft. The official comments to the government's 1952 bill, which eliminated such criminal penalties, acknowledges that "in neither the German public nor concerned business circles . . . is there at this point in time a vital sense that contracts and business practices that restrict competition are improper and morally wrong."[139] The official comments expressly left open, however, the possibility of a change in attitudes and the strengthening of sanctions in the future, and no opponent of criminal sanctions for antitrust has violations argued—at least openly—that anticompetitive conduct should be treated as a *Kavaliersdelikt*. Even the most active supporters of strong antitrust enforcement, on the other hand, have expressed doubts about the appropriateness of criminal stigma for those who violate the GWB.[140] As consensus changes, criminal sanctions may become appropriate. The recent amendment of the German Criminal Code to include bid rigging as a crime can be interpreted as a reflection that the German public now believes that certain collusive acts do warrant the stigma of criminality. Whether the German public would support more general criminal proscription of antitrust violations remains uncertain.

Finally, both the efficacy of criminal sanctions as a deterrent in antitrust enforcement and the need for additional sanctions have been questioned.[141] What is needed, it was argued, was to make existing sanctions more effective.[142] The 1972 commission had before it information on the success, or lack of it, of the American experience with criminal sanctions.[143] Nonetheless, no attempt was made to resolve either doubt empirically.[144]

On one issue there was little if any disagreement. The maximum fine originally fixed in the GWB was much too low to have any meaningful deterrent effect. Consequently, the provisions of the 1980 amendments of section 38(4) increased the limit tenfold to DM 1 million or treble any gain realized as a result of illegal conduct. The result was to raise the maximum fine to the original level provided in the government's 1952 bill.[145] The principal factor taken into consideration in the amount actually levied is the size of the respondent enterprise.[146]

German law requires the same evidentiary burden for conviction for both criminal sanctions and administrative fines. In either case, in proceedings against natural persons, proof is necessary not only of individual responsibility but also of willful or negligent conduct in violating the law.[147]

In the area of sanctions, the Japanese depart in significant respects from both German and American patterns. Not having adopted the strict controls of German law over prosecutorial discretion, the Japanese have not had to create a system of noncriminal and therefore discretionary administrative offenses.[148] Not having a substitute for contempt, they forgo the civil enforcement alternative of American practice and are left to rely on criminal sanctions. If criminal sanctions in any society, as we have noted in Germany, are unwieldy tools in antitrust enforcement, in Japan they are even less useful as a penalty. However, recent cases suggest that criminal prosecution itself rather than the punishment imposed plays a significant didactic role in educating the public and fosters consensus against anticompetitive behavior. Japan exemplifies a system of extraordinarily weak formal law enforcement coupled with an equally notable system of strong social controls.[149] Selective criminal prosecution may accomplish more than any penalty, no matter how severe, as a catalyst for consensus.

The principal statutory sanctions against antitrust violations in Japan are criminal penalties.[150] Except for possible imprisonment and the most recent increase (1991) of the maximum fine that can be levied against corporate offenders and trade associations, such penalties remain trivial. Criminal fines—even the maximum—do not reach the level of attorney fees in major antitrust cases in the United States. The 1977 amendments, as noted, increased the maximum amount of all fines in the statute to their current levels. Prior to the amendment they were one-tenth of the current amount. The amounts remained small by any standard. The maximum criminal fine for illegal price fixing, for example, was raised to only ¥500,000 (approximately U.S. $2,000 in 1977). These levels have remained unchanged except for the maximum fine that can be levied against enterprises and trade associations for private monopolization and unreasonable restraints of trade, which was increased in 1991 from ¥5 million to 100 million (approximately U.S. $833,333 at current exchange rates). Violations of the prohibitions against holding companies, unlawful shareholding, and interlocking directorships and officerships, as well as failure to file required reports, are subject to a maximum fine of ¥2 million (approximately U.S. $16,667). Failure to comply with an FTC order and conclusion of an illegal international agreement are subject to fines not to exceed ¥3 million (U.S. $25,000).

A maximum term of three years' imprisonment can be imposed for private monopolization and unreasonable restraints under article 3. Unlawful holding companies, shareholding violations, and unlawful interlocking directorates and officerships carry a maximum term of one year, and conclusion of an unlawful international agreement a maximum term of two years. Imprisonment cannot be imposed for failure to file a report.

No criminal sanction is imposed for unfair business practices, despite inclusion for amendment of such penalty in the 1974 proposals by the FTC, which formed the basis of the 1977 amendments. This was the only major feature of the original FTC proposal not enacted into law. The significance of its deletion is evident in the agency reliance on the proscription against unfair business practices in articles 19, 8, and 6 as the principal mechanism to police antitrust violations other than the most blatant cases of horizontal price fixing or output restrictions.

Unique to the Japanese system are the provisions giving the FTC the exclusive right to file criminal referrals under the law[151] and giving the Tokyo High Court exclusive jurisdiction to try criminal antitrust actions.[152] Criminal actions are initiated solely by the FTC, but they are subject not only to FTC discretion but also to the general discretion over prosecution enjoyed by the Japanese procuracy.[153]

The most telling problem with criminal sanctions has been atrophy, not lack of severity. In fifty years only nine criminal actions have been brought for antitrust violations. Three were brought in 1949 but not decided until three to four years later:[154] *Kuni* [Japan] *v. Ōkawa K. K.*,[155] *Kuni* [Japan] *v. Yamaichi Shōken K. K.*,[156] *Kuni* [Japan] *v. Nōrin Renraku Kyōgōkai*,[157] and *Kuni* [Japan] *v. Sanintochi K. K.*[158] The oil cartel of the mid 1970s resulted in two separate criminal actions: *Kuni* [Japan] *v. Sekiyu Renmei*[159] and *Kuni* [Japan] *v. Idemitsu Kōsan K. K.*[160] For nearly two decades the FTC filed no further criminal referrals. American pressures in the late 1980s for more active antitrust enforcement was the apparent catalyst for a recent revival. Since 1989 there have been four referrals and prosecutions, all resulting in convictions: *Kuni* [Japan] *v. Mitusi Tōatsu Kagaku K. K.*,[161] *Kuni* [Japan] *v. Toppan Moore K. K.*,[162] *Kuni* [Japan] *v. K. K. Hitachi Seisakusho*,[163] *Kuni* [Japan] *v. K. K. Kanemon Seisakusho.*[164]

The *Ōkawa* case involved failure to obey an FTC order to dispose of corporate stock. It was dismissed before trial in the general amnesty at the end of the Allied occupation. The facts are not reported. The complete facts of the *Yamaichi Shōken* case are also unreported. Not prosecuted at the procurator's discretion, it apparently involved alleged violations of the restrictions on mergers and acquisitions of articles 15 and 16. The third action, against Nōrin Renraku Kyōgōkai, concerned violations of the 1948 Trade Association

Law[165] (repealed in 1953). The nature of the violations is not clear from the reported decision, but the association was found guilty and fined ¥10,000 (approximately U.S. $40 at prevailing exchange rates). Two individual defendants were fined a mere ¥500 (less than U.S. $2). The first prosecution after 1952 was a 1969 case against a real estate firm, Sanintochi K. K., for unfair advertising in selling lots in suburban Tokyo in violation of articles 90(3) and 95 of the Antimonopoly Law as well as articles 4, 6, and 9(1) of the Unfair Premiums and Misleading Representations Prevention Law.[166] The company was fined ¥200,000 (U.S. $800). An individual defendant was fined ¥100,000 (U.S. $400) and sentenced to imprisonment for one year, which was suspended with three years' probation.[167]

The most important criminal enforcement actions brought by the FTC remain the actions against Japan's domestic petroleum industry for price fixing and output restrictions. In 1974 the FTC filed criminal referrals against the Petroleum Industry Federation and two other defendants for output restrictions and twelve Japanese oil companies and fourteen individuals for price fixing. The prosecutions resulted in acquittals in the output-restriction case for lack of criminal intent, but in convictions for price fixing, making these cases the most important antitrust actions in Japan during the past five decades. The corporate defendants were fined between ¥1.5 and 2.5 million[168] and the individual defendants were sentenced from ten to six months in prison, suspended with two years' probation.[169]

The Tokyo High Court decisions, handed down in September 1980, were promptly hailed as landmark cases.[170] Never before had such prominent antitrust offenders in Japan been so severely penalized. Moreover, in both cases the defendants' illegal activities had been carried out with the overt approval of and supervision by MITI pursuant to special legislation to stabilize the supply of petroleum.[171] Finding that the defendants in the output-restriction case had acted as a result of close MITI supervision and guidance under an erroneous assumption that their conduct was lawful, the court held the defendants lacked the requisite criminal intent for conviction.[172] In the price-fixing case the court found that MITI had acquiesced but not mandated the agreement to raise prices; hence the illegality of the arrangements resulted in convictions.[173] Only the price-fixing case was appealed, and on February 24, 1984, the Second Petty Bench of the Supreme Court unanimously affirmed the High Court's judgment.[174]

Despite the oil cartel cases, most could in the 1980s reasonably doubt whether criminal sanctions were likely to prove effective in Japan in the long run. The oil industry was an exceptionally apt target, particularly in the early 1970s. It did not enjoy the level of general support given to most manufacturing and service industries in Japan from labor or the public. Moreover, the actions were brought during a period of acute inflation for which rising oil prices were blamed. Although, as in the United States in the wake of the 1960 electrical equipment conspiracy cases,[175] the oil cartel cases produced in Japan a heightened awareness of the criminality of antitrust violations and the potential for prosecution, such sensitivity does not necessarily endure. No criminal prosecutions were brought thereafter for nearly two decades.

The dearth of criminal prosecutions ended during the U.S.-Japan Structural Impediment Initiative talks. In 1991 the FTC filed a criminal referral with the Ministry of Justice against eight polyvinyl chloride stretch film (plastic wrap) manufacturers and fifteen executives for price fixing. Criminal charges were filed and hearings began on December 20. A year and a half later the Tokyo High Court convicted all of the defendants. The eight defendant firms were each fined ¥6–8 million (approximately U.S. $50–67 thousand). The fifteen individual defendants were given suspended sentences of six months' to one year's imprisonment.

Within two years a second case was brought against four printing companies for bid rigging in public contracts for personal seals used by the Social Insurance Agency. A Ministry of Justice investigation had investigated and successfully prosecuted the individuals involved under the Criminal Code. The case prompted the FTC to act to refer criminal charges against Toppan Moore K. K. and the three other firms under the Antimonopoly Law. On December 14, 1993, they were convicted and each fined ¥4 million (approximately U.S. $34,000 at current exchange rates).

Two years later the FTC referred the third case in four years to the Ministry of Justice. The agency charged K. K. Hitachi Seisakusho and eight other electrical-equipment manufacturers, seventeen of their employees, and one employee of the Japan Sewage Works Agency with bid rigging in connection with the installation of equipment for the Sewage Works Agency. The Tokyo High Court handed down convictions of all of the defendants in the case on May 31, 1996. Five of the nine corporate defendants were each fined ¥60 million (approximately U.S. $500,000 at current rates). The other four were each ordered to pay ¥40 thousand (U.S. $333) in criminal fines. Seventeen of the eighteen individual defendants received sentences of ten months' imprisonment. One was sentenced to eight months. All of the prison sentences were suspended with two years' probation.

The FTC referred the fourth case to the Ministry of Justice in February 1997. The referral accused K. K. Kanemon Seisakusho and twenty-four other firms as well as thirty-four individuals with bid rigging in sales of water meters to Tokyo Prefecture. The Tokyo High Court again convicted all of the defendants. Twenty-four companies were fined ¥6 million (approximately U.S. $50,000 and one, ¥5 million U.S. $41,667). Each individual defendant was sentenced to imprisonment with terms ranging from six to nine months, all of which were suspended with two years' probation.

These recent referrals and the resulting prosecutions and convictions suggest a renewed willingness by the FTC to use criminal prosecutions as an antitrust sanction. They do not, however, demonstrate the effectiveness of criminal sanctions as a deterrent. The fines in these cases remained negligible by most standards. No individual actually served a term in prison. In light of Japanese criminal practice, the outcomes are not surprising. Nor in view of even American experience are the results unusual.

In the United States, as Elzinga and Breit note, the prediction in the wake of the 1960 electrical equipment convictions that "antitrust would never be the same again" proved false.[176] They echo in particularized terms the concern of German lawmakers over community consensus as to the criminality of antitrust violations in concluding that "until judges and juries are convinced beyond a reasonable doubt that the well-dressed, wealthy, articulate pillar of the community facing them is in actuality the real instigator and director of a conspiracy to cut back production, rig prices, and rob consumers and taxpayers just as effectively as a common mugger or bank robber, it is unlikely that prison sentences often will be imposed for violation of the antitrust laws."[177]

If the criminal penalties are not a realistic deterrent to corporate immorality, as Elzinga and Breit conclude for the United States, their efficacy in Japan is even more subject to question. The effective use of criminal sanctions as penalties to control corporate conduct in Japan could well be considered an impossible task. Criminal prosecutions engender severe political and intra-agency conflict as a result of the clientele relationship between each economic ministry and the industries within its jurisdiction. Resort to criminal actions is similarly precluded except in rare instances by the social density that results from the intricate personal ties that connect the leaders of Japanese business, politics, and bureaucracy.

Institutional limitations are also a factor. The members of the FTC are cabinet appointees and have since 1953 come exclusively from the ranks of government officials, especially the Ministry of Finance and its affiliated agencies.[178] They are subject, therefore, to political pressures, and their monopoly of the right to file criminal charges is exercised with great caution. In addition, the Japanese procuracy must also exercise its wide legal discretion to prosecute. There are fewer than 2,200 prosecutors in Japan,[179] less than half as many per capita as in Germany, to handle all criminal and most administrative litigation. Winnowing cases by means of broad prosecutorial discretion is thus a necessity. Although the rate of convictions in criminal cases is 99.5 percent, the rate of prosecution averages less than 66 percent.[180] For statutory crimes the rate of prosecution is a mere 33 percent and less than 20 percent for crimes involving public officials. Similar discretion over sentencing is exercised by judges; less than 2 percent of all of those who are convicted are ever imprisoned. Judges regularly suspend over two-thirds of all jail sentences. The criminal justice system in Japan does not operate as a penalty-imposing process but a corrective one in which defendants are given the opportunity and incentive to repent, compensate the victims, and be absolved.[181] Incarceration is not a deterrent when it becomes a highly improbable outcome in any rational calculation of costs and benefits by potential offenders.

The four recent criminal convictions did mark a change—not that incarceration is more likely in the future or that the fines will increase to the point that either will operate as a deterrent. Regardless of the actual penalty imposed, criminal prosecution and conviction do have consequences. The resort to criminal prosecution in selected cases has two important effects. First, public prosecution and conviction invite social opprobrium and stigma. Second, they educate and foster consensus about the "wrongfulness" of the condemned conduct.

The balance between leading and following public opinion can be delicate. Referrals for prosecution of conduct the public condones or otherwise tolerates carries risks. Prosecutors may not prosecute. Judges may not convict. Adverse political reaction may follow. And public trust in the fairness and good judgment of the enforcement authorities may diminish. In Japan not less than Germany, criminal prosecution is apt to lose utility unless the community believes that the offending behavior warrants so drastic a sanction. Adherence to the "sense of society" is indeed a defining norm of judicial decision making in Japan.[182]

Public opinion is seldom, even in Japan, so homogeneous or constant. Most often divided and in flux, public attitudes are influenced by the actions of those in authority. The measures that law enforcement authorities take function in part as social signals that direct and shape consensus. The criminal prosecutions in the three bid-rigging cases illustrate the dual role of criminal prosecution as both a response to public concern and a catalyst for consensus. As in the oil cartel cases, the prosecutions took place in the midst of political upheaval and widening public concern over political corruption. Charges of massive bribery had tainted the most influential politicians. The Liberal Democratic Party was in disarray. Public outrage was growing. The procuracy notably acted first, filing charges of bid rigging under the Criminal Code.[183] Politically enabled by this action or perhaps simply less equipped to act earlier, the FTC followed with the three referrals for prosecution of the offense as an antitrust violation. The prosecutions in these cases also parallel the German response to bid rigging—only, unlike Germany, existing statutory provisions for criminal prosecutions enabled the procuracy and the FTC to act. The German authorities did not have their options. The public consensus and political decision to make bid rigging a crime had to come first.

ADVERSE PUBLICITY

Even if until recently the formal sanctions of German and Japanese antitrust law have failed to provide fully effective deterrents to antitrust violations, it does not necessarily follow that antitrust enforcement has been a failure. Although impressionistic conclusions that businessmen in both countries have been less sensitive to the antitrust consequences of their conduct than their counterparts in the United States, are probably correct,[184] their awareness of the consequences and concern to avoid prohibited conduct has increased, at least in Japan, along with the increase in the number of criminal prosecutions and other enforcement actions. As a theoretical proposition the argument that suspended sentences and fines that do not cover the actual profits gained from a violation do not provide effective sanctions may be sound.[185] Reality is more complex. There is at least one additional element to add to the calculus: the effect of education and adverse publicity.

In both Germany and Japan publicity of violations appears to be the most significant sanction imposed on offenders, and the most effective deterrent. The use of publicity to educate and to punish has not been fully analyzed in either country (or anywhere else). We still know too little, therefore, to reach definite conclusions and can only offer some general, speculative observations.

During the debate over the introduction of criminal sanctions in Germany in the 1970s, those involved directly with antitrust enforcement were unanimous in the opinion that aside from an increase in the maximum fines, no additional sanctions were necessary. Helmut Gutzler, as vice-president of the FCO, repeatedly asserted that adverse publicity was not only the most effective sanction available, but also sufficient to provide the necessary deterrent.[186] The FCO's president, Wolfgang Kartte, apparently considered adverse publicity more important than any monetary penalty and argued that the addition of criminal sanctions could severely restrict the authorities' ability to use publicity effectively,[187] apparently because of legal limitations on publicizing criminal actions.[188] Giving credence to such views was the chorus of criticism over the FCO's use of press releases and other forms of publicizing decisions about administrative fines.[189]

The Japanese FTC also makes full use of publicity as a means of enforcement. Merely the announcement of an FTC investigation may confirm public suspicions about illicit business activity or may otherwise tarnish the reputation of the firm being investigated. Adverse publicity in turn may lead to political pressure on the firm to seek accommodation with the enforcement authorities. In addition, officials in the various ministries who view their responsibility broadly to include oversight of industry activities may become involved out of a desire to curtail improper activities of a particular firm in order to protect the reputation of the industry as a whole, or the ministry, or both. Their status and authority depend on public trust. The reaction of MITI denouncing the result of the oil cartel cases[190] illustrates the sensitivity of the economic ministries to publicity regarding their role in the formation of covert cartels. Such responses belie the impression by many foreign observers[191] that administrative guidance to foster cartels has been accepted in Japan as a legitimate exercise of governmental power. In recent years the FTC has made full use of the publicity tool for enforcement. There is, however, another facet to adverse publicity as a sanction in Japan.

Until the FTC issues its formal recommendation, the enforcement process may be carried out with little public disclosure. Under article 45(3), the Antimonopoly and Fair Trade Law currently requires the FTC to notify the party reporting a violation of the decision to proceed to a formal investigation. This requirement was not added to the statute until 1977. Under regulations before 1977, the FTC was not required to inform the complainant, although it was allowed to do so and generally did. Despite the apparent purpose—to ensure that the FTC responds to complaints and thus to permit greater public scrutiny of its handling of cases at a preliminary stage—the effect is as likely to be an increase in the number of unreported cases dealt with informally, with officials delaying any formal report of the complaint until the matter has been thoroughly considered internally. As noted in chapter 4, several thousand complaints are made to the FTC each year. Hardly more than a few hundred are fully investigated. Of these no more than a handful result in formal decisions.

Several concerns underlie the desire to control public information about a case. Some violations pose considerable political problems for the staff. This has been especially true in the case of potential violations by banks and other financial institutions regulated by the Ministry of Finance. The relationship between the Ministry of Finance and the commissioners, many of whom were formerly Finance Ministry officials, has been quite close, and some cases are simply too controversial to handle. The staff has had an understandable if not laudable interest in preventing the agency from getting caught in a cross fire between consumer and other organizations (especially those with political ties to opposition parties) and major ministries or the ruling party. A more legitimate concern is that advance publicity about a pending investigation may ruin the chances for successful prosecution inasmuch as the agency is forced to rely in many instances on spot inspections and searches and seizures to gather evidence of a violation. Publicity in such instances forewarns and may lead to the destruction of vital documents.

More broadly, publicity as a sanction raises two separate issues. The first is the dilemma of any liberal legal order: how can law enforcement be truly effective in a society with significant constitutional restraints on governmental power? Yet without adequate means of enforcement, how can the public policies served by the law—including those limiting the government—themselves be effectively maintained? If it is true that adverse publicity is as meaningful a penalty as a fine, must its use be subject also to the procedural restrictions applied to the imposition of other penalties to protect the citizens from arbitrary governmental action? The use of publicity, for example, precludes even the most fundamental protection, such as judicial review. Such questions are left unanswered by those who assert that the enforcement authorities are obligated to provide the public with information or consider that the procedural safeguards of the proceedings being publicized provide adequate protection to the parties.[192]

Whether concern over the "due process" implications of adverse publicity are frivolous or deserve careful thought depends ultimately on how serious a sanction adverse publicity imposes and how it functions as a sanction. If publicity is not in fact a significant penalty or one that cannot be made subject to legal control, further discussion seems pointless. Unfortunately, even these fundamental questions remain unexplored. In Japan, the argument can be made that loss of reputation and trust operates as a substitute for formal legal sanctions throughout the legal system and can be viewed both as a contributing factor and consequence of the inadequacy of the formal institutionalized system to provide effective sanctions and legal relief.[193] In Germany, however, the issue is apparently hardly even raised.[194] More is at stake, says Helmut Gutzler,[195] than corporate "image," but what that is remains unanswered.

# A Concluding Assessment

To assess the contribution of antitrust law in Germany and Japan over the course of the past half century is considerably more difficult than it may first appear. Statistics on antitrust enforcement actions, exempt cartels, or merger controls do not accurately measure the effect of antitrust on the economy of a nation. Unlike ordinary crimes, such as theft or arson, antitrust violations are not widely reported. Not knowing the extent of even the most common violations, such as price fixing, in any market, we cannot calculate clearance rates or the effectiveness of policing. Seldom do consumers know when they are victims of monopoly power. And the more expansive the reach of enforcement authorities or severe the sanction, the greater the effort to obscure or to hide any violation. At a more abstract level, we can measure to some limited extent barriers to entry and degrees of concentration in an industry, but even these figures do not tell us very much about the capacity of any firm to determine prices. The best that we can do is to hazard guesses based on what information is available.

We also need to avoid overstating the effect of even the most expansive antitrust controls. First, competitive economic markets are generally too dynamic for the law to keep pace. All legal systems, even the most efficient—of which Germany is surely one—suffer from delay. By the time a violation is identified and prosecuted, competitive conditions are apt to have changed significantly. In industries characterized by rapid technological advances—such as communications—even the most prompt enforcement actions are unlikely to keep pace with the changes.

The number of formal enforcement actions does not accurately measure the extent of compliance. Successful legal regimes depend upon voluntary obedience to legal rules. Without widespread community acceptance, few legal rules remain viable. Persuasion rather than coercion is nearly always the primary prerequisite for compliance. Germany and Japan reflect the tensions. Without prior public acceptance of the wrongfulness of the proscribed conduct, law enforcement, especially criminal prosecution, puts at risk the legitimacy of the legal regime. Yet, at least in democratic political systems, law enforcement is also a didactic means of persuasion. Criminal prosecution in particular does not simply transmit preexisting social attitudes condemning the conduct in question; it also helps to create, promote, and sustain these attitudes. The didactic effect of law and law enforcement is not, however, easily measured. In the end, we only guess at the answers.

Even more significant factors add to the difficulty in assessing the effect of antitrust. The most obvious include the extent to which other economic and social legislation restrain market competition. Among the most prominent are trade regulations, such as dumping regulations, that restrict price competition by foreign firms. Others include overly protective labor laws and social welfare schemes that unduly add to the risks of expansion and thus in effect create significant barriers to new entry or more intense firm rivalry. Less apparent government actions may be equally significant. The Japanese experience demonstrates that informal government pressures may initiate or aid anticompetitive conduct and that, especially in the case of bid rigging, political corruption may sustain criminal behavior.

What then can be said with at least some degree of certainty about the role of antitrust in postwar Germany and Japan? A few conclusions are apparent.

First, more irony. The features of German law that figure so prominently in antitrust legislation around the world reflect an incongruous political compromise between opposing approaches: cartel prohibition versus abuse regulation. The incorporation of these elements along with merger controls first into European law and subsequently into antitrust legislation throughout Europe and beyond illustrates again a point made by Alan Watson[196] on the extent to which law is made less by a priori design than by imitation and adaptation. Antitrust is one of the best examples of legal transplants and convergence.

Convergence does not mean the elimination of all difference. Fundamental contrasts in origins, statutory language, political and legal culture, and the process and procedures for enforcement preclude total harmony. The degree of convergence notwithstanding, these differences makes German and Japanese antitrust law all the more remarkable. That German and Japanese law have tended to converge despite their differences deserves some attention.

No contrast between the two systems is greater or more significant than their intellectual contexts. German law developed within an intellectual tradition that encouraged those who drafted and enacted the GWB to respond to economic theory. The continuing influence of the ordo-liberals in Germany owes as much to this tradition as their political success in the German public's identification of the role of competition in the "social market economy" with Germany's postwar economic recovery and growth. Subject of course to countervailing political and theoretical concerns, ordo-liberal economic theory shaped German competition policy, the law, and the institutions assigned the task of enforcement.

No similar debate—indeed no similar tradition—is evident in Japan. With the exception of a handful of American advisors, economists had almost no role in the formation of Japanese antitrust law. Its making was almost entirely left to American lawyers and law-trained Japanese officials. Japanese economists would have had in any event little to offer those who were compelled to draft the legislation. A very different tradition prevailed. Only gradually did economists and legal scholars emerge from the constraints of their predominately Marxist orientations to provide the intellectual foundations for sustained antitrust policy. With their contributions by the 1970s Japan had begun a new era.

As in so many other areas of Japanese law, learning from abroad is a recurring thread running through the fifty years of Japanese antitrust. The ideas and the institutions of antitrust are as Japanese today as cellular telephones and digital television. But they did not originate in Japan. The capacity to identify and adapt foreign technology in law as much as electronics has a millennium of supportive history. What was important was less the ideas themselves than their effect and suitability. For the postoccupation makers of antitrust law, German legislation was an obvious source. German law satisfied all requirements. Internationally, the choice of German law would at least mollify some who might otherwise vehemently protest any change in the occupation-imposed law—particularly those Americans who praised German legislative efforts. Who at home could argue with proposals that placed a recovering Japan on a similar course as an economically resurgent Germany? Despite the more basic constitutional and other legal reforms undertaken under the supervision of American military occupiers, Japan's legal system remained firmly within a predominately German-based civil law tradition. Perhaps the greatest irony is that credit for Japan's postwar economic "miracle" would go to those who sought to ensure an "industrial policy" freed from the constraints of antitrust.

Ironies and contrasts aside, in both countries the most significant contribution of antitrust law is its educational role. Market competition and firm rivalry are today widely viewed as essential conditions for economic growth, efficiency, and the production and distribution of wealth. In Germany in particular, industrial cartels are no longer considered, at least by the public, as an appropriate response to economic instability. Most existing exemptions are justified in terms of balancing the bargaining leverage between small and large enterprises. In Japan, fears of "excessive competition" appear to have similarly abated. And as evidenced by recent legislation, Japan has moved a considerable distance from its immediate postwar past.

Concerns remain. One is the gradual diminution of German antitrust law in terms of cartel exemptions and the diminishing prominence of the FCO in terms of staff and influence. For Japan, contrast has replaced convergence as the number of legally exempt cartels decreases and the FTC continues to grow in size and influence.

The Japanese experience is not necessarily as prominent or permanent as it may appear. However great the advances in antitrust legislation and enforcement may seem, they have all taken place during periods of significant political tumult and weak political leadership. Yet to emerge in Japan is a strong political commitment to antitrust within the dominant political parties.

As the war ended, Eleanor Hadley was among the first to recognize that government controls, including licensing, functioned as a predominant barrier to competition. The Edwards Mission similarly identified a concentrated banking industry as a "stronghold" of *zaibatsu* power, enabling the largest conglomerates to exclude competitors. Its warnings were not heeded. The occupation reforms did not fully dismantle the wartime controls over the economy. New and more expansive economic controls over foreign exchange, international trade, and foreign investment were introduced. Business and occupation licensing regimes were extended. A half-century later Japan is paying the price of the inefficiencies in industries long protected from competition by formal and informal government measures that more competitive markets might have prevented.

New entry remains the key. As evidenced by Japanese manufacturing industries in the 1950s and 1960s, new entrants and fear of eventual foreign competition provided incentives for Japanese automobile, steel, electronics, and other manufacturers to compete to become among the world's most efficient firms. In contrast, Japan's financial institutions remained strictly controlled in segmented markets into which new entry was barred by an obdurately rigid licensing regime. Thus side by side with Toyota, Kobe Steel, and Sony were Japan's financial institutions, which remained uncompetitive and woefully inefficient despite their enormous wealth, which was generated by Japan's expanding manufacturing industries. On this score, an opportunity missed is among the lessons of the origins of antitrust in Japan.

Antitrust policy does not create the conditions for new entry. Directed at the private sector, it deals with barriers created by dominant enterprises or through private collective action. The more serious barriers are those imposed by law and regulation. Far more significant than antitrust controls is the commitment of governments to the vision on which they are founded. The concerns of Walter Eucken and other ordo-liberals come to mind. An economic order in which government actively promoted competition was their goal. Antitrust law was merely one means to that end. Their vision for a more inclusive competition policy remains for the second half-century of antitrust in Germany and Japan.

# Notes

## 1 / ERROR AND IRONY—THE AMERICAN IMPETUS

1. See "The Task of the Allied Occupation Forces" (author unnamed but possibly T. A. Bisson), *Amerasia*, vol. 8, no. 22 (December 1, 1944), proposing state ownership of the *zaibatsu*.

2. Bavarian High Court Judgment of July 4, 1888, *Seuffert's Archiv*, vol. 43 (1888), p. 16, cited and discussed in Rainer Schröder, *Die Entwicklung des Kartellrechts und des kollektiven Arbeitsrechts durch die Rechtsprechung des Reichsgerichts vor 1914* [The development of cartel law and labor union law through the decisions of the imperial supreme court before 1914] (Ebelsbach: Gremer, 1988), pp. 9–11.

3. *Entscheidungen des Reichsgerichtshofs* [Decisions of the imperial supreme court], vol. 38, p. 155.

4. For two interwar studies in English, see Rudolf K. Michels, *Cartels, Combines and Trusts in Post-war Germany* (New York: Columbia University Press, 1928), and Doreen Warriner, *Combines and Rationalization in Germany, 1924–1928* (London: F. S. King & Son, 1931). Neither study, it should be noted, found that German cartels resulted in significantly higher prices, but each concluded that German cartels were effective in stabilizing prices and reducing the "costs" of competition.

5. Heinz Müller and Gerhard Gries, *Kommentar zum Gesetz gegen Wettbewerbsbeschränkungen* [Commentary on the law against restraints of competition] (Frankfurt am Main: Schwenk, 1st ed., 1957), p. xxviii [hereinafter Müller and Gries, *Kommentar*; Peter Giessler replaced Gries as co-editor in subsequent editions, which will be cited as Müller and Giessler, *Kommentar*].

6. *Verordnung gegen Mißbrauch wirtschaftlicher Machtstellungen*, November 2, 1923

(*Reichsgesetzblatt* [*RGBI.*] 1923 I 1067). For contemporaneous commentary, see Rudolf Isay and Siegfried Tschierschky, *Kartellverordnung* [Cartel decree] (Mannheim: Bensheimer, 2d ed., 1930). For later legislation, see Hanspeter Brunner, *Zwangskartelle* [Mandatory cartels] (Zurich: Nauch; Berlin: Heymann, 1937); Rudolf Callman, *Das Deutsche Kartellrecht* [German cartel law] (Berlin: Philo, 1934), and Heinz Müllensiefen and Wolfram Dörinkel, *Kartellrecht* [Cartel law] (Berlin: Heymann, 1938). For a summary of the cartel decree in English, see Kurt Stockmann and Volkmar Strauch, "Federal Republic of Germany," *World Law of Competition*, vol. B5 (New York: Matthew Bender, 1981), § 1.02.

7. George W. Stocking and Myron C. Watkins, *Cartels or Competition?* (New York: Twentieth Century Fund, 1948), p. 47.

8. Ibid., p. 68.

9. Ibid., pp. 93, 407.

10. See National Archives, Diplomatic Section, Notter Files [hereinafter, Notter Files], Box 34, Cartel Memo 11a, dated September 1944.

11. See, e.g., Harm G. Schröder, "The International Dyestuffs Cartel, 1927–39, with Special Reference to Developing Areas of Europe and Japan;" Takeshi Ōshio, "Conflict and Cooperation between the International Nitrogen Cartel and Japan's Aluminum Sulfate Industry"; and Shin Hasegawa, "Competition and Cooperation in the Japanese Electrical Machinery Industry," in *International Cartels in Business History*, ed. Akira Kudō and Terushi Hara (Tokyo: University of Tokyo Press, 1992), pp. 33–52, 76–94, 165–86.

12. The most detailed contemporaneous and postwar studies all note the relative failure of cartel activity in prewar Japan to restrict prices or output prior to the 1930s. See, e.g., Minobe Ryōkichi, *Karuteru, Torasuto, Kontsuerun* [Cartels, trusts, concerns], vol. 2 (Tokyo: Kaizōsha, 1931); Yoshida Jinbu, *Nihon no karuteru* [Japanese cartels] (Tokyo: Tōyō Keizai Shubōsha, 1964); Keizo Fujita, "Cartels and Their Conflicts in Japan," *Journal of the Osaka University of Commerce*, vol. 8 (1935), pp. 65–109; J. Mark Ramseyer, "Cartels: Cotton-Spinning," in *Odd Markets in Japanese History: Law and Economic Growth* (Cambridge: Cambridge University Press, 1996), pp. 135–62.

13. Yoshida, *Karuteru*, p. 20.

14. Minobe, *Karuteru*, pp. 16–64; Yoshida, *Karuteru*, pp. 20–25.

15. Fujita, "Cartels," pp. 66–68.

16. See Minobe, *Karuteru*, p. 28, on industrial growth and new entrants. W. Mark Fruin's study of the Kikkoman Company is illustrative. A cartel-like association of soy sauce brewers in the region of Noda in Chiba Prefecture was an initial phase leading to incorporation of the Noda Shōyu Company. The association permitted cost-savings efficiencies and the introduction of new technology enabling the resulting firm to become a major competitor. The association did not stifle competitors even among the Noda producers much less represent a step toward industrywide restric-

tions. W. Mark Fruin, *Kikkoman: Company, Clan, and Community* (Cambridge, Mass.: Harvard University Press, 1983).

17. See Minobe, *Karuteru*, pp. 532–34, 572.

18. Ibid., p. 572.

19. Compare Ramseyer, "Cartels: Cotton-Spinning," with Robert M. Uriu, *Troubled Industries: Confronting Economic Changes in Japan* (Ithaca, N.Y.: Cornell University Press, 1996), p. 50.

20. *Jūyōyushutsuhin dōgyō kumiai hō* (Law No. 47, 1897; repealed by Law No. 35, 1900).

21. *Jūyū bussan dōgyō kumiai hō* (Law No. 35, 1900).

22. Yoshida, *Karuteru*, p. 21.

23. *Ginkō hō* (Law No. 21, 1927).

24. *Jūyō sangyō no tōsei ni kansuru hōritsu* (Law No. 40, 1931, decreed ineffective as of August 11, 1942).

25. William W. Lockwood, *The Economic Development of Japan* (Princeton, N.J.: Princeton University Press, 1954), p. 230.

26. Ibid.

27. Eleanor M. Hadley, *Antitrust in Japan* (Princeton, N.J.: Princeton University Press, 1970), p. 21.

28. Mitsui, Mitsubishi, Sumitomo, and Yasuda, as the Big Four, plus Nissan, Hsano, Furukawa, Okura, Nakajima, and Nomura were the ten *zaibatsu* initially designated for dissolution by the Holding Company Liquidation Commission, established by the Japanese government under order by the Supreme Commander of the Allied Powers (SCAP). Four other combines were excluded: Shibusawa, Matsushita, Kawasaki, and Okochi. Hadley, *Antitrust*, p. 22.

29. Ibid., pp. 23, 322–27.

30. Ibid., p. 23.

31. Ibid., pp. 18–19. Hadley rejects the view that competition was generally suppressed. Ibid., p. 16.

32. See G. C. Allen, *Japanese Industry: Its Recent Development and Present Condition* (New York: Institute of Pacific Relations, 1939); G. C. Allen, "Japanese Industry: Its Organization and Development to 1937," in *The Industrialization of Japan and Manchukuo, 1930–1940*, ed. E. B. Schumpeter (New York: Macmillan, 1940), pp. 477–786.

33. See Tony Freyer, *Regulating Big Business: Antitrust in Great Britain and America, 1880–1990* (Cambridge: Cambridge University Press, 1992), pp. 241–49.

34. Allen, "Japanese Industry," pp. 625–46.

35. Allen, *Japanese Industry*, p. 44.

36. Ibid.

37. Allen, "Japanese Industry," p. 681.

38. Ibid.

39. See, e.g., Mira Wilkins, "The Contributions of Foreign Enterprises to Japanese Economic Development," in *Foreign Business in Japan before World War II*, ed. Takeshi Yuzawa and Mosaru Udagawa (Tokyo: University of Tokyo Press, 1990), pp. 35–56.

40. The generally accepted view is that Kishi shared the hostility of the Kwangtung Army toward the *ziabatsu* but disagreed with the military's plans to encourage small and medium enterprises. Kishi believed in state planning and privately managed industrial concentration as the surest and most rapid means to industrial development. He thus favored Aikawa's Nissan as a "new" and presumably more nationalist entrant. Nissan was also publicly owned rather than closely held by a family. See, e.g., Yoshimoto Shigeyoshi, *Kishi Nobusuke* (Tokyo: Tōyō Shokan, 1957), pp. 96–100. One of Kishi's biographers explains the decision in terms of the failure of Mitsui, Mitsubishi, and other *zaibatsu* to cooperate with the industrial policy for Manchuria. Hosokawa Ryūichirō, *Kishi Nobusuke* (Tokyo: Jiji Tsūshinsha, 1986), p. 30. For a generally sympathetic English-language biography of Kishi, which includes a detailed account of Kishi's experience in Manchuria, including the decision to give Aikawa's company a Manchurian monopoly, see Dan Kurzman, *Kishi and Japan* (New York: Ivan Obolensky, 1960), pp. 122–44.

41. For a brief summary of Hiranuma's professional career and influence as a prosecutor, see John Owen Haley, *The Spirit of Japanese Law* (Athens: University of Georgia Press, 1998), pp. 63–65.

42. See, e.g., Arthur E. Teidemann, "Big Business and Politics in Prewar Japan," in *Dilemmas of Growth in Prewar Japan*, ed. James W. Morley (Princeton, N.J.: Princeton University Press, 1971), pp. 267–316.

43. Jerome B. Cohen, *Japan's Economy in War and Reconstruction* (Minneapolis: University of Minnesota Press, 1949), pp. 508, 509.

44. Noguchi Yukio, *1940 nen taisei* [1940 system] (Tokyo: Tōyō Keizai Shinpōsha, 1995).

45. See Fujita, "Cartels," pp. 98–109.

46. Law No. 62, 1931.

47. Cohen, *Japan's Economy*, p. 28.

48. Ibid., p. 76.

49. Schecter Poultry Corp. v. United States, 295 U.S. 495 (1935).

50. See Freyer, *Regulating Big Business*, pp. 202, 206, 220, 223–25.

51. Thurman Arnold, "Antitrust Enforcement, Past and Future," *Law and Contemporary Problems*, vol. 8, no. 1 (Winter 1940), p. 7.

52. Ben W. Lewis, "The Status of Cartels in Post-war Europe," in *A Cartel Policy for the United Nations*, ed. Corwin D. Edwards (New York: Columbia University Press, 1945), pp. 33–34.

53. Temporary National Economic Commission [TNEC], *Investigation of Concentration and Economic Policy*, Monograph no. 40, Senate Committee Panel, 76th Congress, 3d session (1941).

54. See, e.g., Charles Bunn, "Concerning Cartels," *Department of State Bulletin*, vol. 11, no. 277 (October 15, 1944), pp. 433–35, 438; William A. Fowler, "Post-War Trade Policy," *Department of State Bulletin*, vol. 11, no. 272 (October 15, 1944), pp. 436–38.

55. See Notter Files, Box 34, Cartel Memo 16a, "A Positive International Cartel Program," dated December 7, 1943, approved at committee meeting on December 16 and 17, 1943. Notter Files Box 34, File 1, December 23, 1943; Box 35, Cartel Memo 30 (January 19, 1944) on Proposed International Office for Business Practices; Cartel Memo 48 (April 28, 1944, combined proposals); Box 36, Cartel Memo 62d (ECEFP D-38/45) (March 9, 1945, draft Convention on Restrictive Trade Practices and draft Convention on Objectionable Practices by International Cartels and Combines).

56. Notter Files, Box 34, Cartel Memo 8.

57. Notter Files, Box 34, Cartel Memo 7, September 20, 1944.

58. Corwin D. Edwards, "What Is the International Cartel Problem?" [address to the Consumer's Union, June 30, 1944], *Department of State Bulletin*, vol. 11, no. 262 (July 2, 1944), pp. 25–31.

59. Letter from President Franklin D. Roosevelt to Cordell Hull, secretary of state, dated September 6, 1944, *Department of State Bulletin*, vol. 11, no. 272 (September 10, 1944), p. 254.

60. For a concise summary of the Morgenthau Plan and the related dispute over U.S. occupation in Germany, see John H. Backer, *Priming the German Economy* (Durham, N.C.: Duke University Press, 1971), pp. 3–30. For an account in German, see Wernhard Möschel, *Entflechtung im Recht der Wettbewerbsbeschränkungen* [Divestiture in the law on restraints of competition] (Tübingen: J. C. B. Mohr, 1979), p. 5.

61. The final version of JCS/1067 was issued on May 14, 1945, but not made public until October 17, 1945.

62. Potsdam protocol, section B, paragraph 12.

63. The most complete account of the inclusion of *zaibatsu* dissolution in presurrender U.S. plans for military occupation of Japan is Marlene J. Mayo, "American Economic Planning for Occupied Japan: The Issue of Zaibatsu Dissolution," in *The Occupation of Japan: Economic Policy and Reform*, ed. Lawrence H. Redford (Norfolk, Va.: The MacArthur Memorial, 1980), pp. 205–28. See also Marlene J. Mayo, "American Wartime Planning for Occupied Japan: The Role of Experts," in *Americans as Proconsuls: United States Military Government in Germany and Japan, 1944–1955*, ed. Robert Wolfe (Carbondale and Edwardsville: Southern Illinois University Press, 1984), pp. 3–51. Among the most thorough sources in Japanese is Iokobe Makoto, *Beikoku no nihon senryō seisaku* [America's Japan occupation policy] (Tokyo: Chūō Kōronsha, 1985), especially vol. 1, pp. 178–85, 249–56; vol. 2, pp. 4–9, 104–23.

64. For a biographical sketch of Grew and his influence on occupation policies, see Howard B. Schonberger, *Aftermath of War: Americans and the Remaking of Japan, 1945–1952* (Kent, Ohio; and London: Kent State University Press, 1989), pp. 11–39.

65. Notter Files, T-1221, Reel 3, CAC-222, June 22, 1944.

66. Ibid.

67. Joseph C. Grew, *Ten Years in Japan* (New York: Simon and Schuster, 1944), p. xi.

68. *Department of State Bulletin*, vol. 7, no. 174 (October 24, 1942), p. 848; also quoted in part in Schonberger, *Aftermath of War*, p. 20.

69. Schonberger, *Aftermath of War*, p. 12.

70. On December 29, 1932, Grew noted in his diary that the "deliberate building up of public animosity against foreign nations in general and the United States in particular . . . to strengthen the hand of the military in the face of foreign and especially American, opposition" reminded him of the efforts of the imperial German government "to build up a public war psychology" prior to 1914. Grew, *Ten Years in Japan*, p. 64 (diary entry of December 29, 1932). He was also to write on September 1, 1940, that under a "New Structure" being built up, "Japan is rapidly becoming a regimented nation, although in its main outlines this regimentation cannot be said to be either Fascism or Nazism." Ibid., p. 327.

71. For an excellent biographical essay on Bisson and his tragic career, see Schonberger, *Aftermath of War*, pp. 90–110.

72. Schonberger, *Aftermath of War*, p. 94. *Amerasia* is best remembered by many as the periodical that had obtained and published a classified Office of Strategic Studies (OSS) document on Thailand in January 1945. Subsequent OSS (clandestine) and FBI (with warrants) searches uncovered several hundred classified OSS and State Department reports. Most related to China. Jaffe and several others were prosecuted, including John S. Service, the foreign service officer who had allegedly provided the papers. Jaffe entered a guilty plea. All but one of the remaining defendants, including Service, were cleared by the grand jury or otherwise acquitted. The incident led five years later in March 1950 to charges against Service and other China specialists by Senator Joseph McCarthy. For Service's account of the incident, see John S. Service, *The Amerasia Papers: Some Problems in the History of U.S.-China Relations*, China Research Monographs, no. 7, (Berkeley: University of California, Center for Chinese Studies, 1971).

73. On the Institute for Pacific Relations, see John H. Thomas, *The Institute for Pacific Relations: American Scholars and American Politics* (Seattle: University of Washington Press, 1974).

74. See T. A. Bisson, *Yenan in June 1937: Talks with the Communist Leaders*, China Research Monographs, no. 11 (Berkeley: University of California, Center for Chinese Studies, 1973). Bisson recalls Lattimore's having invited him and Jaffe to accompany

him to Yenan, a trip that had been arranged by Edgar Snow (p. 13). Lattimore rather pointedly states that Bisson had asked him to join them. Owen Lattimore, *China Memoirs: Chiang Kai-shek and the War against Japan* (Tokyo: University of Tokyo Press, 1990), p. 56.

75. T. A. Bisson, "China's Part in a Coalition Loan," *Far Eastern Survey,* vol. 12, no. 14 (July 14, 1943), pp. 135–41.

76. "Problems of War Production Control in Japan," vol. 16 (1943), pp. 301–10; "The Price of Peace for Japan," vol. 17 (1944), pp. 4–25; "Japan as a Political Organism," vol. 17 (1944), pp. 392–420; "Increase of *Zaibatsu* Predominance in Wartime Japan," vol. 18 (1945), pp. 55–61; and "The *Zaibatsu's* Wartime Role," vol. 18 (1945), pp. 355–67.

77. Bisson's radical Marxist orientation is not disputed. Presumably he was the unnamed author of *Amerasia* articles on postwar Japan that recommended Susumu Okano, the Yenan-based leader of the Japanese People's Emancipation League, along with Yukio Ozaki, the progressive, octogenarian critic of the Japanese military, as two ideal candidates for prime minister in postwar Japan. Bisson repeated the recommendation of Okano, Ozaki, and others in an article he wrote for *The New Republic* days after Japan's surrender. T. A. Bisson, "Japan's Strategy for Revival," *The New Republic,* vol. 113, no. 9 (August 7, 1945), pp. 243–44.

78. Ibid. editorial at pp. 235–36.

79. Edwin O. Reischauer, *The Japanese* (Cambridge, Mass.: Harvard University Press, 1977), pp. 107–8.

80. T. A. Bisson, *Zaibatsu Dissolution in Japan* (Berkeley: University of California Press, 1954).

81. Cartel Memo 168, prepared by Eleanor Hadley, dated November 1945, described below.

82. Notter Files, Box 81, E-135 (T-348), quoted in Mayo, "American Economic Planning," pp. 207, 253.

83. "Japan: The Large, Family Concerns in Japanese Industry: Pre-War Structure and Power: Wartime Developments," Memo T-470, March 25, 1944, provided to author by Robert A. Fearey, November 12, 1997.

84. See Mayo, "Wartime Planning for Japan," p. 39.

85. See Mayo, "American Economic Planning," pp. 222–26.

86. Notter Files, Box 92, E-155 (T-354), cited and quoted in Mayo, "American Economic Planning," pp. 207, 255.

87. Notter Files, Box 39, Cartel Memo 168, dated November 15, 1944.

88. Elmer Plischke, "Denazification in Germany: A Policy Analysis," in *Americans as Proconsuls,* p. 214.

89. See John O. Haley, "Toward a Reappraisal of Occupation Legal Reforms," in Kōichirō Fujikura ed., *Eibeihō ronshū* [Essays on Anglo-American law] (Tokyo: University of Tokyo Press, 1987), pp. 543–67.

90. Hans H. Baerwald, "The Purge in Occupied Japan," in *Americans as Proconsuls,* pp. 189, 196.

91. Jerome B. Cohen, "Japan's Economy Under Occupation," *Foreign Policy Reports,* vol. 24, no. 18 (February 1, 1949), p. 216.

92. For a firsthand account of such attitudes and reforms, see Alfred C. Oppler, *Reform in Occupied Japan: A Participant Looks Back* (Princeton, N. J.: Princeton University Press, 1976).

93. JCS/1067, April 26, 1945, made public on October 17, 1945. *Department of State Bulletin,* vol. 8, no. 330 (October 21, 1945), pp. 596–607.

94. SWNCC/150, September 6, 1945, made public on September 22, 1945. *Department of State Bulletin,* vol. 8, no. 326 (September 23, 1945), pp. 423–27.

95. Office of the Military Government (U.S.), Economics Division, Decartelization Branch, *Report on German Cartels and Combines, 1946,* 3 vols. (1947).

96. See, e.g., a U.S. embassy assessment of British attitudes reviewed by the Committee on Private Monopolies and Cartels in 1943: Richard A. Jamison, "Post-war Implications of the Trend Toward Monopoly in Great Britain," American embassy, London, August 6, 1943, Notter Files, Box 34, Cartel Memo 4. For further discussion of British views, see Freyer, *Regulating Big Business,* pp. 256–65.

97. On British attitudes and policy in the Ruhr, see Isabel Warner, *Steel and Sovereignty: The Deconcentration of the West German Steel Industry, 1949–54* (Mainz: Verlag Philipp von Zabern, 1996).

98. Law No. 56, February 12, 1947 (U.S. zone) and Ordinance No. 78, February 12, 1947 (British zone).

99. November 4, 1945, quoted with SCAPIN 244, November 6, 1945, MacArthur's official response, in Bisson, *Dissolution,* pp. 241–44, and Hadley, *Antitrust,* appendix 3, pp. 460–63.

100. Ministry of Foreign Affairs, Special Survey Committee, *Postwar Reconstruction of the Japanese Economy* (transl. Saburo Okita; Tokyo, September 1946), p. 27, translated in Harry First, "Antitrust in Japan: The Original Intent," *Pacific Rim Law and Policy Journal,* vol. 9, no. 1 (2000), pp. 1–71. First's study provides the most detailed and thorough analysis of the drafting of the Antimonopoly Law available in any language.

101. Ibid., pp. 82–85, noted in First, "Original Intent," pp. 32–34.

102. Ibid., p. 46, n. 60, quoted in First, "Original Intent," p. 29.

103. SCAPIN 244, November 6, 1945, in Bisson, *Dissolution,* pp. 241–44; and Hadley, *Antitrust,* appendix 3, pp. 460–63.

104. Ibid.

105. The Mission on Japanese Combines (also known as the *Zaibatsu* Mission as well as the Edwards Mission) was sent to Japan in January 1946. It was chaired by Corwin Edwards. Robert Dawkins, legal advisor and consultant to the Federal Trade

Commission, served as its chief of staff. The members included William B. Dixon, James M. Henderson, and Samuel Neel from the Antitrust Division of the Justice Department; R. M. Hunter, a legal consultant to the Federal Trade Commission and professor of law at Ohio State University; Raymond Vernon, of the Securities and Exchange Commission; and Benjamin Wallace, a special advisor to the Tariff Commission.

Apparently, different versions of the Edwards Mission report exist. Harry First cites a copy in the National Diet Library microfilm collection of the SCAP archives without a date, but ostensibly transmitted to the Joint Chiefs of Staff on May 28, 1946. First, "Original Intent," p. 35. Another version, dated March 1946, available through the University of North Carolina (Chapel Hill) Library, is referred to here.

106. The nineteen *zaibatsu* combines were Mitsui, Mitsubishi, Sumitomo, Yasuda, Kawasaki, Nissan, Asano, Fuji Industrial, Shibusawa, Furukawa, Okura, Nomura, Riken, Nippon Soda, Nippon Nitrogenous, Hitachi, Nichiden, Manchurian Investment, and Oji Paper. First, "Original Intent," p. 37. The language quoted by First is not included in the March 1946 version of the Edwards Mission report.

107. Ibid. pp. 37–38. The March 1946 version of the Edwards Mission report makes the point at pp. 53–55. The report emphasizes *zaibatsu* ownership of Japan's principal commercial banks as a principal source of their capacity to restrict new entry.

108. Edwards Mission report (March 1946), pp. 1–14 (Summary of Recommendations), pp. 173–258 (Outline of Recommendations).

109. This account of the drafting process is based on First, "Original Intent."

110. Salwin was not an antitrust lawyer. In 1948 he wrote one very brief summary of the new Antimonopoly Law for publication ("Japanese Anti-Trust Legislation," *Minnesota Law Review*, vol. 32, no. 6 [1948], pp. 588–605). He is best remembered today for his contribution to the 1950 Commercial Code revisions, for which he took considerable pride. See Lester N. Salwin, "The New Commercial Code of Japan: Symbol of Gradual Progress toward Democratic Goals," *Georgetown Law Journal*, vol. 50 (1960), pp. 478–512. For a more critical view, see Thomas L. Blakemore and Makoto Yazawa, "Japanese Commercial Code Revisions Concerning Corporations," *American Journal of Comparative Law*, vol. 2 (1952), pp. 12–24. Salwin is recalled by many who worked with him as being overbearing and less than gracious to those he disagreed with or considered to be overly sympathetic to Japanese concerns, especially members of the Court and Law Division of Government Section (later the Legal Section) who were responsible for the reforms of the civil, criminal, and two procedure codes, as well as administrative litigation and the judiciary. Conversations with Thomas Blakemore, Kurt Steiner, and Eleanor Hadley.

111. First, "Original Intent," pp. 58–114.

112. Ibid. p. 61.

113. Ibid., pp. 96–97.

114. Ibid. pp. 91–92.

115. Ibid. p. 92, n. 219.

116. Ibid. p. 102.

117. *Shiteki dokusen no kinshi oyobi kōsei torihiki no kakuho ni kansuru hōritsu* (Law No. 54, 1947).

118. *Jigyō sha dantai hō* (Law No. 191, 1948).

119. *Kado keizairyoku shūchū haijo hō* (Law No. 207, 1947). Several recent studies by Japanese scholars describe in detail the controversy over the *zaibatsu* dissolution program and FEC 230: Masahiro Hosoya, "Economic Democratization and the 'Reverse Course' during the Allied Occupation of Japan, 1945–1952," *Kokusaigaku ronshū*, no. 11 (July 1983), pp. 59–104 (based on Masahiro Hosoya, "Selected Aspects of the *Zaibatsu* Dissolution in Occupied Japan 1945–1952: The Thought and Behavior of *Zaibatsu* Leaders, Japanese Government Officials, and SCAP Officials" ([Ph.D. dissertation, Yale University, Department of History, 1982]); Toshihiro Uchiyama, *The U.S. Occupation Policy for Japan: The Deconcentration Controversy and the Origins of the "Reverse Course,"* Student Working Paper no. 1 (Niigata: International University of Japan, 1985).

120. See, e.g., Watanabe Takeshi, *Watanake Takeshi nikki* [Watanabe diary] (Tokyo: Keizai Shinpōsha, 1983). Takeshi Watanabe was the Ministry of Finance officer with principal responsibility for liaison with SCAP. SCAP officials and visiting Americans kept him fully informed of the conflicts within SCAP and in Washington over the dissolution efforts. Over dinner on August 26, 1947, for example, Watanabe listened as lawyer James Lee Kauffman described his meeting with Welsh. *Watanabe Diary*, pp. 114–15. In October a leading American business executive assured him that SCAP would be told by Washington to end the efforts to have Law 207 enacted. Ibid., p. 141. In November he was being briefed on the controversial report that Kauffman had written attacking the dissolution program. Ibid., pp. 146, 147–48. And by December Watanabe was fully cognizant of Draper's concerns. Ibid., p. 153. See also Uchiyama, *The Deconcentration Controversy*, pp. 52–53.

121. See Hadley, *Antitrust*, p. 22.

122. Uchiyama, *The Deconcentration Controversy*, p. 44.

123. Ibid.

124. Ibid., pp. 44–45.

125. See, e.g., ibid., p. 47, citing Ministry of Finance interview with Welsh of March 21, 1974.

126. First, "Original Intent," p. 5.

127. Uchiyama, *The Deconcentration Controversy*, p. 48; Hosoya, "Economic Democratization," pp. 88–90.

128. Letter from Clay for Byrnes, April 20, 1945, in Jean Edward Smith, ed., *The Papers of General Lucius D. Clay*, vol. 1 (Bloomington: University of Indiana Press, 1974), pp. 5–6.

129. Letter from Clay to McCloy, April 26, 1945, ibid., p. 8.

130. See Backer, *Priming the German Economy*, pp. 124, 201.

131. The Hoover mission made three separate reports: Herbert Hoover, The President's Economic Mission to Germany and Austria, "Report No. 1—German Agriculture and Food Requirements" (for public release, February 28, 1947); "Report No. 2—Austrian Agriculture and Food Requirements" (for public release, March 11, 1947); "Report No. 3—The Necessary Steps for Promotion of German Exports, so as to Relieve American Taxpayers of the Burdens of Relief for the Economic Recovery of Europe" (March 18, 1947) [hereinafter Hoover Mission reports].

132. Memo (CC 19760) from Clay to War Department, December 2, 1945, *Papers*, vol. 1, p. 127.

133. Letter from Clay to McCloy, June 1945, ibid., p. 45.

134. James S. Martin, *All Honorable Men* (Boston: Little, Brown 1950), p. 234.

135. Hoover Mission report no. 3, p. 18. Martin later expressed dismay over the language of the report, recalling that during the briefing Hoover remarked favorably on Law No. 56. Martin, *Honorable Men*, pp. 228–29.

136. *Congressional Record*, vol. 93 (House, July 16, 1947), pp. 8981–85.

137. Ibid., pp. 8983, 8995.

138. *Congressional Record Appendix*, vol. 93 (1947), A3798.

139. Ibid., A4066.

140. U.S. Federal Trade Commission, Report of the Committee Appointed to Review the Decartelization Program in Germany, April 15, 1949, p. 57 [hereinafter 1949 FTC Decartelization Report].

141. Ibid. pp. 57–59.

142. The principal controversies in addition to Henschel involved Vereinigte Kugellager Fabriken A.G. (VKF bearings), Robert Bosch (automotive equipment), and the Gutehoffnungshütte (Good Hope steel and machinery). The cases are summarized in the 1949 FTC Decartelization Report, pp. 51–63. See also Martin, *All Honorable Men*, pp. 246–63.

143. See *New York Times*, March 14, 1948, p. 27; March 16, 1948, p. 8.

144. Letter from Clay to Draper, March 14, 1948, *Papers*, p. 379.

145. Martin, *Honorable Men*, p. 257.

146. *Congressional Record*, vol. 93 (House, March 25, 1947), pp. 3552–56.

147. 1949 FTC Decartelization Report.

148. Edwin W. Pauley, the U.S. representative to the Allied Commission on Reparations, headed two missions to study reparations, first in Germany and later in Japan. His report on Japan recommended that "plants should be removed and in some cases whole industries eliminated in such a manner that Japan will no longer be able to control the economic life of neighboring countries by acting as the lay industrial consumer of their raw material." Edwin W. Pauley, Report on Japanese Reparations

to the President of the United States, November 1945 to April 1946 (April 1, 1946). The differences of opinion between Pauley and MacArthur on the propriety of using Japanese industrial equipment as reparations reveals MacArthur's more realistic appraisal of the Japanese economy and his commitment to recovery.

149. Memorandum by Ambassador Edwin W. Pauley to the assistant secretary of state for economic affairs (Clayton), April 30, 1946, *Foreign Relations of the United States, 1946*, vol. 8, p. 506.

150. Comments on Ambassador Pauley's Report to the president, dated September 26, 1946, noted with Pauley's reply, in Pauley's letter of December 28, 1946, to the secretary of state, ibid., p. 603.

151. Uchiyama, *The Deconcentration Controversy*, p. 63.

152. Theodore Cohen, *Remaking Japan: The American Occupational as New Deal* (New York: Free Press, 1987), p. 36.

153. Ibid., p. 362.

154. Uchiyama, *The Deconcentration Controversy*, p. 44, citing T. A. Bisson, *Nihon senryō kaisōki* [Japan occupation reforms] (Tokyo: Sansei-dō, 1983), pp. 81–109 (a translation by Masanori Nakamura and Yōichi Miura of an unpublished manuscript titled "Reform Years in Japan, 1945–1947: An Occupation Memoir," 1975) [hereinafter, Bisson, "Occupation Memoir"]. Bisson recalled that he, Cyrus Peake, and Eleanor Hadley formed a "Democratic economics" group. Bisson, "Occupation Memoir," p. 99.

155. Forrestal was the former president of Dillon Read, the New York investment banking firm of which Draper had been a partner.

156. Uchiyama, *The Deconcentration Controversy*, p. 73.

157. For excellent summaries of Draper's role, see Hosoya, "Economic Democratization," pp. 70–73, and Schonberger, *Aftermath of War*, pp. 161–97. Neither Hosoya nor Schonberger deals with Draper's experience in Germany and his overriding concern for German economic recovery.

158. On August 25 and 26, 1947, *Watanabe Diary*, p. 298.

159. *Congressional Record*, vol. 93 (Senate, December 19, 1947), pp. 11686–88.

160. Ibid., vol. 94 (January 19, 1948), p. 298.

161. Discussed in Uchiyama, *The Deconcentration Controversy*, pp. 136–37.

162. Ibid.

163. Having played an instrumental role in defining U.S. policy in Europe, Kennan viewed his visit in Japan as primarily an opportunity to extend "containment" to Asia with Japan's playing the German role in East Asia against the Soviet Union and, perhaps, China. See George F. Kennan, *Memoirs, 1925–1950* (Boston: Little, Brown, 1967), pp. 368–96.

164. See, e.g., Eleanor M. Hadley, "Trust Busting in Japan," *Harvard Business Review*, vol. 26, no. 4 (July 1948), pp. 425–40. Hadley, like most of those who were closely involved with the dissolution program, blamed Kauffman and conservatives in Con-

gress. They were apparently unaware of the parallel episode in Germany or of Draper's role and his influence on the views of others in the War and State Departments.

165. See address by Edward H. Levi to the Chicago chapter of the New Council of American Business on March 13, 1947, *Congressional Record*, vol. 93 (1947), pp. A1553–56, inserted at the request of Senator Wayne Morse of Oregon. Levi also identified German cartels with German industrial and military strength. These attitudes changed at least in Germany as occupation legislation began to be implemented and German voices, heard. See, e.g., comments by Sidney H. Willmer, chief of the Decartelization and Deconcentration Division under John J. McCloy as Allied high commissioner, on the reorientation of the American rationale for decartelization and deconcentration in positive terms "in the sense that its objective was an expanding German economy with a progressive raising of the standard of living as the basis for a viable democracy," in Wolfgang Friedman, *Anti-Trust Laws: A Comparative Symposium* (Toronto: Carswell, 1956), p. 176.

## 2 / TRANSFORMATION AND CONVERGENCE— THE GERMAN AND JAPANESE RESPONSES

1. Rüdiger Robert, *Konzentrationspolitik in der Bundesrepublik—Das Beispiel der Entstehung des Gesetzes gegen Wettbewerbsbeschränkungen* [Concentration policies in the Federal Republic of Germany—Example of the enactment of the Law against Restraints of Competition] (Berlin: Duncker & Humblot, 1976). Robert's study is a thorough and detailed account of the enactment of the GWB. For an equally thorough study of the development of German competition policy and its influence in Europe, see David J. Gerber, *Law and Competition in Twentieth-Century Europe: Protecting Prometheus* (New York and London: Clarendon Press, 1998). For a study that covers much of the same ground with an emphasis on deconcentration measures and merger control, see Möschel, *Entflechtung*.

2. See, e.g., Franz Böhm, *Wettbewerb und Monopolkampf* [Competition and the struggle against monopoly] (Berlin: Heymann, 1933); Franz Böhm, *Kartelle und Koalitionsfreiheit* [Cartels and freedom to collude] (Berlin: Heymann, 1933); Franz Böhm, *Freiheit und Ordnung in der Marktwirtschaft* [Freedom and order in the market economy], ed. Ernst-Joachim Mestmäcker (Baden-Baden: Nomos, 1980); Leonhard Miksch, *Wettbewerb als Aufgabe: Grundsätze einer Wettbewerbsordnung* [Competition as the mission: Principles of an order of competition] (Godesberg: Küpper, 2d ed., 1948 [1st ed., 1937]); Walter Eucken, *Die Grundlagen der National-ökonomie* [Foundations of the national economy] (Jena: Fischer, 1943 [subsequent editions, Berlin: Springer]); and Walter Eucken, *Grundsätze der Wirtschaftspolitik* [Principles of economic policy] (Tübingen: J. C. B. Mohr, 1952). Few ordo-liberal contributions have been translated or are otherwise available in English. The exceptions include

Walter Eucken, *Foundations of Economics: History and Theory in the Analysis of Economic Reality,* trans. T. W. Hutchison, (Edinburgh, London, and Glasgow: William Hodge, 1950), and idem, *This Unsuccessful Age,* intro. John Jewkes (Chicago: University of Chicago Press, 1951). For a brief essay by Franz Böhm on the development of antitrust policy in West Germany between 1945 and 1954, see Franz Boehm, "Monopoly and Competition in Western Germany," in *Monopoly and Competition and Their Regulation,* ed. Edward H. Chamberlin (London: Macmillan, 1954), pp. 141–67.

3. For an excellent introduction to ordo-liberal ideas and their influence, see David J. Gerber, "Constitutionalizing the Economy: German Neo-Liberalism, Competition Law and the 'New Europe,' *American Journal of Comparative Law,* vol. 42, no.1 (1994), pp. 25–84. See also Gerber, *Law and Competition in Twentieth-Century Europe,* pp. 232–65; Jan Tumlir, "Franz Böhm and the Development of Economic-constitutional Analysis," in *German Neo-Liberals and the Social Market Economy,* ed. Alan Peacock and Hans Willgerodt (London: Macmillan, 2nd. ed., 1955), pp. 125–78; Geoffrey Denton, Murray Forsyth, and Malcolm MacLennan, *Economic Planning and Policies in Britain, France and Germany* (London: George Allen & Unwin, 1968), pp. 34–79.

4. Eucken, *Grundsätze,* p. 336, quoted in Denton, Forsyth, and MacLennan, *Economic Planning,* p. 39.

5. On the continuity of ordo-liberal ideas and the ideology of the "social market economy" with German social economic policy since the late nineteenth century, see Gerhard Lehmbruch, "The Institutional Framework of German Regulation," in *The Politics of German Regulatton,* ed. Kenneth Dyson (Aldershot, U.K.: Dartmouth, 1992), pp. 33–35. Critics of the Freiburg School give them credit not only for the enactment of the GWB but also the manner of its enforcement, but this seems meant as criticism not compliment. See, e.g., Fritz Ottel, *Zwei Jahre deutsche Kartellpolitik* [Two years of German competition policy] (Frankfurt: Knapp, 1960).

6. *Entwurf zu einem Gesetz zur Sicherung des Leistungswettbewerbs und einem Gesetz öber das Monopolamt mit Stellungnahme des Sachverständigen-Ausschusses und Minderheitsgutachten* [Draft of a law to protect efficient competition and for a law for the monopoly office with comment of a panel of experts and minority opinions] (Frankfurt: Printed for the Federal Minister of Economics, July 5, 1949). The term *Leistungswettbewerb* or "performance competition" reflects the influence of a legal distinction between competitive conduct enhancing consumer choice (performance competition) and competitive behavior directed toward a rival's ability to compete (impediment competition) that had developed in the 1920s under German unfair competition law, particularly in the work of Hans Carl Nipperdey. See Gerber, *Law and Competition in Twentieth-Century Europe,* pp. 253, 273.

7. Robert, *Konzentrationspolitik,* p. 112.

8. For confirmation of Böhm's influence, see the comments by Ludwig Erhard in his contribution to the *Festschrift* celebrating Böhm's eightieth birthday: Ludwig Erhard,

"Franz Böhms Einfluss auf die Politik" [Franz Böhm's political influence], in *Wirtschaftsordnung und Staatsverfassung: Festschrift für Franz Böhm* [Economic order and national constitution: Commemorative volume for Franz Böhm], ed. Heinz Savermann and Ernst-Joachim Mestmäcker, (Tübingen: J. C. B. Mohr, 1975), pp. 15–21.

9. Conversation with Ernst-Joachim Mestmäcker, Hamburg, July 9, 1997. In a letter to the author dated December 12, 1998, Wolfgang Fikentscher notes an "almost unknown" draft deconcentration law issued by the Reich Economics Ministry. Deconcentration would be necessary, it was argued, to reinstitute sound competition in the wake of the high degree of concentration that wartime condition had required. Fikentscher adds, "It must have been a lonely follower of the Freiburg School who dared propagate such a Draft when the catastrophic end of the war was visible and Berlin, the seat of the Ministry, was largely destroyed."

10. See Ludwig Erhard, *Prosperity through Competition* [translation by Edith Temple Roberts and John B. Wood into English of *Wohlstand für Alle*] (New York: Praeger, 1958), p. 117. Erhard's postwar speeches and essays are collected in Ludwig Erhard, *Deutsche Wirtschaftspolitik: Der Weg der Sozialen Marktwirtschaft* (Düsseldorf and Vienna: ECON, 1962): trans. into English as *The Economics of Success* by J. A. Arengo-Jones and D. J. S. Thomson, by (London: Thames and Hodson, 1963)

11. Erhard, Prosperity, pp. 124–25.

12. See, e.g., *id.*, p. 125. In *Germany's Comeback in the World Market* (London: George Allen & Unwin, 1954) [translation by W. H. Johnson of *Deutschland's Rückkehr zum Weltmarkt* (1953)], Erhard wrote that his currency reform of June 1948 was the "initiation of the market economy that awakened the entrepreneurial impulse" (p. 21).

13. The dramatic removal of price controls was not entirely an Erhard affair. Clay appears to have given Erhard considerable support. Clay described the results in the most positive terms. In a letter to Byrnes, he wrote, "The immediate benefits of currency reform have been unbelievable. Almost overnight hoarded goods appeared on the shelves as the stores had to sell to meet payrolls. Likewise hoarded goods in manufacturing plants began to move to the stores. Even fruits and vegetables from the farm once more went on sale in the market place. In one month the production output increased from 50 percent of 1936 to 60 percent of 1936—an increase of 10 percent." Letter from Clay to Byrnes, September 18, 1948, Clay, *Papers*, vol. 2, p. 858. Wolfgang Fikentscher also notes that Erhard carefully considered specific market conditions and elasticities of supply and demand before removing price controls. Some rationing continued in West Germany through 1952. Letter to author dated December 22, 1998.

14. Letter from Clay to Byrnes, September 18, 1948, Clay, *Papers*, vol. 2, p. 858.

15. Robert, *Konzentrationspolitik*, is the principal source for the description that follows. For a brief but informative summary of the debate, see Harold Rasch, *Wettbewerbsbeschränkungen: Kartell- und Monopolrecht* [Restraints of competition: Cartel and monopoly law] (Berlin: Neue Wirtschafts-Briefe, 2d ed. 1958), pp. 3–12.

See also Eberhard Günther, "Die geistigen Grundlagen des sogenannten Josten Entwurfs" [Intellectual foundations of the so-called Josten drafts], in *Festschrift für Franz Böhm*, pp. 183–204; and Wolfgang Fikentscher, "Die deutsche Kartellrechts-wissenschaft 1945–1954: Eine kritische Übersicht" [German cartel jurisprudence, 1945–1954: A critical review], *Wirtschaft und Wettbewerb* [Economics and competition; hereinafter, *WuW*], vol. 5, no. 4 (1955), pp. 205–29.

16. *Regierungs-Entwurf eines Gesetzes gegen Wettbewerbsbeschränkungen*, June 13, 1952, BT-Drucksache, I/3462. For an English translation of the 1952 bill and abbreviated translation of the official comments, see "Germany II: Draft Law of 1952," in *Anti-Trust Laws: A Comparative Symposium*, pp. 189–237.

17. Robert, *Konzentrationspolitik*, p. 111.

18. See Wolfram Dörinkel, "Das Lebenswerk von Rudolf Isay" [The life-work of Rudolf Isay], in *Beiträge zum Wirtschaftrecht: Festschrift für Rudolf Isay*, ed. Eduard Reimer (Cologne: Carl Heymanns, 1956), pp. 1–7. Isay and Böhm, who had submitted a separate draft of his own, exchanged views on antitrust policy in a noteworthy series of essays published in *WuW*, the leading German periodical on competition policy. See Isay's critique (*Gegenvorschlag*) in *WuW*, vol. 4, no. 2 (1954), pp. 100–17, followed by Böhm's reply, "Kartelle und Krise" [Cartels and crisis], *WuW*, vol. 4, nos. 6 and 7 (1954), pp. 367–87, and Isay's responses, "Soziale Marktwirtschaft und Kartellgesetzgebung" [Social market economy and cartel legislation], *WuW*, vol. 4, no. 9 (1954), pp. 557–80, and "Wirtschaftliche und rechtliche Konsequenzen des Böhm-Entwurfs" [Economic and legal consequences of the Böhm draft], *WuW*, vol. 5, no. 6 (1955), pp. 339–52.

19. Erhard had impeccable prewar credentials as an economist with strong liberal (neoclassical) views. See his "Einfluss der Preisbindung auf die Qualität und Quantität des Angebots und der Nachfrage" [Influence of price controls on the quality and quantity of supply and demand], (1939) in *Marktwirtschaft und Wirtschaftswissenschaft: Eine Festgabe aus dem Kreise der Nürnberger Schule zum 60. Geburtstage von Wilhelm Vershofen* [Market economy and economics: A commemorative work of the Nuremberg school for the sixtieth birthday of Wilhelm Vershofen], ed. George Bergler and Ludwig Erhard (Berlin: Deutscher Betriebswirteverlag, 1939). Also Ludwig Erhard, *Der Weg des Geistes in der Technik* [The path of intellect in technology] (Berlin: VDI, 1929).

20. See Robert, *Konzentrationspolitik*, p. 115–19. Knut Wolfgang Nörr adds that the proponents of the Josten drafts tended to be insensitive to the demands of a pluralist political order, which required compromise and acceptance of contrary points of view. Knut Wolfgang Nörr, "Law and Market Organization: The Historical Experience in Germany from 1900 to the Law Against Restraints of Competition," *Journal of Institutional and Theoretical Economics* [*Zeitschrift für die gesamte Staatswissenschaft*], vol. 151, no. 1 (1995), p. 17.

21. Conversation with Ernst-Joachim Mestmäcker, Hamburg, July 9, 1997.

22. The occupation legislation (Law No. 56 and its British and French equivalents) continued in force after the Federal Republic had regained complete sovereignty in May 1955 pursuant to German legislation. The October 15, 1954, Protocol about the Termination of the Occupation Regime in the Federal Republic of Germany, ending the occupation in West Germany, provided in an annex that except for regulations concerning the coal and steel industry and I. G. Farben, the occupation deconcentration and decartelization measures would cease to be effective. However, the supplementary October 23, 1954, Convention on the Settlement of Matters Arising out of the War and the Occupation (*United States Treaties and Other International Agreements* [*TIAS*]. vol. 6 part 4, pp. 4411–52 [*Vertrag zur Regelung aus Kreig und Besatzung entstandener Fragen, Bundesgesetzblatt (BGB)*; 1954 II 157]) empowered Federal and *Land* authorities to repeal or amend occupation legislation, but such legislation would remain in force until repeal (chapter 2). In 1957 the Bonn government by ordinance formally implemented each of the three occupation regulations. *BGBI.* 1957 II 377, 378. They were repealed and ceased to have effect as of January 1, 1958, the effective date of the GWB, under GWB section 109. For a German perspective on the implementation of the Allied antitrust regulations, see Henrich Karl Bock and Hans Korsch, "Decartelization and Deconcentration in the West German Economy since 1945," in *Anti-Trust Laws*, pp. 138–75; published a year later in German as "Kartellauflösung und Konzernentflechtung in der westdeutschen Wirtschaft seit 1945," *WuW*, vol. 7, nos. 7 and 8 (1957), pp. 411–37.

23. For a contemporaneous essay on the effect of Law No. 56, Ordinance No. 78, and Ordinance No. 95 as German law, see Alfred Gleiss and Wolfgang Fikentscher, "Weitergeltung des Dekartellierungsrechts" [Continued effect of decartelization law], *WuW*, vol. 5, no. 9 (1955), pp. 525–33.

24. See, e.g., Kurt Zweigert, "Die Zweite und Dritte Gewalt im Kartellrecht," in *Beiträge zur Wirtschaft*, p. 132.

25. German courts continued to enforce and review decisions made pursuant to Law No. 56 See, e.g., Federal Supreme Court Judgment of March 5, 1953 (5th Criminal Bench), holding that a horizontal price-fixing agreement was subject to criminal sanctions. *WuW*, vol. 3, nos. 7 and 8 (1953), pp. 474–78. See also Federal Supreme Court Judgment of May 20, 1953 (1st Civil Bench), *Entscheidungen des Bundesgerichtshofs in Zivilsachen* [hereinafter *BGHZ*], vol. 10, p. 22; Federal Supreme Court Judgment of November 30, 1954 (1st Civil Bench), *BGHZ*, vol. 15, p. 338; Federal Supreme Court Judgment of February 15, 1955 (1st Civil Bench), *BGHZ*, vol. 16, p. 296; Federal Supreme Court Judgment of March 8, 1955 (1st Civil Bench), *BGHZ*, vol. 17, p. 41; Federal Supreme Court Judgment of November 18, 1955, in *WuW*, vol. 6, no. 3 (1956), p. 227. See also Hamm High Court Judgment of September 13, 1956, in *WuW*, vol. 6, no. 12

(1956), p. 796. Other decisions are reported in *WuW*, vol. 6, no. 3 (1956), p. 20. For a detailed review of the jurisprudence produced in the process, see Ernst-Joachim Mestmäcker, "Dekartellierung und Wettbewerb in der Rechtspinechung der deutschen Gerichte" [Decartelization and competition in the decisions of German courts], ORDO, vol. 9 (1957), pp. 99–130.

26. See Warner, *Steel and Sovereignty*; Gerber, *Law and Competition in Twentieth-Century Europe*; Möschel, *Entflechtung*; Ernst-Joachim Mestmäcker, *Europäisches Wettbewerbsrecht* [European competition law] (Munich: C. H. Beck, 1974). For a study of European Court decisions, see Stuart A. Scheingold, *The Rule of Law in European Integration: The Path of the Schuman Plan* (New Haven, Conn.: Yale University Press, 1965). On the pivotal role of the Schumann Plan as well as the Havana Charter and the 1953 United Nations draft convention on restrictive practices, see Eberhard Günther, "Die Regelung des Wettbewerbs im Vertrag zur Gründung der europäischen Wirtschaftsgemeinschaft" [The rules on competition in the treaty for the formation of the European economic community], *WuW*, vol. 7, no. 5 (1957), p. 277.

27. See Werner von Simon, "Kartelle und Zusammenschlüsse in der Montanunion" [Cartels and consolidation in the iron and steel community], *WuW*, vol. 5, nos. 7 and 8 (1955), pp. 401–21. The French concern is also apparent from contemporaneous press accounts and speeches.

28. Allied High Commission Law No. 27, May 16, 1950, reproduced in Warner, *Steel and Sovereignty*, appendix 1, pp. 237–47.

29. In September 1993 the Kohl government announced that it hoped to enact the sixth amendment during that legislative session. See *Bericht der Bundesregierung zur Zukunftssicherung des Standortes Deutschland*, September 3, 1993. *BT Drucksache*, 12/5620, p. 43. The legislation was finally enacted in 1998 and became effective on January 1, 1999.

30. Amendment (*Novelle*) of September 15, 1965 *BGBI*. 1965 I 1363).

31. Amendment of August 3, 1973 (*BGBI*. 1973 I 917).

32. Amendment of June 28, 1976 (*BGBI*. 1976 I 1697).

33. Amendment of April 26, 1980 (*BGBI*. 1980 I 458).

34. Amendment of December 22, 1989 (*BGBI*. 1990 I 235).

35. Amendment of August 26, 1998 (*BGBI*. 1998 I 2512).

36. Takafusa Nakamura, *Postwar Japanese Economy* (Tokyo: University of Tokyo Press, 1981); and Chalmers Johnson, *MITI and the Japanese Miracle: The Growth of Industrial Policy, 1925–1975* (Stanford, Calif.: Stanford University Press, 1982). See also Noguchi, *1940 System*.

37. Chalmers Johnson, "Japan: Who Governs? An Essay on Official Bureaucracy," *Journal of Japanese Studies*, vol. 2, no. 1 (1975), pp. 1–28.

38. For a concise description of "revisionist" bureaucrats and their reformist views,

see Robert M. Spaulding, Jr., "Bureaucracy's Political Force, 1920–45," in *Dilemmas of Growth in Prewar Japan*, ed. J. W. Morley (Princeton N. J.: Princeton University Press, 1971), p. 62.

39. Elimination of Excessive Concentration of Economic Power Law (*Kado keizairyoku shūchū haijo hō*), Law No. 207, 1947, repealed by Law No. 87, 1955.

40. Trade Association Law (*Jigyōsha dantai hō*), Law No. 191, 1948.

41. Law No. 529, 1953.

42. Hiroshi Iyori, "A Comparative Analysis on Japanese Competition Law: An Attempt to Identify German and American Influences," in *Die Japanisier ung des westlichen Rechts* [The Japanization of western law], ed. Helmut Coing, Ryuichi Hirano, Zentaro Kitagawa, Junichi Murakami, Knut Wolfgang Nörr, Thomas Oppermann, and Hiroshi Shiono (Tübingen: J. C. B. Mohr, 1990), p. 238. See also Kojima Seiichi, "Kōtori'in no dokkinhö keiseian ni tsuite" [Concerning the FTC bill to revise the antimonopoly law], *Kōsei torihiki*, no. 2 (1953), p. 1, criticizing the proposals for revision based on the proposed 1952 German bill.

43. See Kozo Yamamura, "Success That Soured: Administrative Guidance and Cartels in Japan," in *Policy and Trade Issues of the Japanese Economy*, ed. Kozo Yamamura (Seattle: University of Washington Press, 1982), p. 82.

44. The full text of the revised designation as adopted is reported in *Kōsei torihiki*, no. 381 (1982), p. 4. The background is reported in *Kōsei torihiki*, no. 379 (1982), p. 16, and no. 382 (1982), p. 4. For English translations of the 1982 General Designations, see Hiroshi Iyori and Akinoru Uesugi, *The Antimonopoly Laws and Policies of Japan* (New York: Federal Legal Publications, 3d ed., 1994), pp. 443–46. For a critique, see Joel Davidow, "The New Japanese Guidelines on Unfair Practices in Patent and Know-how Licenses: An American View," *World Competition*, vol. 12, no. 4 (1989), pp. 5–22.

45. Under the 1952 Export Transactions Law (Law No. 299, 1952), all export cartels were subject to FTC approval. The law was amended in 1953 (Law No. 188, 1953) to cover import cartels as well and renamed the Export and Import Transactions Law (*Yushutsunyū torihiki hō*). Further amendment in 1955 (Law No. 140, 1955) transferred the FTC's authority to approve export cartels to MITI. The FTC was left with little more than a filing and reporting role. The standards governing approvals remained intact. MITI was not granted any authority to compel or in any manner initiate the formation of export or import cartels. Under the statute exempt export or import cartels were to be formed voluntarily. The law was substantially amended under omnibus legislation in 1997 to eliminate export and import cartels. *Shiteki dokusen no kinshi oyobi kōsei torihiki ni kansuru hōritsu no tekiyōgai seido no seiri to ni kansuru hōritsu* [Law concerning the adjustment of the system of exemptions to the law concerning the prohibition of private monopoly and preservation of fair trade] (Law No. 96, 1997).

46. Kōsei Torihiki I'inkai (Fair Trade Commission), *Dokusen kinshi seisaku nijū-nenshi* (Twenty-year history of antimonopoly policy) (Tokyo: Ministry of Finance Printing Office, 1968), p. 152, [hereinafter, *Twenty-Year History*].

47. *Id.*, pp. 152–53.

48. For the text of the bill, see *id.*, pp. 484–519.

49. Shōda Akira, *Dokusen kinshi hō* [Antimonopoly law] (Tokyo: Nihon Hyōron-sha, 1966), p. 50 [2d ed. published in 1980 in two volumes].

50. *Id.*, pp. 42–45.

51. Leon Hollerman, *Japan's Dependence on the World Economy: The Approach toward Economic Liberalization* (Princeton, N.J.: Princeton University Press, 1967), p. 171.

52. See, e.g., Kozo Yamamura, *Economic Policy in Postwar Japan* (Berkeley: University of California Press, 1967), p. 70; Johnson, *MITI*, p. 226.

53. John O. Haley and Hunter Hale, "Recent Developments: Antimonopoly Law," *Law in Japan: An Annual*, vol. 9 (1976), p. 159.

54. Kenji Sanekata, Masu Uekusa, and Joji Atsuya, "Karuteru no tettei-teki kenkyū" [Complete analysis of cartels], *Chūo kōron*, vol. 14, no. 3 (1975), p. 126.

55. In the case against Sony, Sony agreed to end its resale price arrangements; as a result, no formal action was taken. For the second, see *In re* Matsushita Denki Sangyō K. K., 17 *Kōsei Torihiki I'inkai Shinketsushū* [hereinafter, *Shinketsushū*] 187 (FTC [Consent], no. 4, 1967, March 12, 1971).

56. *In re* Sanyo Denki K. K. et al. 25 *Shinketsushū* 37 (FTC [Ruling], no. 6, 1966, July 27, 1978). The proceedings, which lasted for more than a decade, were discontinued after the initial decision for lapse of time.

57. *In re* Yawata Seitetsu K. K. and Fuji Seitetsu K. K., in 16 *Shinketsushū* 46 (FTC [Consent], no. 2, 1969, October 30, 1969).

58. *In re* Asahi Kasei Kōgyō K. K. et al., 19 *Shinketsushū* 124 (FTC [Consent] December 27, 1972).

59. The first case was *In re* Sekiyu Renmei et al., 20 *Shinketsushū* 355 (FTC [Decision], no. 4, 1971, March 28, 1974). The appeals from this decision were rejected on first (24 *Shinketsushū* 155 [Tokyo High C., August 15, 1977]) and second appeal (*Hanrei jihō*, no. 1037, p. 3 [Sup. C., 2d P.B., March 9, 1982].) It involved the 1971 price-fixing arrangements approved by MITI. The second case, *In re* Sekiyu Renmei et al. in 20 *Shinketsushū*, 312 (FTC [Recommendation], no. 7, 1974, February 22, 1974, involved output restrictions approved and supervised by MITI in the wake of the 1973 oil crisis. The third case was *In re* Idemitsu Kōsan K. K. et al., 20 *Shinketsushū* 300 (FTC [Recommendation], no. 6, 1974, February 22, 1974. Separate appeals by six of the twelve respondents in this case were dismissed by both the Tokyo High Court (122 *Shinketsushū* 220 [Tokyo High C., September 19, 1974]) and the Supreme Court (25 *Shinketsushū* 59 [Sup. C., 3d P.B. April 4, 1978]). The case involved price fixing by

twelve of Japan's domestic petroleum firms in consultation with MITI officials in 1972 and 1973.

60. Kuni [Japan] v. Sekiyu Renmei et al., *Hanrei jihō*, no. 988, p. 22 (Tokyo High Ct., September 26, 1980). In this decision 1973 output restrictions were deemed illegal, but the defendants were acquitted for lack of criminal intent as result of reliance on MITI guidance. Kuni [Japan] v. Idemitsu Kōsan K. K. et al., *Hanrei jihō*, no. 985, p. 3 (Tokyo High Ct., September 26, 1980). In this decision, 1972 and 1973 price fixing was held illegal, and both corporate and individual defendants were convicted of criminal antitrust offenses.

61. Idemitsu Kōsan K. K. et al., v. Kuni [Japan], 38 *Keishū* 1287 (Sup. Ct., 2d P.B., February 24, 1984).

62. *In re* Tōyō Rayon K. K. et al., *Shinketsushū* 17 (FTC [Decision], no. 2, 1952, August 6, 1953), and *In re* Noda Shōyu K. K., 7 *Shinketsushū* 108 (FTC [Decision]. no. 2, 1954, December 27, 1955).

63. See *United States–Japan Structural Impediments Initiative (SII)*: Hearing before the Senate Subcommittee on International Trade, Committee on Finance, 101st Cong., 2d sess. (1990). For a detailed analysis of the variety of issues raised by the SII negotiations, see Kozo Yamamura, ed., *Japan's Economic Structure: Should It Change?* (Seattle: Society for Japanese Studies, 1990), pp. 1–12. For an extract of the final report issued, on May 22, 1991, see Iyori and Uesugi, *Antimonopoly Laws of Japan* (1994 ed.), pp. 553–64.

64. See Laura D'Andrea Tyson, *Who's Bashing Whom? Trade Conflict in High Technology Industries* (Washington, D.C.: Institute for International Economics), esp. pp. 81, 99–100. One of the more elegant presentations of this view is found in Kozo Yamamura and Jan Vandenberg, "Japan's Rapid Growth Policy on Trial: The Television Case," in *Law and Trade Issues of the Japanese Economy: American and Japanese Perspectives*, ed. Gary R. Saxonhouse and Kozo Yamamura Seattle and Tokyo: University of Washington Press and University of Tokyo Press, 1986), pp. 238–83.

## 3 / PROHIBITIONS AND APPROVALS

1. Fritz Rittner, *Wettbewerbs- und Kartellrecht* (Heidelberg: C. F. Müller, 1995), p. 211.

2. Federal Supreme Court Judgment of July 12, 1973, *Entscheidungen des Bundesgerichtshofs in Strafsachen [BGHSt]*, vol. 25, p. 208, *WuW/E BGH*, p. 1276.

3. *Begründung des Gesetzentwurfes zu # 10 Nr. 8, BT Drucksache 2/1158*, cited in Eugen Langen, Ernst Niederleithinger, and Ulrich Schmidt, eds., *Kommentar zum Kartellrecht* [Commentary on cartel law] (Neuwied and Darmstadt: Luchterhand, 5th ed., 1977).

4. See, e.g., Federal Supreme Court Judgment of September 23, 1975, *WuW/E BGH*,

p. 1404 (*EDV-Zubehör*), and Federal Supreme Court Judgment of October 29, 1970, *WuW/E BGH*, p. 1168 (*Blitzgeräte*).

5. Criminal procedure scholar John Langbein uses the term "petty offenses" for *Ordnungswidrigkeiten*. See, e.g., John H. Langbein, "Controlling Prosecutorial Discretion in Germany," *Chicago Law Review*, vol. 41, no. 3 (1974), p. 439. Because such offenses are not necessarily minor and the procedures for levying fines are administrative not criminal, the translation "administrative" or "regulatory" offenses seems preferable. The standard Japanese translation is *chitsujo ihan*, construing the term *Ordnung* as "public order" rather than "regulation." The English conveys more accurately the sense of the term if not its literal translation.

6. Law on Administrative Offenses of January 2, 1975 (*BGB1*. 1975 I 80). For an excellent description of the OWiG and its operation in English, see Tilmann Schneider, "The German Code of Regulatory Offenses," in *Studies in Comparative Criminal Law*, ed. Edward M. Wise and Gerhard O. W. Moeller (Springfield, Ill.: Charles C. Thomas, 1975), pp. 253–80.

7. See chapter 5, p. 154.

8. *Strafgesetzbuch*, § 298, as amended by *Gesetz zur Bekämpfung der Korruption* [Law to combat corruption], August 13, 1997, *BGB1*. 1997 I 2038.

9. Kanazawa Yoshio, "Kokusai karuteru ni taisuru kokunai hōteki kisei" (Domestic legal regulation of international cartels), *Kōsei torihiki*, no. 126 (1961), p. 6. See also Michiko Ariga, "Regulation of International Licensing Agreements under the Japanese Anti-Monopoly Act," in *Patent and Know-how Licensing in Japan and the United States*, ed. Teruo Doi and Warren Shattuck (Seattle: University of Washington Press, 1977), pp. 278–309.

10. Guidelines concerning the Activities of Trade Associations under the Antimonopoly Law (*Jigyō dantai no katsudo ni kansuru dokusen kinshi hōjo no shishin*) (FTC, August 1979), *Law in Japan: An Annual*, vol. 12 (1979), p. 118.

11. *In re* Baishō Shisetsu Konpō Onyu Kumiai, 1 *Shinketsushū* 10 (FTC [Decision] no. 2, 1947, March 27, 1948); *In re* Kimura et al., 1 *Shinketsushū* 133 (FTC [Decision] no. 3, 1947, March 27, 1947); *In re* Saitama Ginkō K. K. et al., 2 *Shinketsushū* 74 (FTC [Decision] no. 30, 1950, July 13, 1950); *In re* Noda Shōyu K. K., 7 *Shinketsushū* 108 (FTC [Decision] no. 2, 1954, December 29, 1955); *In re* Yukijirushi Nyugyō K. K. et al., 8 *Shinketsushū* 12 (FTC [Decision] no. 4, 1954, July 23, 1956); *In re* Tobu Tetsudō K. K. et al., 11 *Shinketsushū* 1 (FTC [Decision] no. 5, 1952, April 17, 1962) [no violation]; *In re* Kanegafuchi Bōseki K. K. et al., 13 *Shinketsushū* 18 (FTC [Decision] no. 7, 1965, June 1, 1965) [no violation]; *in re* Tōyō Seikan K. K., 19 *Shinketsushū* 87 (FTC [Decision] no. 11, 1972, September 18. 1972). *In re* Nihon Iryōshoku Kyōkai et al., 43 *Shinketsushū* 209 (FTC [Recommendation] no. 14, 1996, May 9, 1996).

12. *In re* Noda Shōyu K. K. (1955). Noda Shōyu, Japan's largest soy sauce producer, had set the resale prices for its highest-quality brand, Kikkoman. Thereafter, Japan's

three other leading producers followed suit, raising the prices of their competing brands. The FTC prosecuted the case on the theory that vertical price fixing by a leading manufacturer in an oligopolistic industry constituted control over the pricing decisions of its competitors in cases where consumers identified quality with price. On appeal, the Tokyo High Court affirmed the FTC decision. Noda Shōyu K. K. v. Kōsei Torihiki I'inkai, 9 *Shinketsushū* 57 (Tokyo High Ct., December 25, 1957). The court accepted the FTC's argument but suggested that the extent of customer identification of quality with price might be unique to the soy sauce industry. The case is further complicated by the role of an exempt wholesale cooperative, which distributed the products of all four producers.

13. *In re* Tōyō Seikan K. K. (1972). In this case the FTC found that the respondent, Japan's largest can manufacturer, had engaged in private monopolization by limiting the output and territories of subsidiaries. Broken up under the *zaibatsu* dissolution program, by the early 1970s Tōyō Seikan had reestablished control over several former subsidiaries.

14. The facts are not elaborated in the two earliest cases—*In re* Baishō Shisetsu Konpō Unyu Kumiai (1948) and *In re* Kumura (1948). Two of the three remaining cases involved loans conditioned on borrowers' selling through an agent or to buyers designated by the lender. In the first, *In re* Saitama Ginkō (1950), the respondent bank had conditioned loans to silk manufacturers on their agreement to export through an export sales company organized and controlled by the bank. In the second, *In re* Yukijirushi Nyugyō K. K. [Snow Brand Dairy] (1956), an agricultural cooperative bank required dairy farmers receiving loans in order to finance their purchase of cows to sell their raw milk to either one of two dominant dairy product manufacturers. The third and most recent case—the first private monopolization decision in twenty-four years—involved an association of hospital food suppliers and food equipment manufacturers that had attempted to exclude new entrants. *In re* Nihon Iryōshoku Kyōkai et al., 43 *Shinketsushū* 209 (FTC [Recommendation] no. 14, 1996, May 9, 1996).

15. *In re* Yuasa Mokuzai Kōgyō K. K. et al., *Shinketsushū* 62 (FTC [Decision] no. 2, 1948, (August 3, 1949).

16. Shōda (1980 ed.), vol. 1, pp. 227–34.

17. K. K. Asahi Shinbunsha v. Kōsei Torihiki I'inkai, 4 *Shinketsushū* 145 (Tokyo High Ct., March 9, 1953).

18. An implication to the contrary appears in Yoshihiko Tsuji, "Regulation of Resale Price Maintenance in Japan," *New York Law Forum*, vol. 18, no. 2 (1972), p. 397, fn. 3, probably as a result of editorial error. The examples of resale price maintenance cases and other violations involving article 3 cited by Tsuji include 211 trade association cases and other examples of horizontal price fixing.

19. Federal Supreme Court Judgment of October 14, 1976 (*Fertigbeton*), BGHZ, vol. 68, p. 6; *WuW E/BGH* (1977), p. 1458.

20. See *FTC / Japan Views*, no. 28 (June 1997), pp. 49–51.

21. See chap. 2, n. 45.

22. Council Regulation No. 4064/98, O. J. Eur. Comm. (No. I. 395) 1 (1989).

23. Unless otherwise noted, the statistics included in this section were compiled from official Japanese and German reports: Kōsei Torihiki I'inkai, *Nenji hōkoku;* Bundeskartellamt, *Bericht des Bundeskartellamtes über seine Tätigkeit sowie über die Lage und Entwicklung auf seinem Aufgabengebiet* [hereinafter, FTC of FCO annual reports].

24. Helmut Gutzler, "Die Ermittlungstätigkeit des Bundeskartellamtes" [The investigatory functions of the Federal Cartel Office], *Grundlagen der Kriminalistik,* vol. 13, no. 1 (1974), p. 537.

25. Exports account for 11 percent of its gross national product (GNP). In 1997, 55.4 percent of German exports went to countries within the European Union (including Finland, Austria, and Sweden). Federal Statistical Office for Germany, "Germany as a Trading Partner," <http://www.statistik-bund.de/basis/e/extrixt.htm>.

26. See, e.g., Mark Tilton, *Restrained Trade: Cartels in Japan's Basic Materials Industries* (Ithaca, N.Y.: Cornell University Press, 1996).

27. Stockmann and Strauch, *World Law of Competition,* §10.01.

28. See *Fifty-Year History,* vol. 2, pp. 420–29.

## 4 / PROCESSES AND PROCEDURES

1. Ulrich Immenga and Ernst-Joachim Mestmäcker, eds., GWB: *Kommentar zum Kartellgesetz* [Commentary on the GWB] (Munich: C. H. Beck, 1st ed., 1981), §48, pp. 1508–9.

2. See Fritz Rittner, "Das Ermessen der Kartellbehörde" [Discretion of the cartel authorities], in *Beiträge zum Wirtschaftsrecht: Festschrift für Heinz Kaufmann* [Contributions to economic law: Commemorative volume for Heinz Kaufmann], ed. Horst Bartholomeyczik, Kurt H. Biedenkopf, and Helmuth von Hahn (Cologne-Marienburg: O. Schmidt, 1972), pp. 307–25.

3. See, e.g., Ulrich Immenga, *Politische Instrumentalisierung des Kartellrechts* [Political instrumentalization of cartel law] (Tübingen: J. C. B. Mohr, 1976), p. 13; also Wolfgang Kartte, "Wettbewerbspolitik im Spannungsfeld zwischen Bundeswirtschafts-ministerium und Bundeskartellamt" [Competition policy in the areas of tension between the Federal Ministry of Economics and the Federal Cartel Office], in *Wettbewerb im Wandel: Festschrift für Eberhard Günther* [Competition in transformation: Commemorative volume for Eberhard Günther], ed. Helmut Gutzler, Wolfgang Herion, and Joseph H. Kaiser (Baden-Baden: Nomos, 1976), p. 55, fn. 30.

4. Directive on application of § 22 GWB with respect to concerted actions of July 9, 1971, *Bundesanzeiger,* no. 107, June 15, 1971; directive on stricter supervision of ver-

tical price fixing and resale price recommendations of November 30, 1972, *Bundesanzeiger*, no. 231, December 9, 1972; directive on publication of consents in merger control proceedings of March 25, 1976, *Bundesanzeiger*, no. 66, April 3, 1976; directive on the treatment of foreign mergers of May 30, 1980, *Bundesanzeiger*, no. 103, June 7, 1980.

5. The directive involved a controversial instruction that the FCO should refrain from acting against voluntary restrictions of heating oil production by petroleum firms. For details and critique, see Kurt H. Biedenkopf, "Zur Selbstbeschränkung auf dem Heizölmarkt" [On voluntary restrictions in the heating oil market], *Betriebs-Berater* [*BB*], vol. 28, no. 21 (1966), pp. 1113–20.

6. Eberhard Günther, "Brauchen wir eine neue Wettbewerbspolitik?" [Do we need a new competition policy?] *WuW*, vol. 17, no. 1 (1967), p. 99; Kartte, "Wettbewerbspolitik," p. 54.

7. See, e.g., Wolfram Dörinkel, "Zur kartellpolitischen Lage in der Bundesrepublik" [On the status of cartel policy in the Federal Republic], *WuW*, vol. 16, no. 12 (1966), p. 942.

8. See, e.g., Ernst Forsthoff, "Die Verfahrensvorschriften im Kartellgesetz" [Procedural provisions in the cartel law], in [Law reprint restraints of competition and European cartel law] *Isay Festschrift*, p. 96.

9. Werner Junge, in Hans Müller-Henneberg and Gustav Schwartz, eds., *Gesetz gegen Wettbewerbsbeschränkungen und europäisches Kartellrecht* [Law against Restraints or Competition and European Cartel Law] (Cologne: Carl Heymanns, 1st ed., 1958), p. 48 [hereinafter, Müller-Henneberg and Schwartz, GWB]; Alexander Reisenkampff and Joachim Gres, *Law against Restraints of Competition: Text and Commentary in English and German* (Cologne: Otto Schmidt, 1st ed., 1977), p 171.

10. Information provided the author by the various *Land* authorities. See also Stockman and Strauch, *World Law of Competition: Federal Republic of Germany*, at § 23.02[2]. The role of the *Land* authorities has been generally ignored in both the German and English literature.

11. See, e.g., Bayerisches Staatsministerium für Wirtschaft und Verkehr (als Landeskartellbehörde), *Kartellbericht* [Cartel report], (1977–80).

12. Semiannual conferences are held by the FCO with the *Land* authorities. Also section 49(1)2 of the GWB requires each *Land* authority to notify the FCO with respect to any administrative or *Bußgeld* proceedings initiated. Under section 49(1) the FCO must similarly inform the competent *Land* authority of any case that would also be within its jurisdiction. Finally, under section 54(3) the FCO may also participate in *Land* proceedings.

13. Rittner, "Das Ermessen," p. 319.

14. FCO annual reports, 1980–97.

15. Bernhard Griesbach, "Jurist und Volkswirt vor der Fusionskontrolle" [Lawyers and economists in merger control], *WuW*, vol. 21, nos. 11 and 12 (1971), pp. 813–19.

16. *Deutsches Richtergesetz* [*DRiG*] of April 19, 1972 [*BGB1.* 1972 I 713], §§ 5, 5a

17. *DRiG* § 7.

18. *Bundesbeamtengesetz* [*BBG*], of July 14, 1953 [*BGB1.* 1957 I 551], § 19.

19. For a biographical sketch of Eberhard Günther and an assessment of his contribution to German antitrust law, see "Eberhard Günther," in *Wettbewerb in Wandel: Festschrift für Eberhard Günther,* pp. 11–24.

20. Immenga and Mestmäcker, *Kommentar,* § 37a.

21. See Werner Junge, "Das Verfahrensrecht in der Zweiten Kartellgesetznovelle," *WuW,* vol. 23, no. 12 (1973), pp. 834–36; also the government's official comment on section 37a, *Begründung, BT-Drucksache,* 6/2520, p. 35.

22. See *Kammergericht* Judgment of June 7, 1974 (*AGIP* I), *Wirtschaft und Wettbewerb/Entscheidungssammlung Oberlandesgerichte* [hereinafter, *WuW/E OLG*], p. 1497; Judgment of July 4, 1974 (*AGIP* II), *WuW/E OLG,* p. 1499; and Judgment of July 9, 1974 (*Chemie Grundstoffe II*), *WuW/E OLG,* pp. 1507, 1509, 2510.

23. See Federal Supreme Court Judgment of July 3, 1976, *Neue Juristische Wochenschrift* [hereinafter, *NJW*] (1976), p. 2259; and Federal Supreme Court Judgment of December 16, 1976 (*Valium*), *Wirtschaft und Wettbewerb/Entscheidungssammlung Bundesgerichtshof* [hereinafter, *WuW/E BGH*], p. 1445, construing similar prohibitions under § 22(5).

24. See Wada Hideo, "Gyōsei-i'inkai" [Administrative commissions], *Jurisuto,* no. 361 (1967), p. 70; Kawakami Katsumi, "Gyōsei-i'inkai" [Administrative commissions], in *Gyōseihō kōza* [Administrative law lectures], ed. Tanaka Jirō, Hara Ryūnosuke, and Yanase Yoshimoto (Tokyo: Yūhikaku, 1965), vol. 4, p. 50; Nathaniel L. Nathanson and Yasuhiro Fujita, "Right to Fair Hearing in Japanese Administrative Law," *Washington Law Review,* vol. 45, no. 2 (1970), p. 295.

25. Wada, "Gyōsei-i'inkai," p. 71.

26. See, e.g., Imamura Shigekazu, "Kōsei Torihiki I'inkai no kokuhatsu gimu ni tsuite" [The duty of the Fair Trade Commission to file criminal charges), *Jurisuto,* no. 733 (1981), p. 100.

27. Kōsei Torihiki I'inkai Jimu Sōkyoku, ed., *Dokusen kinshi seisaku sanjū nenshi* [Thirty-year history of antimonopoly policy] (Tokyo: Fair Trade Commission, 1977), p. 55 [hereinafter, Thirty-Year History].

28. Ibid., p. 55.

29 *Id.* See also Richard W. Rabinowitz, "Antitrust in Japan," in *Current Legal Aspects of Doing Business in Japan and East Asia,* ed. John Owen Haley (Chicago: American Bar Association, 1978), p. 107.

30. Kōsei Torihiki I'inkai Jimu Sōkyoku, ed., *Dokusen kinshi seisaku goju nenshi* [Fifty-year history of antimonopoly policy], vol. 2 (Tokyo: Fair Trade Commission, 1997), pp. 92–93 [hereinafter, *Fifty-Year History*].

31. See, e.g., the investigation of shareholding by financial institutions discussed

in Hideharu Hisabayashi, "Kinyū kaisha no kabushiki shōyū no jōtai ni tsuite" [Concerning shareholding by financial institutions], *Kōsei torihiki,* no. 374 (1981), p. 16.

32 Between 1947 and 1997 the FTC handed down formal decisions (recommendation, consent, or contested) against financial institutions—banks, insurance companies, securities firms—as the principal respondents in only fourteen cases. Five were initiated during the occupation and five were brought against separate securities firms in the wake of the securities industry scandals of the late 1980s and early 1990s. No decisions were issued against financial institutions between 1961 and 1991: *In re* K. K. Teikoku Ginkō et al., 1 *Shinketsushū* 1 (FTC [Decision] No. 11947, December 22, 1947); *In re* K. K. Saitama Ginkō et al., 2 *Shinketsushū* 74 (FTC [Decision] No. 30, 1950, July 13, 1950); *In re* K. K. Sanwa Ginkō, 2 *Shinketsushū* 91 (FTC [Recommendation] No. 2, 1950, August 25, 1950); *In re* K. K. Chiyoda Ginkō, 2 *Shinketsushū* 113 (FTC [Recommendation] No. 4, 1950, September 19, 1950); *In re* Toa Kaji Kaijō Saihūken K. K. et al., 2 *Shinketsushū* 235 (FTC [Decision] No. 18, 1950, February 20, 1951); *In re* K. K. Nihon Kōgyō Ginkō, 5 *Shinketsushū* 61 (FTC [Recommendation] No. 4, 1953, November 6, 1953); *In re* K. K. Mitsubishi Ginkō, 9 *Shinketsushū* 1 (FTC [Recommendation] No. 3, 1957, June 3, 1957); *In re* K. K. Daiwa Ginkō, 10 *Shinketsushū* 36 (FTC [Recommendation] No. 3, 1961, June 26, 1961); *In re* Nomura Shōken K. K., 38 *Shinketsushū* 115 (FTC [Recommendation] No. 1, 1990, November 21, 1991); *In re* Nomura Shōken K. K., 38 *Shinketsushū* 134 (FTC [Recommendation] No. 20, 1991, December 2, 1991); *In re* Daiwa Shōken K. K., 38 *Shinketsushū* 138 (FTC [Recommendation] No. 21, 1991, December 2, 1991); *In re* Nikkō Shōken K. K., 38 *Shinketsushū* 142 (FTC [Recommendation] No. 22, 1991, December 2, 1991); *In re* Yamaichi Shōken K. K., 138 *Shinketsushū* 146 (FTC [Recommendation] No. 23, 1991, December 2, 1991); *In re* Nihon Kikai Hoken Renmei, 43 *Shinketsushū* 339 (FTC [Recommendation] No. 1, 1996, February 5, 1997). Private actions against banks alleging antitrust violations include K. K. Miyakawa v. Gifu Shōkō Shinyō Kumiai, 24 *Shinketsushū* 291 (Sup. Ct., 2d P.B., June 20, 1977); Yachiyo Mishin v. Chuō Shinyō Kinkō, 24 *Shinketsushū* 362 (Tokyo High Ct., May 29, 1975); Tabuchi v. Yachiyo Shinyū Kinkō, 25 *Shinketsushū* 264 (Tokyo Dr. Ct., July 11, 1977).

33. See, e.g., Misonō Hitoshi, *Kōsei Torihiki I'inkai* [Fair Trade Commission] (Tokyo: Nihon Keizai Shinbunsha, 1968), pp. 163–66.

34. FTC annual report, 1977, pp. 11–12.

35. *Shitauke daikin shiharai chien tō boshi hō* (Law No. 120, 1956).

36. *Futō na keihinrui oyobi futōhyōji boshi hō* (Law No. 134, 1962).

37. FTC annual report, 1978, pp. 159–60.

38. *Fifty-Year History,* p. 441.

39. See Research and Training Institute, Ministry of Justice (Japan), *Summary of White Paper on Crime* (Tokyo, annual).

40. *Nihon keizai shinbun,* April 2, 1977, p. 1.

41. The term "administrative proceedings" is frequently defined as formal actions. The following actions are subject to administrative proceedings: approvals under §§ 4, 5(2) and (3), 6(2), 7, 8, 11(2), 14, 19(3), 20(3), 24(3), and 91(1)2; restrictions or withdrawal of approvals under § 11(4) and (5); registration or deregistration of competition rules under §§ 28(3) and 31(1) and (3); objections under §§ 2(3), 3(3), 5a(3), and 5b(2); actions taken in connection with the authorities' powers to police abuse of market power under §§ 3(4), 12(2), 17(1), 18, 22(4), and 27; and the issuance of prohibition orders under §§ 37a and 47(2)2. They do not include fine proceedings.

42. Fritz Rittner, *Einführung in das Wettbewerbs- und Kartellrecht* [Introduction to competition and cartel law] (Heidelberg: C. F. Müller, 1st ed., 1981), p. 312. See also Immenga and Mestmäcker, GWB *Kommentar*, p. 1788; Langen, Niederleithinger, and Schmidt, *Kommentar*, p. 707.

43. Riesenkampff and Gres, *Law against Restraints of Competition*, pp. 226, 227.

44. See Immenga and Mestmäcker, GWB *Kommentar*, p. 1788; Langen, Niederleithinger and Schmidt, *Kommentar*, p. 706.

45. Such combination of functions has been strongly criticized by some. See, e.g., Peter Erlinghagen and Klaus Zippel, "'Presseinformationen' des Bundeskartellamtes über Bußgeldfestsetzungen" [FCO's press releases on fine proceedings], *NJW*, vol. 26, nos. 1 and 2 (1973), p. 12.

46. See, e.g., Riesenkampff and Gres, *Law against Restraints of Competition*, p. 175; for an abstract of the informal, preventative activities of the FCO, see the summary by Karsten Schmidt, in Immenga and Mestmäcker, GWB *Kommentar*, pp. 1790–94.

47. See, e.g., *Kammergericht* Judgment of December 6, 1968 (*Autoschmiermittel*), *WuW/E OLG*, p. 964, in which the court deemed formal proceedings to have begun once a letter requesting information pursuant to section 46 was sent.

48. See, e.g., Federal Supreme Court Judgment of November 14, 1968 (*Taxiflug*), *WuW/E BGH*, p. 499, in which the court held that the petitioner did not have any right to compel the enforcement authorities to act pursuant to a complaint, in connection with an abuse of market power. To same effect, see Düsseldorf High Court Judgment of December 17, 1960, *WuW/E OLG*, p. 1171, and Stuttgart High Court Judgment of May 4, 1971, *WuW/E OLG*, p. 1177. For general discussion, see G. Malzer, "Zum Antragsrecht und Rechtsanspruch auf Einschreiten der Kartellbehörde" [On the right to petition and make legal claims in response to initiatives by cartel authorities], *Der Betrieb* [hereinafter, *DB*], vol. 25, no. 41 (1972), pp. 1955–56.

49. Düsseldorf High Court Judgment of December 17, 1970.

50. Felix Stark, "Anhörung und Beiladung in Kartellverfahren" [Hearing and participation in cartel procedures], *BB*, vol. 15, no. 12 (1960), pp. 465–68.

51. *Verwaltungsgerichtsordnung* (VWGO).

52. *Id.;* Junge, in Müller-Henneberg and Schwartz, *Kommentar*, § 53, ¶ 3; Schmidt, in Immenga and Mestmäcker, GWB *Kommentar*, pp. 1827–28. See also Langen,

Niederleithinger, and Schmidt, *Kommentar*, p. 721; Riesenkampff and Gres, *Law against Restraints of Competition* p. 179.

53. Junge, in Müller-Henneberg and Schwartz, *Kommentar*, § 53, ¶ 3.

54. See, e.g., *Kammergericht* Judgment of June 24, 1960 (*Exportförderung*), *WuW/E OLG*, p. 393; Judgment of February 16, 1960 (*Bergbau*), *WuW/E OLG*, p. 339; and Judgment of November 7, 1969 (*Triest-Klausel*), *WuW/E OLG*, p. 1071 (disqualification caused by parties). Also Rittner, "Das Ermessen," p. 307.

55. See, e.g., Erlinghagen and Zippel, "'Presseinformationen'", p. 12; Otfried Lieberknecht, "Probleme des Verfahrensrechts in Kartellsachen" [Problems of procedural rights in cartel cases], in *Schwerpunkte des Kartellrechts 1977/78* [Cologne: Carl Heymanns, 1979), p. 77.

56. Heinz Kaufmann and H. G. Rautmann, *Kommentar zum Gesetz gegen Wettbewerbsbeschränkungen* [hereinafter, *Frankfurter Kommentar*] (Cologne: Otto Schmidt, 4th ed., 1980), § 53, ¶ 13. In practice, most proceedings are open. Siegfried Klaue, in Immenga and Mestmäcker, GWB Kommentar, p. 1757.

57. *Frankfurter Kommentar* § 53, ¶ 4; Riesenkampff and Gres, *Law against Restraints of Competition*, p. 179, citing FCO decision of July 30, 1980 (*Ofen III, Wirtschaft und Wettbewerb/Entscheidungssammlung Bundeskartellamt* [*WuW/E BKartA*], p. 261.

58. *Frankfurter Kommentar*, § 53, ¶ 4; Junge, in Müller-Henneberg and Schwartz, *Kommentar*, § 53, ¶ 1; Schmidt, in Immenga and Mestmäcker, GWB, pp. 1821–22. See also Langen, Niederleithinger, and Schmidt, *Kommentar*, pp. 719–20.

59. Strafprozeßordnung (STPO).

60. For general discussion of requirements under the OWIG, see *Rotberg Ordnungswidrigkeitengesetz Kommentar* (Munich: Verlag Vahlen, 5th ed., 1975), pp. 271–74.

61. *WuW/E BGH*, p. 858.

62. *Id.*, p. 859. See also *Rotberg OWiG Kommentar* (3d ed., 1964), pp. 205–22.

63. *WuW/E BGH*, p. 860.

64. *Id.*, at 861. For comparison with U.S. law see Administrative Procedure Act, 60 Stat. 237 (1946), 5 U.S.C.A. § 1001 et seq. (1946). Section 5(1) excludes matters subject to "a subsequent trial as the law and facts de novo in any court" from the requirements of an administration adjudication.

65. Günther, "Brauchen wir eine neue Wettbewerbspolitik?" p. 99.

66. Letter to author from Frank D. Reh of the FCO, October 30, 1981.

67. Information provided author by various *Land* authorities.

68. *Kōsei Torihiki I'inkai no shinsa oyobi shinpan ni kansuru kisoku* (FTC Regulation No. 5, October 10, 1953, as amended).

69. Ebisu Shokuhin K. K. v. Kōsei Torihiki I'inkai, 19 *Shinketsushū* 215 (Sup. Ct., November 16, 1972); Zenkoku Shōhisha Dantai Renrakukai v. Kūsei Torihiki I'inkai, 10 *Shinketsushū* 124 (Tokyo High Ct., July 27, 1960); Udagawa v. Kōsei Torihiki I'inkai 27 *Shinketsushū* 255 (Tokyo High Ct., August 26, 1980).

70. Shōda, *Dokusen kinshi hō* (1980 ed.), vol. 2, p. 468; Abe Yoshihisa, *Shinketsu dokusen kinshihō: Kōsei Torihiki I'inkai Shinketsu no bunseki* [Decisional antimonopoly law: Analysis of FTC decisions] (Tokyo: Hōgaku Shoin, 1974), p. 619.

71. For the analogous practice in criminal investigations and the admissibility of prosecutorial protocols in criminal proceedings, see Shigemitsu Dando, *Japanese Criminal Procedure*, trans. B. J. George (Hackensack, N.J.: Rothman, 1968), p. 306.

72. *In re* Meiji Shōji K. K., 15 *Shinketsushū* 63 (FTC [Decision] No. 1, 1966, October 11, 1968).

73. Toshiba Chemical K. K. v. Kōsei Torihiki I'inkai, *Hanrei jihō* (no. 1493) 54 (Tokyo High Ct., February 25, 1994).

74. Kanazawa City in *In re* Maruka Ishikawa Chūo Seika, 18 *Shinketsushū* 149 (FTC [Ruling] December 28, 1971).

75. See, e. g., *In re* K. K. Chōbu Nihon Shinbunsha et al., 6 *Shinketsushū* 16 (FTC [Decision] No. 41, 1950, February 15, 1955); *In re* K. K. Asahi Shinbunsha et al., 6 *Shinketsushū* 44 (FTC [Decision] No. 42, 1950, February 15, 1955).

76. *In re* Sanyo Denki K. K. et al., 25 *Shinketsushū* 37 (FTC [Ruling] No. 6, 1966, July 27, 1978) [the 1966 *Television Cartel* case].

77. *In re* Tōbu Tetsudō K. K. et al., 11 *Shinketsushū* 1 (FTC [Decision] No. 5, 1952, April 12, 1962) [the *Tōbu Railways* case].

78. For comment in English on the failure of the FTC to develop antitrust doctrine in the cases, see Rabinowitz, "Antitrust in Japan."

79. The GWB uses the term *wirtschaftlichen Verhältnisse*, which is perhaps best translated in this context as "economic matters." The term has been construed to include the information relevant to the provisions of the GWB being enforced, *inter alia* prices, customers and suppliers, pricing methods, and production including that for overseas affiliates if relevant to competition in the German domestic market. *Kammergericht* Judgment of October 7, 1969, *WuW/E OLG*, p. 1046 (*Kopierautomaten*); Judgment of January 29, 1971, *WuW/E OLG*, p. 1160 (*Haushaltspanels*); Judgment of June 18, 1971, *WuW/E OLG*, p. 1189 (*Import-Schallplatten*).

80. Rittner, *Einführung*, p. 320; Ferdinand Hermanns, *Ermittlungsbefugnisse der Kartellbehörden nach deutschem und europäischem Recht* [Investigatory authority of the cartel authorities under German and European law] (Cologne: Deutscher Wirtschaftdienst, 1978), pp. 18, 19. See also *Frankfurter Kommentar*, § 46, ¶ 10–13; Müller-Henneberg and Schwartz, *Kommentar*, § 46, ¶ 2. Siegfried Klaue disagrees with the more extreme statement that the information-gathering authority under the section can only be used in connection with formal enforcement actions. Siegfried Klaue, in Immenga and Mestmäcker, GWB *Kommentar*, p. 1756.

81. Federal Supreme Court Judgment of December 15, 1960, *WuW/E BGH*, p. 425. This case involved an appeal from an FCO ruling seeking information from the association of accountants with respect to their fee schedules. The *Kammergericht* in Berlin

upheld the ruling on first appeal but the Federal Supreme Court reversed on the second on the grounds that no appeal was available insofar as an appeal from such rulings would be interlocutory in effect since section 46 can only be used in connection with the formal investigation of a particular violation and the GWB did not provide for interlocutory appeals.

82. *Frankfurter Kommentar,* §46, ¶¶3 and 4; Langen, Niederleithinger, and Schwartz, *Kommentar,* pp. 696–99; Müller and Giessler, *Kommentar,* § 46, ¶3; Werner Junge, in Müller-Henneberg and Schwartz, *Kommentar,* § 46, ¶ 2. Junge notes that the Adenauer government and the Bundestag expressly rejected a suggestion made in the upper house during consideration of the GWB bill that section 46 apply to assist the FCO to prepare its annual report under section 50. This, the opponents argued, would have given the agency open-ended authority and in effect would have turned section 46 into a general fact-finding provision.

83. Stuttgart High Court Judgment of April 30, 1979 (*Zwangskombinationstarif II*), *WuW/E OLG,* p. 2130.

84. *Id.,* p. 2131.

85. The applicable legislation governing compulsory disclosure of economic information by agricultural, commercial, and industrial enterprises is the *Verordnung über Auskunftpflicht,* July 3, 1923 (*RGBl.* 1923 I 723). Originally enacted to aid officials of the Weimar Republic in their attempts to control inflation, this regulation has been considered sufficiently important by subsequent regimes, totalitarian and democratic alike, for it to be kept in force. Karl Eugen Thomä, *Auskunfts- und Betriebsprüfungsrecht der Verwaltung: Seine rechtstaatlichen Grenzen: Recht und Wirtschaft* [Administrative right to information and examination of business records: The rule-by-law boundary of law and economics] (Stuttgart: Verlagsgesellschaft, 1955), pp. 18–22.

86. Federal Supreme Court Judgment of December 15, 1960, *WuW/E BGH,* pp. 425, 426.

87. As a technical issue the debate centered on whether the specific provisions for investigation of violations of regulatory statutes under the OWIG which apply to antitrust violations under GWB section 81, override the provisions of section 59 (former §46). See, e.g., Wolfram Klemp, "Übergang vom kartellrechtlichen Verwaltungsverfahren zum Bußgeldverfahren" [Transition from administrative proceedings to administrative fine proceedings in cartel law], *BB,* vol. 31, no. 20 (1976), pp. 912–14. Authorities argued that the section should not be considered so limited. See, e.g., *Frankfurter Kommentar,* § 46, ¶¶ 10–13; Müller and Giessler, *Kommentar,* §46; Müller-Henneberg and Schwartz, *Kommentar,* § 46, ¶4. However, Langen, Niederleithinger, and Schmidt, *Kommentar,* p. 693, states that it is unclear whether the section can be used in connection with a fine proceeding. At least four early commentators argued that the section did not apply. Helmuth Lutz, "Die Ermittlungen

der Kartellbehörden im Bußgeldverfahren und die Rechtsstellung des Betroffenen" [Investigations by the cartel authorities in administrative fine proceedings and the legal status of the respondents], *NJW*, vol. 14, no. 28 (1961), pp. 1241–44; Felix Stark, "Das Auskunfts-verlangen der Kartellbehörden" [Requests for information by the cartel authorities], *BB*, vol. 14, no. 6 (1959), pp. 216; Herbert Krüger, "Auskunftspflicht und Betriebsprüfung in der Regelung des Gesetzes gegen Wettbewerbsbeschränkungen" [Reporting duties and company audits under the regulations of the law against restraints of competition], *DB*, vol. 11, no. 3 (Jan. 22, 1958), pp. 71–73, arguing that section 46 should apply only at a preparatory stage, before the commencement of any formal proceeding; K. E. Thomä, "Das Auskunftsrecht der Kartellbehörden in den Entwürfen zu einem Gesetz gegen Wettbewerbsbeschränkungen" [Right to information of the cartel authorities under the bills for a law against restraints of competition], *BB*, vol. 10, no. 12 (1955), pp. 359–62. For a similar view that material disclosed under section 46 cannot be used in a merger approval proceeding because of the confidentiality provisions of the GWB, see Werner Kleinmann, "Verwaltungsverbote für das Bundeskartllamt, insbesondere im Anschluß du Fusionsverfahren" [Procedural prohibitions imposed on the FCO, in particular in merger proceedings], *DB*, vol. 27, no. 23 (1974), pp. 1097–99.

88. See, e.g., Rittner, *Einführung*, p. 320; Hermanns, *Ermittlungsbefugnisse*, pp. 12, 19.

89. *WuW/E BGH*, p. 347. See also the critical comment by Werner Benisch, *WuW/E BGH*, pp. 348, 349.

90. Rittner, *Einführung*, p. 320; Langen, Niederleithinger, and Schmidt, *Kommentar*, p. 695.

91. Mainz District Court Judgment of July 22, 1971, in FCO annual report, 1971, p. 101.

92. See, e.g., Langen, Niederleithinger, and Schmidt, *Kommentar*, p. 707.

93. See, e.g., Benisch, *WuW/E BGH*, p. 429. Also conversation with Fritz Rittner, July 20, 1981.

94. See comments by Benisch, *WuW/E BGH*, pp. 429–32. Benisch makes a strong case in arguing that the provisions of the OWIG are less appropriate for *Bußgeld* proceedings in the context of an antitrust case than section 46 of the GWB, but the catalogue of differences he cites illustrate more the lack of any serious practical impairment of the enforcement authorities' ability to obtain necessary information given the existing procedural restrictions of section 46.

95. See *Frankfurter Kommentar*, § 46, ¶84; Müller-Henneberg and Schwartz, *Kommentar*, § 46, ¶ 21.

96. See also Krüger, "Auskunftspflicht," p. 73.

97. See, e.g., *Kammergericht* Judgment of October 7, 1969 (*Kopierautomaten*).

98. Müller-Henneberg and Schwartz, *Kommentar*, §46, ¶7.

99. Forsthoff, "Verfahrensvorschriften im Kartellgesetz," p. 100.

100. *Kammergericht* Judgment of 29 January 1971 (*Haushaltspanels*), Langen, Niederleithinger, and Schmidt, *Kommentar*, p. 696; Junge, in Müller-Henneberg and Schwartz, *Kommentar*, §46, ¶¶14–16.

101. *Frankfurter Kommentar*, § 46, ¶ 51.

102. Uwe Jessen, "Das Auskunftsverweigerungsrecht gegenüber einem Auskunfts-verlangen der Kartellbehörde" [Right to refuse to disclose information in response to requests by the cartel authorities], *BB*, vol. 17, no. 2 (1962), pp. 278–81.

103. Comment by Helmut Gutzler as vice president of FCO before the 1976 ad hoc commission to study the expansion of economic crimes (*Sachverständigen kommission zur Bekäampfung der Wirtschaftskriminalität*), *Tagungsbericht* (Commission hearings), vol. 8, appendix 7, p. 23. For more details on the commission, see note 530.

104. Klaus Westrick and Ulrich Loewenheim, *Gesetz gegen Wettshewerbs-beschränkungen: Kommentar* [Commentary on the law against restraints of competition] (Herne: Verlag Neue Wirtschafts-Briefe, 4th ed., 1977), § 46, ¶ 14, state emphatically that these protections do not apply to juristic persons. But *Frankfurter Kommentar*, § 46, ¶ 53, argues in favor, citing the Federal Constitutional Court decision of February 26, 1975, *Wirtschaft und Wettbewerb/Entscheidungssammlung Bunlesv erfassungsgericht* [WuW/E VG], p. 263, on the constitutional right to silence asserted on behalf of a corporation.

105. One of the most telling decisions is *Kammergericht* Judgment of February 2, 1981, which upheld the appeal by Metro, one of Europe's largest cash-and-carry retailers, from an FCO ruling seeking information related to the respondent's purchase of a 24 percent interest in Kaufhof, at that time Germany's second-largest retailer. The court in Berlin held that the ruling was appealable and found that the disclosure demand was unjustified in relation to the purpose of the investigation. The FCO sought information to confirm that Metro acted in collusion with the United Bank of Switzerland, which also acquired 24 percent of Kaufhof in December 1980, thus evading the GWB's merger control provisions. See *WuW*, vol. 3 (1981), p. 163. The case and its background is reported in *The Economist*, vol. 279, no. 7191 (June 27, 1981), p. 80. See, also, *Kammergericht* Judgment of October 7, 1969 (*Kopierautomaten*), and Judgment of July 7, 1977; Munich High Court Judgment of September 29, 1977, in FCO annual report, 1977, p. 95.

106. Fritz Rittner, conversation on June 11, 1981.

107. Karlheinz Liekefelt, "Das informelle Auskunftsersuchen des Bundes-kartellamtes" [Informal requests for information by the FCO], *DB*, vol. 28, no. 8 (Feb. 21, 1975), pp. 339–41.

108. *Id.*, p. 339. See also Otfried Lieberknecht, "Probleme des Verfahrensrechts in Kartellsachen" [Problems of procedural rights in cartel proceedings], in *Schwerpunkte des Kartellrechts 1977/78*, pp. 68–69.

109. The most comprehensive comparative study of discovery in the United States and Japan remains Kōji Harada, "Civil Discovery in Japan," *Law in Japan: An Annual*, vol. 16 (1983), pp. 21–53. For an example of Japanese difficulties with U.S. discovery, see the contempt citation against Mitsubishi Electric Co., Ltd., for failure to deliver documents subject to discovery in the United States: United States v. Westinghouse Corp., 1974–2 *Trade Cases*, ¶ 75, 312 (N.D. Cal. 1974).

110. The problem of access to information by the Japanese government is generally ignored in most studies of Japanese law and public administration. Japan has few reporting requirements. In the United States they number in the thousands.

111. See, e.g., Hideo Tanaka and Akio Takeuchi, "The Role of Private Persons in the Enforcement of Law: A Comparative Study of Japanese and American Law," *Law in Japan: An Annual*, vol. 7 (1974), pp. 34–50.

112. Shōda (1966 ed.), p. 775; see also FTC Investigation and Hearings Regulations, section 15, which requires that the FTC return all materials that become unnecessary before the end of a case.

113. See Abe, *Shinketsu dokusen kinshi hō*, pp. 246–47.

114. *Id.*, p. 247.

115. See, e.g., John Henry Merryman, *The Civil Law Tradition* (Stanford, Calif.: Stanford University Press, 1967); Fritz Bauer, "Introduction," in *Bibliography of German Law* (1964), pp. 34–50.

116. Code of Administrative Courts (*Verwaltungsgerichtsordnung* or, simply, VWGO), January 21, 1960 (*BGB1*, 117), § 40. See also Carl Hermann Ule, *Verwaltungsprozeßrecht: Ein Studienbuch* [Law of administrative process: A treatise] (Munich: C. H. Beck, 9th ed., 1987), p. 20. Prior to 1945 the jurisdiction of the administrative courts was limited to specific cases designated by statute under the "enumeration" principle (*Enumerationsprinzip*). Section 40 of the VWGO, however, is a "general clause" (*Generalklausel*) in conformity with the constitutional guarantee of judicial review in article 19(4). See Dieter Lorenz, *Rechtsschutz des Bürgers und die Rechtsweggarantie* [Legal protection of citizens and the right to legal redress] (Munich: C. H. Beck, 1973), p. 246; Karl August Bettermann, "Der Schutz der Grundrechte in der ordentlichen Gerichtsbarkeit" [Constitutional protections in the regular courts], in *Die Grundrechte*, ed. Karl August Bettermann, H. C. Nipperdey, and Ulrich Scheuner (Berlin: Duncker & Humblot, 1959), vol. 3 pt. 2, pp. 779, 782; Christian Friedrich Merger, "Der Schutz der Grundrechte in der Verwaltungsgerichtsbarkeit" [Constitutional safeguards in administrative courts], ibid., p. 717.

117. Rittner, *Einführung*, p. 324.

118. The high courts in Karlsruhe (Baden-Württemberg), Munich (Bayern [Bavaria]), Berlin [the *Kammergericht*], Potsdam (Brandenburg), Bremen, Hamburg, Frankfurt (Hessen [Hesse]), Schwerin (Mecklenburg-Vorpommern [Mecklenburg-Western Pomerania]), Celle (Niedersachen [Lower Saxony]), Düsseldorf, Hamm and

Cologne (Nordrhein-Westfalen [North Rhine–Westphalia]), Koblenz (Rheinland-Pfalz [Rhineland-Palatinate]), Saarbrücken (Saarland), Dresden (Sachen [Saxony]), Magdeburg (Sachsen-Anhalt [Saxony-Anhalt]), Kiel (Schleswig-Holstein), and Erfurt (Thuringen [Thuringia]).

119. See, e.g., Berlin-Tiergarten Local Court Judgment of June 26, 1972, *Wirtschaft und Wettbewerb/Entscheidungssammlung Landgerichte Amtsgerichte [WuW/E LG/AG]*, p. 335; and Judgment of August 16, 1974, *WuW/E LG/AG*, p. 397, involving appeals under section 68(1) of the OWiG from fines levied by the FCO against witnesses who refused to testify.

120. For a description of the German approach to administrative appeals in English, see Dieter Lorenz, "The Constitutional Supervision of the Administrative Agencies in the Federal Republic of Germany," *Southern California Law Review*, vol. 53, no. 2 (1980), pp. 543–82; Ernst K. Pakuscher, "Administrative Law in Germany: Citizen v. State," *American Journal of Comparative Law*, vol. 16, no. 3 (1968), pp. 309–31.

121. The emphasis on the proper application of law corresponded to the viewpoint of the "Prussian" school (particularly of Gneist and Otto Mayer). Menger, "Der Schutz der Grundrechte," p. 723.

122. The concern for protection of citizens reflected the emphasis of the "southern German" school (especially Jellinek), ibid.

123. See, e.g., discussion in Hans J. Wolf and Otto Bachof, *Verwaltungsrecht: Ein Studienbuch* [Administrative law: A hornbook] (Munich: C. I. Beck, 9th ed., 1974), pp. 369–389 (§ 46).

124. Fritz Bauer (as translated by Peterson) defines the term to recall "a directive or some other measure, issued or taken by a public official for the disposition of an individual case arising in the area of public law." Bauer, "Introduction," p. 124.

125. Erich Eyermann and Ludwig Fröhler, *Verwaltungsgerichtsordnung: Kommentar* [Administrative court order: Commentary] (Munich: C. H. Beck, 8th ed., 1980), p. 233. See also Otto Bachof, *Die verwaltungsgerichtliche Klage auf Vornahme einer Amtshandlung* [Administrative court appeal from actions by administrative offices] (Tübingen: J. C. B. Mohr, 1951), pp. 10, 20.

126. Bachof, *Verwaltungsgerichtliche Klage*, p. 23; Wolff and Bachof, p. 380.

127. *Frankfurter Kommentar*, § 57, ¶ 3.

128. Federal Supreme Court Judgment of May 17, 1973 (*Asbach Uralt*), *WuW/E BGH*, pp. 1264, 1265. Any "sovereign measure" can be an administrative act.

129. For example, Karsten Schmidt, *Gerichtsschutz in Kartellverwaltungssachen* [Judicial protection in cartel proceedings] (Heidelberg: C. F. Müller, 1980), p. 10.

130. See, e.g., Federal Supreme Court Judgment of November 16, 1970 (*Feuerfeste Steine*), *WuW/E BGH*, p. 1161; *Kammergericht* Judgment of July 12, 1974 (*Sicherheitsglas*), *WuW/E OLG*, p. 1515. Many commentators view the term *Verfügung* of sections 61 and 63 (former §§ 57 and 62) to be the same as administrative act. See, e.g., Junge, in

Müller-Henneberg and Schwartz, *Kommentar*, § 57, ¶ 11; Michael Hoffmann-Becking, "Kein Rechtsschutz gegen eine Aufforderung der Kartellbehörde nach § 24 GWB?" [No legal safeguards against a summons by the FCO under section 24 of the GWB?], *BB*, vol. 27, no 11, (April 20, 1972), pp. 475–77. Under this view, the Federal Supreme Court's reference to the reviewability of "sovereign measures" other than a *Verfügung* in *Asbach Uralt* represents a radical departure from the accepted restrictions on reviewability. The court's comment has thus been sharply criticized by some. See, e.g., *Frankfurter Kommentar*, § 62, ¶ 9.

131. *Kammergericht* judgment of July 12, 1974.

132. Federal Supreme Court decision of November 16, 1970 (*Feuerfeste Steine*). For critical comment, see Hoffmann-Becking, "Kein Rechtsschutz?"

133. VWGO, § 42. On the development of these categories of appeals, see Bachof, *Verwaltungsgerichtliche Klage*, p. 7. Bachof's use of this terminology has apparently had decisive influence. See, e.g., Christian-Friedrich Menger, *System des verwaltungsgerichtlichen Rechtsschutzes* [System of legal protections in administrative courts] (Tübingen: J. C. B. Mohr, 1954), p. 97, fn. 1.

134. See Schmidt, *Gerichtsschutz*, p. 17.

135. Rittner, *Einführung*, p. 325.

136. See, esp., Schmidt, *Gerichtsschutz*.

137. See Ule, *Verwaltungsprozeßrecht*, pp. 200–15.

138. See *Frankfurter Kommentar*, § 66, ¶ 1.

139. On the more restrictive general rule, see Ule, *Verwaltungsprozeßrecht*, p. 203.

140. *Id.*, pp. 366–72.

141. *Kammergericht* Judgment of June 9, 1974 (*Chemische Grundstoffe II*), *WuW/E OLG*, p. 1507.

142. No German court adjudicates with a full court of all judges. Even for the Federal Supreme Court, with more than ninety judges, *en banc* proceedings are impracticable. For uniformity of decisions on the construction as well as application of law, special branches for each major field of law, such as the *Kartellsenat,* have been established. See, e.g., *Gesetz zur Wahrung der Einheitlichkeit der Rechtsprechung der obersten Gerichtshöfe des Bundes,* June 19, 1968 [*BGBl.* 1968 I 661].

143. See, e.g., K. K. Miyakawa v. Gifu Shōkō Shinyō Kumiai, 31 *Saikō saibansho minji hanreishū* [hereinafter, *Minshū*] 449 (Sup. Ct., 2nd P.B., June 20, 1977).

144. See, e.g., Satō v. Sekiyu Renmei, *Hanrei jihō*, no. 997, p. 18 (Yamagata Dist. Ct., Mar. 31, 1981).

145. The problem of administrative appeals is not even mentioned in the published reports by the Law and Courts Division of Government Section, which supervised the basic postwar reforms in Japan's legal system to insure conformity with the new constitution. See, e.g., Government Section, Supreme Commander for the Allied Powers, *Political Reorientation of Japan* (Report covering September 1945–September

1948), p. 227. This is surprising since the head of the division, Alfred C. Oppler, was a former German administrative law judge under the Weimar Republic. See Alfred C. Oppler, *Legal Reform in Occupied Japan: A Participant Looks Back* (Princeton, N.J.: Princeton University Press, 1976).

146. *Gyōsei jiken sōsho tokurei hō* (Law No. 81, 1948).

147. *Gyōsei jiken sōsho hō* (Law No. 139, 1962).

148. Administrative Case Litigation Law, art. 3. For general discussion in English, see Ichirō Ogawa, "Judicial Review of Administrative Actions in Japan," *Washington Law Review*, vol. 43, no. 5 (1968), p. 1075, reprinted in Dan F. Henderson, ed., *The Constitution of Japan: Its First Twenty Years, 1946–1967* (Seattle: University of Washington Press, 1969), p. 185; Kiminobu Hashimoto, "The Rule of Law: Some Aspects of Judicial Review of Administrative Action," in *Law in Japan: The Legal Order in a Changing Society*, ed. Arthur T. von Mehren (Cambridge: Harvard University Press, 1963; Tokyo: Tuttle, 1964), p. 185; Ichirō Ogawa, "Several Problems Relating to Suits for the Affirmation of the Nullity of Administrative Acts," *Law in Japan: An Annual*, vol. 6 (1973), p. 73.

149. The substantial evidence rule applies to findings by the Radio Regulatory Council under the Airwaves Law (*Dempa hō*), Law No. 131, 1950; and the Japanese FTC under article 80 of the Antimonopoly Law. It also applied to the Land Use Adjustment Commission under article 52 of the Land Use Adjustment Commission Establishment Law (*Tochi chōsei i'inkai setchi hō*), Law No. 292, 1950, until its repeal. For critique in English of the rule in its application to Japan, see Hidetoshi Asakura, "The Substantial Evidence Rule: A Search for the Grounds for the Adoption in the United States and Japan" (unpublished L.L.M. paper, University of Washington, 1979).

150. *In re* Nihon Shuppan Kyōkai, 2 *Shinketsushū* 27 (FTC [Decision] No. 5, 1949, May 9, 1950); *In re* Tōhō K. K., 2 *Shinketsushū* 146 (FTC [Decision] No. 10, 1950, September 29, 1950); *In re* Ōsaka Kyōgō Shokuhin K. K. et al., 2 *Shinketsushū* 138 (FTC [Decision] No. 10, 1949, September 29, 1950); *In re* K. K. Asahi Shimbunsha et al., 3 *Shinketsushū* 4 (FTC [Decision] No. 20, 1949, April 7, 1951); *In re* Tōhō K. K. et al., 3 *Shinketsushū* 44 (FTC [Decision] No. 11, 1950, June 5, 1951); *In re* K. K. Hokkaidō Shimbunsha, 5 *Shinketsushū* 5 (FTC [Decision] No. 9, 1951, May 18, 1953); *In re* Nihon Sekiyū K. K. et al., 7 *Shinketsushū* 70 (FTC [Decision] No. 1, 1953, December 1, 1955); *In re* Nōda Shōyu K. K., 7 *Shinketsushū* 108 (FTC [Decision] No. 2, 1954, December 27, 1955); *In re* K. K. Mitsubishi Ginkō, 9 *Shinketsushū* 1 (FTC [Recommendation] No. 3, 1957, June 3, 1957); *In re* Tōbu Tetsudō K. K., et al., 11 *Shinketsushū* 1 (FTC [Recommendation] No. 5, 1952, April 12, 1962); *In re* Meiji Shōji K. K., 15 *Shinketsushū* 67 (FTC [Decision] No. 1, 1966, October 11, 1968); *In re* Morinaga Shōji, 15 *Shinketsushū* 84 (FTC [Decision] No. 2, 1966, October 11, 1968); *In re* Wakōdō K. K., 15 *Shinketsushū* 98 (FTC [Decision] No. 3, 1966, October 11, 1968); *In re* Yawata Seitetsu K. K. et al., 16 *Shinketsushū* 46 (FTC [Decision] No. 2, 1969, October 30 1969); *In re* Amano Seiyaku

K. K., 16 *Shinketsushū* 134 (FTC [Decision] No. 22, 1969, January 12, 1920); *In re* Sekiyu Renmei, 20 *Shinketsushū* 355 (FTC [Decision] No. 4, 1971 March 28, 1974); *In re* Idemitsu Kōsan K. K., et al., 20 *Shinketsushū* 300 (FTC [Recommendation] No. 6, 1974, February 22, 1974).

151. Ōsaka Kyōgō Shokushin K. K. v. Kōsei Torihiki I'inkai, 3 *Shinketsushū* 196 (Tokyo High Ct., November 30, 1951), reversed in part and remanded in part; Tōhō K. K. v. Kōsei Torihiki I'inkai, 5 *Shinketsushū* 118 (Tokyo High Ct., December 7, 1953), reversed in part and remanded in part. K. K. Tōyō Seimai Kisei Sakusho v. Kōsei Torihiki I'inkai, *Kōsei torihiki tokuho*, no. 627 (Tokyo High Ct., February 17, 1984), reversed and remanded for lack of substantial evidence.

152. Tōhō K. K. v. Kōsei Torihiki I'inkai, 3 *Shinketsushū* 166 (Tokyo High Ct., September 19, 1951); K. K. Asahi Shinbunsha v. Kōsei Torihiki I'inkai, 4 *Shinketsushū* 145 (Tokyo High Ct., March 9, 1953), reversed in part; Nihon Shuppan Kyōkai v. Kōsei Torihiki I'inkai, 5 *Shinketsushū* 88 (Tokyo High Ct., August 29, 1953); K. K. Hokkaidō Shimbunsha v. Kōsei Torihiki I'inkai, 6 *Shinketsushū* 89 (Tokyo High Ct., December 23, 1954); Nihon Sekiyu K. K. v. Kōsei Torihiki I'inkai, 8 *Shinketsushū* 65 (Tokyo High Ct., November 9, 1956); Nōda Shōyu K. K. v. Kōsei Torihiki I'inkai, 9 *Shinketsushsū* 57 (Tokyo High Ct., December 25, 1957); Yoshikawa v. Kōsei Torihiki I'inkai, 9 *Shinketsushū* 57 (Tokyo High Ct., November 24, 1958), third-party appeal of *Mitsubishi Bank* case); Tōbu Tetsudō Kōnai Eigyōnin Sōgō v. Kōsei Torihiki I'inkai, 11 *Shinketsushū* 146 (Tokyo High Ct., May 21, 1963), third-party appeal of *Tobu Railways* case; Zenkoku Kinzoku Rōdō Kumiai v. Kōsei Torihiki I'inkai, 17 *Shinketsushū* 221 (Tokyo High Ct., December 12, 1970), third-party appeal of *Yawata-Fuji Merger* case; Novo Industri A/S v. Kōsei Torihiki I'inkai, 17 *Shinketsushū* 297 (Tokyo High Ct., May 19, 1971), third-party appeal of *Amano Seiyaku* case; Meiji Shōji K. K. v. Kōsei Torihiki I'inkai, 18 *Shinketsushū* 167 (Tokyo High Ct., July 17, 1971); Wakōdō K. K. v. Kōsei Torihiki I'inkai, 18 *Shinketsushū* 214 (Tokyo High Ct., July 17, 1971); Morinaga Shōji K. K. (Tokyo High Ct., July 17, 1971), unreported; Shell Sekiyu K. K. v. Kōsei Torihiki I'inkai, 22 *Shinketsushū* 220 (Tokyo High Ct., September 29, 1975); in addition, five companion cases decided and reported together involving Taiyō Sekiyu K. K., Idemitsu Kōsan K. K., Shōwa Sekiyu K. K., Kyōwa Sekiyu K. K., and Maruzen Sekiyu K. K.

153. Tōhō K. K. v. Kōsei Torihiki I'inkai, 8 *Shinketsushū* 119 (Sup. Ct., May 25, 1954); K. K. Hokkaidō Shimbunsha v. Kōsei Torihiki I'inkai, 10 *Shinketsushū* 97 (Sup. Ct., January 26, 1961); Yoshikawa v. Kōsei Torihiki I'inkai, 10 *Shinketsushū* 91 (Sup. Ct., July 8, 1960); Zenkoku Kinzoku Rōdō Kumiai v. Kōsei Torihiki I'inkai, 19 *Shinketsushū* 231 (Sup. Ct., March 1, 1973); Meiji Shōji K. K. v. Kōsei Torihiki I'inkai, 22 *Shinketsushū* 198 (Sup. Ct., July 10, 1974); Wakōdō K. K. v. Kōsei Torihiki I'inkai, 22 *Shinketsushū* 173 (Sup. Ct., July 10, 1975); Novo Industri A/S v. Kōsei Torihiki I'inkai, 29 *Minshū* 1592 (Sup. Ct., November 28, 1975). *In re* Idemitsu Kōsan was split into six

separate appeals brought by Shell Sekiyu K. K., Taiyō Sekiyu K. K., Idemitsu Kōsan K. K., Shōwa Sekiyu K. K., Kyōwa Sekiyu K. K., and Maruzen Sekiyu K. K. The official reporters' decision is Idemitsu Kōsan K. K. v. Kōsei Torihiki I'inkai, 32 *Minshū* 515 (Sup. Ct., 3d P.B., April 4, 1978). One other case, Shūfu Rengōkai v. Kōsei Torihiki I'inkai, 24 *Shinketsushū* 202 (Sup. Ct., March 14, 1978) involved an appeal from an FTC designation on labeling of fruit juices. Both the Tokyo High Court and the Supreme Court held that the appellant consumer group (Federation of Housewives) did not have standing. The most recent decision is Sekiyu Renmei v. Kōsei Torihiki I'inkai, 36 *Minshū* 265 (Sup. Ct., 3d P.B., March 28, 1982).

154. In the order named the respondents were Idemitsu Kōsan K. K., Nihon Sekiyu K. K., Taiyō Sekiyu K. K., Daikyō Sekiyu K. K., Maruzen Sekiyu K. K., Kyōdō Sekiyu K. K., Kigunasu Sekiyu K. K., Kyūshū Sekiyu K. K., Mitsubishi Sekiyu K. K., Shōwa Sekiyu K. K., Shell Sekiyu K. K., and General Sekiyu K. K.

155. Kawagoe, in Kawagoe and Mitsuo Mitsushita, "Sodan: Sekiyu Karuteru Tōkyō Kōsai hanketsu o megutte" [Discussion of the high court decisions in the oil cartel cases], *Jurisuto*, no. 729) 15 (1980). *In re* Sekiyu Renmei K. K., 20 *Shinketsushū* 312 (FTC [Recommendation] No. 7, 1974, February 22, 1974). A month later the FTC entered a contested final decision against the federation for earlier price-fixing activities on a case originally brought in 1971.

156. *In re* Sekiyu Renmei, 20 *Shinketsushū* 355 (FTC [Decision] No. 4, 1971, March 28, 1974). The later case was appealed to the Tokyo High Court and to the Supreme Court.

157. Idemitsu Kōsan K. K., Shell Sekiyu K. K., Kyōdō Sekiyu K. K., Shōwa Sekiyu K. K., Maruzen Sekiyu K. K., and Taiyō Sekiyu K. K.

158. Shell Sekiyu K. K. v. Kōsei Torihiki I'inkai, 22 *Shinketsushū* 220 (Tokyo High Ct., September 29, 1975).

159. Idemitsu Kōsan K. K. v. Kōsei Torihiki I'inkai, 32 *Minshū* 515 (Sup. Ct., 3d P.B., April 4, 1978), is the officially reported case. The decisions as to all six appellants are reported in 25 *Shinketsushū* 59 (1977).

160. *Saibansho hō* (Law No. 59, 1947).

161. See, e.g., Suzuki v. Kuni [Japan], 6 *Minshū* 783 (Sup. Ct., G.B., October 8, 1952); Tomabechi v. Kuni [Japan], 7 *Minshū* 305 (Sup. Ct., G.B., April 15, 1953).

162. There have been three antitrust cases besides the *Novo Industri* case: Yoshikawa v. Kōsei Torihiki I'inkai, 10 *Shinketsushū* 94 (Tokyo High Ct., November 24, 1958), affirmed 10 *Shinketsushū* 91 (Sup. Ct., July 8, 1960), appeal dismissed on grounds that Yoshikawa shareholders in corporation subject to Mitsubishi Bank's illegal control did not have sufficient legal interest to justify suit; Tōbu Tetsudō Kōnai Eigyōnin Sōgō v. Kōsei Torihiki I'inkai, 11 *Shinketsushū* 146 (Tokyo High Ct., May 21, 1963), appeal dismissed on ground that employees of respondent railways company lacked standing to challenge FTC decisions; Zenkoku Kinzoku Rōdō Kumiai

v. Kōsei Torihiki l'inkai, 17 *Shinketsushū* 221 (Tokyo High Ct., December 12, 1970), affirmed 19 *Shinketsushū* 231 (Sup. Ct., Mar. 1, 1973), appeal dismissed on grounds that union opposing consent decisions approving Yamata–Fuji Steel merger lacked sufficient legal interest.

163. See, e.g., Tofoku-in v. Kōsei Daijin [Minister of Health and Welfare], 22 *Minshū* 3147 (Sup. Ct., 3d P.B., December 24, 1968).

164. See, e.g., Ōkawa v. Matsushita Denki Kōgyō K. K., *Hanrei jihō*, no. 863, p. 20 (Tokyo High Ct. Sept. 19, 1977), summarized in English in *Law in Japan: An Annual*, vol. 10 (1977), p. 165.

## 5 / REMEDIES AND SANCTIONS

1. An article by Jürgen Baumann and Gunther Arzt in 1970 was one of the first academic expressions of concern with the issue of whether antitrust violations had become in effect minor, excusable offenses and therefore harsher sanctions were necessary. Jürgen Baumann and Gunther Arzt, "Kartellrecht und allgemeines Strafrecht" [Cartel law and general criminal law], *Zeitschrift für das gesamte Handels- und Wirtschaftsrecht [ZHR]*, vol. 134 (1970), p. 24. The authors argued for the imposition of criminal penalties for most antitrust violations. This article was the catalyst for intense academic and political debate. The issue was a principal theme in the 49th Conference of German Jurists in 1972. For the proceedings of the conference, see generally *Verhandlungen des 49 deutschen Juristentages* (1972). For the views expressed at the conference by Professor Klaus Tiedemann, one of the panelists and principal proponents of criminalization of German antitrust law, see Klaus Tiedemann, *Welche strafrechtlichen Mittel empfehlen sich für eine wirksame Bekämpfung der Wirtschaftskriminalität?* [What criminal law mechanism is best to combat economic crimes effectively] (1972). See also Wolfgang Kartte and Alexander von Portius, "Kriminalisierung des Kartellrechts" [Criminalization of cartel law], *BB* (1975), p. 1169, fn. 1. The federal minister of justice responded, as noted, by appointing a special commission to study the issue of criminal sanctions for antitrust violations in the context of criminal law reforms to prevent various economic offenses.

2. See, e.g., "Zadankai, Korekara no dokusen kinshi seisaku" [Panel discussion: Antimonopoly policy for tomorrow], *Kōsei torihiki*, no. 243, (1972), pp. 4–11.

3. *Strafgesetzbuch* § 298?, as amended August 13, 1997, *BGBl*. 1997I 2038.

4. The maxims are based on the 1764 treatise *Dei Dellitti e delle Pene* (translated into English in 1776 as *An Essay on Crimes and Punishments*) by Caesar Bonesana, Marquis di Beccaria (1735–94). They were incorporated in nearly all nineteenth-century European constitutions (as well as the 1889 Constitution of the Empire of Japan) and continue today in most legal systems based on continental European law. See Constitution (*Grundgesetz*), art. 103(2), and Weimar Constitution (1919), art. 116.

Japan's postwar constitution, which reflects the influence of its American drafters, is not explicit. The principles are nonetheless accepted.

5. Antimonopoly Law, arts. 7(1), 8-2(1), 17-2(1), 20.

6. ZPO section 890 provides for a maximum fine of DM 500,000 (approximately U.S. $280,000 at current rates) and imprisonment for six months for violations of court orders. It is made applicable to administrative orders under VWGO section 167.

7. See, e.g., *In re* Asahi Kasei Kenzai K. K., 23 *Shinketsushū* 30 (FTC [Recommendation] No. 12, June 14, 1976); *In re* Asahi Kasei Kenzai K. K., 24 *Shinketsushū* 62 (FTC [Recommendation] No. 18, November 28, 1977). For discussion and statistics on repeat offenders, see Yamamura, "Success That Soured," pp. 77, 90 fn. 16.

8. Antimonopoly Law, art. 97.

9. *Id.,* art. 86.

10. *Id.,* arts. 67, 86. Similar provisions are found in the *Shōken torihiki hō* [Securities transactions law], Law No. 25, 1948, art. 187, and the *Shōhin torihikisho hō* [Commodity exchange law], Law No.239, 1950, art. 143.

11. *In re* K. K. Asahi Shimbunsha, 7 *Shinketsushū* 163 (Tokyo High Ct., April 6, 1955); *In re* Itoka, 7 *Shinketsushū* 181 (Tokyo High Ct., December 23, 1955); *In re* K. K. Osaka Yomiuri Shimbunsha, 7 *Shinketsushū* 169 (Tokyo High Ct., November 5, 1955); *In re* K. K. Hokkaido Shimbunsha, 8 *Shinketsushū* 82 (Tokyo High Ct., July 11, 1958); *In re* K. K. Chubu Yomiuri Shimbunsha, 22 *Shinketsushū* 301 (Tokyo High Ct., April 30, 1975).

12. *In re* Yawata Seitetsu K. K., petition for temporary injunction to block merger (filed by the FTC on May 7, 1969, and withdrawn on May 30, 1969).

13. *In re* Ōsaka Yomiuri Shimbunsha, 7 *Shinketsushū* 169 (Tokyo High Ct., November 5, 1955).

14. GWB § 38(4); see also Heinz Mayer-Wegelin, in Müller and Giessler, *Kommentar* (3d ed., 1974), § 8, ¶ 109.

15. GWB § 38(4).

16. Mayer-Wegelin, in Müller and Giessler, *Kommentar* (3d ed., 1974), § 8, ¶ 109.

17. Rittner, *Einführung,* p. 312 (by implication).

18. *Id.;* Rosemarie Werner, "Rechtsfolgen bei Wettbewerbsverstößen im GWB" [Legal consequences of competition violations], *Schwerpunkte des Kartellrechts 1977/78,* p. 54.

19. The cost of both prosecuting and defending antitrust damage actions in the United States is well known. See, e.g., Kenneth G. Elzinga and William Breit, *The Antitrust Penalties: A Study in Law and Economics* (New Haven, Conn.: Yale University Press, 1976), p. 71.

20. Gutzler, *Commission Hearings,* vol. 10, app. 4, p. 36.

21. *Id.,* vol. 8, app. 7, p. 36.

22. *Kammergericht* Judgment of *November* 28, 1972 (*Linoleum*), *WuW/E OLG,* pp. 1349, 1350; *Kammergericht* Judgment of November 7, 1980 (*Programmzeitschriften*), *WuW/E OLG,* pp. 2369, 2375.

23. *Kammergericht* Judgment of November 28, 1972 (*Linoleum*), *WuW/E OLG,* pp. 1349, 1350.

24. *Id.*

25. *Id.*

26. This point was raised in the 1970s by Peter Erlinghagen and Klaus Zippel, "Der 'Mehrerlös' als Grundlage der Bußgeldgestsetzung bei Kartellverstößen" ["Excess proceeds" as basis for an administrative fine for cartel violations], *DB* (1974), pp. 953, 954. But see Erich Göhler, *Gesetz über Ordnungswidrigkeiten* [Law on administrative offenses] (Munich: Beck, 4th ed., 1975), § 17, ¶ 4E, p. 111 (dismissing such questions in the context of the similar provision of the OWIG).

27. A considerable volume of literature exists on the methods for calculating the excess proceeds surcharge. Among the most often cited is Harald Albuschkat, "Zur Problematik der Bestimmung des Mehrerlöses bei Kartellverstößen" [On the problem of determining excess proceeds for cartel violations], *Wettbewerb in Recht und Praxis* (1976), p. 666. See also Horst Albach, *Als-Ob-Konzept und zeitlicher Vergleichsmarkt* [As-if concept and comparable market in time] (Tübingen: J. C. B. Mohr, 1976); A. H. von Oertzen, "Methoden probleme bei der Bestimmung des Mehrerlös nach § 38 Abs. 4 des Gesetzes gegen Wettberwerbsbeschränkungen" [Methodological problems in determining excess proceeds pursuant to section 38, paragraph 4 of the law against restraints of competition] (doctoral diss., Bonn University, 1974); Erlinghagen and Zippel, "Mehrerlös"; Gutzler, *Commission Hearings,* vol. 10, app. 4, p. 32.

28. Albuschkat identifies three separate methods. Albuschkat, "Problematik," p. 667.

29. See *Kammergericht* Judgment of November 28, 1972 (*Linoleum*), *WuW/E OLG,* p. 1349.

30. See *Kammergericht* Judgment of November 7, 1980 (*Programmzeitschriften*), *WuW/E OLG,* pp. 2369, 2375.

31. Gutzler, *Commission Hearings,* vol. 10, app. 4, pp. 34–35.

32. FCO annual report, 1978, p. 45.

33. *Id.*

34. One of the first and best general commentaries on the illegal proceeds surcharge in Japanese law is found in Shōda Akira, *Dokusen kinshi hō* [Antimonopoly law] (Tokyo: Nihon Hyrōnsha, 1980), vol. 1, p. 548. See also Motonaga Tsuyoshi, "Kachōkin seidō no genjō to dōkō" [Current status and trends of the illegal proceeds surcharge system], *Jurisuto,* no. 751 (1981), pp. 43–47.

35. *Seirei* [Cabinet Order No. 317, 1977], arts. 4 and 5.

36. Antimonopoly Law, art. 48-2(1).

37. *Id.*, art. 48-2(4).

38. *Id.*, art. 48-2(5).

39. Shōda, *Dokusen kinshi hō*, vol. 1, p. 563. The FTC order in the case *In re* Rengō K. K., 30 *Shinketsushū* 56 (FTC [Order] February 2, 1984), was the first surcharge levied after a full adjudicatory hearing. For discussion of this case, see Sawada Meirō, "Kachōkin no nōfu o meizuru no saishō no shinketsu" [First decision ordering payment of surcharge], *Kōsei torihiki*, no. 402 (1984), p. 38.

40. Shōda, *Dokusen kinshi hō*, vol. 1, p. 550.

41. *Id.*, p. 558.

42. *Id.*, p. 563.

43. Antimonopoly Law, art. 7-2(5); Shōda, *Dokusen kinshi hō*, vol. 1, p. 557.

44. See Shōda, *Dokusen kinshi hō*, vol. 1, p. 563; Iyori and Uesugi, *Antimonopoly Laws of Japan* (2nd ed., 1983), p. 55. See also Shōda Akira, *Dokusen kinshihō kenkyū* [Antimonopoly law studies] (Tokyo: Dōbunkan, 1976), vol. 2, p. 110 (anticipating the problem under the Diet bill).

45. Shōda, *Dokusen kinshi hō*, vol. 1, p. 563.

46. *Kokuzei chōshū hō* [Law No. 147, 1959].

47. The notion that private actions under the GWB operate as a sanction is not questioned in German literature. Ludwig Linder, *Privatklage und Schadensersatz im Kartellrecht: Eine vergleichende Untersuchung zum deutschen and amerikanischen Recht* [Private actions and compensatory damages in cartel law: A comparative study of German and American law] (Baden-Baden: Nomos, 1980), p. 24. There is also a vast literature on the use of civil remedies in German antitrust enforcement. Much of it tends to emphasize refined, if not rarified, issues of theory that go beyond the scope of this study and do not require elaboration here. But they do provide important insights. The most influential include K. Peter Mailänder, *Privatrechtliche Folgen unerlaubter Kartellpraxis* [Private law consequences of unlawful cartels] (Karlsruhe: Verlag Versicherungswirtschaft, 1964); Hans-Martin Müller-Laube, *Der private Rechtsschutz gegen unzulässige Beschränkungen des Wettbewerbs und missbräuchliche Ausübung von Marktmacht im deutschen Kartellrecht* [Private legal protection against unreasonable restraints of competition and abuse of market power in German cartel law] (Berlin: Duncker & Humblot, 1964); Karsten Schmidt, *Kartellverfahrensrecht- Kartellverwaltungsrecht-Bürgerliches Recht* [Cartel procedural law, cartel administrative law, civil law] (Cologne: Carl Heymanns, 1977); Hans-Joachim Mertens, "Deliktsrecht und Sonderprivatrecht: Zur Rechtsfortbildung des deliktischen Schutzes von Vermögensinteressen" [Tort law and special private law: On legal development of tort protection from influential interests] *Archiv für die civilistische Praxis* [AcP], vol. 178 (1978), p. 227; Ernst-Joachim Mestmäcker, "Das Verhältnis des Rechts der Wettbewerbs-

beschränkungen zum Privatrecht" [The law on restraints of competition as private law], *DB* (1968), p. 787; Ernst-Joachim Mestmäcker, "Über das Verhältnis des Rechts der Wettbewerbsbeschränkungen zum Privatrecht" [On the law on restraints of competition as private law], *AcP*, vol. 168 (1968), p. 235.

48. The limitations on declaratory judgments found in American law do not apply to Germany. In practice, a judicial declaration (*Feststellung*) of the validity or effect of a legal relationship is among the most common forms of judicial relief.

49. Based on author's review of the complete collection of cases in *WuW/E LG/AG*, pp. 109—457. Not included are cases in which a violation of the GWB was a subsidiary issue, particularly to alleged violations of European Union antitrust regulation under articles 85 or 86 of the Treaty of Rome.

50. Ernst Steindorff, *Commission Hearings*, vol. 8, app. 6, pp. 5–10; Linder, *Privatklage*, p. 126; Karsten Schmidt, *Aufgaben und Leistugen der Gesetzgebung im Kartellrecht: Eine rechtspolitische Studie zu den außerstrafrechtlichen Sanktionen im* GWB [Legislative functions and performance in cartel law: A legal policy study on the non-criminal sanctions in the GWB] (Baden-Baden: Nomos, 1978).

51. The proceedings in two-thirds of all civil cases in district courts (*Landgerichte*) are completed within six months. Less than 13 percent require more than one year. Statistisches Bundesamt, *Statistical Yearbook 1997 for the Federal Republic of Germany* (1998), p. 365.

52. The date of the violation is unclear in many cases, but in only eight cases could it *possibly* have been longer than three years from the date of the decision.

53. Steindorff, *Commission Hearing*, app. 6, p. 8.

54. On the use of antitrust litigation as a predatory practice to impose costs on competitors, see Gary Myers, "Litigation as a Predatory Practice," *Kentucky Law Journal*, vol. 80, no. 3 (1991–92), pp. 565–629.

55. See, e.g., Bauer, "Introduction," pp. 54, 55. On the comparative problems of evidence, see Linder, *Privatklage*, p. 134.

56. Bauer," Introduction," pp. 58, 59. For a German reaction to the cost of U.S. antitrust litigation, see Steindorff, *Commission Hearings*, app. 6, p. 10.

57. Rittner, *Einführung*, p. 310.

58. BGB § 823 provides:

(1) A person who, willfully or negligently, unlawfully injures the life, body, health, freedom, property or other right of another is bound to compensate him for any damage arising therefrom.

(2) The same obligation is placed upon a person who infringes a statute intended for the protection of others. If, according to the provisions of the statute, an infringement of this is possible even without fault, the duty to make compensation arises only in the event of fault.

59. Hans-Joachim Mertens, in Kurt Rebmann and Franz-Jürgen Säcker, eds., *Münchener Kommentarzum bürgerlichen Gesetzbuch* [Munich commentary on the civil code], vol. 3/2 (ed. Peter Ulmer) (Munich: C. H. Beck, 2d ed., 1980), § 823, ¶ 140, p. 1183.

60. *Id.*

61. *Id.*

62. See Benisch, in Müller-Henneberg and Schwartz, *Kommentar*, § 35, ¶ 3; *Frankfurter Kommentar*, § 35, ¶ 3, fn. 11; Langen, Niederleithinger, and Schmidt, *Kommentar*, p. 618; Müller and Giessler, *Kommentar*, § 35, ¶ 13. See also Linder, *Privatklage*, p. 30. The first reported decisions on section 1 of the GWB were at odds with all the commentaries. These decisions held that an injunction or compensation under section 35 could be awarded for violations of section 1 since the section could be considered a "protective provision" when read in connection with section 38(1). Düsseldorf District Court Judgment of September 8, 1959 (*Filmtransport*), *WuW/E LG/AG*, p. 146; Mannheim District Court Judgment of December 18, 1964 (*Zweittaxi*), *WuW/E LG/AG*, p. 259.

63. *Frankfurter Kommentar*, § 35, ¶ 12. The 1980 amendments added a new paragraph 2 that explicitly subjects violations of administrative and court orders to damage actions and private injunctive relief. The purpose of the revision was to permit recovery or damages from the time the order was served rather than from the time when all appeals were completed. Riesenkampff and Cres, *Law against Restraints of Competition* (1981 ed.), p. 73. See also Karlsruhe High Court Judgment of June 8, 1977 (*Objektschutz*), *WuW/E OLG*, p. 1952. Bo.2 are now included in section 33.

64. Benisch, in Müller-Henneberg and Schwartz, *Kommentar*, § 35, ¶ 3. Benisch also lists violations of GWB sections 38(1)9 and 38(2) prior to the 1973 amendment of section 38, and the duty to respond truthfully to disclosure demands and investigation under sections 46 and 47, citing Albrecht Spengler, "Zivilrechtliche Auswirkungen des Kartellgesetzes" [Civil law effects of the cartel law], *WuW* (1960), p. 428.

65. See Benisch, in Müller-Henneberg and Schwartz, *Kommentar* (2d ed., 1963), p. 869; *Frankfurter Kommentar*, § 35, ¶¶ 3–11; Müller and Giessler, *Kommentar*, B5, ¶ 13.

66. Federal Supreme Court Judgment of October 8, 1958 (*4711*), *WuW/E BGH*, p. 753 (§ 15 held not to be a "protective provision"); Federal Supreme Court Judgment of October 22, 1973 (*Strombezugspreis*), *WuW/E BGH*, p. 1299 (§ 22 not a "protective provision"); *Kammergericht* Judgment of January 12, 1976 (*Weichschaum*), *WuW/E OLG*, p. 1637 (§ 24 not a "protective provision").

67. See discussion and works cited in Spengler, "Zivilrechtliche Auswirkungen," p. 419. See also Spengler, "Über die Tatbestandsmäßgkeit und Rechtswidrigkeit von Wettbewerbsbeschränkungen" [On findings of fact and violation of law of restraints of competition], *Wirtschaft und Wettbewerb-Schriftenreihe* (1960), p. 29.

68. Federal Supreme Court Judgment of December 17, 1970, *BGHSt*, vol. 24, p. 54,

*WuW/E BGH*, p. 1147 (holding that the GWB did not proscribe tacit assent or concerted action for unlawful restraints of trade).

69. Rittner, *Einführung*, p. 219.

70. *BGHZ*, vol. 64, p. 232, *WuW/E BGH*, p. 1361, *aff'g* Düsseldorf High Court Judgment of April 9, 1974, *WuW/E OLG*, p. 1523, *aff'g* Cologne District Court Judgment of February 20, 1973, *WuW/E LG/AG*, p. 348.

71. *Gesetz gegen den unlauteren Wettbewerb* [UWG], Law of June 7, 1909 (*RGBI.* 499).

72. For comment on the case, see Linder, *Privatklage*, p. 26; and Steindorff, *Juristenzeitung* [*JZ*], vol. 31 (1976), pp. 29–31. For one of the strongest critiques, see Werner Benisch, "Private Verfolgung von Wettbewerbsbeschränkungen und Allgemeininteresse" [Private pursuit of restraints of trade and the general interest], in *Wettbewerbsordnung im Spannungsfeld von Wirtschafts- und Rechtswissenschaft: Festschrift für Gunther Hartmann* [Competition order in the field of tension between economics and legal science: Commemorative volume for Gunther Hartmann], ed. Forschungsinstitut für Wirtschaftsverfassung und Wettbewerb (Cologne: Carl Heymanns, 1976), p. 38.

73. Karlsruhe High Court Judgment of May 25, 1977 (*Zeitschriftenvertrieb*), *WuW/E OLG*, p. 1855.

74. Celle High Court Judgment of February 15, 1963 (*Brückenbauwerk*), *WuW/E OLG*, pp. 559, 561.

75. Hans Goll, "Verbraucherschutz im Kartellrecht" [Consumer protection in cartel law], *Gewerblicher Rechtsschutz und Urheberrecht* [GRUR] (1976), pp. 456, 491.

76. Rittner, *Einführung*, p. 308.

77. *Id.*, p. 310.

78. Theo Mayer-Maly, in *Münchener Kommentar* (1st ed., 1978), vol. 1 (ed. Franz Jürgensäcker) § 134 ¶¶ 66, 801.

79. Steindorff, *Commission Hearings*, vol. 8, app. 6, p. 7.

80. Shōda, *Dokusen kinshi hō*, vol. 2, p. 355.

81. *Id.*, p. 357.

82. Antimonopoly Law, art. 2(1) provides, "The term 'entrepreneur' as used in this Law means a person who carries on a commercial, industrial, financial or any other business."

83. Shōda, *Songai baishō*, p. 2, translated in *Law in Japan: An Annual*, vol. 16 (1983), p. 3.

84. See Takaaki Hattori and Dan F. Henderson, *Civil Procedure in Japan* (New York: Matthew Bender, 1983), § 7.06(8)(b).

85. Ōkawa v. Matsushita Denki Sangyō K. K., *Hanrei jihō*, no. 863, p. 20 (Tokyo High Ct., September 19, 1977), summarized in English in *Law in Japan: An Annual*, vol. 10 (1977), p. 165.

86. See Imamura Shigekazu, *Dokusen kinshi hō* [Antimonopoly law], in *Hōritsugaku zenshū*, vol. 52, p. 84 (rev. ed., 1967). For a recent comparison between Civil Code and Antimonopoly Law damage actions, see Murakami Masahiro, "Dokusen kinshi hō ihan ni tsuite no tokubetsu songai baishō seido no igi" [Significance of the special system of compensatory damages with respect to violations of the antimonopoly law], *Hanrei taimuzu*, no. 959 (1998), pp. 4–11.

87. Satō v. Sekiyu Renmei, *Hanrei jihō*, no. 997, p. 18 (Yamagata Ct., March 31, 1981).

88. Sekiyu Renmei v. Satō, *Hanrei jihō*, no. 1340, p. 1 (Sup. Ct., 2nd P.B., December 8, 1989).

89. Shōda, *Dokusen kinshi hō*, vol. 2, p. 357.

90. The first case settled by compromise was K. K. Kosaka Seikyoku v. Taishō Seiyaku K. K., 9 *Shinketsushū* 162 (1957) (reopened even though settled by compromise). The second case arose out of the oil cartel cases. See Miyasaka Tominosuke, "Shōhisha ni yoru tōyu karuteru ni tsuite no songai baishō seikyū soshō" [Consumer litigation for compensation for damages resulting from the kerosene cartel], *Jurisuto*, no. 768 (1982), p. 252. See also J. Mark Ramseyer, "Japanese Antitrust Enforcement after the Oil Embargo," *American Journal of Comparative Law*, vol. 31, no. 3 (1983), p. 418.

91. Kotō v. Kansai Surippa Seizō Kaisha, *Keizai hō*, vol. 2 (1958), p. 60 (Tokyo High Ct., November 24, 1958).

92. Shōda, "Dokusen kinshi hō ihan kōi to songai baishō" [Antimonopoly law violations and compensatory damages], *Keizai hōgaku nenpō*, vol. 1 (1982), p. 1; translated in *Law in Japan: An Annual*, vol. 16 (1983), p. 1. See also Ramseyer, "Antitrust Enforcement after the Oil Embargo."

93. *Hanrei jihō*, no. 863, p. 20 (Tokyo High Ct., September 19, 1977).

94. See Kaneko Akira, "Sekiyu yami karuteru songai baishō sekiyu jiken Tōkyō kōsai hanketsu o megutte" [Concerning the Tokyo high court decision in the secret oil cartel damage action], *Kōsei torihiki*, no. 372 (1981), p. 26.

95. K. K. Kosaka Seikyoku v. Taishō Seiyaku K. K., 9 *Shinketsushū* 162 (1957).

96. For a critical analysis of these cases and their implications, see J. Mark Ramseyer, "The Costs of the Consensual Myth: Antitrust Enforcement and Institutional Barriers to Litigation in Japan," *Yale Law Journal*, vol. 94, no. 3 (1985), pp. 604–45.

97. Kai v. Nihon Sekiyu K. K., *Hanrei jihō*, no. 1005, p. 32 (Tokyo High Ct., July 7, 1981).

98. Kai v. Nihon Sekiyu K. K., *Hanrei jihō*, no. 1239, p. 3 (Sup. Ct., 1st P.B., July 2, 1987).

99. Dejikon Denko K. K. v. Nihon Yūgijōjū Kyōdō Kumiai, *Hanrei jihō*, no. 1629, p. 70 (Tokyo Dist. Ct., April 9, 1997).

100. Jiji Press Ticker Service, September 30, 1997 ("MITI eyes civil procedures for antitrust violations"); Jiji Press Ticker Service, March 11, 1998 ("FTC to study personal antitrust suits").

101. The 1998 edition of *Justice in Japan*, published annually by the Supreme Court of Japan, indicates that the total number of judges in Japan as of 1997 was 2,545, including 15 Supreme Court justices, 280 high court judges, 910 district court judges, 530 assistant judges, and 810 summary court judges. The 1998 directory of licensed attorneys in Japan published by the Japanese Federation of Bar Associations lists 16,852 lawyers (*bengoshi*) and 87 "foreign special members" (*gaikoku tokubetsu kai'in*) as of July 1, 1998. Nihon Bengoshi Rengōkai, *Kai'in meibo* [Member directory] (Tokyo, 1998).

102. Statistisches Bundesamt, *Statistical Yearbook 1997 for the Federal Republic of Germany* (Bonn: Metzler Poeschel, 1998), p. 364.

103. *Gaikoku kawase oyobi gaikoku bōeki kanri hō* (Law No. 228, 1949) (repealed in 1997).

104. Tomita v. Inoue, *Hanrei jihō*, no. 435, p. 38 (Sup. Ct., 1st P.B., December 23, 1965); Ryūkyū Ginkō K. K. v. Tōkai Denki Kōji K. K., *Hanrei jihō*, no. 782, p. 19 (Sup. Ct., 3d P.B., July 15, 1975); summarized in English in *Law in Japan: An Annual*, vol. 9 (1976), p. 158.

105. See, e.g., Imamura, *Dokusen kinshi hō*, p. 172; Shōda, *Dokusen kinshi hō*, vol. 1, p. 500.

106. 31 *Minshū* 449 (Sup. Ct., 2d P.B., June 20, 1977).

107. Fair Trade Commission Notification No. 11, 1953, translated in Iyori and Uesugi, *Antitrust Laws of Japan* (1983), p. 265. As noted previously, the 1953 General Designation was superseded in 1982.

108. *Miyagawa* case, 31 *Minshū*, p. 459.

109. *Risoku seigen hō* (Law No. 100, 1954).

110. *Miyagawa* case, 31 *Minshū*, p. 459.

111. For comment on this point, see Shōda, *Dokusen kinshi hō*, vol. 1, p. 501.

112. Fukumitsu Ienobu, "Dokusen kinshi hō ihan kōi no kōryoku" [Validity of acts in violation of the antimonopoly law], *Kokumin keizai zasshi*, vol. 82 (December 1950), p. 25 (pt. 1); *Kokumin keizai zasshi*, vol. 83 (January 1951), p. 14 (pt. 2).

113. Josten Draft Law for Protection of Competition, §§ 66, 67, 68.

114. Formally titled the Sachverständigen kommission zur Bekämpfung der Wirtschaftskriminalität, the commission was appointed on July 25, 1972, by the federal minister of justice to study criminal law reforms as a means to prevent economic offenses. Chaired by the attorney-general for Baden-Württemberg in Stuttgart (Weinmann), its members included representatives from the legislature, the government, and the Federal Supreme Court as well as practitioners (one lawyer and one accountant) and several leading scholars, two of whom, Professors Peter Raisch (Hagen) and Peter Ulmer (Heidelberg), were antitrust and economic law specialists,

and one, criminal law professor Klaus Tiedemann (Freiburg), the most prolific and ardent proponent of the use of criminal sanctions to deter antitrust violations. The commission met on ten occasions from October 1972 through November 1976 and explored the greater use of criminal penalties in preventing tax evasion, computer crimes, credit fraud, unfair competition, and consumer fraud in addition to antitrust violations. See generally Bundesrepublik Deutschland, Bundesministerium der Justiz, *Tagungsberichte der Sachverständigenkommission zur Bekämpfung der Wirtschafts-kriminalität* (1972–76) [cited, as noted, as *Commission Hearings*].

115. Ibid., vol. 1 (1979), p. 126.

116. With the exception of some commission members themselves, no scholar or practitioner appearing before the commission fully supported the introduction of criminal sanctions. Compare submissions by commission members Tiedemann, Raisch, and Ulmer (*Commission Hearings*, vol. 10) (supporting criminal sanctions) with the submission by Steindorff (vol. 8, app. 6) (opposing criminal penalties) and by Cramer (vol. 10, app. 6) (same). The vice-president of the Federal Cartel Office was equally unenthusiastic. See submissions of Gutzler, vols. 8 and 10, app. 4. The president of the Federal Cartel Office at the time, Wolfgang Kartte, was apparently no more supportive of the use of criminal sanctions. See Kartte and von Portius, "Kriminalisierung des Kartellrechts."

117. STPO, §§ 152(2), 160, 170. For discussion in English of the limits of prosecutorial discretion in Germany, see Mirjan Damaska, "The Reality of Prosecutorial Discretion: Comments on a German Monograph," *American Journal of Comparative Law,* vol. 29, no. 1 (1981), pp. 119–38; Joachim Herrmann, "The Rule of Compulsory Prosecution and the Scope of Prosecutorial Discretion in Germany," *University of Chicago Law Review,* vol. 41, no. 3 (1974), pp. 468–505; Hans-Heinrich Jescheck, "The Discretionary Powers of the Prosecuting Attorney in West Germany," *American Journal of Comparative Law,* vol. 18, no. 3 (1970), pp. 508–17; Langbein, "Controlling Prosecutorial Discretion in Germany." See also Abraham Goldstein and Martin Marcus, "The Myth of Judicial Supervision in Three 'Inquisitorial' Systems: France, Italy, and Germany," *Yale Law Journal,* vol. 87, no. 2 (1977), pp. 240–83 (asserting that prosecutors must exercise at least de facto discretionary power to prosecute without judicial supervision); the response, John H. Langbein and Lloyd L. Weinreb, "Continental Criminal Procedure: 'Myth' and Reality," *Yale Law Journal,* vol. 87, no. 8 (1978), pp. 1549–69 (maintaining that German prosecutors exercise little prosecutorial discretion); and the rebuttal, Abraham Goldstein and Martin Marcus, "Comment on Continental Criminal Procedure," *Yale Law Journal,* vol. 87, no. 8 (1978), pp. 1570–77. Much of the argument on both sides rested on speculation for lack of empirical data. A subsequent study conducted under the auspices of the Max-Planck-Institut für ausländisches und internationales Strafrecht (Freiburg im Breisgau) fills much of this gap. Erhard Blankenburg, Klaus Sessar, and Weibe Steffen, *Die Staatsanwaltschaft in*

*(prozeßstrafrechtlicher Sozialkontrolle* [Prosecution in social control through the criminal process] (Berlin: Duncker and Humblot, 1978) (a summary in English appears at pp. 336–50). This study supports the argument made by Langbein and Weinreb that the German principle of mandatory prosecution does effectively limit prosecutional discretion.

118. STPO § 374, described in English by Langbein, "Controlling Prosecutorial Discretion," pp. 461–62; and Herrmann, "Scope of Prosecutorial Discretion," p. 478.

119. STPO §§ 172–177 (Langbein, "Controlling Prosecutorial Discretion," p. 463). Apparently, however, resort to such petitions rarely if ever occurs. Blankenburg, Sessar, and Steffen, *Staatsanwaltschaft,* p. 347.

120. STPO §§ 153–154d. See generally Herrmann, "Scope of Prosecutorial Discretion."

121. For a concise description of the judge's role, see Peterson's note as translator to Bauer, "Introduction," p. 136. See also Damaska, "Reality of Prosecutorial Discretion," p. 125.

122. See Joachim Herrmann, "Bargaining Justice: A Bargain for German Criminal Justice?" *University of Pittsburgh Law Review,* vol. 53, no. 3 (1992), pp. 755–76.

123. The accuracy of this conclusion lies at the heart of the debate between Goldstein and Marcus, who oppose the notion that in fact German prosecutors exercise little real discretion, and Langbein and Weinreb, who support it. The empirical data support Langbein and Weinreb's view. To quote from the Freiburg Study (emphasis in original),

> It is characteristic of the *prosecutor's decision making that he displays a marked lack of interest in the individuals affected by his decisions.* . . . His decisions are based on data contained in dossiers, which are often incomplete and only rarely give useful information on the personality of the subject. *The prosecutor generally takes into account very few criteria to substantiate and legitimate his decisions,* and he has only very little information about the individuals who are affected by his decision. Blankenburg, Sessar, and Steffen, *Staatsanwaltschaft,* p. 343. See also Thomas Weigend, *Anklagepflicht und Ermessen: Die Stellung des Staatsanwalts zwischen Legalitäts- und Opportunitätsprinzip nach deutschen und amerikanischen Recht* [Duty to prosecute and discretion: The position of prosecutors between the principles of mandatory and discretionary prosecution in German and American law] (Baden-Baden: Nomos, 1978), p. 41.

124. The Freiburg Study provides some support for this view, although it concludes that the seriousness of the offense is a factor in the charging decisions of German procurators. Blankenburg, Sessar, and Steffen, *Staatsanwaltschaft,* p. 340.

125. Federal Statistical Office of Germany (December 16, 1998) <http://www.statsitik-bund.de/basis/e/justueb.htm>.

125. Kartte and von Portius, "Kriminalisierung des Kartellrechts"; and submissions by Gutzler, *Commission Hearings,* vol. 8, app. 7; vol. 10, app. 4.

127. See Weigend, *Anklagepflicht und Ermessen,* and its critique by Damaska, "Reality of Prosecutorial Discretion."

128. Although seldom expressed so baldly, the importance of expertise is apparent from the efforts to deal with the problem by proponents of criminal sanctions. See, e.g., submission by Klaus Tiedemann, *Commission Hearings.* vol. 10, app. 1, p. 6.

129. On the role of the police in criminal investigations, see Blankenburg, Sessar, and Steffen, *Staatsanwaltschaft,* pp. 291, 338.

130. See submissions of Peter Cramer and Peter Ulmer in *Commission Hearings,* vol. 10, apps. 6 and 2. See also comments by Wolfgang Kartte before a seminar conducted by Professors Fritz Rittner and Klaus Tiedemann on Antitrust Violations and Criminal Law (*Kartellrechtverstosse und Strafrecht*) in the Law Faculty of Freiburg University, spring semester 1975. Comments by Wolfgang Kartte of May 28, 1975; Dieter Lutz, reporter, in Seminar Records (provided to author by Professor Fritz Rittner).

131. In one of the few empirical studies in English on the German criminal process, professors Gerhard Casper and Hans Zeisel determined that roughly one-half of all criminal trials last one-third of a day or less. Gerhard Casper and Hans Zeisel, "Lay Judges in the German Criminal Courts," *Journal of Legal Studies,* vol. 1, no. 1 (1972), pp. 149–50. The Federal Statistical Office (Statistisches Bundesamt) reports (December 16, 1998) that the time between the offense and conviction has become considerably longer than in the 1970s. In 44 percent of all criminal cases in 1976, conviction occurred in the year of the offense. By 1996 the percentage had decreased to 38 percent <http://www.statsitik-bund.de/basis/e/justueb.htm>.

132. Fredrich Berckhauer, "Wirtschaftskriminalität und Staatsanwaltschaft" doctoral diss., Freiburg University, 1977).

133. See, e.g., Kartte and von Portius, "Kriminalisierung des Kartellrechts." See also Gutzler, *Commission Hearings,* vol. 8, app. 7, p. 8.

134. See, e.g., Gutzler, *Commission Hearings,* vol. 8, app. 7, p. 8.

135. Gutzler, "Ermittlungstätigkeit des Bundeskartellamtes," p. 537.

136. The distinction was first explored in the now classic study by James Goldschmidt. James Goldschmidt, *Das Verwaltungsstrafrecht* [Administrative criminal law] (Berlin: Carl Heymanns, 1902; reprint, Aalen: Scientia, 1969). Erik Wolf, however, is considered its most persuasive and articulate conceptual explicator. Erik Wolf, "Die Stellung der Verwaltungsdelikte im Strafrechtssystem" [The position of administrative delicts in the criminal law system], in *Beiträge zur Strafrechtswissenschaft: Festgabe für Reinhard von Frank* [Essays on criminal jurisprudence: Commemorative work for Reinhard von Frank, ed. August Hegler, Max Grunhut, and Theodor Rittler (Tübingen, 1930; reprint, Aalen: Scientia, 1969), pp. 516–88. Eberhard Schmidt is credited with giving life to these early works in postwar legislation. See Eberhard Schmidt, *Das neue westdeutsche Wirtschaftsstrafrecht* [The new West German economic criminal law]

(Tübingen: J. C. B. Mohr, 1950). For a critical analysis, see Klaus Tiedemann, *Kartellrechtsverstöße und Strafrecht* [Cartel law violations and criminal law] (Cologne: Carl Heymanns, 1976), p. 99; and Klaus Tiedemann, *Wettbewerb und Strafrecht* [Competition and criminal law] (Karlsruhe: C. F. Müller, 1976), p. 117.

137. See, e.g., Erich Göhler, *Gesetz über Ordnungswidrigkeiten* [Law on administrative offenses] (Munich: Beck, 4th ed., 1975), pp. 3–6; Kurt Rehmann, Werner Roth, and Siegfried Hermann, *Gesetz über Ordnungswidrigkeiten: Kommentar* [Law on administrative offenses: Commentary] (Stuttgart: Kohlhammer, 1968), § 1, ¶ 6; *Rotberg OWiG Kommentar* (5th ed., 1975), p. 43.

138. Federal Supreme Court Judgment of November 4, 1957, *BGHSt*, vol. 11 (1958), pp. 263, 264; see also Langbein, "Controlling Prosecutorial Discretion," p. 453, citing Karl Peters, *Strafprozeß* [Criminal procedure] (2d ed., 1966), p. 31. Langbein's description of the differences between *Ordnungswidrigkeiten* and criminal offenses is excellent. As he notes, the distinction "reflects the view that the essence of the criminal process is the moral condemnation attaching to its formal sanctions and its procedures." *Id.* (footnote omitted). As noted above, Langbein's use of the term "petty infractions" for *Ordnungswidrigkeiten* seems less appropriate than "administrative" or "regulatory" offenses since many, such as antitrust violations, are not minor or petty. Rather, as explained above, criminal sanctions in such cases are considered to be impractical out of procedural considerations or too harsh for lack of consensus about the appropriateness of the criminal stigma.

139. *Begründung des Gesetzentwurfes. BT Drucksache*, 11/1158, p. 28.

140. In addition to previously cited works, see Rittner, *Einführung* (1981), p. 305.

141. Steindorff, *Commission Hearings*, vol. 8, app. 6; reprinted as Steindorff, "Gesetzgeberische Möglichkeiten zum verbesserten Durchsetzung des GWB" [Legislative possibilities for improving the effectiveness of the GWB], *ZHR*, vol. 138 (1974), p. 504.

142. Gutzler, *Commission Hearings*, vol. 8, app. 7.

143. Steindorff, *Commission Hearings*, vol. 8, app. 6 (citing works by Packer, Elzinga, and Breit, and other American research).

144. Professor Tiedemann offered the only concrete examples of the failure of sanctions to provide an effective deterrent. He simply details, however, a number of antitrust decisions to show that the fines were insignificant relative to the violation. Tiedemann, *Commission Hearings*, vol. 10, app. 1.

145. For a brief description of the political decision by the government not to follow the draft in all respects, especially to limit the maximum fine (and eliminate criminal sanctions), see Müller-Henneberg and Schwartz, *Kommentar*, p. 661 (portion written by Mayer-Wegelin). Unless a higher fine is expressly allowed by other statutes, the maximum administrative fine under the OWiG is DM 1,000 (about U.S. $555 at current exchange rates). OWiG § 17(1).

146. Federal Supreme Court Judgment of October 7, 1959 (*Nullpreis II*), *WuW/E BGH*, pp. 352, 353.

147. See Gutzler, *Commission Hearings*, vol. 8, app. 7, p. 36.

148. Japan's most celebrated prewar constitutional and administrative law scholar, Tatsukichi Minobe, introduced the German distinction between administrative and criminal offenses in the 1940s. See, e.g., Minobe Tatsukichi, *Keizai kēihō no kiso riron* [The theoretical basis for economic criminal law] (Tokyo: Yūhikaku, 1934). His observations made hardly a ripple and have been almost totally ignored because the underlying need for the dichotomy, the *Legalitätsprinzip*, was one of the few significant features of German law the Japanese did not borrow.

149. John O. Haley, "Sheathing the Sword of Justice in Japan: An Essay on Law without 464 Sanctions," *Journal of Japanese Studies*, vol. 8, no. 2 (1982), pp. 265–81.

150. Antimonopoly Law, arts. 87 to 91-2.

151. *Id.*, art. 96.

152. *Id.*, art. 85.

153. *Keiji soshōhō* [Code of criminal procedure] (Law No. 131, 1948), art. 248.

154. The account of early criminal antitrust cases in Japan is based on Stephen F. Clayton, "Criminal Prosecution of Antitrust Violations in Japan" (seminar paper, University of Washington, 1982).

155. Tokyo High Ct., May 12, 1953, noted in *Twenty-Year History*, p. 107.

156. Prosecution suspended, December 28, 1952, noted ibid.

157. 17 *Shinketsushū* 244 (Tokyo High Ct., February 2, 1951).

158. 17 Shinketsushū 232 (Tokyo High Ct., January 29, 1972).

159. *Hanrei jihō*, no. 983, p. 22 (Tokyo High Ct., September 26, 1980). For comment and partial translation, see J. Mark Ramseyer, "The Oil Cartel Criminal Cases: Translations and Postscript," *Law in Japan: An Annual*, vol. 15 (1982), pp. 57–72. (Volume 15 of *Law in Japan: An Annual* contains a symposium on the oil cartel cases.)

160. *Hanrei jihō*, no. 985, p. 3 (Tokyo High Ct., September 28, 1980). For comment and partial translation, see Ramseyer, "Oil Cartel Cases," pp. 66–75.

161. 46 Kōsai keishū (no. 2), 108 (Tokyo High Ct., May 21, 1993); also reported in *Hanrei jihō*, no. 1474, p. 31.

162. 46 Kōsai keishū (no. 3), 322 (Tokyo High Ct., December 14, 1993); also reported in *Hanrei taimuzu*, no. 840, p. 81.

163. 49 Kōsai keishū (no. 2), 320 (Tokyo High Ct., May 31, 1996); also reported in *Hanrei taimuzu*, no. 912, p. 139.

164. *Hanrei taimuzu*, no. 959, p. 140 (Tokyo High Ct., December 24, 1997).

165. *Jigyō dantai hō* (Law No. 191, 1948; repealed by Law No. 259, 1953).

166. *Futō keihinrui oyobi futō hyōji bōshi hō* (Law No. 134, 1962).

167. 17 Shinketsushū 232, 233.

168. Idemitsu Kōsan K. K. and Nihon Sekiyu K. K. were fined ¥2.5 million

(approximately U.S. $10,000 at prevailing exchange rates). Taiyō Sekiyu K. K. was fined ¥1.5 million U.S. $6,000), and the remaining nine companies were fined ¥2 million (U.S. $8,000). Ramseyer, "Oil Cartel Cases," p. 66.

169. The individual defendants were all high-level managers. The heaviest sentences (ten months) were meted out to Jun'ichi Saitō, director and former head of Idemitsu's sales department, and Ichiyuki Okada, who had a similar position with Nihon Sekiyu. Ramseyer, "Oil Cartel Cases," p. 66.

170. Few antitrust cases in Japan have produced as much commentary. See bibliography, *Law in Japan: An Annual,* vol. 15 (1982), p. 99, app. A.

171. *Sekiyugyō hō* [Petroleum industry law] (Law No. 128, 1962).

172. The decisions did not reflect a significant change in the law about the legal effect of administrative guidance. Prior FTC decisions had consistently held that administrative guidance, even if itself lawful, did not provide exemption or immunity for private conduct that violated the antitrust law. The "guidance cartels" of the 1960s and early 1970s were long recognized as the means used by MITI working together with industry representatives to evade the proscriptions of the Antimonopoly Law following the defeat of the proposed 1958 amendments. The overt and widespread use of "guidance cartels" had nonetheless tended to endow them with a sort of de facto legitimacy, especially for foreign observers. See, e.g., Wolfgang Pape, *Gyōseishidō und das Anti-Monopol-Gesetz in Japan* [Administrative guidance and the antimonopoly law in Japan] (Cologne: Carl Heymanns, 1980). The decisions did take many scholars by surprise. The court's acceptance of the notion that a defendant's mistake of law could operate as an exculpatory excuse reflected a change in the law. See, e.g., Itakura Hiroshi, "Sekiyu yami karuteru jiken keiji hanketsu no igi" [Significance of the secret oil cartel criminal decision], *Kōsei torihiki,* no. 361 (1980), p. 24. Not all scholars were surprised. The court adopted an argument first put forth by Hideo Fujiki, "Gyōsei shidō to dokkin hō ihan no tsumi" [Administrative guidance and the crime of antimonopoly law violations], *Jurisuto,* no. 566 (1974), p. 46.

173. Ramseyer, "Oil Cartel Cases," p. 72.

174. Idemitsu Kosan v. Kumi, 38 *Keishū* 1287 (Sup. Ct., 2d P.B., February 24, 1984).

175. See generally John Herling, *The Great Price Conspiracy: The Story of the Antitrust Violations in the Electrical Industry* (Washington, D.C.: R. B. Luce, 1962).

176. Elzinga and Breit, *Antitrust Penalties,* p. 32.

177. *Id.,* p. 43.

178. Richard W. Rabinowitz, "Antitrust in Japan," in *Current Legal Aspects of Doing Business in Japan and East Asia,* ed. John O. Haley (Chicago: American Bar Association, 1978), p. 107.

179. In 1996 there were 2,164 public prosecutors in Japan. Statistics Bureau, Office of the Prime Minister, *Japan Statistical Yearbook 1997* (Tokyo, 1998), p. 747.

180. See Shigemitsu Dando, "System of Discretionary Prosecution in Japan," *American Journal of Comparative Law,* vol. 18 (1970), p. 525. Dando, Japan's leading criminal law scholar and later Supreme Court justice, was the first to detail the extent to which prosecutorial discretion was used to suspend prosecution. For annual statistics, see the Ministry of Justice of Japan, *Summary of White Paper on Crime* (Tokyo, annual). For more detailed discussion, see Haley, *Spirit of Japanese Law,* pp. 72–76.

181. See John O. Haley, "Apology and Pardon: Learning from Japan," in *Civic Repentance,* ed. Amitai Etzioni (Lanlam, Boulder, New York, and Oxford: Rowman & Littlefield, 1999), pp. 97–120.

182. See Haley, *Spirit of Japanese Law,* pp. 156–76.

183. On the procuracy's response to political corruption historically, see Richard H. Mitchell, *Political Bribery in Japan* (Honolulu: University of Hawaii Press, 1996), Haley, *Spirit of Japanese Law,* 156–76.

184. In a major price-fixing enforcement action brought by the FCO in the mid 1970s, the chairman of the industry association argued on appeal that he did not even know that there was an antitrust statute in Germany. Gutzler, "Ermittlungstätigkeit des Bundeskartellamtes," p. 530.

185. See, e.g., Steindorff, *Commission Hearings,* vol. 8, app. 6, p. 22.

186. Gutzler, *Commission Hearings,* vol. 8, app. 7, p. 38; vol. 10, app. 4, p. 49; Wolfgang-Gutzler, "Zur Begründung und Durchsetzung des Kartellverbots" [The establishment and implementation of cartel prohibition], in *Festschrift für Eberhard Günther,* p. 177; Gutzler, "Ermittlungstätigkeit des Bundeskartellamtes," p. 537.

187. Kartte and von Portius, "Kriminalisierung des Kartellrechts," p. 1171.

188. *Id.*

189. See, e.g., Erlinghagen and Zippel, "'Presseinformationen' des Bundeskartellamtes," p. 10 (sharply criticizing the practices of the FCO). For a response, see Scholz, "Informationspolitik des Bundeskartellamtes und Informationsrecht der Öffentlichkeit" [Information policy of the FCO and the public's right to information], *NJW* (1973), p. 481. Scholz cites a series of critical articles and replies thereto that appeared in *Handelsblatt* (Commercial news) in 1972.

190. See Tsusanshō [MITI], "Gyōsei shidō ni tsuite no kangaekata o matomeru" [Thoughts on administrative guidance), *Shōji hōmu,* no. 902 (1981), p. 87; trans. Lawrence Repeta, "The Limits of Administrative Authority in Japan: The Oil Cartel Criminal Cases and the Reaction of MITI and the FTC," *Law in Japan: An Annual,* vol. 15 (1982), pp. 55–56.

191. See, e.g., Pape, *Gyōseishidō.*

192. Both arguments are made by Scholz, "Informationspolitik." Doubts over the probity of publicity as a sanction have also been raised by Karsten Schmidt. Schmidt, *Kartellverfahrensrecht,* p. 293. But see Klaus Lüderssen, *Erfahrung als Rechtsquelle: Eine*

*Fallstudie aus dem Kartellstrafrecht* [Practice as a source of law: A case study of cartel criminal law] (Frankfurt am Main: Suhrkamp Verlag, 1972), p. 206; Tiedemann, *Kartellverstöße,* p. 34 (discussing the institutionalization of publicity as a formal sanction).

193. See generally John Owen Haley, *Authority without Power: Law and the Japanese Paradox* (New York and London: Oxford University Press, 1991).

194. Lüderssen, *Erfahrung als Rechtsquelle,* p. 207 (attempting a brief explanation based apparently on G. Katona, *Psychological Analysis of Economic Behavior* [1951]).

195. Gutzler, "Ermittlungstätigkeit des Bundeskartellamtes," p. 537.

196. Alan Watson, *Legal Transplants: An Approach to Comparative Law* (Charlottesville: University of Virginia Press, 1974).

# Selected Bibliography

Abe Yoshihisa. *Dokusen kinshihō* [Antimonopoly law]. Tokyo: Daiichi Hōki, 1978.

———. *Shinketsu dokusen kinshihō: Kōsei Torihiki I'inkai shinketsu no bunseki* [Decisional antimonopoly law: Analysis of Fair Trade Commission decisions]. Tokyo: Hōgaku Shoin, 1974.

Allen, G. C. *Japanese Industry: Its Recent Development and Present Condition.* New York: Institute of Pacific Relations, 1939.

———. "Japanese Industry: Its Organization and Development to 1937." In *The Industrialization of Japan and Manchukuo, 1930–1940,* ed. E. B. Schumpeter. New York: Macmillan, 1940.

Backer, John H. *Priming the German Economy.* Durham, N.C.: Duke University Press, 1971.

Berckhauer, Fredrich. "Wirtschaftskriminalität und Staatsanwaltschaft" [Economic crimes and prosecution]. Doctoral dissertation, Freiburg University, 1977.

Bisson, T. A. *Japan's War Economy.* New York: Institute of Pacific Relations, 1945.

———. *Nihon senryō kaisōki* [Japan occupation reforms]. Tokyo: Sansei-dō, 1983.

———. *Zaibatsu Dissolution in Japan.* Berkeley: University of California Press, 1954.

Böhm, Franz. *Freiheit und Ordnung in der Marktwirtschaft* [Freedom and order in the market economy], ed. Ernst-Joachim Mestmäcker. Baden-Baden: Nomos, 1980.

———. *Kartelle und Koalitionsfreiheit* [Cartels and freedom to collude]. Berlin: Heymann, 1933.

———. *Wettbewerb und Monopolkampf* [Competition and the struggle against monopoly]. Berlin: Heymann, 1933.

Brunner, Hanspeter. *Zwangskartelle* [Mandatory cartels]. Zurich: Nauch; Berlin: Heymann, 1937.

Bundeskartellamt. *Bericht des Bundeskartellamtes über seines Tätigkeit sowie über die Lage und Entwicklung auf seinem Aufgabengebiet nach #50 GWB (Tätigkeitsbericht)* [Federal Cartel Office 1959–78 annual, 1979/80 to present, biennial report].

Callman, Rudolf. *Das Deutsche Kartellrecht* [German cartel law]. Berlin: Philo, 1934.

Clayton, Stephen F. "Criminal Prosecution of Antitrust Violations in Japan." Seminar paper, University of Washington (Seattle), 1982.

Cohen, Jerome B. *Japan's Economy in War and Reconstruction.* Minneapolis: University of Minnesota Press, 1949.

Cohen, Theodore. *Remaking Japan: The American Occupation as New Deal.* New York: The Free Press, 1987.

Dando, Shigemitsu. *Japanese Criminal Procedure.* Translated by B. J. George. Hackensack, N.J.: Rothman, 1968.

Denton, Geoffrey; Forsyth, Murray; and MacLennan, Malcolm. *Economic Planning and Policies in Britain, France and Germany.* London: George Allen & Unwin, 1968.

Dyson, Kenneth, ed. *The Politics of German Regulation.* Aldershot, U.K.: Dartmouth, 1992.

Edwards, Corwin, ed. *A Cartel Policy for the United Nations.* New York: Columbia University Press, 1945.

Erhard, Ludwig. *Deutsche Wirtschaftspolitik: Der Weg der sozialen Marktwirtschaft* [German economic policy: The course of Socialist market economics] Düsseldorf and Vienna: ECON, 1962. Translated into English by G. A. Arengo-Sones and D. J. S. Thomson as *The Economics of Success.* London: Thames and Hodson, 1963.

———. *Germany's Comeback in the World Market.* Translated by W. H. Johnson. London: George Allen & Unwin, 1954.

———. *The Economics of Success.* Translated by J. A. Arengo-Sones and D. J. S. Thomson. London: Thames and Hodson, 1963.

———. *Prosperity through Competition.* Translated by Edith Temple Roberts and John B. Wood. New York: Praeger, 1958.

Euchen, Walter. *Die Grundlagen der National-ökonomie* [Fundations of the national economy]. Jena: Fischer, 1943 [subsequent editions, Berlin: Springer].

———. *This Unsuccessful Age.* Edinburgh, London, and Glasgow: William Hodge, 1951.

Eyermann, Erich, and Fröhler, Ludwig. *Verwaltungsgerichtordnung: Kommentar* [Administrative court order: Commentary]. 8th ed. Munich: C. H. Beck, 1980.

Fikentscher, Wolfgang. "Die deutsche Kartellrechtswissenschaft, 1945–1954" [German cartel jurisprudence, 1945–1954]. *Wirtschaft und Wettbewerb* 5 (1955): 205–29.

First, Harry. "Antitrust Enforcement in Japan." *Antitrust Bulletin* 64 (1995): 137–82.

————. "Antitrust in Japan: The Original Intent." *Pacific Rim Law and Policy Journal* 9 (2000): 1–71.

Forschungsinstitut für Wirtschaftsverfassung und Wettbewerb, ed. *Wettbewerbsordnung im Spannungsfeld von Wirtschafts- und Rechtswissenschaft: Festschrift für Gunther Hartmann* [Competition order in the field of tension between economics and legal science: Commemorative volume for Gunther Hartmann]. Cologne: Carl Heymanns, 1976.

Freyer, Tony. *Regulating Big Business: Antitrust in Great Britain and America, 1880–1990.* Cambridge: Cambridge University Press, 1992.

Friedmann, Wolfgang., ed. *Anti-Trust Laws: A Comparative Symposium.* Toronto: Carswell 1956.

Fruin, W. Mark. *Kikkoman: Company, Clan, and Community.* Cambridge, Mass.: Harvard University Press, 1983.

Gerber, David J. "Constitutionalizing the Economy: German Neo-Liberalism, Competition Law and the 'New Europe.'" *American Journal of Comparative Law* 42 (1994): 25–84.

————. *Law and Competition in Twentieth-Century Europe: Protecting Prometheus.* New York and London: Clarendon Press, 1998.

Government Section, Supreme Commander for the Allied Powers. *Political Reorientation of Japan, September 1945–September 1948.* Washington, D.C.: U.S. Government Printing Office, 1949.

Gutzler, Helmut; Herion, Wolfgang; and Kaiser, Joseph H., eds. *Wettbewerb im Wandel: Festschrift für Eberhard Günther:* Commemorative volume for Eberhard Günther [Competition in transformation]. Baden-Baden: Nomos, 1976.

Hadley, Eleanor M. *Antitrust in Japan.* Princeton, N.J. Princeton University Press, 1970.

————. "Trust Busting in Japan." *Harvard Business Review* 26 (1948): 425–40.

Haley, John Owen. "Antitrust in Japan: Problems of Enforcement." In *Current Legal Aspects of Doing Business in Japan and East Asia,* ed. John Owen Haley. Chicago: American Bar Association, 1978.

————. *Authority without Power: Law and the Japanese Paradox.* New York and London: Oxford University Press, 1991.

————. "Japanese Antitrust Enforcement: Implications for United States Trade." *Northern Kentucky Law Review* 18 (1991): 335–66.

————. "Marketing and Antitrust in Japan." *Hastings International and Comparative Law Review* 2 (1979): 51–72.

————. *The Spirit of Japanese Law.* Athens, Ga. University of Georgia Press, 1998.

Haley, John O., and Iyori, Hiroshi. *Antitrust: A New International Trade Remedy?* Seattle: Pacoific Rim Law & Policy Association, 1995.

Hegler, August; Grunhut, Max; and Rittler, Theodor, eds. *Beiträge zur Strafrechtswissenschaft: Festgabe für Reinhard von Frank* [Essays on criminal jurisprudence:

Commemorative work for Reinhard von Frank]. Tübingen, 1930; reprint, Aalen: Scientia, 1969.

Henderson, Dan F., ed. *The Constitution of Japan: Its First Twenty Years, 1946–1967.* Seattle: University of Washington Press, 1969.

Hermanns, Ferdinand. *Ermittlungsbefugnisse der Kartellbehörden nach deutschem und europäischem Recht* [Investigatory authority of the cartel authorities under German and European law]. Cologne: Deutscher Wirtschaftdienst, 1978.

Hollerman, Leon. *Japan's Dependence on the World Economy: The Approach toward Economic Liberalization.* Princeton, N.J.: Princeton University Press, 1967.

Hosokawa Ryūichirō. *Kishi Nobusuke.* Tokyo: Jiji Tsūshinsha, 1986.

Hosoya, Masahiro. "Economic Democratization and the 'Reverse Course' during the Allied Occupation of Japan, 1945–1952." *Kokusaigaku ronshū,* no. 11 (July 1983): 59–104.

———. "Selected Aspects of the *Zaibatsu* Dissolution in Occupied Japan 1945–1952: The Thought and Behavior of *Zaibatsu* Leaders, Japanese Government Officials and SCAP Officials." Ph.D. dissertation, Yale University, 1982.

Imamura Shigekazu. *Dokusen kinshi hō* [Antimonopoly law]. *Hōritsugaku zenshū,* vol. 52. New ed. Tokyo: Yūhikaku, 1978.

Immenga, Ulrich. *Politische Instrumentalisierung des Kartellrechts* [Political instrumentalization of cartel law]. Tübingen: J. C. B. Mohr, 1976.

Immenga, Ulrich, and Mestmäcker, Ernst-Joachim, eds. *Kommentar zum GWB* [Commentary on the GWB]. 1st ed. Munich: C. H. Beck, 1981, 2d ed. 1992.

Iokobe Makoto. *Beikoku no nihon senryō seisaku* [America's Japan occupation policy]. Tokyo: Chūō Kōronsha, 1985.

Isay, Rudolf, and Tschierschky, Siegfried. *Kartellverordnung* [Cartel decree]. 2d ed. Mannheim: Bensheimer, 1930.

Iyori, Hiroshi. *Antimonopoly Legislation in Japan.* New York: Federal Legal Publications, 1969.

———. "A Comparative Analysis on Japanese Competition Law: An Attempt to Identify German and American Influences." In *Die Japaniseriung des westlichen Rechts* [The Japanization of western law], ed. Helmut Coing and others. Tübingen: J. C. B. Mohr, 1990.

Iyori, Hiroshi, and Uesugi, Akinoru. *Antimonopoly Laws of Japan.* 2d ed. New York: Federal Legal Publications, 1983.

———. The *Antimonopoly Laws and Policies of Japan.* 3d ed. New York: Federal Legal Publications, 1994.

Johnson, Chalmers. "Japan: Who Governs? An Essay on Official Bureaucracy." *Journal of Japanese Studies* 1(1) (1975): 1–28.

———. *MITI and the Japanese Miracle: The Growth of Industrial Policy, 1925–1975.* Stanford, Calif.: Stanford University Press, 1982.

Kaufmann, Heinz, and Rautmann, H. G. *Kommentar zum Gesetz gegen Wettbewerbs-beschränkungen* [Commentary on the law against restraints of competition]. 4th ed. Cologne: Otto Schmidt, 1980 [*Frankfurter Kommentar*].

Kōsei Torihiki I'inkai [Fair Trade Commission]. *Dokusen kinshi seisaku nijūnenshi* [Twenty-year history of antimonopoly policy]. Tokyo: Ministry of Finance Printing Office, 1968.

———. *Nenji hōkoku* [Annual reports]. Tokyo: Ministry of Finance Printing Office, annual.

Kōsei Torihiki I'inkai Jimu Sōkyoku, ed. *Dokusen kinshi seisaku goju nenshi* [Fifty-year history of antimonopoly policy]. Tokyo: Fair Trade Commission, 1997.

———. *Dokusen kinshi seisaku sanjū nenshi* [Thirty-year history of antimonopoly policy]. Tokyo: Fair Trade Commission, 1977.

Kudō, Akira, and Hara, Terushi, eds. *International Cartels in Business History*. Tokyo: University of Tokyo Press, 1992.

Langen, Eugen; Niederleithinger, Ernst; and Schmidt, Ulrich, eds. *Kommentar zum Kartellrecht* [Commentary on cartel law]. 5th ed. Neuwied and Darmstadt: Luchterhand, 1977.

Linder, Ludwig. *Privatklage und Schadensersatz im Kartellrecht: Eine vergleichende Untersuchung zum deuschen und amerikanischen Recht* [Private actions and compensatory damages in cartel law: A comparative study of German and American law]. Baden-Baden: Nomos, 1980.

Lockwood, William W. *The Economic Development of Japan*. Princeton, N.J.: Princeton University Press, 1954.

Lorenz, Dieter. *Rechtsschutz des Bürgers und die Rechtsweggarantie* [Legal protection of citizens and the right to legal redress]. Munich: C. H. Beck, 1973.

Lüderssen, Klaus. *Erfahrung als Rechtsquelle: Eine Fallstudie aus dem Kartellstrafrecht* [Practice as a source of law: A case study of cartel criminal law]. Frankfurt am Main: Suhrkamp Verlag, 1972.

Mailänder, K. Peter. *Privatrechtliche Folgen unerlaubter Kartellpraxis* [Private law consequences of unlawful cartels]. Karlsruhe: Verlag Versicherungswirtschaft, 1964.

Martin, James S. *All Honorable Men*. Boston: Little, Brown and Company, 1950.

Matsushita Mitsuo. *Dokusen kinshihō to keizai tōsei* [Antimonopoly law and economic control]. Tokyo: Yūhikaku, 1976.

———. *International Trade and Competition Law in Japan*. London and New York: Oxford University Press, 1993.

Matsushita, Mitsuo, with Davis, John D. *Introduction to Japanese Antimonopoly Law*. Tokyo: Yūhikaku, 1990.

Menger, Christian-Friedrich. *System des verwaltungsgerichtlichen Rechtsschutzes* [System of legal protections in administrative courts]. Tübingen: J. C. B. Mohr, 1954.

Mestmäcker, Ernst-Joachim. ["Dekartellierung und Wettbewerb in der Rechtspechung der deutschen Gerichte" [Decartelization and competition in the decisions of German courts]. *ORDO* 9 (1957): 99–130.

——. *Europäisches Wettbewerbsrecht* [European competition law]. Munich: C. H. Beck, 1974.

Michels, Rudolf K. *Cartels, Combines and Trusts in Post-war Germany.* New York: Columbia University Press, 1928.

Miksch, Leonhard. *Wettbewerb aus Aufgabe: Grundsätze einer Wettbewerbsordnung* [Competition as the mission: Principles of an order of competition]. 2d ed. Godesberg: Küpper, 1948; 1st ed. 1937.

Minobe Ryōkichi. *Karuteru, Torasuto, Kontsuerun* [Cartels, trusts, concerns]. Tokyo: Kaizōsha, 1931.

Minobe Tatsukichi. *Keizai keihō no kiso riron* [The theoretical basis for economic criminal law]. Tokyo: Yūhikaku, 1934.

Misonō Hitoshi. *Kōsei Torihiki I'inkai* [Fair trade commission]. Tokyo: Nihon Keizai Shinbunsha, 1968.

Möschel, Wernhard. *Entflechtung im Recht der Wettbewerbsbeschränkungen* [Divestiture in the law on restraints of competition]. Tübingen: J. C. B. Mohr, 1979.

Mueller, Rudolf; Heidenhain, Martin, and Schneider, Hannes. *German Antitrust Law: An Introduction to the German Antitrust Law with German Text and Synoptic English Translation of the Act against Restraints of Competition.* 1st ed. Frankfurt: Knapp, 1973; 2d ed. 1981, 3d ed. 1984.

Müllensiefen, Heinz, and Dörinkel, Wolfram. *Kartellrecht* [Cartel law]. Berlin: Heymann, 1938.

Müller, Heinz, and Gries, Gerhard. *Kommentar zum Gesetz gegen Wettbewerbsbeschränkungen* [Commentary on the law against restraints of competition]. 1st ed. Frankfurt: Schwenk, 1957.

Müller-Henneberg, Hans, and Schwartz, Gustav, eds. *Gesetz gegen Wettbewerbsbeschränkungen und europäisches Kartellrecht* [Law against restraints of competition and European cartel law]. 1st ed. Cologne: Carl Heymanns, 1958.

Müller-Laube, Hans-Martin. *Der private Rechtsschutz gegen unzulässige Beschränkungen des Wettbewerbs und missbräuchliche Ausübung von Marktmacht im deutschen Kartellrecht* [Private legal protection against unreasonable restraints of competition and abuse of market power in German cartel law]. Berlin: Duncker and Humblot, 1964.

Murakami Masahiro. *Dokusen kinshihō* [Antimonopoly law]. Tokyo: Kōbundō, 1996.

Nakamura, Masanao, ed. *Antimonopoly Legislation of Japan.* Tokyo: Kosei Torihiki Kyokai, 1984.

Nakamura, Takafusa. *Postwar Japanese Economy.* Tokyo: University of Tokyo Press, 1981.

Noguchi Yukio. *1940 nen taisei* [1940 system]. Tokyo: Tōyō Keizai Shinpōsha, 1995.

Nörr, Knut Wolfgang. "Law and Market Organization: The Historical Experience in Germany from 1900 to the Law against Restraints of Competition." *Journal of institutional and Theoretical Economics* [*Zeitschrift für die gesamte Staatswissenschaft*], 151 (1995): 5–20.

Pape, Wolfgang. *Gyōseishidō und das Anti-Monopol-Gesetz in Japan* [Administrative guidance and the antimonopoly law in Japan]. Cologne: Carl Heymanns, 1980.

Peacock, Alan, and Willgerodt, Hans. *German Neo-Liberals and the Social Market Economy.* 2d ed. London: Macmillan, 1955.

Rabinowitz, Richard W. "Antitrust in Japan." In *Current Legal Aspects of Doing Business in Japan and East Asia,* ed. John Owen Haley. Chicago: American Bar Association, 1978.

Ramseyer, J. Mark. "The Costs of the Consensual Myth: Antitrust Enforcement and Institutional Barriers to Litigation in Japan." *Yale Law Journal* 94 (1985): 604–45.

———. "Japanese Antitrust Enforcement after the Oil Embargo." *American Journal of Comparative Law* 31 (1983): 395–430.

———. *Odd Markets in Japanese History: Law and Economic Growth.* Cambridge: Cambridge University Press, 1996.

———. "The Oil Cartel Criminal Cases: Translations and Postscript." *Law in Japan: An Annual* 15 (1982): 57–72.

Rasch, Harold. *Wettbewerbsbeschränkungen: Kartell- und Monopolrecht* [Restraints of competition: restraints Cartel and monopoly law]. 2d ed. Berlin: Neue Wirtschafts-Briefe, 1958.

Redford, Lawrence H., ed. *The Occupation of Japan: Economic Policy and Reform.* Norfolk: The MacArthur Memorial, 1980.

Reimer, Eduard, ed. *Beiträge zum Wirtschaftsrecht: Festschrift für Rudolf Isay* [Essays on economics: Commemorative volume for Rudolf Isay]. Cologne: Carl Heymanns, 1956.

Reisenkampff, Alexander, and Gres, Joachim. *Law against Restraints of Competition: Text and Commentary in English and German.* 1st ed. Cologne: Otto Schmidt, 1977: 2d ed. 1980.

Rittner, Fritz. *Einfürung in das Wettbewerbs- und Kartellrecht* [Introduction to competition and cartel law]. 1st ed. Heidelberg and Karlsruhe: C. F. Müller, 1981; 2d ed. 1985.

———. "Das Ermessen der Kartellbehörde" [Discretion of the cartel authorities]. In *Beiträge zum Wirtschaftsrecht: Festschrift für Heinz Kaufmann* [Contributions to economic law: Commemorative volume for Heinz Kaufmann], ed. Horst Bartholomeyczik, Kurt H. Biedenkopf, and Helmuth von Hahn. Cologne-Marienburg: O. Schmidt, 1972.

———. *Wettbewerbs- und Kartellrecht* [Competition and cartel law] Heidelberg: C. F. Müller, 1995.

Robert, Rüdiger. *Konzentrationspolitik in der Bundesrepublik—Das Beispiel der Entstehung des Gesetzes gegen Wettbewerbsbeschränkungen* [Concentration policies in the Federal Republic of Germany—Example of the enactment of the Law against Restraints of Competition]. Berlin: Duncker & Humblot, 1976.

Sanekata Kenji. *Dokusen kinshihō* [Antimonopoly law]. 1st ed. Tokyo: Yūhikaku, 1987; 2d ed. 1992.

Savermann, Heinz, and Mestmächer, Ernst-Joachim, eds. *Wirtschaftsordung und Staatsverfassung: Festschrift für Franz Böhm* [Economic order and national constitution: Commemorative volume for Franz Böhm]. Tübingen: J. C. B. Mohr, 1975.

Scheingold, Stuart A. *The Rule of Law in European Integration: The Path of the Schuman Plan.* New Haven, Conn.: Yale University Press, 1965.

Schmidt, Eberhard. *Das neue westdeutsche Wirtschaftsstrafrecht* [The new West German economic criminal law]. Töbingen: J. C. B. Mohr, 1950.

Schmidt, Karsten. *Aufgaben und Leistungen der Gesetzgebung im Kartellrecht: Eine rechtspolitische Studie zu den ausserstrafrechtlichen Sanktionen im GWB* [Legislative functions and performance in cartel law: A legal policy study on the noncriminal sanctions in the GWB]. Baden-Baden: Nomos, 1978.

———. *Gerichtsschutz in Kartellverwaltungssachen* [Judicial protection in cartel proceedings]. Heidelberg: C. F. Möller, 1980.

———. *Kartellverfahrensrecht- Kartellverwaltungsrecht-Börgerliches Recht* [Cartel procedural law, cartel administrative law, civil law]. Cologne: Carl Heymanns, 1977.

Schonberger, Howard B. *Aftermath of War: Americans and the Remaking of Japan, 1945–1952.* Kent, Ohio; and London: Kent State University Press, 1989.

Schröder, Rainer. *Die Entwicklung des Kartellrechts und des kollektiven Arbeitsrechts durch die Rechtsprechung des Reichsgerichts vor 1914* [Development of cartel law and labor union law through the decisions of the imperial supreme court before 1914]. Ebelsbach: Gremer, 1988.

Seita, Alex Y., and Tamura, Jiro. "The Historical Background of Japan's Antimonopoly Law." *University of Illinois Law Review* 1 (1994): 115–85.

Shōda Akira, *Dokusen kinshihō* [Antimonopoly law]. 1st ed. Tokyo: Nihon Hyrōnsha, 1966; 2d ed. 1980.

———. *Dokusen kinshihō kenkyū* [Antimonopoly law studies]. Tokyo: Dōbunkan, 1976.

Stocking, George W., and Watkins, Myron C. *Cartels or Competition?* New York: Twentieth Century Fund, 1948.

Stockmann, Kurt, and Strauch, Volkmar. "Federal Republic of Germany." Vol. B5 of *World Law of Competition.* New York: Matthew Bender, 1981.

Thomä, Karl Eugen. *Auskunfts und Betriebsprüfungsrecht der Verwaltung: Seine rechtstaatlichen Grenzen Recht und Wirtschaft* [Administrative right to information and examination of business records: The rule-by-law boundary of law and economics]. Stuttgart: Verlagsgesellschaft, 1955.

Tiedemann, Klaus. *Kartellrechtsverstöße und Strafrecht* [Cartel law violations and criminal law]. Cologne: Carl Heymanns, 1976.

———. *Wettbewerb und Strafrecht* [Competition and criminal law]. Karlsruhe: C. F. Müller, 1976.

Tilton, Mark. *Restrained Trade: Cartels in Japan's Basic Materials Industries.* Ithaca, N.Y. Cornell University Press, 1996.

Uchiyama, Toshihiro. "The U.S. Occupation Policy for Japan: The Deconcentration Controversy and the Origins of the 'Reverse Course.'" Student Working Paper no. 1, 1985. Niigata: International University of Japan.

Ule, Carl Hermann. *Verwaltungsprozeßrecht: Ein Studienbuch* [Law of administrative process: A treatise]. 9th ed. Munich: C. H. Beck, 1987.

Uriu, Robert M. *Troubled Industries: Confronting Economic Changes in Japan.* Ithaca, N.Y.: Cornell University Press, 1996.

U.S. Federal Trade Commission. *Report of the Committee Appointed to Review the Decartelization Program in Germany.* April 15, 1949.

von Mehren, Arthur T., ed. *Law in Japan: The Legal Order in a Changing Society.* Cambridge, Mass.: Harvard University Press, 1963; Tokyo: Tuttle, 1964.

von Oertzen, A. H. "Methoden probleme bei der Bestimmung des Mehrerlös nach § 38 Abs. 4 des Gesetzes gegen Wettberwerbsbeschränkungen" [Methodological problems in determining excess proceeds pursuant to § 38 ¶ 4 of the law against restraints of competition]. Doctoral dissertation, Bonn University, 1974.

Warner, Isabel *Steel and Sovereignty: The Deconcentration of the West German Steel Industry, 1949–54.* Mainz: Vertag Philipp von Zabern, 1996.

Warriner, Doreen. *Combines and Rationalization in Germany, 1924–1928.* London: F. S. King & Son, 1931.

Wolfe, Robert, ed. *Americans as Proconsuls: United States Military Government in Germany and Japan, 1944–1952.* Carbondale and Edwardsville: Southern Illinois University Press, 1984.

Yamamura, Kozo. *Economic Policy in Postwar Japan.* Berkeley: University of California Press, 1967.

———. "Success That Soured: Administrative Guidance and Cartels in Japan." In *Policy and Trade Issues of the Japanese Economy,* ed. Kozo Yamamura. Seattle: University of Washington Press, 1982.

Yoshida Jinbu. *Nihon no karuteru* [Japanese cartels]. Tokyo: Tōyō Keizai Shubōsha, 1964.

Yuzawa, Takeshi, and Udagawa, Mosaru, eds. *Foreign Business in Japan before World War II.* Tokyo: University of Tokyo Press, 1990.

# Index